SAGAS OF IMAGINATION:

A Medieval Icelandic Reader

SAGAS OF IMAGINATION:

A Medieval Icelandic Reader

translated by Ben Waggoner

Troth Publications
2018

An earlier version of *The Saga of Asmund Champions' Bane* has been published as an e-book by The Troth.

An earlier version of *The Saga of Asmund Champions' Bane* was published in *Idunna* #92 and #97.

Portions of an earlier version of *The Saga of Half and his Warband* were published in *Idunna* #105 and #110.

An earlier version of *The Tale of Hedin and Hogni* was published in *Idunna* #87 and #91.

Published by The Troth
325 Chestnut Street, Suite 800
Philadelphia, Pennsylvania 19106
http://www.thetroth.org/

ISBN-13: 978-1-941136-17-1 (hardcover); 978-1-941136-18-8 (paperback); 978-1-941136-19-5 (e-book)

Cover images, clockwise from top left:

Ivory chess piece, ca. 1200, Denmark. Image courtesy of the National Museum of Denmark; released under Creative Commons license CC BY-SA 2.0. (http://samlinger.natmus.dk/DMR/asset/168281)

Stained glass window from Hablingbo, Gotland. Image courtesy of the Swedish Historical Museum; released under Creative Commons license CC BY 2.5 SE. (http://kulturarvsdata.se/shm/object/html/114772)

Bronze statue identified as the god Thor, from Eyrarland, Iceland, now in the National Museum of Iceland. Image from Wikimedia Commons; released under Creative Commons license CC BY-SA 3.0. (https://commons.wikimedia.org/wiki/File:Thor_statue_transparent.png)

Troth logo designed by Kveldulf Gundarsson; drawn by 13 Labs, Chicago, Illinois
Cover design: Ben Waggoner
Typeset in Adobe Garamond Pro 14/12/10

This volume is dedicated
to Jo and Roy Tye,
hinir bezta smiðar,
with deepest thanks for their support
and their wish to pass the stories on

CONTENTS

CHIVALRIC ROMANCES

INTRODUCTION

The next day, he prepared to travel to the ship early in the morning, and he told all his men that he would ride away for good. His men were grieving, but still expected that he would return later. Gunnar bid farewell to his householders when he was ready, and they all went outside with him. He stabbed his long spear downwards and vaulted into the saddle, and he and Kolskegg rode away.

They rode out to Markarfljot. Then Gunnar's horse stumbled and knocked him out of the saddle. He ended up looking up towards the hills and the farm at Hlidarendi, and he said, "So fair is the hillside that I have never seen it looking so beautiful, the golden fields and mowed pastures. I will ride back home and not go anywhere."

"Don't make your enemies happy by breaking the settlement," said Kolskegg, "because no one would expect you to do that. Surely you must see that everything will turn out as Njal has said."

"I will not go anywhere," said Gunnar, "and I want you to do the same."[1]

—*Njáls saga*, ch. 75

Thrain had been king over Normandy in olden days, and gained everything by means of magic spells. He became very wicked. When he was so old that he couldn't do any more harm, he had himself placed alive in the mound, and a great deal of wealth with him.

Now Hromund saw the sword hanging up on a post. He pulled it down, buckled it at his side, and went up to the throne and said, "It must be time for me to leave this mound, since no one's resisting. Say, how's it going for you, old man? Don't you see that I've piled up your wealth, while you were quietly limping along, you mangy dog? What had you turned to look at when I took the sword and necklace and so many of your other treasures?"

Thrain said that he felt it was no great matter if he should stay quietly on his throne. "I knew how to fight once. I must have become rather a weakling if you plunder my wealth by yourself. I want to keep the treasures from you. You should beware of me, since I'm dead."[2]

—*Hrómundar saga Gripssonar*, ch. 4

Far across the North Sea from the mainland, medieval Iceland might seem an unlikely place to develop a literary culture. Yet although Iceland may have been on the fringes of the medieval European world, it holds a central place in any study of medieval European literature. The corpus of Old Norse texts composed, translated, or copied in Iceland between approximately 1150 and 1450 makes up the largest body of literature in any medieval vernacular.

By far the best-known medieval Icelandic texts are the sagas—primarily prose narratives, sometimes but not always including quoted poetry. Sagas range in length from a few thousand words to a hundred thousand words, not counting those that are compilations of semi-independent sagas. The word saga is derived from the same root as "to say" (*segja*), and some sagas probably have roots in oral tradition, although to what extent this is true has been hotly debated. However, while sagas could be recited orally—and often were, if post-medieval practice and accounts in the sagas themselves are at all reliable—the texts that we have are fundamentally literary, created by writers and shaped by copyists who had had exposure to continental European literature.

Pride of place is often given to the *Íslendingasögur*, "sagas of Icelanders", which present episodes from the settling of Iceland in 870 through the first few generations of settlers' families, up to about the year 1100; and the *konungasögur* or "kings' sagas", biographies of the rulers of Norway and Denmark, from legendary times to approximately 1280. These have attracted approving attention for their straightforward, novelistic style. Like a movie camera, these sagas usually report only speeches and actions that could have been seen and heard by observers; they rarely directly relate characters' thoughts or emotions. The impression is one of documentary-style realism, combined, in the best of them, with penetrating characterization and insight. There has been considerable debate over exactly to what extent these sagas can be said to present historical fact. Certainly there is no simple answer: *Haralds saga hárfagra*, written roughly 300 years after the reign of King Harald Fairhair, is less likely to be "sound" history than *Sverris saga*, which was partially dictated to its scribe by King Sverrir itself. But the best of these sagas feel accurate—they report the words and actions of people who seem familiar. Once dismissed by an 18th century Icelander as *bændur flugust á*—"farmers at fisticuffs"[3]—the *Íslendingasögur* give off an aura of psychological realism. Supernatural elements are usually, although not always, kept out of the foreground; they may spice up the narrative, but they are rarely critical to the plot. Even these supernatural elements are often familiar; many of us today have had dreams that seemed portentous, wondered if some event might be an omen, or even carry objects "for luck"—all behaviors that appear in the sagas.

On the other hand, there is a different set of sagas that are full of fantastic and fabulous elements. Dragons, trolls, giants, dwarves, sorcerors and shapeshifters, and the undead all have roles to play. Even the old pagan gods turn up from time to time. Magic spells work spectacular effects, and ancient weapons and magical items have amazing powers. These characteristically fantastic sagas include the so-called *fornaldarsögur* or "sagas of olden times", set in the nebulously defined "heroic past" of the Germanic-speaking world, and the *riddarasögur* or "knightly sagas", translations of European chivalric tales and epics. Overlapping with these categories are the rather nebulously defined "indigenous romances" that draw on elements of both: a hero might display very Viking attributes and attitudes while dispatching enemies in jousting or other forms of knightly combat, for example.

Icelandic churchmen also created sagas on specifically Christian themes, notably translations of the lives of the apostles and saints, along with original biographies of Icelandic saints and holy men. Such sagas could be either "realistic" or "fantastic". The sagas that recount the lives of Icelandic bishops (*biskupasögur*), for example, are generally sober and realistic in tone; some were written by people who had known the protagonists personally. Such sagas may recount miracles, but these were not considered "fantastic" by the people who wrote and read these sagas; furthermore, the miracles appear as solutions to very everyday problems—a lost child, a sickness, and so on. On the other hand, some of the sagas of the more obscure apostles and saints, known as *póstula sögur* and *heilagra manna sögur* respectively, are set in exotic locales and abound in monsters, treasures, and strange magic—although faith and prayer always prove stronger.

While the "sagas of Icelanders" have often been praised for their realism, the more fantastical sagas have often been considered hackneyed. William Ker called the indigenous romances "among the dreariest things ever made by human fancy"[4], while Sigurður Nordal called them "extremely unoriginal and paltry products", and Jón Helgason complained of their writers' "corrupt taste, which takes pleasure in unbridled exaggerations and improbabilities."[5] Medieval Icelanders sometimes agreed that their people really should be reading more uplifting fare—like the late 13th century priest Grímr Holmsteinson, who complained in his saga of John the Baptist about foolish men, *þeira sem allt þickir þat langt, er fra Cristz köppum er sagt, ok skemtaz framarr med skröksögur*—"those who find everything said about Christ's champions to be boring, and prefer to amuse themselves with fables."[6] And yet, judging by the number of surviving manuscripts, the fantastic sagas were far more popular with medieval and post-medieval Icelanders.[7] They continued to be written for much longer, as well; the priest Jón Oddson Hjaltalín was writing original romance sagas as late as the early 19th century.[8] And they are the most numerous sagas; there are roughly 35 original romances known to date from before the Protestant Reformation, and probably well over 100 surviving romances from after the Reformation, compared with 49 "canonical" *Íslendingasögur.*[9]

To look at the origins of fantastic sagas in Iceland, it is useful to define three "strands" of literary influences on medieval Icelandic literature.

The First Strand: Myth, Legend, and Family History

According to the reckoning of Ari Thorgilson in *Íslendingabók*, Iceland was discovered in the year 870 by a Norwegian named Ingolf.[10] Over the next sixty years, the *Landnám* or "land-taking" period, settlers arrived in Iceland and staked claims to land; most of the settlers came directly from Norway, but some were Norse people who had settled in Ireland or the Hebrides. The *Landnám* is traditionally said to have ended in 930, by which time most of the habitable land had been claimed. Tradition has it that in that year, the Althing was established—the annual legislative and judicial assembly, which would make up Iceland's national government until 1262.

Like any settlers in a new land, the settlers of Iceland brought stories with them. Many were no doubt entertaining, but many had a more serious use. Genealogical stories about a family's ancestors revealed their status back in Norway, their reasons for leaving (often a variation on "to escape the tyranny of Harald Fairhair, the first king of all Norway"), and how they came to settle their land in Iceland. For people in a non-feudal society without a king as the ultimate source of rank and distinction, stories like this were politically useful if they supported a family's claim to land or power or prestige—and this became doubly true after 1262, when Iceland entered the Kingdom of Norway and Icelanders had to integrate into the older, established kingdom.[11] Leaders could appeal to the shared history and genealogy of the group they led in order to build a sense of unity and shared purpose.[12] Furthermore, genealogies determined a person's legal and social obligations, range of permissible spouses, and right to inherit property.[13] Stories could present potential problems that might arise society, and explore possible solutions.[14] They were also useful in dealings with foreigners; an often-quoted line from a late recension of *Landnámabók* states that

> Many people say that it is useless knowledge to write about the land-taking. But on the contrary, we think that we know how to answer foreigners, when they accuse us of being descended from slaves or scoundrels, if we know our true ancestry with certainty.[15]

An Icelander might have been more likely to get favorable trading terms from a Norwegian merchant, or gain a position with the Norwegian king, if he could claim kinship with prominent families. Icelanders with poetic skill often visited royal courts or even served as court poets for an extended time, where their success depended on knowing the biographies and family histories of their patrons.[16]

The oldest datable references to Icelandic learning all mention genealogies. Around 1150, the young Thorlak Thorhallarson, who would later become Bishop Thorlak (and Saint Thorlak after his death), learned Christian lore as part of his training for the priesthood, but when he could he also learned *ættvísi ok mannfræði*, "genealogy and family history", from his mother.[17] The *First Grammatical Treatise*, written at some time in the 12th century, mentions the knowledge that was coming to be written down at the time: *bæði lög ok áttvísi eða þýðingar helgar*, "both laws and genealogies, or holy expositions" (or possibly "holy translations").[18] *Hungrvaka*, an account of early bishops of Iceland written in the early 13th century, mentions *þat er á norrænu er ritat: lög, eða sögur, eða mannfræði*—"that which is written in Norse: laws, or sagas, or family histories."[19]

Poetry was also felt to carry accurate information—both because a lying poem would bring no credit on its composer, and because the strict formal requirements of Norse poetry meant that any change in wording would spoil the poem. Snorri Sturluson specifically mentions these in his prologue to *Heimskringla*:

> In this book, I have had old stories written about rulers who held kingdoms in the Northlands and who spoke Norse, just as I have heard wise men tell, and also certain genealogies of theirs, according to what has been taught to me. Some is found in lists of ancestors, because kings and other men of noble descent have traced their ancestors, and some is written according to old poems or lays which men have had as entertainment. But although we don't know the truth of this, we may be certain that old and wise men have accepted such things as true. . . . we have the greatest certainty about what is said in those poems which were recited before the rulers themselves or their sons; we accept everything as true which is found in those poems about their expeditions or battles. It is the custom of skalds to praise those most highly who are standing in front of them, but none of them would have dared to tell the man himself about deeds of his that everyone who heard, and he himself, knew were nonsense and falsehoods. That would have been mockery, not praise.[20]

Snorri adds in the prologue to the *Separate Saga of St. Óláfr* the idea that the complex forms of Norse poetry make it resistant to change and therefore especially reliable.

> And yet I find that most important for veracity, which is said straightforwardly in poems or other poetry that was composed about kings or other chieftains so that they themselves heard it, or in those commemorative poems which the skalds brought to their sons. Those words which stand in poetry are the same as they were in the beginning,

> if the recitation is correct, although each person has since learned it from another; and for that reason nothing can be distorted.[21]

Iceland developed a reputation as a land whose people were especially keen on recording history. At some time between 1177 and 1187, Theodoricus (Þórir munkr) credited Icelanders with special diligence in recording history:

> In this book I have set down the count of years which I ascertained by making the most diligent inquiries I could among those whom we in our language call Icelanders. It is well known that they without doubt have always been more knowledgeable and more inquisitive in matters of this kind than all the other northern peoples. . .[22]

The Danish historian Saxo Grammaticus made the same claim for the Icelanders in the Preface, probably composed between 1208 and 1218, to his *History of the Danes*:

> The diligence of the men of Iceland must not be shrouded in silence; since the barrenness of their native soil offers no means of self-indulgence, they pursue a steady routine of temperance and devote all their time to improving our knowledge of others' deeds, compensating for poverty by their intelligence. They regard it a real pleasure to discover and commemorate the achievements of every nation; in their judgment it is as elevating to discourse on the prowess of others as to display their own. Thus I have scrutinized their store of historical treasures and composed a considerable part of this present work by copying their narratives, not scorning, where I recognized such skill in ancient lore, to take these men as witnesses.[23]

The history that Icelanders preserved included an exceptional amount of pre-Christian mythological material. No one wrote anything like the *Prose Edda*, or compiled and preserved anything like the *Poetic Edda*, in Anglo-Saxon England, continental Germany, or even mainland Scandinavia. In all these areas, as far as we can tell, whatever stories were once told of the old gods were mostly laid aside and forgotten with the arrival of Christianity.

What was different about Iceland?

Many of the genealogies preserved in the sagas make a point of tracing the ancestry of Icelandic families back beyond the *Landnám* generation. Some of these extended genealogies go back to kings or jarls, or to famous heroes, and here they begin to transition into mythology. Some kings were ultimately descended from the gods. Heroes might have famously accepted the gods' help in battle, or otherwise encountered them in some way, or might have faced mythological monsters such as dragons and giants and trolls. A famous passage in *Þorgils saga ok Hafliða*, part of the great compilation known as *Sturlunga saga*, describes the entertainment at a wedding feast at Reykjahólar, Iceland, in the year 1119:

> Hrolf of Skalmarnes told a saga about Hrongvid the Viking and about Olaf King of Warriors, and breaking into Thrain's burial mound, and Hromund Gripsson—and many verses along with it. King Sverrir found this saga amusing, and he called such "lying sagas" the most entertaining. And yet men are able to reckon their ancestry from Hromund Gripsson. Hrolf himself had put this saga together.[24]

The surviving *Hrómundar saga Grípssonar* dates to the 17th century and cannot be the same as whatever tale might have been told at the wedding, but its first four chapters correspond to Þorgils saga, featuring Hrongvid the Viking and the undead Thrain. Even if the account in *Þorgils saga* is fiction, a story corresponding to these first four chapters must have been known when *Þorgils saga* was written in the mid-13th century.25 And while King Sverrir, whose opinion is quoted although he was not born at the time of the wedding, considered such *lygisögur*, "lying sagas", to be entertainment only, at least some Icelanders evidently considered them as part of their family history. According to *Landnámabók*, Hromund Gripsson was the great-grandfather of Ingolf Arnarson, the first permanent settler in Iceland.[26]

Furthermore, a traditional poet had to know myth and legend extremely well in order to compose formal poetry. The *kenningar*, or metaphorical names for persons and things, were commonly derived from myths and legends; the name "embers of the Rhine", *glóða Rínar*, for gold only makes sense in reference to the fabulous golden treasure won by the hero Sigurd and sunk in the Rhine by his killers Gunnar and Högni, while the names "blood of Kvasir" (*dreyra Kvasis*), "shoal-wave of the dwarves' rock" (*grynnilö bergs dverga*), and "beer of the Terrible One" (*bjór Yggjar*) all refer to poetry by means of different episodes in the complex myth of how Odin won the mead which gave inspiration to those who tasted it. One could neither understand the great poems of the past nor compose new ones without a thorough grounding in myth and legend.

The Second Strand: Christian Learning

According to the sagas, there were Christians in Iceland from its earliest settlement, including some who had adopted it while in Britain or Ireland.[27] Other Icelanders were exposed to Christianity during trips to the mainland. Some, like Egil Skalla-Grimsson, allegedly adopted *prima signatio*, the sign of willingness to convert, purely as an advantage in trade. Others were more sincere; Thorvald the Far-Traveler converted during his time serving the King of Denmark, and returned to Iceland in 981 on a mission. By the year 1000, there was a sizable and vocal Christian community in Iceland, increasingly at odds with those who kept to the old religion. To head off civil strife, Iceland formally adopted Christianity.

Christianity brought with it a major cultural shift, because it depended on manuscript culture. Icelanders evidently used the pre-Christian rune alphabet before 1000, but this was never used to write extensive texts; stories and poems were transmitted almost entirely orally. By contrast, Christianity depends on a book—the Bible—and medieval Christianity further relied on liturgies, sermons, Bible commentaries, saints' lives and miracle stories, theological treatises, and other writings intended to confirm and strengthen the faith. For Christianity to survive, Icelanders had to be taught to read and write using the Latin alphabet. Priests had to know Latin, but the early generation of converts could not be expected to learn it fluently, and even after Latin instruction was available in Icelandic monasteries, relatively few had the opportunity to learn it. Translations had to be prepared, both for private devotion and for public preaching.

We have seen the *First Grammatical Treatise*'s mention of *þýðingar helgar* as some of the earliest Icelandic writing; *þýðingar* in this context could mean either "expositions; interpretations" or "translations," and in fact both types of writing were produced in abundance. The oldest known manuscripts in Old Norse, fragments dating from the late 12th century, include a collection of homilies, a compilation of saints' lives, the basic theological textbook *Elucidarius*, and two fragments dealing with computing the date of Easter.[28] The complete Bible was not translated into Icelandic until 1540, but translations of much of the Old Testament, some with considerable additions and commentary, have survived and are collectively known as *Stjórn*, "Steering" or "Direction". The Gospels and Psalms were probably translated separately; no complete manuscripts have survived, but quotations are frequent in Christian literature.[29] The lives and miracles of apostles and saints—including, in time, Iceland's native saints—also had to be made available in the vernacular, as did homilies and lessons. Finally, as manuscript culture and private reading grew, there was a need for theological treatises and writings for private devotion. We get glimpses of this in *Sturlunga saga*, in an incident from the year 1258: Þorgils skarði Böðvarsson spends the night as a guest at a farm, and offered his choice of dancing or saga-reading for entertainment, he chooses to have the life of St. Thomas Becket read aloud to him, "for he loved him more than other holy men."[30]

Churchmen also brought with them various secular texts. Not all of these texts were especially holy or useful, from a Christian perspective—an anecdote relates how Bishop (and later Saint) Jón of Hólar once caught a junior priest reading the erotic poetry of Ovid.[31] But secular medical texts, for example, were useful in monasteries that provided care to the sick. Would-be priests had to read classical Latin literature as part of their studies of the liberal arts of grammar and rhetoric. Texts on astronomy and calendrics were useful in determining the correct dates for Easter and other major feasts. Histories and geographies could also support the Christian message in various ways, clarifying parts of the Bible or furnishing lessons for sermons; for example, the *Physiologus*, a description of familiar and exotic animals with moral lessons drawn from each, is one of the earliest surviving translations into Icelandic.

The Bible itself contains miracles and other "fantastic" seeming events, but it was not a "fantastic" text, as the events related in it were meant to be accepted unquestioningly. The lives of saints mentioned in the Bible, such as the apostles of Jesus, shared in the authority of the Bible to some extent. Lives of Icelandic saints and bishops were often well authenticated, written by people who had known them. Yet some apostles and saints had traveled into far-distant lands, or so it was said; and strange and fantastic things could happen there. Many pious stories were set in exotic countries; some might feature monsters and treasures and battles of the sort that Icelanders would enjoy. Texts on cosmology and history also included fabulous places and peoples and beasts, some of them traceable to classical authors. Theodore Andersson has suggested that Christian myth and mystery may have been more important than suspected in the Icelanders' adoption of Christianity:

> . . . the Icelanders could also have been swayed by a certain liberation of the imagination as they absorbed the new, more potent Christian magic found in the liturgy and the miracles of hagiography. . . . We know that they looked back at their own pagan religion as a fundamentally magical practice, and perhaps they did not at first regard Christianity so much as a displacement of magic but rather more as the advent of a more powerful magic from a distant region in the East, a magic that had captured all the intervening regions from the Holy Land to Iceland.[32]

While the Bible itself was not to be questioned, the more "fantastic" lore and legend transmitted along with it could sometimes be of dubious veracity. The prologue to *Niðrstigninga saga* or *The Saga of the Descent* [into Hell], a partial translation of the non-canonical but widely known Gospel of Nicodemus, almost timidly points out that the book is not said to be dubious, even though it is not canonical.

The Third Strand: Tales of Chivalry

Hákon Hákonarsson (Hákon IV of Norway), who ruled from 1217 to 1263, is credited with sponsoring a series of Norse translations of French or Anglo-Norman *romans*, *lais*, and *chansons de geste*, which probably came to him through trade and diplomatic contacts, especially with Henry III of England.[33] The earliest evidence for Hákon's "translation project" comes from *Tristrams Saga ok Ísönd*, a translation of *Tristan* by Thomas of Britain; its prologue mentions that one Brother Robert translated the saga in the year 1226, when Hákon would have been about twenty-one years old. A translation of the French chanson de geste of *Élie de Saint Gille*, *Elis saga ok Rosamundu*, is attributed to "Abbot Robert"; while we cannot be sure that he was the same man as Brother Robert (presumably with a promotion), no one seems to have any better ideas.[34] Hákon is also credited with sponsoring *Strengleikar*, a translation of the *lais* of Marie de France and other authors;

Ívens saga, a translation of Chrétien de Troyes's *Yvain*; and *Möttuls saga*, a translation of a *fabliau*, *Le lai du cort mantel*. He probably encouraged or oversaw the translation of other romances, such as *Parcevals saga*, although there is less direct evidence.

Hákon's motives are not clear. It is often assumed that he had these texts translated because he wanted to promulgate chivalric ethics—valor, generosity, wisdom, renown, and courtly manners. After a hundred years of fighting between factions who kept setting weak kings on the throne, he may well have wanted to spread the ideals of chivalry, especially the ideal of a strong and just king firmly on top of a stable hierarchy of loyal courtiers, in the mold of King Arthur.[35] On the other hand, several of the translated texts present a rather critical or satirical view of court life, and most do not feature an especially strong king. If Hákon was trying to instill reverence for ideals of feudal rulership, his choice of, say, *Möttuls saga* for translation would be rather odd. Several of the translated tales explicitly state that they were created to entertain, and perhaps they were more valued by their audience as entertainment than as propaganda.

Nonetheless, Hákon may have seen these tales as prestige gifts—not physical gifts, but gifts of entertainment with exotic tales from distant lands—that he could offer his court, increasing his reputation among his courtiers and guests.[36] He may also have felt that his kingdom, remote from European centers of power, had some catching up to do in culture and reputation if it was to be considered the equal of other kingdoms. According to Hákon's biography (*Hákonar saga Hákonarsonar*), the Papal representative at his coronation in 1247, Cardinal William of Sabina, was pleasantly surprised to find that the food, drink, and company were of the highest quality; he had been warned that Norwegians lived like beasts and their food and drink was wretched and scanty. Given the negative stereotypes of Norway that evidently existed at the time, Hákon may have felt that his court needed a touch of class.[37]

Other chivalric tales circulated in Norway and Iceland, and these may have been translated elsewhere. *Karlamagnús saga* is a compilation of sagas about the Matter of France; most are translations of *chansons de geste*, but one was translated from a now-lost Middle English original in 1286 or 1287, under the auspices of King Eirik II of Norway.[38] Another portion of *Karlamagnús saga*, known as *Af Agulando konungi*, seems to have been translated before 1200.[39] Also falling in the "chivalric" category, more or less, is *Þiðreks saga af Bern*, based on a Middle Low German cycle of tales about Theodoric of Verona (Dietrich af Bern). *Þiðreks saga* may have been translated at Hákon's court, or possibly even before his rule began. Supposedly, Hákon's grandson Hákon Mágnússon (Hákon V; reigned 1299-1319) had many romances translated from French and Greek, although if this is true, none of them are known to have survived.[40] Several other sagas may be based on continental romances, but either the material has been considerably reworked or the original romance has been lost. These would include *Mágus saga jarls*, a reworking of *Les quatre fils Aymon*; and *Flóvents saga*, probably a translation of a lost chanson de geste that has little in common with the existing *Floovant*. *Klári saga* claims to be a translation of a Latin poem by the Icelandic bishop Jón Halldórsson, who had found it in France; it has no known analogues in French or Latin literature and may well be an original composition.[41]

Finally, a number of medieval historiographical works, sometimes referred to today as "pseudo-histories", were translated into Old Norse. These overlap in style and subject matter with the chivalric romances to some degree. Examples include *Trójumanna saga* (The Saga of the Trojans), translated from Darius Phrygius's *De excidio Troiae*; *Breta sögur* (The Sagas of the Britons), based on Geoffrey of Monmouth's *Historia regum Britanniae*; *Rómverja saga* (The Saga of the Romans), based on works by Lucan and Sallust; *Gyðinga saga* (The Saga of the Jews), based on the books of Maccabees; and *Alexanders saga* (The Saga of Alexander the Great), based on Walter of Châtillon's *Alexandreis*. Hákon IV's son, Magnús Hákonarson, is credited with commissioning *Alexanders saga* and *Gyðinga saga* from the Icelandic bishop Brandr Jónsson at some time between 1257 and 1263.[42]

Judging by the number of manuscript copies, the translated *riddarasögur* were not the most popular reading in medieval Iceland; many texts survive in only a few copies. Nonetheless, they had considerable influence on Icelandic literature. There are allusions in other sagas to chivalric sagas, including allusions to some works that have been lost but must once have existed.[43] The epilogue to the longer edition of *Mágus saga jarls* in its epilogue mentions that "wise men will want to listen to those stories that they find enjoyable for pleasure, such as *Thidreks saga*, *Flóvents saga*, or other sagas of knights" (*spakir menn. . . vilja heyra þær frásagnir, sem þeim þikki kátligar til gamans, svo sem er Þiðreks saga, Flóvents saga eðr aðrar riddarasögur*).[44]

The translated *riddarasögur* have received less scholarly attention than other saga genres, except when they preserve texts whose original has been lost. The translations vary in their degree of perceived fidelity; some follow the original fairly closely, but others show considerable revision. *Parcevals saga*, for example, has been condensed to about 40% the length of its source, Chrétien de Troyes's *Perceval*, by the deletion of descriptive passages and philosophical digressions. The translator has also added a brief prologue, scattered rhyming couplets throughout the narrative, and an epilogue that brings Chrétien's unfinished tale to a hasty narrative conclusion. Scholars of medieval literature have sometimes dismissed the translated *riddarasögur* as inferior work by incompetent translators who cut passages whose artistic significance they could not grasp. However, when comparative study of multiple manuscripts is possible, it often shows that many of the alterations are the work of later copyists, not the original translator. Different recensions of the same saga may vary so much that it is hard to get an idea of exactly what the original translator wrote, yet it seems clear that the Norwegian translators like Brother Robert were more accurate than they have sometimes been given credit for.[45] Furthermore, in practice it is difficult to draw a line between "translations" and "adaptations" in medieval literature. It would be surprising if the riddarasögur had been translated perfectly literally, with no attempt to make them more relevant to their audience.[46]

Braiding The Strands Together

Many extant sagas, whatever genre they may be placed in, show a "braiding" of two or more of these strands. Motifs were freely borrowed among sagas. To give just a few of the best-known examples: *Völsunga saga* recounts the legend of Sigurd, an ancient tale known in Old English and Middle German literature and traceable to events in the 5th century. However, *Völsunga saga* includes an episode borrowed from *Eliduc*, a *lai* of Marie de France that has not survived in Norse translation but must have been known.[47] *Völsunga saga* also includes a chapter borrowed from *Þiðreks saga af Bern* that recounts the hero's chivalric accomplishments and the blazon of his coat of arms—matters with which the historical Iron Age prototype of Sigurd probably did not concern himself. *Eiriks saga rauða*, an account of the Viking-era discovery of the New World, includes an encounter with a "Plinian race", a uniped or *einfætingr*, while the legendary *Örvar-Odds saga* includes an encounter with monsters from the *Physiologus* and some geographical information from a learned text.[48] A number of "bookish *riddarasögur*" blend the conventions of chivalry with the exotic settings and monsters of Christian learning.[49] Translations of saints' lives and learned texts frequently replace the names of Roman or Greek gods with their Norse counterparts, and even include fragments of their mythological attributes.[50] Many more examples of motif exchange could be listed. On a deeper level, plot types were also freely borrowed; to give one famous example, the "maiden-king", in which the hero tries to win a hostile bride who rules like a man, appears in no fewer than ten Icelandic romances, and may have been borrowed from the translated *Klári saga* and/or *Partalopa saga*.[51] On the other hand, narrative types derived from Norse myths of Odin and Thor end up in Icelandic romances such as *Samsons saga*, *Vilmundar saga*, and *Valdimars saga*.[52]

By the mid-14th century, sagas were being composed that drew on all three strands, blending them to such a degree that they are difficult to classify as one genre or the other. These have been variously classified as *fornaldarsögur* or *riddarasögur*, depending on whether the setting is Viking-age Scandinavia or elsewhere in Eurasia. Stylistically and thematically, however, they are much harder to distinguish, and are sometimes classified together as *Märchensagas*, *lygisögur*, "late prose fiction," "indigenous riddarasögur", or "indigenous romances." The heroes of such sagas may face giants and trolls from ancient myths, yet may also contend in jousting and other chivalric pursuits, while professing Christian devotion and encountering monsters from medieval bestiaries. In the hands of an unskilled compiler, the result could be a mess—and in fact, the later romantic sagas have often been dismissed as boring, jumbled, and derivative. But skilled writers could make such composite stories work well, as entertaining and sometimes edifying tales—and some of the romances are as well-crafted as any Icelandic literature.[53]

There were two places in medieval Iceland where people had the time, tastes, and resources to compose romances: the church, and the estates of secular magnates. However, it must be remembered that during the time that sagas were coming to be written down, there was no fine line between the two.

By the year 930, Iceland's government had taken shape. The chief legal and judicial authorities were the *goðar*, who assembled each year at the Althing to make new laws and hear judicial cases. The word *goði* originally meant "pagan priest," but in Iceland the secular powers of the *goðar* continued even after paganism had been officially abandoned. Yet while paganism lasted, the *goðar* seem to have had the responsibility for communal religious worship. A *goði* might build a temple on his land, hold regular ritual feasts there, and be empowered to collect the *hoftollr* or "temple toll", a fee for maintaining the temple.[54]

This model seems to have been maintained even after the coming of Christianity, when pious landowners began to build churches on their own farms for their family's use. By the 12th century, churches were being endowed with land. A *goði* might choose to endow a church with an entire farm, or at least a large share of a farm; such a church was known as a *staðr.* The arrangement could be lucrative for the *goði*, who was entitled to a quarter of the local tithes to pay for maintenance of the church; if he was the priest or appointed the priest, he was entitled to another quarter of the tithe, and he might also be able to collect additional dues and tolls from churchgoers. Families that controlled *staðir* grew wealthy; this contributed to the situation in the 13th century by which a few powerful families of chieftains (*stórgoðar*, literally "big goðar") came to control most of the *goðorð* (offices of the *goðar*).[55]

Instruction for the priesthood and ordination originally had to be acquired abroad; the first native bishop of Iceland, Ísleifr Gizursson, had been educated at the cathedral school of Herford Abbey in England, and later traveled to Germany for his ordination. Once a bishop and a cadre of priests were available in Iceland, many *goðar* chose to be ordained as priests themselves—despite frequently being married (clerical celibacy was not enforced in Iceland until 1275) and engaging in quite secular political wrangling. As *Kristni saga* relates, when Gizurr Ísleifsson was bishop at Skálholt during the period 1082-1118:

> Bishop Gizur pacified the country so well that there were no conflicts among the chieftains, and the carrying of weapons fell very much into disuse. At that time, most worthy men were educated and consecrated as priests, although they were chieftains.[56]

By the middle of the 12th century, roughly half the goðar were also priests.[57] It was not until 1190 that the Norwegian Archbishop prohibited the ordination of *goðar*; even after that, *goðar* gave their sons clerical education. The situation set up a conflict between the Icelandic chieftains and the Church, known as the *Staðamál*, over whether the Church or the chieftains could claim control of the churches and their revenue. The chieftains actually won the first *Staðamál* in 1179, and it was not until 1297 that the Church gained full control over the *staðir*.[58]

Beginning with the first bishopric at Skálholt, founded in 1056, the cathedrals and monasteries of Iceland became centers of instruction. But some of the *staðir* also became important intellectual centers. To give a famous example, the *staðr* at Oddi was renowned as a center of learning under the ownership of Jón Loptsson (1124-1197), where the famous author and political figure Snorri Sturluson was fostered. Snorri himself went on to acquire the staðir of Reykholt and nearby Stafholt, and by 1220 he controlled two major *staðir*, with a total staff of twelve priests. Even though Iceland had plenty of sheep to provide the parchment, books and manuscripts were relatively rare items, and the time spent in writing, illustrating, and binding books was also valuable. For a *staðr* to own a library would have conferred considerable prestige.[59] A chieftain holding a feast at one of his *staðir* would have enhanced his status if he could offer the reading of excellent sagas as entertainment—preferably painting his own ancestors in a favorable light—along with excellent food and drink.[60]

In the *staðir*, the "strand" of traditional stories and the "strand" of church lore would have come together frequently. The learning available to the Icelandic elite at the *staðir* in the 12th and 13th centuries would have included Latin and Christian theology—but it would also have included extensive training in Icelandic law, as fitting for future chieftains and retainers who had to master the game of power politics. It would also have included training in traditional skaldic poetry, both learning the greatest old poems and composing new ones—and in the knowledge of mythology, legend, and history that was needed in order to understand and compose poems.[61] In fact, by the end of the 12th century, Icelandic chieftains like Jón Loptsson were beginning to surround themselves with praise-poets of their own; poetic skill could be quite useful within Iceland itself, as well as useful in ingratiating oneself with Norwegian magnates.[62] The conflict with the church over the *staðir* may have contributed to a sense that the native lore preserved in Iceland, even the parts that dealt with the old gods, was worthy of being remembered and preserved, equal in some sense to the lore of the church and the chivalric tales from abroad.

With the church's introduction of manuscript culture, chieftains could now write the stories of their ancestors who had settled Iceland, the *Íslendingasögur*—along with sagas and poems of the German and Scandinavian heroic past, creating the heroic *fornaldarsögur*. Both of these could buttress their claims to greatness. Gabriel Turville-Petre argued that the saints' lives introduced by the church inspired the creation of the saga form:

> The saints' lives and the homilies are not among the best or most interesting of Icelandic literature. . . . But they were more important for the Icelanders of the twelfth century than they are for us. They were the first written biographies which the Icelanders came to know. The Icelanders learned from them how biographies and wonder-tales could be written in books. Thus, they helped the Icelanders to develop a literary style in their own language, and gave them the means to express their own thoughts through the medium of letters. It is unlikely that the sagas of kings and of Icelanders, or even the sagas of ancient heroes, would have developed as they did unless several generations of Icelanders had first been trained in hagiographic narrative.[63]

Not all scholars today would agree that saints' lives are the foundation of the saga form, but saints' lives and learned treatises certainly expanded the sagas' horizons, giving them new and exotic settings from Africa to Greece to Babylonia, and new villains and monsters ranging from devils to elephants and flying serpents. They also expanded the stylistic palette of Icelandic literature, as some Icelanders came to adopt Latinate styles and rhetoric.

Meanwhile, leading Icelandic chieftains traveled to and from Norway, where they might well have heard recitations of the chivalric tales commissioned by King Hákon. In the aftermath of Iceland's incorporation into Norway between 1262 and 1264, at the end of Hákon's reign, a few Icelanders had the opportunity to join the royal court and be dubbed knights. Even Icelanders who were not dubbed knights would have wanted to make a good impression at court, or with the royal representatives in

Iceland. An early manuscript of *Flóres saga konungs*—the translation of *Floire et Blancheflor*—makes this suggestion:

> If men are eager to hear old stories, the first thing to pay attention to is that most sagas deal with certain topics. Some are about God and his saints, and one can learn great wisdom there, but most men don't find much amusement in sagas of saints. Other sagas are about powerful kings; from them, one can learn refined, courtly customs, or how to serve powerful rulers. The third division of the sagas concerns those kings who have undergone great trials and gotten out of them in various ways, and people can conduct themselves after the example of those bold men.[64]

It was presumably through the coming and going of Icelanders to and from Norway that the translated sagas found their way to Iceland; in fact, many of Hákon's translations survive only in Icelandic manuscripts, some dating several centuries after their composition. And their style probably furnished models for Icelandic writers; writing in the 13th century, in his *Third Grammatical Treatise*, Óláfr Þórðarson referred to "courtly eloquence" (*hirðlig málsnild*) as one of the three prose styles in Icelandic writing, along with "popular style" (*alþýðligt orðtæki*) and "discourse of scholars" (*ræður spekinga*).[65]

The braiding of these strands together created a space in which the best saga writers could play with different concepts of truth. Christian lore gave Icelanders the vocabulary to discuss the truth or lack thereof in their texts; Isidore of Seville, for one, had written of the difference between *historia*, *argumentum*, and *fabula*:

> And history [*historia*], 'plausible narration' [*argumentum*], and fable [*fabula*] differ from one another. Histories are true deeds that have happened, plausible narrations are things that, even if they have not happened, nevertheless could happen, and fables are things that have not happened and cannot happen, because they are contrary to nature.[66]

> A history (*historia*) is a narration of deeds accomplished; through it what occurred in the past is sorted out.[67]

> Poets named 'fables' (*fabula*) from 'speaking' (*fari*), because they are not actual events that took place, but were only invented in words. . . . Poets have made up some fables for the sake of entertainment, and expounded others as having to do with the nature of things, and still others as about human morals.[68]

While *fabulae* could have their place as vehicles for moral instruction, Icelanders seem to have prided themselves on their reputation for recording historia as truthfully as possible. The earliest historical writings "cite their sources"; Ari Thorgilsson begins the *Íslendingabók* by listing people whom he knew personally and recognized as having excellent memories:

> Iceland was first settled from Norway in the days of Harald Fairhair son of Halfdan the Black, at the time—by the reasoning and reckoning of my foster-father Teitr, the wisest man I knew, son of Bishop Isleif; and my father's brother Thorkel Gellison, who remembered a long way back; and Thurid the daughter of Snorri the Priest, who was both very wise and accurately informed—when Ivar the son of Ragnar Lodbrok had St. Edmund the King of England killed. That was eight hundred and seventy years after the birth of Christ, as is written in Edmund's saga.[69]

Although some sagas contain episodes that seem "fantastic" to us, that does not mean that their original authors, readers, and copyists saw them in that light; criteria for truth were different in the medieval world. Certainly many medieval writers, in Iceland and outside it, had no reason to disbelieve stories about fantastic beasts and where to find them—in the far reaches of the world, or in the distant past when great heroes walked the earth. Claims to veracity that seem humorous today, such as the claim that Homer originally wrote the indigenous romance *Vilhjálms saga sjóðs* on a wall in ancient Babylon, would not have seemed so obviously incorrect to medieval readers.[70] Medieval authors could also invent dialogue and even certain episodes without surrendering their claim to be recording accurate history, and pious authors writing about saints could introduce material that they felt was spiritually "true," even if it was not necessarily historically true. Thus, the inclusion of material that no modern historian would accept as valid does not mean that a saga-writer was intentionally writing fiction. In fact, the words for a story that was not true, *lygisaga* and *skröksaga* ("lie-saga" and "falsehood-saga"), usually had strongly pejorative connotations.[71]

All the same, the assimilation of the chivalric romances into Icelandic culture seems to have created a "space" within which authors could explore different concepts of narrative truth. In particular, the device of the self-conscious narrator, imported from the chivalric romances, allowed Icelandic saga authors to maintain an ironic distance from the narrative. The narrator could occasionally offer humorous comments on the action, or could head off the audience's possible skepticism of fantastic-seeming events with straight-faced avowals of truth. In this way, the narrator could maintain that he was writing, not necessarily a *fabula*, but an *argumentum*—a story that might or might not have happened, but that certainly could have happened. The prologue to *Flóres saga* has already been cited for listing three separate types of saga, but it goes on:

> But it is the habit of many people to call sagas lies that go beyond their own ability, and the reason is that a weak man cannot tell what great deeds men may accomplish who were both strong and had excellent weapons that could cut everything. And we can see many true examples of how strong men have worked, and the huge stones that they have carried. And no one can deny what Fortune grants to those whom she wishes to raise up.[72]

The prologue to *Göngu-Hrólfs saga* makes a similar point:

> Men have composed many tales for entertainment, some according to ancient lays or the knowledge of learned men, and sometimes according to old books, which originally were set down briefly, but were later filled out with words, because most events are quicker in the telling. Men are never equally well informed, because it often happens that what's seen and heard by one isn't seen and heard by another, even though they're present at the same event. And it's also in the nature of many foolish men to believe only what they see with their own eyes or hear with their own ears. They find that what came of the schemes of wise men, or the mighty strength or surpassing skill of great men, is far beyond their own natures—and this is no less the case concerning trickery, or wizardry

> and mighty magic, when they conjured up eternal misfortune or loss of life for some, and for others, worldly reputation, riches, and honors.[73]

It's not entirely clear whether disclaimers like this are intended to be tongue-in-cheek invitations to suspend disbelief, or serious avowals that the fantastic events in the sagas are really true. But whatever attitude towards truth the creators of the indigenous romances may have had, they created a type of literature that was "good to think with"—that could be used to reflect on contemporary issues that they faced.

Icelandic chieftains in the 13th century felt a need to integrate with medieval Christendom, adopting the Christian learned lore and the aristocratic vernacular literature in vogue at European courts. At the same time, they felt a need to show that their own history and lineages were as noble as those of any other country.[74] Hence they had reason for creating and preserving all three "strands" of literature. In 1262-1264, Iceland came under Norwegian rule, and the *goðar* were replaced by royal officers (although many of these were initially drawn from the same leading families). By 1400, Iceland was being relegated to the status of a backwater; it could only watch as Norway came under joint rule with Sweden and Denmark in the Kalmar Union, whose kings took Copenhagen for their capital and focused on continental affairs. The indigenous romances are often said to form an "escapist" literature, enabling Icelanders to forget their waning status as a nation. Yet there is more to the romances than escapism; they must have spoken to contemporary concerns of their writers and listeners or readers. Through their literary heritage, Icelanders could still take pride in their long and glorious past, while wealthy Icelanders with ambitions of improving their status could learn from the courtly sagas of chivalry and the encyclopedic lore preserved and transmitted by the Church. Writers and readers of sagas like these could explore questions of how to contract marriages that might boost one's social status, or how to deal with powerful rivals in the most effective and beneficial way. Thus the blending of literary traditions from distant places and times created a new type of literature that could effectively address concerns of the here and now.

Notes on the Translation

To facilitate comparison with parallel sources in other languages, I have rendered the most familiar personal and place names by their best-known equivalents in English: *Arthur* instead of *Artús*, *Theodoric* instead of *Þiðrek*, *Bartholomew* instead of *Bartholomeus*, *Ravenna* instead of *Rána*, and so on. Even here I've made some exceptions, mostly because they seemed like a good idea at the time. I have tried my best to render different Icelandic prose styles with similar English styles.

I owe a great debt of gratitude to Enbarr Coleman, Ani Greenwood, Thomas de Mayo, and Ann Sheffield, who proofread and critiqued my translations. All remaining errors and shortcomings are entirely my own. I thank Zoe Borovsky, Sean Crist, Matthew Driscoll, Silvia Hufnagel, P. S. Langeslag, Stefan Langeslag, Andy Lemons, Carsten Lyngdrup Madsen, and Jon Julius Sandal for creating freely available electronic resources that were indispensable for my work. I owe a great debt to Dietrich Mateschitz's contribution to completing this book. The redoubtable and long-suffering Tim Purkiss and Amanda Bryant moved mountains to hunt down obscure books and articles that I needed, and Chris Baty has provided inspiration and incentive for years.

Last, but never least, I thank Amanda Waggoner for her love and support, as always.

Þykki mér bezt sóma,
at finna eigi til,
þeir eigi um bæta.

SAGAS OF OLDEN TIMES

The Saga of King Half and his Warband

Hálfs saga ok Hálfsrekka

While King Hálf lacks the fame of Sigurd the Volsung or King Hrolf Kraki, his legend has deep roots. As early as the 9th century, the poem Ynglingatal *used the kenning* Hálfs bani, *"Half's bane", to mean "fire". Half and his kinfolk get brief mentions in* Landnámabók, *in Snorri Sturluson's* Edda, *and in various other sources dating to or before the 13th century.*[1] *The age of his legendarium, and the sizable amount of old poetry, makes* Hálfs saga ok Hálfsrekka *a good example of a "heroic fornaldarsaga".*

The saga contains several episodes borrowed from folklore. The story of the sardonically laughing sea-goblin is a folktale recorded from Scandinavia and Ireland; the wife who unwittingly promises her unborn son in exchange for supernatural assistance is known from the fairy tale "Rumpelstiltskin," among other sources. Even the "Polyphemus motif" from the Odyssey, in which a hero stabs a hostile giant in the eye with a burning spear, puts in an appearance. Hence Hálfs saga *has been written off as an awkwardly assembled hodgepodge. Yet there are common themes that bind the saga into a coherent whole. In particular, strife brought about by marriage—rivalry between men over women, rivalry among competing wives, and rivalry among families related through marriage—drives much of the action in the first part of the saga, and only in the second part does King Half manage to put an end to it.*

Torfi Tulinius points out that Hálfs saga *would have been appreciated in 13th-century Iceland because it spoke to the interests and concerns of the ruling class. Rival Icelandic chieftains held large estates and maintained troops of fighting men, and violence was common—including burning houses with enemies inside. The men of these Icelandic warrior bands would have enjoyed* Hálfs saga *for its battle scenes that reflected the real battles they fought, and for its depiction of King Half as an ideal leader and his men as ideal followers.*[2] *Themes of marital rivalry would have also seemed quite contemporary to the Icelandic chieftains, who could and did take concubines, plural wives in all but name.* Hálfs saga*'s themes of rivalry among wives and extended families* *would have seemed quite timely. Thus, like many* fornaldarsögur, Hálfs saga *was written and understood as a way to discuss social issues at the time in which it was composed.*

The oldest manuscript of the saga is GKS 2845 4to, dating from the middle of the 15th century. I've translated the text as published by Guðni Jónsson and Bjarni Vilhjálmson and checked it against Hubert Seelow's critical edition of the manuscript. Where the verses are ambiguous or indecipherable, I have felt free to choose which textual authority to follow (discussed in the footnotes).

CHAPTER I

There was a king named Alrek who lived at Alreksstad[3] and ruled over Hordaland. He married Signy, the daughter of the king of Vor. He had a retainer named Koll, who traveled north with the king to Sogn, and told him a great deal about the beauty of Geirhild the daughter of Drif, because he had seen her brewing strong ale.[4] Koll told him that he approved of this match.

Hott—who was actually Odin—came to find Geirhild as she was weaving her linen.[5] He struck a bargain with her: King Alrek would marry her, but she had to call on him for everything. The king saw her when he came home, and he held a wedding with her that same autumn. The king rewarded Koll well for his trustworthiness, giving him the title of jarl and a residence on Kollsey, on the south side of Hardsae. That's a heavily populated district.[6]

King Alrek could not stay married to both Signy and Geirhild, because they couldn't get along. He said that he would keep the one who could brew better ale for him when he came home from levying taxes. They contended with each other in brewing ale. Signy called on Freyja, but Geirhild called on Hott. He dropped some spit on the lees, and said that in exchange for coming, he wanted what was between the vat and herself. The ale turned out to be good. Alrek said:

Geirhild my girl,[7]
good is this ale,
if no curses
have come with it.

I see hanging
on a high gallows
your son, woman,
sent to Odin.

Within six months, Vikar was born, the son of Alrek and Geirhild.[8]

CHAPTER II

Ogvald the king of Rogaland lived at Roga, in Josurheid. That's between Rogaland and Telemark; men now call that Vidi. He went out hunting, and his household went with him. There his queen gave birth to a boy named Josur. Gunnvald the Jarl of Stord fostered him.[9]

Haekling the Viking attacked King Ogvald with his forces. King Ogvald fell in that battle, and he was buried in a mound on Ogvaldsnes.[10]

Finn the Wealthy[11] from Akranes, who settled Iceland, anchored off Ogvaldsnes as he was bound for Iceland, and he asked how long it had been since King Ogvald fell. He heard this verse spoken inside the mound:

So long ago,
they steered this way,
a huge host
of Haekling's men,
sailing the salt trail
of the sea-trout.° — *trail of the sea-trout*: ocean
Then I was chosen
as chief of this village.[12]

CHAPTER III

Jarl Gunnvald and Koll both asked to marry the same woman, and Gunnvald got her. Afterwards, Koll secretly landed on Stord with large forces and set Gunnvald Roga's house on fire. Gunnvald ran outside and was killed.

By then, Josur had been king for some time. He moved at once to avenge his foster-father, with a great force. When Koll saw his ships approaching, he rushed on board his warship and sailed north around Hardsae into

Grafdalsvag.[13] King Alrek came to meet Koll with few men, because he wasn't expecting hostility. They fought with King Josur, and King Alrek fell there with the greater part of his forces.

Alrek's son Vikar didn't come with the forces he'd summoned until King Josur had left. On that expedition, Josur subjugated all the realm that Koll had held.

CHAPTER IV

Many years later, King Vikar with many men came against Josur when he was in the realm that Koll had held, and they had a battle. Josur fell before him, along with all the farmers of that district. It's called Women's District[14] because only widows lived there afterwards. Then Vikar took possession of all the realm that Koll had owned. In response to that, Josur's son Hjorr came to battle Vikar. They fought each other for a long time, and first one side and then the other had the advantage. In the end they came to a settlement.

Vikar's son was Vatnar, who was buried in Vatnarshaug. Vatnar's sons were Snjall and Hjall, who lie in Braedrahaug.[15]

CHAPTER V

King Hjorr, Josur's son, was a powerful king. He died of an illness and was buried in a mound in Rogaland. His son was Hjorleif, the king of Hordaland. He also ruled over Rogaland and was a most mighty king. He was called Hjorleif Woman-Chaser. He married Aesa the Shining, the daughter of Jarl Eystein of Valdres.

Hjorleif ran short of money, on account of his open-handedness. He had a ship built with great care, and traveled to Bjarmaland.[16] Hogni the Wealthy lived on Njardey, across from the mouth of Namdalen.[17] He welcomed King Hjorleif, and the king stayed there for three nights. He married Hild the Slender, Hogni's daughter, before he went away. She went with him to Bjarmaland, along with her brother Solvi.

When King Hjorleif came to the mouth of the Dvina River, he divided his forces into thirds. There were ninety men on his ship. A third of his men went with him and fought the inhabitants. Another third of his men guarded the ship along with the steersman, and the final third broke open mounds along with the forecastle-man, and they got a great deal of wealth.

King Hjorleif anchored for the night in a hidden inlet on Gjardey in the south of Finnmark.[18] His cooks built a fire on land, and two men went to fetch water from a brook that plunged over a cliff. There they saw a well-pissing ogre,[19] and they told King Hjorleif. At once the king heated a spiked spear in the fire and thrust it at him. The king said,

Away from the well,
worthless wretch!
Back to your home,
don't banter with me.
I will send you
a sizzling spear,
which will wet down
your whiskers with gore.

They took their water, and the ogre dashed into the cliff. When they were sitting beside the fire, the ogre chanted another song from the cliff:

Your wife, o king,
doesn't clearly know
what will hold back
her happiness.
Hild will grant you
her goodly love,
unworthy Hjorleif.
Stay warm by the fire![20]

Then Hjorleif threw the same spear into that troll's eye.[21]

Hogni invited Solvi and Hild to stay with him, but the king didn't want that. Two serving-maids went with Hild, and twenty men went with Solvi. Aesa was not pleased with the king and his retinue, but everyone else was happy.

CHAPTER VI

King Hjorleif traveled to Konungahella[22] in the same ship that he had taken to Bjarmaland. Hreidar the king of Zealand and his men set up their booths nearby.[23] Heri, the son of King Hreidar, ingratiated himself with King Hjorleif. When they met, he urged his father to invite King Hjorleif to his home. King Hreidar said that that wouldn't turn out to be fortunate, but he gave his permission and a sum of money.

They sailed together to Denmark. At this feast, King Hjorleif saw Hringja, the daughter of King Hreidar, and asked for her hand. She was eager for this marriage, and a ship's crew and all its cargo were her dowry.

King Hjorleif lay becalmed in the Skagerrak. When he went out at sunrise, he looked to the north and saw a huge mountain coming out of the sea in the shape of a man. It said:

I see a howe
for Hringja raised,
and Heri sink,
hit by a spear.
I see Hjorleif
held in bonds,
and for Hreidar
a hewn gallows.

The ships wouldn't move. The king ordered his men to start rowing. Then Hringja fell sick. They gave up rowing. She died at the same time of day that she had fallen ill, and her coffin was thrown overboard. It sailed back southward as quickly as a six-oared ship could be rowed.

Heri found the coffin washed up a short distance from his father's boatshed. He told him about it, and said that King Hjorleif must have murdered her.

CHAPTER VII

That autumn, a father and his son rowed out to fish and hauled in a sea-goblin.[24] One of them was named Handir, and the other was Hrindir. They brought the goblin to Hjorleif. The king put him in the care of one of his female retainers and ordered her to treat him well. No one got a word out of him.

The pageboys were wrestling, and they put out the candle. At that moment, Hild knocked a drinking horn onto Aesa's mantle. The king struck her with his hand, but Hild said that the dog that was lying on the floor was to blame. The king beat the dog. Just then the goblin laughed. The king asked why he was laughing. He answered, "Because you were foolish, since they'll save your life."[25] The king asked him further, but he didn't answer.

At once the king said that they would return him to the sea, and asked him to tell him what he needed to know. When the goblin went to the sea, he said:

> I see light on the sea
> a long way to the south:
> the Danish king vows
> vengeance for his daughter.
> He has set sail
> with ships uncounted,
> he calls on Hjorleif
> to come and fight him.
>
> Beware this warning,
> if you will. . . .
> I want to go back to the sea.

But when they rowed with him to the spot where they had hauled him up, he said:

> There's a very good tale
> I can tell to the sons
> of Haleyg, if they're willing
> to hear what I say:
> up from the south,
> soaked in blood,
> the daughter of Hogni[26]
> from Denmark comes.

She has on her head
a helmet clasped,
Hedin's grim sign
of strife on her hair.[27]
I see that the lads
won't have long to wait
for Hild to wend
her way right here.

The ring-land° will be ruined,
there rises before my eyes
a fearsome felling of
defenders of these lands.[28]
Every swordsman's mate must
have many spears readied,[29]
before the storm of steel
stretches forth to reach us.

ring-land: shield

If this is true,
there's trouble ahead;
a high price to pay
for a prosperous spring.

King Hjorleif let him over the side. Then a man seized him by the hand and asked, "What is best for a man?" The sea-goblin answered:

Cold water for eyes,
whale's flesh[30] for teeth,
linen for the body.
Let me back in the sea!
No man shall drag me
in days to come
from the ocean floor
up into a ship.

The king gave Handir and Hrindir land to settle on, and slaves and bondsmaids along with it.

CHAPTER VIII

At once King Hjorleif sent out the war-arrow[31] and summoned his forces. In the night, King Hreidar arrived with his host and surrounded King Hjorleif's estate. That same night, Hjorleif's dog Floki barked—he never barked unless he knew that the king was in danger. King Hjorleif broke through the ring of men and flung a spear back at his enemies, and he heard someone call out that Heri had fallen. From the forest, the king saw the burning of his home, and King Hreidar sailing away with a great deal of plunder.

That same autumn, King Hjorleif came in a single ship to King Hreidar's estate in the night. He went alone into the sleeping quarters, but all the women had left their beds, except for Aesa alone.[32] The king told her to get him close to King Hreidar. She locked him in her wardrobe chest, and went and told King Hreidar at once that Hjorleif was there. On Aesa's advice, King Hjorleif was strung up by his own shoelaces between two fires in the king's hall,[33] but the king's retainers sat drinking.

In the meantime, Hild stayed awake and poured beer on the fires. She released Hjorleif by cutting his shoelaces with a sword. King Hreidar was sitting in the high-seat asleep, and Aesa sat on his lap. King Hjorleif stabbed him in the chest, and at once ran to his ship for his men. He had King Hreidar's retainers tied up, but granted them a truce. But he had dead King Hreidar hanged on the gallows that Hreidar had meant for him.

That same evening when King Hjorleif came, King Hreidar heard this recited:

Remember, Hreidar,
who felled Heri.[34]
Woe was wakened
by the western door.
She's heading again
to your hall, a woman
with winds at her back—
just you wait, king!

King Hjorleif laid under his rule all the realm that King Hreidar had held. He appointed Hogni's son Solvi to rule it, and gave him the title of jarl. But King Hjorleif traveled to Norway and brought Hild and Aesa with him, and he summoned the assembly. The people of the land ruled that Aesa was to be drowned in a bog, but King Hjorleif sent her away to the highlands with her dowry.

The son of Hjorleif and Aesa was Oblaud, the father of Otrygg, the father of Hogni the White, the father of Ulf the Squint-Eyed, from whom the people of Reykjanes are descended.[35]

CHAPTER IX

King Hjorleif and Hild the Slender had two sons. The older son was named Hjorolf, and the younger son was Half.[36]

King Hjorleif fell while on a raid. Asmund was the name of the king who married Hild the Slender and fostered King Hjorleif's sons.

When Hjorolf was thirteen years old, he prepared to set out raiding. He kept every ship that he could get, whether small or large, new or old; and he kept every man that he could get, whether free men or conscripts. They had lots of things to use as weapons: posts and poles, cudgels and clubs. That's why anything unwieldy has been called "Hjorolf's gear," ever since.

When he came to battle against Vikings, he trusted in his superior numbers and went on the attack. His forces were unskilled and unarmed, and many of his men fell, but some fled. He returned in the autumn and never amounted to anything.

CHAPTER X

The next spring, Half was twelve years old, and no man was as tall or as strong as he.[37] He prepared to set out raiding. He had one ship, new and well built.

In Hordaland lived the jarl named Alf the Old. He married Gunnlod, the daughter of Hromund the Berserk, the sister of hersir[38] Hamund the Bold. They had two sons, and both of them were named Stein. The elder son was eighteen years old at this time, and he was King Half's counsellor. No one who was younger or more childish than he could go on this raid. A large stone stood in the courtyard, and no one could go who hadn't lifted this stone from the ground. No one could go who wasn't such a valiant man that he never felt fear or spoke timid words or winced from wounds. Gunnlod's younger son Stein wasn't allowed to go on account of his age, because he was twelve years old.

The hersir Hamund had two sons. One was named Hrok the Black, and the other was Hrok the White.[39] They were chosen for this expedition.

Aslak was the name of a powerful farmer. His sons were Egil and Erling. They were excellent men. Vemund was the name of King Half's standard-bearer. Four men from the household came with him. Then eleven shires were searched, and twelve men were found. There were the two brothers Hauk and Val,[40] Styr the Strong, Dag the Splendid, Bork and Brynjolf, Bolverk and Haki, Hring and Halfdan, Stari and Steingrim, Stuf and Gauti, Bard and Bjorn. There were twenty-three men who set out.

The first evening, when they were laid up at an anchorage, there was a heavy rain. Stein asked for a tent. The king answered, "Do you still want a roof over your head, just like at home?" Since then, they called him Innstein.

The next day, they rowed around a certain headland in a brisk wind. A man stood on the headland and asked for passage. The king ordered him to stand on the rudder post till evening. He said that was well spoken, and said that he felt he'd been honored with a position near the king. And so it was done. This person was the younger Stein, Gunnlod's son. He was called Utstein[41] ever since.

Many prohibitions were made in their laws, for the sake of valor. One was that they could not have swords longer than one ell,[42] so that they would have to come close to their enemies. They had knives made so that their blows would have to be more powerful. None of them had less strength than twelve ordinary men. They never took women or children captive.[43] None of them was allowed to bandage a wound until an entire day had passed. No one was accepted who was any less in strength and valor than what has been stated. They raided lands far and wide, and always won victory.

King Half spent eighteen summers raiding. It was their custom to alays anchor off headlands.[44] It was another of their customs never to put up awnings over their ships, and never to reef sails before a gale. They were called Half's Warband, and he never had more than sixty on board.

CHAPTER XI

King Half was returning to his own kingdom from raiding. They were struck by a great storm in harbor, and their ship couldn't be bailed out.

Their decision was to draw lots for a man to jump overboard, but this wasn't necessary, because each man offered to go overboard for his fellows. As they stepped overboard, they said, "There's no straw over the gunwales."[45]

When King Half came to Hordaland, King Asmund came to meet him. He became his liegeman and swore an oath to him, and invited him to a feast, along with half of his men. The next morning, when the king made ready and said that half of his men had to stay behind on the ship, Innstein said:

> All of us men,
> mightiest warriors,
> must make landfall,
> leaving our ships.
> We must let this host
> of heroes burn,
> end the lives
> of Asmund's men.

The king said,

> We'll pay our visit
> with a pledge of truce,
> head from the harbor
> with half our men.
> Asmund has
> offered to us
> golden rings,
> gifts such as we wish.

Innstein said:

> You don't see all
> that Asmund's thinking,
> this folk-ruler
> is false at heart.
> If we had our way,
> war-king, you'd have

much less faith
in your family relation.

The king said:

Asmund has
offered to us
many pledges,
as people know.
No wise king
nor warrior, either,
should seek settlement
on deceitful terms.

Innstein said:

Odin has grown
angry with you,
if you fully
place faith in Asmund.
He'll deceive all
of us, your men,
unless you keep
a careful watch.

The king said:

You always wish
to speak words of fear.
That king won't break
the bonds of truce.
There we'll get gold
and good treasures,
red-gold rings
from his rich estates.

Innstein said:

Half, I dreamed—
think deeply on this—
that flames flickered
on our fighters' heads;
it was no good
getting free of them.
What say you, king,
signifies that dream?

The king said:

I'll give a gleaming
golden helmet
to every fighter
who follows me.
That will look
like licking flames
on hair-mountains°
of the men of the king.

hair-mountains: heads

Innstein said:

A second time
I saw in dreams
that flames were blazing
on our broad shoulders.
I have misgivings
that good will come.
What say you, king,
signifies that dream?

The king said:

Down from the shoulders
of the shield-wall fighters,

guards of the king,
fall gilded mailcoats.
That will seem bright
as burning flames
at play, on the shoulders
of the prince's friends.

Innstein said:

A third time I dreamed,
and this I saw:
we had sunk down
into the sea's depths.
Surely this tells
of treacherous dealing.
What say you, king,
signifies that dream?

The king said:

That's quite enough
of this nonsense talk.
Here's what I say:
such things mean nothing.
From now on, don't tell
these dreams of yours
in any place
where I can hear.[46]

Innstein said:

Hear my words,
Hrok brothers,
also Utstein,
in the army of the king:
We all should go
up from the shore;

we can't make sense
of the king's orders.

Utstein said:

Let's let our warlike
leader give orders,
choose for our folk
where we're faring to.
Brother, let's risk
our lives with him,
stand by the proud king
as it pleases him.

Innstein said:

The host's commander
has heeded my counsel
many times before
as we've made journeys.
Now I say that
since we came here,
he won't heed
what I have to say.

CHAPTER XII

King Half went up to King Asmund's estate with one half of his forces. There was a great multitude already there. The feast was bountiful and the drink was so strong that Half's warband soon fell asleep. King Asmund and his retainers set fire to the hall.[47]

The first man in Half's warband to awaken saw the hall almost filled with smoke. He said "It must be smoking around our hawks now." Then he lay down and fell asleep.

Then another man woke up and saw that the hall was burning, and he said, "Now the wax will drip from our long knives."[48] He lay down.

Then King Half awoke. He stood up and awakened his men and ordered them to arm themselves. Then they rushed at the walls so hard that the iron fittings fell from the timbers. Innstein said:

There's smoke around the hawks
in the hall of the king,
I daresay the wax
drips from our knives.
It's time to give out
gold and treasures,
hand out helmets
to Half's Warband.

Half, I urge you
to open your eyes;
flames have been lit,
we're not lacking fire.
Necklace-breaker,°
now you are forced
to pay for the gifts
of your grim-hearted kinsman.

necklace-breaker: generous king

Let's briskly batter
the boards of the walls.
Now the pillars are
at the point of breaking.
Half's band's journey
to the hall of this prince
will always be remembered
until the end of the world.

We must boldly advance
and not back away;
with knives we'll kill
this king's troops.
They themselves must bear
bloody wounds,

ere the din of battle
can die away.

Get away quickly,
glorious companions,
escape the blaze
with the breaker of wealth.° *breaker of wealth*: generous king
He is no warrior
who wants to live forever.
The breaker of rings° *breaker of rings*: generous king
will not blanch at death.

CHAPTER XIII

It is said here that King Half and his warband escaped the flames, and King Half and his band fell against overwhelming forces. When the king had fallen, Innstein said:

Here I saw
all the sons of heroes,
equal in firmness,
follow one man.
Hearty our meetings,
when from here we pass;
death's no more burden
to bear than life is.

Then Half's warriors who had stayed by the ships entered the battle. A great part of Half's warband fell there. The fighting went on until nightfall before Innstein fell. Innstein said,

Bold Hrok lies
by his lord's side,
fallen at the feet
of the folk's chieftain.
We'll pay back Odin
with evil in exchange,

since he stole victory
from such a king.

I have followed
a fearless man,
bloodied arrows
for eighteen summers.
I'll never have
another lord
so keen for battle;
nor become old.

Here wise Innstein
to earth will sink,
fallen at the head
of the host's commander.
Men will say
in the sagas they tell
how our lord Half
laughed as he died.

CHAPTER XIV

Gunnlod went among the slain in the night to search for her sons. She found Innstein dead, but Utstein was wounded to the point of death, along with Bard and Bjorn. She drove them to a farm and healed them in secret, and then sent them south to Sweden. Bjorn and Bard went to find King Solvi, King Half's mother's brother, but Utstein went to Denmark to his kinsman King Eystein.

Hrok the Black had many severe wounds. He left the battlefield in the night and came to a cottager named Skogkarl.[49] He stayed there, and his wounds were bandaged. The old man brought him north to Sogn to the hersir Geirmund, his father's brother. There he was healed in secret, and in the autumn he went to Uppland and eastward to Gautland. He came to King Haki in Scania and stayed with him over the winter.

CHAPTER XV

Utstein stayed with King Eystein. King Eystein's counsellor was named Ulf the Red. He had eight sons, and they were all the greatest champions, but envious men. They treated Utstein badly, and a battle of words broke out between them as they were drinking. This was before Utstein had told of the fall of King Half. He said:

One matter most
makes me laugh:
Asmund's sorrow
hasn't slept yet.
From these forces,
fallen are three
of Eynef's offspring°—
but one still lives.

Eynef: a legendary sea-king;
his *offspring*: warriors

When Ulf compared him to himself and egged him on, Utstein said:

Up shall we rise,
out shall we go,
and strong shields
we'll shove together.
Our own disir[50]
have all arrived
in Denmark, holding
helmets for us.

Ulf said:

All your disir
are dead, I say.
Your warband's luck
is lost forever.
This morning I saw
my sons in a dream,

winning victory
wherever you meet.

Utstein said:

I expect to gain
far greater victory
than Ulf would want
to wish for Stein.
Soon, when swords
from scabbards are drawn,
I'll slice off your head,
slop your neck with blood.

Ulf said:

Ulf's sons will hold
the upper hand:
Odd and Ornolf,
Ati the Black,
Bork and Brynjolf,
Bui, Hardskafi,
Raud the Strong,
if you struggle with them.

Utstein said:

Stein and Stari
wouldn't stoop to fear
a battle against
these boys of Ulf's;
our brothers soon saw
how simple it was
to lay them low,
those little shits.[51]

Neither Hrok
nor Halfdan found it
a burden to battle
against bitch-men,[52]
when the four of us
felled to earth
eight jarls in all,
off Annisnes.[53]

Let the sons of Ulf
set out to battle,
eight heroes against
one head alone.
I won't step back,
though Stein may have
somewhat fewer
fighters with him.

I dreamed that Half
dared me to fight,
the staunch ruler said
that he'd stand beside me—
the king in dreams
has been kind to me—
wherever we had
to hold our battle.

Then Ulf's sons and Utstein went out and fought. Utstein killed all of Ulf's sons. Then he came before the king, and said:

I have entered
that Ulf may know
how his sons lie,
hewn to earth.

Let more warriors—
if you're willing, Eystein—
come test the mettle
of this tree of spears.°

tree of spears: warrior

Eystein said:

I must forbid
any more testing:
Half's heroes
are highest of all.
I know you as finest
by far of men,
you alone stoutest,
since you struck down eight.

Utstein said,

All Eystein's men
I would mow down,
strike with my sword
in the same way,
if I were compelled
to press the attack,
or else if spite
had sprung up between us.

Let no one be eager
to offer me violence,
for my doom was shaped
in the days of my youth.
A hardened heart
I have in my breast,
since Odin marked me out
when I was a child.

CHAPTER XVI

Hrok the Black stayed with King Haki. King Haki's daughter was Brynhild. Svein the Victorious was the name of the king who had asked to marry Brynhild, but King Haki denied it. Svein swore an oath to bring death to whichever man married Brynhild, and also to her father.

King Haki's jarl was named Hedin, and Vifil was his son. He asked for Brynhild, and she was promised to him if he would guard the land against Svein.

Hrok the Black was not recognized there, and he was not honored and sat in the guests' seat. One day, the king's men went out hunting, and the women went gathering nuts. The king's daughter Brynhild saw a tall man standing against an oak. She heard him say:

Now Hamund's son
will have his say,
speak of our brothers,
what sort they were:
My own father
was far more bold,
a keen-hearted hawk,
than that Haki of yours.

No one would vie
to be Vifil's equal,
not even the herdsman
of Hamund's flocks.
I've never seen
a swine-herding lad
who had less boldness
than Hedin's boy.

Loftier by far
my life seemed
when we went
with wise King Half.

We acted as one,
all together,
and every realm
our raiding felt.

All our forces
were fierce as hawks
where the prudent man
put proof to his fame.
In steel-gray helms
we struck throughout
nine powerful
native realms.

I saw Half lash
to left and right;
the king bore no shield
to shelter himself.
Though far I may fare,
I'll find no man
with sterner heart
and stouter courage.

Men who know
nothing better say
that Half's fame
was foolishness.
He who counts
his courage as foolish
has no understanding
of Halogaland's king.

He ordered his troop
not to tremble at death,

nor to speak words
of wavering fear.
None could follow
our folk's ruler,
unless he would hold
to our helmsman's° fate.

helmsman: king

They could not cry out,
the king's friends,
though terrible wounds
they might take in battle,
nor could they have
their hurts bandaged
until they'd lasted
the length of a day.

No one could cause
captives to weep,
nor could do harm
to a husband's wife.
Each man had to pay
his maiden's bride-price,
give out fine gold,
get father's consent.

There weren't so many
warriors on ships
that we had to flee
from facing them,
though far fewer
fighters we'd have,
eleven of them
against one of us.

All of us had
the upper hand,
wherever Hild's shelters°
we shoved together;
I know only
one prince as valiant:
Sigurd the hero
in the halls of Gjuki.

Hild; a valkyrie; *Hild's shelters*: shields

Many were the men,
mighty and bold,
who sailed our ships
beside the king:
Bork and Brynjolf,
Bolverk and Haki,
Egil and Erling,
Aslak's sons.

Greatest regard
I gained from these men:
Hrok my brother
and Half the king,
Styrr and Steinar,
strong men both,
steady and sure,
sons of Gunnlod.

Hring and Halfdan,
hawk-hearted men,
deeming wisely;
Dag the Splendid,
Stari and Steingrim,
Styrr and Gauti.
You'll never find
finer companions.

Val and Hauk
on Viking raids
were both most brave,
the bold king's friends.
Few retainers
following Haki
would seem higher than
those heroes with our king.

In those ranks
I rarely seemed
to be my family's
blackest sheep.[54]
They called me
the keenest man,
for each one sought
the others' praise.

Battle-hardy Vemund
bore the standard
with Bjorn and Bersi[55]
for the brave one to see.
As long as he lived,
he led his hosts
in battle array,
boldest of kings.

The great land-guardian°
never grew to old age,
as he should have, for
his shining deeds.
Twelve winters old,
he took up raiding;
when he lost his life,
the lord was thirty.

land-guardian: king

I've learned from this
to get little sleep,
stand on watch
in the still of the night:
when my brother
was burned alive,
when he died in flames
with fellow warriors.

That day was the most
doleful for me
in all the world,
as the wise know.
We never felt
we'd find joy again,
we who would follow
our faithful kin.

All my grief would
grow much lighter,
if I had my vengeance
for Half my king,
if I could break
the breast of Asmund,
ring-breaker's° killer,
with a keen blade.

ring-breaker: generous king

Vengeance is vowed
for valiant Half;
under truce they tricked
the trusting king.
The murderer,
the maker of slaughter,
was Asmund the King
in an evil hour.

If we fight against Svein
in the fury of battle,
it will be proved
and put to the test
which one for battle
is better suited:
Hamund's boy,
or Haki's thanes.

To the wise woman
these words I'd speak:
I would bid fair
for Brynhild's hand,
if I were sure
that she would give
her heart to Hrok,
Hamund's son.

If we two had sons,
I trust they'd be
wise lads with
their wits about them;
in all the lands,
no lady I've found
with deeper mind
than the daughter of Haki.

I have never found,
though far I've roamed,
a dearer maid
than the daughter of Haki.
In every way
she is as I desire.

Under Haki's rule,
I realize now
that I am cast out[56]
from every folk.
All the heroes
may have places
to sit in the hall,
save Half's band.

King Haki's daughter Brynhild told her father what she had heard, and said that one of Half's warband must have come there. When the king realized that, he led Hrok to a seat on the high bench, and the king treated him with the greatest friendliness. Hrok the Black married Brynhild, daughter of King Haki.

The next spring, Hrok took a host of men and attacked Svein the Victorious, and they had a battle. Svein fell there, and Hrok returned to King Haki with the victory. The next summer, King Solvi and King Haki and Hrok the Black set out with their forces, along with King Eystein and Utstein with him. They traveled to Norway and battled King Asmund and killed him.

Hjor was the name of King Half's son, who was king over Hordaland at the time. Hrok and Utstein went out on Viking expeditions for a long time afterwards, and were the greatest of men. The daughter of Hrok the Black and Brynhild was Gunnlod, the mother of Hromund Gripsson.[57]

CHAPTER XVII

King Hjor, the son of Half, married Hagny, the daughter of Haki son of Hamund.[58] King Hjor went to an assembly of kings, and while he was there Hagny gave birth to two sons, who were dark-skinned and dreadfully ugly. One was named Hamund, and the other was Geirmund. A bondswoman also bore a son at that time, who was named Leif. He was the most beautiful child. The queen swapped sons with the bondswoman and brought him to the king.

On another occasion, the king went away to levy troops. The boys were three years old at the time. Leif had become timid as he grew older, but Hamund and Geirmund were uncommonly big and clever. Bragi the skald came to a feast there. One day, all the men went to the forest, and the women to the nut grove. There was no one in the hall except for Bragi sitting on the high seat—and the queen was hiding there, covered up with a cloth. Leif was sitting in the high seat and playing with gold, but Hamund and Geirmund were down in the straw on the hall floor. They came up to Leif and shoved him out of the seat and took all the gold away. He cried. Then Bragi stood up and went to where the queen was lying, and struck the cloth with a staff and said:

Two are inside—
I trust in both well—
Hamund and Geirmund,
Hjorvi's children,
but Leif, the third,
is Lodhott's son.
You never bore
that baby, woman.[59]

Then Hagny took her sons back from the bondswoman. When King Hjor came home, she brought the boys to him and said that they were his sons. The king replied, "Take them away! I've never seen such Hell-skins."

They were both called that afterwards. They were mighty men who achieved great deeds, and a great family in Iceland is descended from them. Thorir of Espihol was Hamund's son, and the Esphæling clan is descended from him.[60] Geirmund Hell-Skin claimed land at Medalfellsstrond in Breidafjord. His daughter was named Yri, and a great family is descended from her.[61]

The Saga of Asmund Champions'-Bane

Ásmundar saga kappabana

Folklorists recognize variants of a tragic story in which a warrior is forced to fight a challenger who turns out to be his own son. Sometimes neither father nor son knows of their relationship until it is too late; sometimes the father or son knows, but can do nothing to stop the fight. Such tales are sometimes called "Sohrab and Rustam" stories, after an episode in the Persian epic Shahnameh *in which the hero Rustam fights and kills his son Sohrab. The Irish* Aided Óenfhir Aífe *[The Death of Aife's Only Son]*[1] *and Russian* byliny *of Il'ja Muromets are additional examples.*[2] *The 7th–8th-century Old High German* Hildebrandslied *tells a similar story: Hildebrand is challenged to fight by his son Hadubrand and cannot decline the challenge. The poem breaks off just as the fight begins, but it is usually assumed that Hildebrand kills his son.*[3] *Hildebrand's tale is also told in the Middle High German* Jüngeres Hildebrandslied,[4] *and in* Þiðreks saga af Bern*; in these, father and son are reconciled at the last moment. Several Icelandic sagas feature unwitting fights between a father and son,*[5] *but* Ásmundar saga kappabana *is specifically derived from the Hildebrand legend, although not directly derived from any known German version. However, the combatants have been changed to half-brothers, not a father and son—although the saga awkwardly mentions that Hildibrand kills his own son, probably because that part of the legend was too well-known to leave out.*

Ásmundar saga *is relatively young; the oldest manuscript dates to the early 1300s. However, the Danish historian Saxo Grammaticus quotes poetry from the saga—translated into Latin hexameters and considerably expanded, but still recognizable—in his* Gesta Danorum, *composed around 1200. The saga and Saxo's account agree on most details that are directly spelled out in the poetry; however, they diverge in every detail that is not found in the poetry. For example, since the poems themselves mention few personal names, each author apparently devised his own names for the characters—Hildibrand and Asmund in the saga correspond to Saxo's Hildiger and Haldan, the saga's King Budli is Saxo's King Regnald, and so on. This suggests how the saga, and perhaps many legendary sagas were composed: by adding explanatory prose passages to much older poems, creating a mixed genre known as* prosimetrum.[6]

Ásmundar saga *has not always been treated kindly by critics.*[7] *The saga author borrowed names and plot elements from other sagas to fill out his work, and there are a few plot holes. But the heart of this saga remains the way in which fate, set in motion by King Budli's avarice, traps his grandsons between their obligations to kin and the code of warrior honor. The saga has been praised for its growing sense of suspense as the inevitable conflict draws nearer and nearer.*

The Norse text I used was published by Ferdinand Detter and reprinted by Guðni Jónsson and Bjarni Vilhjálmsson, based on the oldest surviving manuscript, Perg. 4to no. 7 in the Royal Library in Stockholm. The verses are possibly corrupt in several places; I consulted Finnur Jónsson's Skjaldedigtning *and Heusler and Ranisch's* Eddica Minora *for alternate readings.* Ásmundar saga kappabana *has been published in translation by W. Bryant Bachman and Guðmundur Erlingsson, by Alison Finlay, and by George L. Hardman. W. H. Auden and Paul Taylor translated the poems and connecting prose;*[8] *Lee Hollander also translated the poems, adding conjectural missing stanzas based on Saxo's text.*[9] *I've consulted all of these, but have tried to find my own way through the text.*

CHAPTER I

There was a king named Budli who ruled over Sweden, mighty and renowned. It was his custom to honor craftsmen very highly, whenever he received a most skilled one who made treasures for him.[10] He had a queen, and a daughter named Hild. It so happened that the queen had died, and the king had no wife.

It is said that one evening, two men arrived at the king's hall, and came before him and greeted him. The king asked who they might be. One gave his name as Olius, and the other as Alius[11]—"and we would like to have lodging here for the winter." He asked if they were any sort of craftsmen, or if they knew any skills. They said that they could skillfully make anything that might need to be crafted. The king showed them to their seats and invited them to stay.

At that time, the king was giving a feast. In the evening, the king's smiths came into the hall and showed him their handiwork, gold jewelry or weapons. They always did this if visitors were there, to honor the king.

Everyone praised their work—except for the guests; they had little to say about it. There was a certain elaborate knife among the pieces that the smiths had made.

The king was told about this, and he said that he didn't suppose that his guests would be able to make anything better. He called them over and said, "Why are you so unwilling to praise the craftwork that's been brought out here? Could you do better?"

They told the king that if he were willing, they could prove that this work would be worthless, compared to their own. The king ordered them to forge something of the highest quality—"if you don't want to be liars."

They said that they would quickly prove that this work was worthless and no good. They stuck the knife in the edge of the table, in front of the king, and the blade fell right off. They asked the king to take his own treasure, and said that they would try to make another knife. The king ordered them to do so.

Soon they made a knife and brought it to the king. He swung it at his mustache, and it cut off the mustache and the skin, sticking into the flesh.[12]

The king said, "It must be true that you're both skillful men. Now you must make me a gold ring."

They did so, and brought it to the king. He examined it and said, "It's the truth: I've never seen a more precious gold ring." Everyone who saw it said the same.

The king said that such servants were excellent men. Then he said, "Now you must make me two swords, which must be no less superior to other smithwork than the things you have already made, and which shall never strike without cutting."

Olius said that he didn't want to do that. He said that it wasn't unlikely that some terrible curse would be placed on the swords if they were forced into making them, and he said that it was best to make something more modest. The king said that they had to do it, willingly or not. They set to work at their smithing, and each of them forged a sword. Then they went before the king and showed him the swords.

The king examined them, and they seemed excellent to him—"but what good qualities do they have?"

Olius spoke up and told him that they would never strike anything that they couldn't cut. "I think that there will be no flaws."

The king said, "That's good, but we'll have to test how well this one is tempered." He stuck the point into the high-seat pillar, and the sword bent a little. Then he bent it straight in a window-frame. The smith said that that was too harsh a test for the sword, and said that it was made for striking, not bending. The king said that it wouldn't withstand blows if it broke in such tests. Now he tested the sword that Alius had made, and it sprang back, as straight as a plank. In every respect it was finer than the other, and it withstood both tests that the king made.[13]

The king said, "This one that Alius has made is better, but both of them are good. But what nature do they have?"

Alius said, "This, lord: if the swords clash with each other, and are borne against each other, my sword will prevail. Yet one might call their quality one and the same."

Then the king took the sword that Olius had made and tried to break it, and the sword broke at the hilt. The king ordered Olius to make a better sword. He angrily went straight to the smithy, forged a sword, and brought it to the king. The king put it through all the same tests as the first one, and it withstood them all.

The king said, "Now you have done well. But are there any problems with it?"

Olius said, "The sword is made of good steel, but now some flaws will be laid on it to break your good fortune, because it will cause the death of the noblest of brothers: your daughter's sons."[14]

The king said, "Make your prophecies, wretch. Now the sword shall be the death of brothers, but not noble ones." He struck at him, but they quickly disappeared down into the underworld.

The king said, "These are powerful enemies. I must see to it that the sword harms no one." The king had a lead case made for the sword, and he had it sunk in Lake Mälaren, near Agnafit.[15]

CHAPTER II

Helgi was the name of a renowned king. He was a mighty warrior. Helgi sailed with his warships to meet King Budli and sent word that he would keep the peace there, saying that he wanted to make his acquaintance and be given a feast by him. The king welcomed the news. King Helgi went up to the hall and was warmly received there. The father of King Helgi was named Hildibrand, ruler of the Hunnish lands.

King Helgi said, "I want to reveal my intentions to you—to ask for a marriage with your daughter. I can see that it will do us both honor, for me to defend your lands and inherit your kingdom in return."

King Budli said, "With her consent, I will agree to your request." This proposal was brought before her right away, and she agreed to go along with her father's will. Now the feasting was redoubled, according to the custom of noble men, and King Helgi married Budli's daughter Hild. Then the father-in-law and his son-in-law were allied, and King Budli placed great trust in King Helgi.

Hild and Helgi had a son named Hildibrand, who was the most promising of men. As soon as he could toddle, his father King Helgi said, "Your foster-father shall be Hildibrand the Mighty, my father, in Hunland. And then it's likeliest that you'll achieve the most fitting destiny."

King Helgi sent the boy there. King Hildibrand received him splendidly, and said that he hoped that a champion would grow up there. After that, King Helgi went raiding, and King Budli grew old as he ruled his lands.

CHAPTER III

There was a king named Alf who ruled Denmark. His daughter was named Aesa the Fair. She was famed throughout lands far and wide for her beauty and her handiwork.

Aki was the name of a mighty champion in Denmark. He was a very dear friend of the king, and King Alf had the greatest trust in him. The king called him and said, "We wish to set out raiding in the summer, and claim the kingdom which lies unguarded for our own. We'll increase our power, if it can be done."

The champion answered, "My lord, where do you know of such a kingdom to be had?"

The king said, "King Budli is elderly now, and we want to conquer his kingdom."

Aki said, "I won't discourage you from accomplishing great deeds. As it was before, so it will be again: after a great exploit, you'll be disposed to reward your friends for their trouble."

Then King Alf and Aki readied their forces and invaded King Budli's kingdom in Sweden and ravaged it, slaying men and plundering wealth. When King Budli heard, he summoned his forces. He got few men, since the forces of his son-in-law Helgi were far away. Nonetheless, he persisted in attacking, and he was overwhelmed and fell in the battle. King Alf took Budli's daughter and a huge amount of wealth as plunder. Having done that, he went home.

Then Alf said, "So it has come about that we have plenty of power and wealth. In return for your assistance, Aki, I will betroth Budli's daughter Hild to you, even though she's had a husband before."

Aki said, "What other reward could be more to my taste than this one? Even though King Helgi was formerly married to her, she seems no worse to me."

After that, Aki went to marry Hild, and they had one son. His name was Asmund. He was big and strong from an early age. He set out raiding as soon as he could, and he forced a great many warriors to submit to him.

CHAPTER IV

Now the tale turns to his brother Hildibrand, the son of King Helgi. King Helgi fell in battle. Hildibrand forced many men to submit to him, and wandered far and wide with his host. He was related by marriage to a certain king named Lazinus, the very mightiest of kings. He set out to meet his kinsman with friendly greetings, and there he was well received. He began to grow quite ambitious as his power increased.

At the time, there were mighty dukes of noble lineage in Germany. Hildibrand the Huns' Champion moved against them, saying that he wanted them to grant him whatever honors he asked for—or else they, like others, would face dire consequences. The dukes had a sister, and she was the best at giving counsel, because she was the wisest of them. At once they had a private conversation and considered their options. She said that it was more advisable to submit to him and pay tribute, than to give battle—"it's best to show restraint, but switch to resistance when we have the strength." She said that it would happen here, as in other places, that he would be victorious. Then the dukes said that they were willing to agree to pay him tribute. He said that that was prudent of them, and they reached an agreement.

Hildibrand the Huns' Champion now forced many nations to submit to him. He heard the news of the fall of King Budli, his mother's father. He summoned his forces again and called for an assembly. He spoke, and said that it was usual for men to go raiding, regardless of their family obligations. But he said that it wasn't fit for him to harry Vikings or other men for little cause or none, yet not avenge his own mother's father. After that, he transported his forces to King Alf's kingdom, and said that the Danes had found out about the onslaught against their homes. He made sparks fly, setting fires far and wide. King Alf came against him with his own forces, and they fought as soon as they met. Hildibrand the Huns' Champion had a berserk's nature, and the berserk fit came upon him. Duke Aki was not in this battle, because he was on a raid. Hildibrand the Huns' Champion broke right through King Alf's ranks, and it wasn't good to stand in front of him. He struck to the left and right and attacked the king's standard, howling, and King Alf fell in this battle along with many of his men. After that, the Huns went back to their land.

Hildibrand became the most renowned of all men. He always stayed on his estates in winter, but raided in summer.

CHAPTER V

Now the story turns to Asmund the son of Aki, who was out raiding. The Vikings found him to be fierce and hardy in battle.

There was a man of Danish descent named Eyvind Skin-Peg,[16] a handsome man, powerful and wealthy, who bore himself proudly. When Aki and his son Asmund came home from their raiding, they were told the news of the fall of King Alf. For the time being, they stayed home quietly. Asmund didn't know of the kinship between him and Hildibrand, because his mother never told him about it.

Eyvind Skin-Peg went to meet the king's daughter Aesa the Fair, saying that he wanted to propose marriage to her. He said that his honor and wealth, his descent and prowess, were known to her. She said that she would have to give him an answer on the advice of her friends. Afterwards, she brought up the matter before Aki and Asmund, her foster-brother. Aki said that he would not wish for this to happen.

Then Asmund said, "You shall not marry Eyvind. You shall marry me."

She said, "Foster brother, he has greater excellence in lands and splendid estates, but I would think that you have greater manliness."

Asmund said, "Lend me your own luck, and then this marriage may bring glory to both of us."

"I shall marry the one who brings me beautiful hands,"[17] she said, "when you return from raiding in the autumn."

They ended their discussion, and both set out raiding as usual. Asmund often put himself in great danger in order to win plunder, and so he gained wealth and fame. But Eyvind usually stayed with the cooks, and didn't let his gloves come off his hands.

When autumn came, they both went to meet the king's daughter, each with his own men. Eyvind came forward first, and asked the king's daughter to look at his hands. Aesa the Fair said, "These hands have been well protected, and they're white and fair. They have hardly been stained with blood, nor marred by wounds. Let us see your hands now, Asmund."

He stretched out his hands, and they were scarred and quite darkened by scabs and wounds. But when he rolled up his sleeves, his arms were covered with gold rings up to the armpits.

The king's daughter said, "It is my ruling that Asmund's hands are fairer in every way. You, Eyvind, are dismissed."

Asmund said, "Then I must be the one you've chosen, lady."

She said, "First you must avenge my father, because this alone is right for me: to marry the man who rights this wrong, and wins fame for himself, by killing Hildibrand Hun-Champion."

Asmund said, "How can he be beaten, since no one has ever triumphed over him? What advice can you offer?"

She said, "I have heard that a sword is concealed in Lake Mälaren, next to Agnafit. I have heard it said that if that sword were to clash with the one that Hildibrand owns, his sword would have to give way. An old farmer, a friend of mine, lives near the lake, and I will arrange for him to direct you to the place."

Asmund said that it must be obvious that he was eager to marry her, if he undertook this perilous endeavor. After that, Asmund went to the farmer by himself, and told him his mission and the king's daughter's message. The farmer bid him welcome. He frequently turned to look at Asmund that evening.

Asmund said, "Why are you staring at me?"

He said that there was a reason.

Asmund said, "How long have you lived here?"

He said that he had lived there all his life—"and I think the messengers of King Budli stayed here, a long time ago, when they brought Hildibrand to be fostered with King Hildibrand. But I see that you are even more handsome than he, and most like him in appearance."

Asmund said, "I don't know of any ties between us. But what do you know about this sword whose excellence is spoken of? Where is it hidden?"

He said, "I was here when it was sunk, and I've clearly marked the place where it's concealed. It must still be undamaged, or so I think."

Asmund said, "Then by order of the king's daughter, take me there."

He said that it would be so. He brought a large side of bacon and a burning log with him. Asmund said, "What will you do with those, farmer?"

He answered, "You'll feel cold enough when you come up, even if you warm yourself with these."

Asmund said, "You're a shrewd man."

Then they went out in a boat, and when Asmund least expected it, the farmer said, "It's right here."

Asmund leaped overboard and dived down, and when he came up, he wanted to go down a second time. The farmer said, "That's not a good idea for you. Warm yourself now and have some food," and he did so. The second time that he dived, he recognized the case and raised it a bit, and swam up and warmed himself. Then he dived a third time, and he picked up the case and brought it to land. Asmund chopped up the case with an ax, and a corner of the axehead fell off when it touched the sword's edge.

Asmund said, "You've been helpful, old man. Accept this gold ring from me for your trouble, and call on me as a friend, if you need me." The old man thanked him very much, and they parted.

Afterwards, Asmund went home and told the king's daughter. She said, "A great thing has been accomplished, and you will be a man of renown. Now here is the plan at hand: I want to send you to the dukes in Germany who have lost their realm at the hands of Hildibrand—and to their sister, for she is a wise woman. My advice is to set about doing whatever they put in your hands, for I suspect that most will have a hard time against your courage and your excellent weapon."

Then Asmund went away.

CHAPTER VI

Now we must tell what happened in Germany. One day, the dukes' sister spoke up: "My dreams have shown me that a bold man will seek us out, who will bring great fortune to us and our realm." The brothers were glad to hear that.

That same day, in the evening, they saw a tall man with splendid weapons riding towards their hall. The dukes went to meet him and invited him to stay there. He said that he would accept. They seated him between them; their sister served them drink, and then sat down to speak with him and her brothers. She said, "We know little concerning your affairs, but we can see that there is an air of nobility about you, and we trust that something good will come to us from you and your coming here. You must have heard what distress we are suffering from the tyranny of Hildibrand Hun-Champion. At first, we were forced to pay tribute, but now we must respond to a challenge to a duel from his berserks every half-year, and an estate must always be wagered on every duel. And so we have lost both our men and our estates, and now there are no more than twelve estates left in our dukedom."

Asmund replied, "My lady, you complain to me of great suffering. It will be necessary to hold back the storm. I have come here to defend your realm, if I can."

The dukes said that it wouldn't be long before he would be challenged to a duel. Asmund replied, "Then I will have to give an answer." He stayed there, highly honored.

CHAPTER VII

Now the story turns to King Lazinus and his son-in-law Hildibrand Hun-Champion. Hildibrand said, "Isn't it time to fight a duel with the dukes and their men? To take their remaining estates wouldn't be difficult now."

The king said, "Instead, we'll send a man to them and find out if it can be done easily."

The man who was sent was named Vogg. Nothing is said about his journey until he came to the dukes. He entered their hall and came before their table, and said, "King Lazinus and the mighty Hildibrand Hun-Champion want to know whether you will accept a challenge to a duel, or abandon your remaining estates without a struggle."

The dukes answered, "It's come to this: If our landholdings seem too large, then it's a small matter to surrender them, rather than losing good men."

Asmund said, "Why are you talking like this? Wouldn't there be all the more need to hold on to your property when less of it remains?"

Vogg turned and looked at him. Asmund said, "Why are you staring at me so persistently?"

He said, "As it happens, I've never seen a third man as excellent as you and Hildibrand. He is fairer, but you're no less mighty. Hildibrand has heard that an unknown man has come here with a fine weapon. I must see your sword."

Asmund told him to do as he wished. He looked at it and said, "The weapons match the appearance of those who own them. The other one is brighter and better made, but no keener."

Asmund said that he didn't know about that—"but you'll want to know the answer to your message."

He said that that was correct. Asmund said, "Tell your chieftains that a man will accept the challenge on behalf of the dukes."

Now Vogg rode home and greeted the king and Hildibrand. Hildibrand said, "What can you tell us about the dukes' plans?"

Vogg answered, "I don't believe they'll fail to answer the challenge."

Hildibrand said, "But have they mustered up a lot of courage now, or is this unknown man the cause? How did he look to you? You're clear-sighted."

Vogg said, "His bearing is well-mannered, and his eyes look exactly like yours. I think it likely that he'd be fearless. And he has that sword—I have never seen another one like the one you have, and I think it must have come from the same forge."

Hildibrand said, "You admire this man very much. Don't you think that my sword would be equal to his sword, or that he would be my equal?"

Vogg answered, "I don't know whether he is your equal. I know this: whoever fought him would have a hard time of it. He is certainly a doughty man."

Hildibrand said, "You speak highly of him."

Now Hildibrand had one of his champions ride to the duel.

CHAPTER VIII

Asmund was told the news. He called for his horse and armor. The dukes said, "We offer you our men." He said that one should fight against one.

He rode to where the duel was to be, and they rode at each other with swords drawn. With the first blow, Asmund chopped him in two at the middle. He flung the pieces out into the river, and they drifted past the king's castle.

Hildibrand said, "Our comrade is taking his time to deal with this stranger."

Then a man spoke up. "My lord," he said, "here's your chance to see him, since he's drifting down the river, and he's in two pieces now."

Hildibrand said, "That was quite a mighty blow. Let two of our men prepare themselves and get him off our hands as fast as possible."

They said that that was not a great task. Hildibrand said, "It's to our advantage if you two can beat him quickly."

The next day, the two of them rode to the battlefield against Asmund. He said, "The berserks have strange laws here, allowing two swords to clash with one. But I'm quite prepared to take on this fight with both of you."

They felt that it was unworthy for the two of them to hang back from fighting one man.[18] They both struck at him, but he parried with his shield, and struck each one a fatal blow. Then he rode back to the dukes, who came to meet him and welcomed him. He said that he thought that three estates had come back into their hands on his expedition. The dukes' sister said, "Our dreams of this man's coming have not proven false." He stayed there in high honor, and won great fame from this deed.

Hildibrand was told the news, and he said, "Even if one man beats two men, that doesn't seem surprising to me. Now I shall ready four men to go against him." The champions said that it was obvious that they would chop him into four pieces. They rode to the battlefield, with good helmets and shining mailcoats and sharp swords.

The news reached Asmund and the dukes. They asked him to go with an equal number of men. He said that he didn't want that, and said that it was most likely that they would fight one against one again, and said that it would be a great bargain if four estates could be had.

Then they met. Asmund said, "It's obvious that you think you're poor fighters, sending four against one. They can't call you champions. Instead, you're common foot soldiers." They grew furiously angry at his words and attacked him at once, but the sword that he carried sliced mailcoats and helms as smoothly as cutting birchbark, and spared neither human bones nor flesh—and he who wielded it had a strong arm and a stout heart. In short order they suffered terrible wounds from him. He killed all four and shoved them out into the river, along with their horses.

Now Hildibrand heard this and said, "It's one or the other: either our men are less warlike than we thought, or this is an outstanding man." He then summoned five of the fiercest champions, and said that triumphing over one man was not too great a task for them. They said that they meant to cut his pride down to size and feed his flesh to the beasts. Then they went out.

When Asmund heard, he said, "Today I intend to earn my keep." The dukes said that they felt afraid that he was intent on doing too much, and said that they had to reward him with all honor. Then they encountered each other and fought immediately. Asmund struck strong and frequent blows, and in the end he killed them all.

When Hildibrand heard this, he said, "It takes a long time for his arm to tire, but it won't be long before he'll get to fight." In the halls there was a rumbling sound coming from the berserks, bellowing that this one man should overcome so many men.

Hildibrand said, "Let six of our men prepare now, and may they win the honor of avenging our men." They went straight to the dueling ground. When Asmund heard that, he quickly made ready and said, "I have the sword that's just as good for killing six men as three."

Then they met. The champions said that he should drop his sword and give himself up. He said, "That won't happen without shields getting hacked. And you have quite a need to avenge your men." At once they fought, and he attacked fiercely. He was able to use the same technique to strike down the swordsmen as before. Despite being wounded, he didn't soften his sword-blows, cutting some in two in the middle. In the end he killed them all and returned to the dukes. There were a great many people who wanted to have the realm under the dukes' rule forever, and now there was talk about those champions in every man's house.

Again the news came to Hildibrand, and he said, "The number of our men is getting meager. How many are left?"

"My lord," they said, "there are twenty-six left."

Hildibrand answered, "Now this is how his reputation will be from now on: this unknown man will be counted as one of the mighty champions, and he'll pick off my men until the two of us will have to fight. But I shall send seven more, who have long been in my service." At once they made ready.

Asmund was told that there was no time for resting now. He said, "If seven estates can be won, there'll be time for a meal."

Then he went out, and seven champions came against him. Asmund said, "Why is Hildibrand pushing his men out, while he himself sits at home and makes little men fight me?"

They were enraged at his words and said that he would never get to fight Hildibrand under any circumstances. At once they fought, and however it happened, he killed them all. Then he pushed them out into the river.

When Hildibrand heard of that, he said, "Our situation has become far worse than we imagined. Now eight berserks must go after him, because none of us will be worthy to live if they aren't avenged." They howled loudly and took bites out of the shields that they seized.

Asmund was with the dukes, and the news came to him that he would have to fight yet again. The dukes' sister said, "The honor that we surrendered has now completely returned, and with greater power than we expected."

Asmund said, "We must risk it, because he wants to set a trap with the berserks, but he has no control over them. It would be better for their holdings to be added to our realm, because you lost them unjustly." Then he rode out against them, and as soon as they met, they fought. That encounter took longer, but in the end he killed them all.

When Hildibrand heard that, he raged furiously and said, "That man has powerful luck, since a host of men haven't prevailed against him. Now the eleven remaining men must face him."

When Asmund heard that, he fell silent. The dukes said, "Now we want to send our men with you. Be their leader, and then you'll be victorious—but you can't counter such a bold stroke by yourself."

Asmund didn't answer. Evening came, and men had their meal and then went to lie down and sleep. Asmund dreamed that women were standing over him holding weapons, and they said, "What's the meaning of your fearful expression? You are meant to be a leader of others, but you're afraid of eleven men. We are your guardian spirits,[19] and we will grant you protection against the dukes' enemies, whom you must test yourself against."

At that, he sprang up and got ready, though most tried to dissuade him. He rode out at once against the champions. They thought that they had his fate in their grip, and told him that it would be better for him to surrender to Hildibrand than to perish. He told them that they were no less doomed to death than the first man he had killed, and said that there would clearly be a great difference in fame between killing one and killing eleven. Then they fought, and he was surrounded, but he was hard to overcome. Weapons didn't land many blows on him, but his sword cut everything before it that it touched, and in the end he dealt death to them all. The dukes had gone with him and said that his glorious deed would never be forgotten. Word spread among the people that Asmund would never turn and flee, even though Hildibrand Hun-Champion himself, the most renowned man in those days, should come against him.

CHAPTER IX

When Hildibrand heard that his champions were slain, a berserk rage came over him, and he turned and left, saying, "It shall not be said that I risk my men, but don't dare to fight myself." In the fury that seized him as he went on his way, he saw his own son and killed him at once.[20] Then he drove up along the Rhine River to find Asmund. He had a shield, on which were depicted the many men he had killed.

When Asmund heard that, he prepared to meet him. As soon as they encountered each other, they fought, and most of their blows were quite powerful. When they had fought for a long time out of great wrath, Hildibrand summoned his strength and struck at Asmund with all his might, with both hands. But as the sword landed on his helmet, it broke apart at the hilt, and the blade fell howling into the river. By then, Hildibrand was wounded with many wounds. Then he spoke these verses:

It's hard to guard
against this fate:
to be slain in battle
by some other man.[21]

The lady[22] of Denmark
gave life to you,
and myself
in Sweden she bore.

There were twin
treasures of Budli,
eager for war—[23]
one is now broken.
Dwarves once smithed
Dainsleif thus,[24]
such as never was forged
before nor since.

At my head lies
the hacked shield
on which eight tens
are tallied up:
all of the men
whose murder I wrought.

My sweet son[25] lies
slain at my head,[26]
the heir I sired,
my house's scion;
it was not my will
to waste his life.

Brother, I beg
one boon from you;
do me one favor,
and don't refuse!
In your own cloak
cover my body,
since I'm fated to fell
few other men.

Now I must lie,
left here dying,
bloodied by the blade
which brings great wounds.

CHAPTER X

After that, Hildibrand Hun-Champion died. Asmund made his funeral a worthy one, and felt that what he had done was bad. He didn't meet with the dukes, and went to the estate which his mother owned together with the king's daughter Aesa the Fair. There a man was intending to ask for her hand. Asmund spoke when he came through the hall doors:

I didn't expect
to be deemed this way,
ranking second
to someone else,[27]
when the Hunnish kindred
called me out
to fight eight duels
for the dukes' realm.[28]

I faced the first one
and fought against two,
then four and five warriors,
fierce when safe at home;[29]
soon against six
and seven on the field,
alone against eight;
yet I live still.

Then in my breast
the boldness wavered,
when eleven thanes
threatened battle,

until in a dream
my disir told me
I must take my part
in the play of swords.° *play of swords*: battle

Then came Hildibrand
the Hun-Champion;
the grizzled one
couldn't grapple with me,
and with my blade[30]
I branded him
beneath his helm
with harsh battle-signs.° *battle-signs*: wounds

After that, men gave him a warm welcome, and he was called Asmund Champions' Bane. The king's daughter begged him not to be angry, even though she had arranged to marry that man. She asked for mercy, and said that a powerful enchantment had come with the swords. Although Asmund had been angry with her, he remembered his love for her, and he held his wedding feast and went to marry Aesa the Fair. But he killed the man who had asked for her hand; he isn't named.[31]

Asmund Champions' Bane later became a famous man, renowned far and wide.

Here ends this saga.

The Tale of Sorli

Sörla þáttr

The largest and finest surviving manuscript from medieval Iceland is Flateyjarbók, *"The Book of Flatey". Compiled between 1387 and 1394, it contains sagas of the kings of Norway, notably Olaf Tryggvason (reigned 995-1000) and Olaf Haraldsson (reigned 1015-1028). The* Flateyjarbók *sagas are based on those in Snorri Sturluson's* Heimskringla, *expanded by the addition of tales and even entire sagas about the kings and their followers.* Flateyjarbók *was probably written to be a gift for the young Olaf Hákonarson (1370-1387), who'd become king of Denmark at the age of five and king of Norway at ten. It was intended not just to entertain him, but to provide him with moral lessons on how a Christian monarch should rule, drawn from the lives of his famous namesakes.*[1] *However, the boy king Olaf died before the book could be presented to him, and* Flateyjarbók *stayed in Iceland until it was purchased by Icelandic bishop Brynjólfur Sveinsson and sent to Denmark in 1656, one of thousands of Icelandic manuscripts to end up in Danish collections. Its repatriation to Iceland in 1971, on a Danish warship, was a nationally televised event.*[2]

Sörla þáttr *(The Tale of Sorli) or* Heðins saga ok Högna *(The Saga of Hedin and Hogni) is found only in* Flateyjarbók, *inserted into the saga of King Olaf Tryggvason.* Sörla þáttr *is one of several "pagan-contact tales" in* Flateyjarbók, *in which a Christian king encounters a survivor from the heathen past, showing his superiority to the "bad old days". In the form that we have it,* Sörla þáttr *is a collage of at least four different myths or legend: a goddess committing sexual infidelity to gain a treasure; Loki's theft of Brisingamen; the tale of Sörli and his son; and the Everlasting Battle. All of these can be traced in older sources.*[3] *Nonetheless,* Sörla þáttr *shows skillful construction. The plot is dominated by three parallel struggles, each driven by obsession with a precious object: first Freyja's necklace, then the ship Skrauti, and finally the girl Hild who unwittingly causes the Everlasting Battle.*[4]

The Everlasting Battle or Hjaðningavíg *is particularly well-known; several versions of the story exist in Norse literature,*[5] *and both the continental Germans and the Anglo-Saxons were familiar with it.*[6] *In the oldest versions of the story, Hild deliberately resurrects the slain warriors and forces them to fight, reminiscent of the myth of the endless fighting and feasting in Odin's hall Valhöll. The* Flateyjarbók *compilers reworked the old tales to show the superiority of Christian virtue. In particular, they turned the Everlasting Battle from a reward for heroes into a ghastly punishment inflicted by the machinations of uncaring gods, with Hild as nothing but a pawn in their game. The warriors fight out of the old pagan virtue of loyalty to their kings—but it brings them nothing but suffering. Not only is there no rest and no feasting, there is no higher purpose to the fighting: it all happens because of Odin's petty quarrel with his unfaithful mistress. This, the compilers are saying, is all that the old gods can offer; only Christianity can bring relief.*[7]

The Norse text that I have used was published in Guðni Jónsson and Bjarni Vilhjálmsson's Fornaldarsögur Norðurlanda, *checked against Vigfusson and Unger's edition of* Flateyjarbók.

CHAPTER I

The land east of the fork in the Vana River, in Asia, was called Asialand or Asiaheim. The people who lived there were called Æsir, and they called their capital city Asgard.[8] Odin was named king over that land. There was a great place for sacrifices there. Njord and Frey were appointed by Odin to be sacrificial priests. Njord's daughter was named Freyja. She went with Odin and was his concubine.

There were some men in Asia: one was named Alfrigg, the second was Dvalin, the third was Berling, and the fourth was Grer. They had a home a short distance from the king's hall. They were men so skillful that they could turn their hand to anything. Men such as these were called dwarves by the people. They lived in a certain stone. They mingled more with humans then, than now.

Odin loved Freyja very much, and she was the fairest of all women at that time. She had a bower for herself. It was both beautiful and strong, so that people say that if the door was closed and locked, no man could come into the bower against Freyja's will.

One day, when Freyja had gone to the stone, it was open. The dwarves were about their work, smithing a gold necklace. It was quite finished by then. Freyja liked the necklace well. And the dwarves liked Freyja well. She asked to buy the necklace from the dwarves, and offered gold and silver and other fine treasures in exchange. They said that they weren't in need of money. Each one said that he was willing to sell his own share in the necklace—and they wanted nothing other than for her to lie with each of them for a night. And whether it was for better or worse that she acquired it, they struck this bargain.

When four nights had passed and all conditions were met, they handed over the necklace to Freyja. She went home to her bower and kept quiet about herself, as if nothing had happened.

CHAPTER II

There was a man named Farbauti. He was an old man, married to the old woman named Laufey. She was both slender and frail, and for that reason she was called Needle. They had one boy-child; he was named Loki. He wasn't very tall, but from an early age he was a fast talker, and quick at devising schemes. More so than other men, he had that wisdom which is called cunning. He was very deceitful from a young age, and for that reason he was called Loki the Crafty. He entered the service of Odin in Asgard and became his man. Odin spoke up for Loki, whatever he got up to, yet he often set hard tasks before him, and he accomplished all of them better than expected. He found out about nearly everything that happened, and he told Odin everything that he found out.

It's also said that Loki found out that Freyja had gotten the necklace—and what she had given in exchange. He told that to Odin. When Odin found out, he said that Loki should take the necklace and bring it to him. Loki said that that wasn't likely to succeed, because no man could get into Freyja's bower except by her will. Odin said that he had to go and not come back until he had taken the necklace. Loki turned away and left, wailing. Most people were happy that it was going badly for Loki.

He went to Freyja's bower, and it was locked. He tried to get in and couldn't manage it. There was a strong cold wind outside, and he quickly began to feel the chill. Then he turned into a fly. He fluttered around all the latches and along all the boards, and never managed to find space so that he could get inside. All the way up by the gable, he found a hole, although it was no larger than a needle could be stuck into. He crept in by the hole. When he came in, he stared all around and watched out for whether anyone was awake, but he could see that everyone in the bower was asleep. He went inside to Freyja's bed and discovered that she had the necklace on her neck, and that the catch was underneath. Then Loki turned into a flea. He sat on Freyja's cheek and bit so hard that Freyja awoke and turned and went back to sleep. Then Loki cast off the flea-shape, slipped the necklace off of her, opened the bower doors and went away, and brought it to Odin.

Freyja awoke in the morning and saw that the doors were open but not broken, and the fine necklace was missing. She realized what sort of trickery this must be. As soon as she was dressed, she went into the hall before King Odin and told him that he had permitted evil to be done by stealing her treasure from her, and she begged him to give her back her treasure. Odin said that she would never get it, considering how she had acquired it—"unless you arrange it so that two kings, with twenty kings serving each one, should become enemies and fight, under such spells[9] and incantations that they should stand up and fight just as quickly as they fall—unless some Christian man should be so bold, and such great luck from his liege-lord go with him, that he should dare to enter their battle and kill these men with his weapons. Then their labors shall finally be ended by whichever leader is destined to release them from the bondage and suffering caused by the terrible things they have done."

Freyja agreed to this, and accepted the necklace.

CHAPTER III

At the time when twenty-four years had passed since the death of Peace-Frodi,[10] a king named Erling ruled over Oppland in Norway.[11] He had a queen and two sons; the elder was named Sorli the Strong, and Erlend was the younger. They were promising men, but Sorli was the stronger one. They set out raiding as soon as they came of age. They battled Sindri the Viking, the son of Sveig, the son of Haki the sea-king of the Elfar Skerries, and Sindri and all his men fell there. Erling's son Erlend also fell in that battle. After that, Sorli set sail for the Baltic Sea and raided there, and accomplished so many mighty deeds that it would take a long time to write them all down.

CHAPTER IV

There was a king named Halfdan who ruled over Denmark. His royal seat was at the place called Roskilde. He married Hvedna the Older, and their sons were Hogni and Hakon. They were remarkable for their size and strength and all their accomplishments. They set out raiding as soon as they were grown.

Now we must tell about how Sorli sailed to Denmark one autumn. King Halfdan had intended to go to an assembly of kings then. He was very much bowed down by great age when this story took place. He owned a dragon-ship so good that another one like it was not to be found in the Northlands, on account of its sturdiness and skillful construction. It was afloat, tied up in the harbor, but King Halfdan was on land and had ordered ale to be brewed for his departure. When Sorli saw the dragon-ship, such great greed filled his heart that he wanted to own the dragon-ship himself, in any way he could. And what most people say is that there has never been a more excellent ship in the Northlands than this one, with the exception of the dragon-ships *Ellidi*, *Gnod*, and *The Long Serpent*.[12] He told his men that they should prepare for battle—"because we must kill King Halfdan and take the ship for ourselves."

The man named Saevar answered his speech—he was Sorli's steersman and marshal. "That is unwise, lord," he said, "because Halfdan is a great chieftain and a renowned man. He also has two sons who are resolved to avenge him, for each of them is now the most renowned of men."

"Even if they were bolder than the gods," said Sorli, "I shall fight, all the same."

Now they prepared for battle. The news came to King Halfdan. He lost no time and went to the ship with all his men, and at once they prepared for battle. Some men proposed to Halfdan that it was unwise for him to fight, and that he should retreat and get help. The king said that every man would fall, one across another, before he would flee. Now both sides prepared to fight, and the fiercest battle broke out. In the end, King Halfdan and all his men fell. Sorli took the dragon-ship and all the riches on it.

Then Sorli heard that Hogni had come home from his raiding and was anchored off Odense. Sorli set his course there, and as soon as they met, he told him of the fall of Halfdan his father, and he offered him a settlement and self-judgment and his sworn brotherhood along with that, but Hogni refused all that. At once they fought, as is told in the poem *Sorli's Piece*. Hakon bravely advanced and killed Saevar, Sorli's standard-bearer and steersman. After that, Sorli killed Hakon, but Hogni killed King Erling, Sorli's father. At once, Hogni and Sorli fought, and Sorli fell before Hogni from exhaustion and wounds. Hogni then had him healed, and they swore brotherhood with each other, and they held to it firmly as long as they both lived. But Sorli had the shorter life of the two; he was killed by Vikings in the Eastern realms[13], as it says in *Sorli's Piece* and says here:

Bold and battle-eager,
braving the Eastern realms,
the fierce one was first slain,
falling down to Hel's bench;
dead lay the deed-famed one
in the dale-trout's mildness;° *dale-trout:* snake; its *mildness:* summer
the mail-spike° struck deeply *mail-spike*: sword
at sword-moot° of Vikings. *sword-moot*: battle

As soon as Hogni heard of the fall of Sorli, he invaded the Eastern realms that same summer. He won victories everywhere and became king over all those lands. People say that twenty kings had to yield tribute to King Hogni, and they held their kingdoms in fief from him. Hogni became so famous from his mighty deeds and battles that his name was just as well-known in Lapland in the north as it was in far-off Paris, and everywhere in between.

CHAPTER V

There was a king named Hjarrandi, who ruled over Arabia.[14] He had a queen and one son who was named Hedin. From an early age, Hedin was outstanding for his strength, size, and achievements. He set out raiding in his youth and became a sea-king, and raided so far and wide in Spain and Greece and all the neighboring kingdoms that he forced twenty kings to pay tribute to him, and they all held their lands in fief from him. Hedin stayed home in Arabia in the winter.

It's said that on one occasion, Hedin went to the forest with his household. He had stopped in a grove by himself. He saw a woman sitting on a throne in the grove, very tall and beautiful to look upon.[15] She greeted Hedin courteously. He asked her name, and she said that her name was Gondul. Then they began to converse. She asked him about his mighty deeds, and he told her everything openly. He asked whether she knew of any king who equalled him in prowess and hardiness, renown and success. She said that she knew one who was no less than he, and no fewer than twenty kings served him. She said that his name was Hogni and that he reigned in Denmark, to the north.

"I know that we must test which one of us is superior," said Hedin,

"You must tell your men," said Gondul, "they'll be looking for you."

Then they parted, and he went to his men, and she stayed behind. As soon as spring came, Hedin prepared for his journey; he had one dragon-ship and three hundred men on it. He set his course to the north, and sailed all summer and winter. When spring came, he arrived in Denmark.

CHAPTER VI

King Hogni was staying at home at the time. When he heard that a noble king had come to his land, he invited him home to a splendid feast. Hedin accepted. And when they sat down to drink, Hogni asked why Hedin had come, that he should have wanted to sail such a long way to the north. Hedin said that his purpose was to test their courage and prowess in sports and all skills. Hogni said that he was ready.

Early the next day, they went swimming and shooting at targets. They also competed in jousting and fencing and all sports, and they were so evenly matched in all their skills that no one could tell which one was foremost. After that was done, they swore brotherhood with each other. They had to share everything equally.

Hedin was young and unmarried, while Hogni was somewhat older. He was married to Hervor the daughter of Hjorvard, the son of Heidrek Wolfskin.[16] Hogni had a daughter named Hild. She was the loveliest and wisest of all women. Hogni loved his daughter very much. He had no other children.

CHAPTER VII

It is said that some time later, Hogni went raiding, but Hedin stayed behind and had to oversee the kingdom. One day, Hedin went into the forest to amuse himself. The weather was fine. He wandered away from his men again. He came into a grove. There he saw the same woman that he had seen before in Arabia, sitting on a throne, and he found her much more beautiful than before. She addressed him as before, and spoke cheerfully. She held a horn with a cover over it. The king was attracted to her. She invited him to drink, and the king was thirsty because he felt warm, so he took the horn and drank. But when he had drunk, a very strange feeling came over him, because he didn't remember what had happened before. Then he sat down, and they talked.

She asked whether Hogni's skill and prowess had been shown to be just as she had told him previously. He said that it was true—"because he was no less than I in any achievement that we tried, and thus we may be called equals."

"But the two of you are not equals," she said.

"Why do you say that?" he said.

"I believe that Hogni has a queen of noble lineage," she said, "and you have no wife."

He answered, "Hogni would give me his daughter Hild at once, if I wanted to ask for her, and then I would be no less well married than he."

"Your honor will be diminished," she said, "if you ask Hogni for the girl. It would be better—if you're not lacking courage or valor, as you claim—to kidnap Hild, and to kill the queen this way: take her and lay her down in front of your dragon-ship's prow, and let it cut her in two when it's launched."

Hedin was so caught up by wickedness and forgetfulness from the ale he had drunk that this seemed to be the only thing to do. He didn't remember that he and Hogni had sworn brotherhood.

Then they parted, and Hedin went to his men. The end of summer was approaching. Hedin set his men to prepare the dragon-ship, because he said that he wanted to go home to Arabia. Then he went to the bower and seized the queen with one hand and Hild with the other, and went out with them. His men took Hild's clothes and belongings. The men in the kingdom didn't dare to offend Hedin and his men, because he was scowling fiercely.

Hild asked Hedin what he meant to do, and he told her. She begged him not to do that—"because my father will betroth you to me, if you're willing to to ask for my hand."

"I don't want to ask for you," said Hedin.

"Even if you want nothing but to kidnap me," she said, "you and my father can still reach a settlement. But if you do such a wicked and unmanly deed as to kill my mother, then you and my father will never be reconciled. I have seen in my dreams that you two will fight each other and strike each other down, and yet something is coming that will be even harder to bear.

It will be a terrible grief to me if I have to see my father subjected to agony and powerful spells[17]—and yet, to see you in such trouble and toil would be no happiness for me."

Hedin said that he would never care, whatever might happen, and said that he would do what he'd said.

"You can't set this right," said Hild, "because you're not in control of yourself now."

Hedin got to the beach, and the dragon-ship was launched. He threw the queen down underneath the prow. She lost her life there, and Hedin boarded the dragon-ship. When he was all ready, one of his own men urged him to go on to land, into the same forest which he had entered before. When he came out into the clearing, he saw Gondul sitting there on a throne. They greeted each other as friends. Hedin told her about his deeds, and she approved. She had the horn that she had used before, and she invited him to drink. He took it and drank, but when he had drunk, sleep came over him, and he slumped down on her lap. And when he was asleep, she slipped out from underneath his head, and she said, "Now I hallow you all, both you and Hogni and all your men, according to all the decrees and terms that Odin pronounced."

At once Hedin woke up and caught a glimpse of Gondul, and she appeared black and monstrous to him. Hedin now remembered everything, and felt that he had suffered great misfortune. Now he thought he would go somewhere far away, so that he might not hear reproach every day for his vile deeds. He went to the ship and quickly cast off. A favorable wind was blowing seaward, and so he sailed away with Hild.

CHAPTER VII

Now Hogni came home and found out the truth: Hedin had sailed off with Hild and the dragon ship *Halfdan's Gift*, and the queen had been left behind, dead. Hogni grew furious at that, and ordered his men to set to work at once and sail after Hedin. They did so, and got the most favorable wind, and that evening they came to the harbor that Hedin had sailed away from in the morning.

One day, as Hogni was sailing towards land, Hedin's sails could be seen against the ocean. Hogni and his men sailed towards them. It's true that Hedin got a headwind against him, but the same favorable wind persisted for Hogni. Hedin headed for the island called Hoy[18], and he tied up there. Hogni came after him swiftly, and when they met, Hedin greeted him cheerfully.

"I must tell you, sworn brother," said Hedin, "that such a terrible misfortune has befallen me that no one but you can amend it. I have stolen your daughter and your dragon-ship, and caused your queen's death—yet not by my own wickedness, but rather from wicked prophecies and evil spells. Now I want you alone to settle and arrange matters between us. I will offer to surrender Hild and the dragon-ship to you, along with all my men and wealth, and go so far away that I will never come to the Northlands, nor into your sight, as long as I live."

Hogni answered, "I would have given you Hild if you had asked for her. Even now, though you've kidnapped Hild, we two might yet come to terms for that. But now that you've done such a wicked deed, treating the queen shamefully and killing her, it can't be expected that I would accept a settlement. Here and now, we'll find out which one of us can strike most strongly."

Hedin answered, "If all you want is to fight, it's best that the two of us should fight each other, because you have no case against any man here but me. It's not right that undeserving men should pay for my foolishness and wicked deeds."

But all their followers answered with one voice that each of them would fall dead at the others' feet, rather than let them fight in single combat. And when Hedin saw that Hogni wanted only to fight, he ordered his men to come onto land: "I shall no longer avoid Hogni, nor excuse myself from the battle. Let each man help as his courage allows."

Now they went onto land and fought. Hogni was furious, but Hedin was skilled with weapons and struck mighty blows. It is truthfully said that such great sorcery and evil accompanied these spells, that although they cleaved each other down to the shoulders, they stood up and fought as before. Hild sat in a grove and watched the fight.

This toil and bondage went on without ceasing, from the moment they began to fight until Olaf Tryggvason became king over Norway. Men say that that was one hundred forty-three years before it was destined that this noble man, King Olaf, would have his liegeman release them from this wretched damnation and agonizing trial.

CHAPTER IX

It is said that in the first year of King Olaf's reign, he came to the island of Hoy and put into an anchorage there one evening. It was usual on this island that watchmen disappeared there every night, so that no one knew what became of them. Ivar Beam-of-Light had to stand watch on this night. When all the men on the ship were asleep, Ivar took the sword that Jarnskjold had owned, which his son Thorstein had given him[19], and all his armor, and landed on the island. When he landed on the island, he saw a man coming to meet him. The man was very tall and covered in blood, with a very grave expression.

Ivar asked the man his name. He said that he was called Hedin, the son of Hjarrandi, a native of distant Arabia. "It's true what I tell you: if watchmen have disappeared here, I'm to blame, and so is Hogni Halfdan's son, because we and our men are compelled by such powerful magic and oppression that we fight both night and day. This has gone on for many a man's lifetime, and Hogni's daughter Hild sits and watches us. Odin has laid this on us, and there will be no redemption unless some Christian man were to fight with us. Then anyone whom he kills shall not get up, and every man will be released from his bondage. Now I want to ask you to come fight us, because I know that you are a good Christian, and also that the king whom you serve has great luck. My heart tells me that we will get some good from him and his men."

Ivar agreed to go with him. Hedin was glad to hear that, and he said, "You must be careful to not go in front of Hogni, and not to kill me before Hogni, for no human being can face Hogni or kill him, once I am dead—because he has the Helm of Awe[20] in his eyes, and he spares no one. The only thing for it is for me to go in front of him and fight with him, but you go behind his back and strike him a deadly blow, because it won't be difficult for you to kill me, though I live the longest of us all."

Then they went to battle, and Ivar saw that everything that Hedin had told him was true. He went behind Hogni's back and struck at his head and cleaved him down to the shoulders. Hogni fell dead and never stood up again. He killed all the men that were there in the battle. Finally he killed Hedin, and it wasn't difficult for him. Then he went to the ship, and day was breaking. He went to the king and told him. The king approved of his deed, and said that he had succeeded through good fortune.

Later that day, they landed and went to where the battle had been, and saw no trace of what had happened there. But blood was seen on Ivar's sword as a sign—and ever since then, watchmen have never disappeared there. The king went home to his kingdom afterwards.

CHRISTIAN LORE AND LEARNING

The Saga of the Apostle Bartholomew

Bartholomeus saga postola

During the first few centuries after the death of Christ, traditions grew up about his apostles' lives and deaths. Traditions about the apostle Bartholomew were slow to develop—probably because the Bible has almost nothing to say about him. Nonetheless, legends eventually appeared about Bartholomew's missionary activities and eventual martyrdom. The apostles had supposedly divided up the known world into regions for missionary activity, and Bartholomew had been assigned to the most distant parts of India.[1] *By the 4th century CE, Eusebius and Jerome claimed that Bartholomew had left a Hebrew copy of the Gospel of Matthew in India, where it was found in the second century.*[2] *By about 600 CE, lives of all the apostles had been compiled in a collection known as* Historia Apostolica, *attributed (falsely) to one Abdias, the first bishop of Babylon.*[3] *Bartholomew's life, known as* Passio Bartholomaei, *was probably written between 450 and 550 CE*[4] *and incorporated into the* Historia Apostolica *soon after. At least part of the* Historia Apostolica *reached Scandinavia early; a fragment of the life of Matthew (AM 655 IX 4to) goes back to an original translation made before the year 1150.*[5]

The Norse translation of the Passio Bartholomaei, Bartholomeus saga postola, *has attracted some attention because a devil mentions* Hel drottning vara, *"Hel our queen", which just might show the influence of pre-Christian myth, in which Hel is both the realm of the dead and the goddess who rules it.*[6] *The vivid physical description of a devil probably influenced the figure of the* blámaðr *in the legendary sagas: a savage trollish fiend.*[7] *Aside from these occasional echoes of folk belief,* Bartholomeus saga *and other sagas of the Apostles were evidently enjoyed in Iceland for their exotic settings, foreign peoples, and dangerous monsters, all in the service of religious devotion.*[8] *The translation is generally very close, but the translator has rendered the Latin text in a plainer style, similar to the style of the "sagas of Icelanders," with few Latinisms or rhetorical flourishes.*

I translated the text as published by Unger in Postola sögur, *based on a late 17th- or early 18th-century manuscript (AM 630), a copy of a now-fragmentary*

13th-century manuscript known as AM 652.[9] *I have checked it against the text from the great* Skarðsbók *manuscript as published by Ólafur Halldórsson, which agrees with it in all but a few minor details.*[10] *The AM 630 text adds a prologue, as well as an epilogue concerned with the* translatio *of the saint's relics to Lipari and then to Benevento; these are not part of the* Passio Bartholomaei *proper and have been added from other sources.*

CHAPTER I

We celebrate Mass on the feast day of the Apostle Bartholomew in memory of his martyrdom, and of the splendid triumphal journey which he made on this day, through his painful tortures into the glory of Heaven.[11]

We have not found in books what his occupation was before the Lord called him to his following. Certain wise men have said that the Apostle Bartholomew was the most high-born of all the Apostles—that he bore that name because he was of royal descent. For long ages, kings in Egypt were named Ptolemy, one after another, and *bar* means "son" in our language.[12] Thus some men say that on this day, during Mass, the Gospel is to be read in which the Apostles were disputing over which of them was greater.[13] But the Lord said that whatever the lineage of each of them might be, and whatever occupation they had formerly followed, the company in which they followed the Lord, and the commandments that he gave them, and the distinction that he gave them above all other men, made them all equal. No other distinction could be like the glory that he offered them.

Many things are apparent from Bartholomew's actions. He was a powerful man by the standards of this world. He was a strong and steadfast man, well-dressed and watchful, cleanly and courageous.[14]

CHAPTER II

There are three nations in India. One of them lies next to Africa, the second lies next to Arabia, and the third is located at the world's end, and that is called Furthest India in books. When the Apostles were assigned to nations, the holy Apostle Bartholomew was sent by God to Furthest India.[15]

When he arrived there, an idol was receiving sacrifices there, one called Astaroth. There was a devil inside the idol, who was said to heal sick people—but he only healed those whom he had sickened, because the people of India did not know the true God, and so they had been deceived by false gods. The lying god deceived those who did not believe in or know the true God—so much that he struck them with illnesses and injuries and hurts, and gave answers from the idol that they should sacrifice to him. The foolish people felt that he healed them when he stopped harming them. He saved no one; instead he caused hurt, and he appeared to save when he ceased to hurt.

But when the Apostle Bartholomew arrived, Astaroth could not give any answers or any aid to his people whom he had harmed. The temple was full of sick men who had come a long way to that place. Astaroth could not give any answers to his people, even though they made sacrifices and poured out their own blood, as was their custom. The people went to other cities, where another devil, named Berith, was worshipped. There the people sacrificed to him and asked why their god Astaroth gave them no answers. Berith answered them and said, "Your god was taken captive and bound in fiery chains so that he does not dare to speak or breathe, as soon as the Apostle Bartholomew arrived there."

The priests said, "Who is this Bartholomew?"

Berith answered, "He is a friend of Almighty God, and he has come here in order to put an end to all the sacrifices in India."

The priests said, "Tell us his features so that we may find him, because we cannot recognize him among many thousands of men."

Berith answered them, "His hair is black in color and curly. He has a straight nose, and his ears are covered by the hair on his head. He has a long beard with some grey hairs in it. He is of medium height, such that he does not seem either tall or short. He wears white clothing, ornamented with purple dye and gemstones. For twenty-six years his clothes have not been soiled or worn out, and neither his clothes nor his shoes are torn. One hundred times each night and one hundred times each day he falls to his knees and praises his God. His voice is like a terrifying trumpet. God's angels travel with him and do not allow him to tire or to hunger. He is ever in the same mood; he is always cheerful and glad. He knows and foresees everything, and he can speak and understand all nations' languages. He knows what you are asking me now, and what I tell you about him, because God's angels serve him and tell him everything. If you seek him out, you will only find him if he is willing, but otherwise not. And if you find him, beg him not to come here, so that God's angels may not do such things to me as they did to my friend Astaroth."

CHAPTER III

The devil fell silent when he had said this. The priests returned, and they scrutinized the dress and appearance of every foreigner. They searched for two days for the apostle and didn't find him.

Just then, it happened that a possessed man shouted and said, "Bartholomew, Apostle of God, your prayers are burning me!"

The apostle said, "Be silent, unclean spirit, and go away from him!" Then the man, who had been mad for many years, was healed.

The king was told about the healing of this sick man. The king's name was Polimius, and he had a daughter who was mad. He sent men for the apostle and addressed him: "My daughter is in a bad way, and I ask that just as you healed Seustium, who has been mad for many years, you also heal my daughter."

The apostle stood up and went with him. And when the apostle saw her, fettered in chains, he called out and asked her to be released. But the servants answered, "No one will dare raise a hand to her, for she bites and rips everything that she can catch."

The apostle said to then, "I have bound the enemy that tormented her, but you are still afraid of her. Go and release her and give her food, and bring her to me early in the morning." They did as the apostle ordered, and the devil was never able to torment her again.

CHAPTER IV

King Polimius had camels and horses loaded up with gold and silver, gemstones and costly clothes, and he searched for the apostle and could not fine him. The treasure was then brought back to his hall.

But when the night had passed and day was breaking,[16] the apostle appeared to the king where he was lying in his bedchamber behind locked doors. He said to him, "Why did you search for me all day with gold and silver and gemstones and costly clothes? Those who love earthly matters feel that they need these gifts, but I desire nothing corporeal or earthly. But I want you to know that God's Son allowed himself to be born into this world by the Virgin Mary, and he became a man in the womb of a virgin. When this holy virgin had God with her, the one who created heaven and earth and sea and all that lies between them, he took human nature upon his divine nature. He began his life among men through birth, he who had never had a beginning to his divine nature; rather, he himself is the beginning of all things and gave a beginning to all creation, visible and invisible. That virgin first swore this oath to God: to keep her virginity unspoiled and never be married. No one had ever before made that oath to God: that virgin was the first woman to swear to God to keep her virginity. She took this up not on account of the judgments or words of mankind; rather, she did this in imitation of the angels of life, for the love of God. For that reason, the angel Gabriel appeared to her within closed doors, shining like the sun. When she was afraid, the angel spoke to her: 'Do not be afraid, Mary; for you shall bear a son.' She laid aside her fear and spoke steadfastly: 'How can that be, because I do not intend to be betrothed to a man?'[17] The angel answered, 'Because of this, the Holy Spirit shall come over you, and the holy child that you bear will be called the Son of God.'

"That Son of God, when he was here, a man among men, allowed the devil to tempt him. That devil had overcome the first man and managed to tempt him to eat the fruit of the tree that God had forbidden him. But just as the devil told the first man to eat, and he ate, and because of this he was driven from Paradise and made an outlaw in this world, and all mankind is descended from him—in the same way, the devil told God's Son that he should turn rocks and stones into bread and eat it and not allow himself to suffer hunger. The Lord answered him, 'Man does not live by bread alone, but rather by all of God's Word.' That devil who overcame the one who ate, that adversary lost his victory on account of the one who fasted and despised his temptations. For it was right that a virgin's son should overcome the one who formerly had overcome a virgin's son."

King Polimius answered, saying, "How can you say that the mother of God's Son is a virgin, if another man was the son of a virgin first?"

The apostle answered, "I give thanks to God, because you have listened to me attentively."

CHAPTER V

"The first man was created from earth, and because of this the earth was his mother. She was a virgin when she was not yet defiled by mankind's sins, and not opened up by the digging of graves for dead men. What I told you was correct: a virgin's son would overcome the one who first overcame a virgin's son and made him bewail his trickery, that he should eat of the forbidden tree and straightaway be driven from Paradise and shut out. But this virgin's son allowed the devil to tempt him. This was the devil's trickery: he wanted to destroy this virgin's son, but did not dare to tempt him as long as he did not see that he was hungry, because he thought it must be certain that Jesus was the Son of God if he was not hungry after forty days. But just as he is the true Son of God, he is also a man, and only those men who love him with a pure heart and good deeds are able to recognize him. When the devil saw that the Lord was hungry after forty days, he thought it was certain that he was not God, and he said to him, 'Why do you let yourself be hungry? Command that these stones become bread, and eat.' But the Lord answered him, 'Listen, you enemy! If you have power over mankind because Adam the father of all mankind gave in to your temptation and disobeyed God's commandments, I will keep God's laws and overcome you fasting and drive you from the rulership that you have held on account of the sins of the man who ate.'

"When the devil found himself overcome in this trial, he showed him gold and silver and all the glories of the world, and said to him, 'All this will I give you, if you bow down to me.' The Lord answered him, 'Flee away, enemy! For so is it written: You shall bow down to your Lord God alone and serve only him.'

"The third temptation was again pride, when the Enemy lifted the Lord up onto a high temple and told him to step off, if he were God's son. But he who once had overcome a virgin's son was now triply overcome by a virgin's son. And just as you see that a king overcomes his enemy, and sends his knights and soldiers to all the places where his enemy had ruled, and places his signs and his ownership on everything—Jesus Christ did the same when he overcame the devil: he sent us into all countries, so that we might drive out all servants of the devil that dwell in temples and in idols, and we might free men from their enslavement and from the power of the one who was overcome. And we despise gold and silver, as Christ despised it, because we wish to be wealthy where He has his kingdom for eternity. There is neither sickness nor sorrow there; there is eternal joy and blessing without end and eternal delight. When I entered your temple, the angels of my Lord, who sent me, bound the devil that gave you answers from the idol. But if you let yourself be baptized and accept the faith, I will arrange it so that you will see him, and you will know how great is the God whom you have been lacking. And you shall hear about the tricks that the devil used to appear to heal all those who were lying sick in the temple. As soon as he overcame the first man, he began to have power over men, and he has greater power over those who transgress more, and less power over those who transgress and offend less. The devil himself gives men illnesses by his trickery and urges men to believe in him and in idols, so that he may have rulership over their souls. He leaves off harming them when they call a stump or a stone their god. The devil that was in this image cannot answer his own priests, since he is bound and overcome by me. But if you want to prove that what I tell you is true, I will command him to come out of his image and answer you."

The king replied, "Early in the morning, the high priests[18] will be ready to sacrifice, and I will come there to see these wonders that you speak of."

CHAPTER VI

When the next morning came and the priests sacrificed, the devil shouted and said, "Stop sacrificing to me, wretched men, or it will be the worse for you. I am bound with fiery chains by the angels of Jesus Christ, whom the Jews crucified and thought was a man who would be held by death. But he attacked Hel our queen, and bound the prince of Hell himself in fiery chains, and arose from death on the third day, and gave the sign of his Cross to his apostles and sent them into all the corners of the world. Now one of them has come here, and he has bound me. I beg this of you: he must let me go to another district, at your request."

Bartholomew spoke. "Say, unclean spirit, who is the one who injured all these men who are lying here sick?"

The devil said, "Our prince sent us to injure men—first their bodies, as long as we did not have power over their souls. But when they sacrifice to us for the health of their bodies, we leave off harming their bodies, because then we have power over their souls. We appear to heal them when we give up harming them, and we are worshipped as gods. But we are devils and servants of the one whom the crucified Son of the Virgin bound. Since the day that that apostle of his came here, I have been tormented and bound in fiery chains. Now I speak because he has ordered me to speak, for not even our prince himself would dare to speak, if he were here."

Bartholomew said, "Why did you not heal these men who came to you?"

The devil answered, "When we hurt their bodies, we allowed their pains to continue for as long as we could not injure their souls."

The apostle said, "How did you injure their souls?"

The devil answered, "When men believe that we are gods and offer sacrifices to us, God turns away from them, and we turn a sickness of the body into a sickness of the soul."

Then Bartholomew spoke to the crowd: "Now you can see the one whom you thought was a god and healed you. Hear now who the true God is, your Creator, who lives in Heaven, not in stones or stumps. If you wish for me to pray for you and for all who are sick to recover their health, then cast down this idol and smash it, and I will consecrate the temple in the name of Christ and baptize you in this temple with Christ's baptism."

On the advice of the king, the entire crowd got ropes and tied them to the idol, and they wanted to drag it out of the temple, but they never could move it from its place. Then the Apostle said to them, "Loosen all the bonds from the idol." When they had released all the bonds from it, the Apostle spoke to the devil that was inside the idol, "If you do not want me to send you into the abyss, come out of this graven image and break it up completely. Then go into the wilderness, to the place where no birds fly and no human speech is heard!"

Then Astaroth came out and broke up all the idols that were inside, both greater and lesser, and he took away from the temple all the painted heathen images that were there. All the people shouted with one voice: "There is one Almighty God, whom the Apostle Bartholomew proclaims!"

Then the Apostle Bartholomew raised his hands to Heaven, and he spoke: "God of Abraham, God of Isaac, God of Jacob, You who sent your only begotten son, our Lord Jesus Christ, for our redemption, so that he might free us by his blood when we were slaves of sin, and make sons of us—you are the one true God: one unbegotten Father; one only begotten Son our Lord Jesus Christ; one Holy Spirit, illuminator and comforter of our souls; one indivisible God. Our Lord gave us the power, in His name, for us to heal the sick and give sight to the blind and cast out devils from madmen and cleanse lepers and give life to the dead, and we receive all of that from God, whom we beseech in the name of Jesus Christ. In His name, I ask that this entire multitude of sick people become well, and that all know that you are the One God in Heaven and on earth and on the sea, who restores the health of all for the sake of our Lord Jesus Christ himself, for the sake of your honor and glory throughout all ages."

All the people answered and said "Amen."

CHAPTER VI

Then an angel of God appeared, as bright as the sun. He flew into the four corners of the temple and inscribed the sign of the Cross with his finger on the four cornerstones. He spoke: "Thus says God, who sent me: Just as He has cleansed you of your sicknesses, so has He cleansed you and this temple of all the pollution of the devil, because His Apostle has driven this fiend away from men, the one who inhabited this temple. The Lord commanded me that I should reveal him to you. You must not fear when you see him. Rather, make the same sign on your forehead with your fingers that I made on the stones, and all evil things shall flee from you."

Then he showed them a huge and terrifying shadow, blacker than a raven.[19] His nose was sharp and his beard was long; his hair reached all the way down to his feet. Fire blazed forth from his eyes, and sparks flew out of his mouth as if from glowing iron, and burning brimstone smoldered from his nose. His feathers were like thorns, but his hands were bound behind his back with flaming bonds. God's angel said to him, "Because you heeded the Apostle's words and destroyed all the idols that were in the temple, I will release you, as the Apostle promised you. But you must go into the wilderness where men cannot live, and stay there until Judgment Day."

The black spirit flew from the temple and disappeared, howling in a dreadful voice. God's angel flew up to Heaven, and everyone saw it. Then the king laid down the crown from his head and his purple robes, and he became a disciple of the Apostle. He accepted baptism, along with his wife and his two sons and all his household, and all those who had received healing there, and all those who were under his command.

CHAPTER VIII

The chief priests of all the temples assembled together, and they went to meet the king's brother, who ruled over half of India. He was called Astriges. They spoke with him: "Your brother has become a disciple of a sorceror who took possession of our temple and smashed all our gods."

When they had said that, weeping, some more chief priests came and told the same story with tears. King Astriges grew angry, and he sent a thousand fully armed men with the chief priests. They were to capture the Apostle and bring him there in fetters, if they could find him.

When they had done that, King Astriges spoke to him. "Are you the one who has deluded my brother?"

The Apostle said, "I did not delude him; rather, I led him out of delusion."

The king said, "Are you the one who smashed our gods?"

The Apostle said, "I gave the devils that lived in the idols the power to break their own idols themselves, so that the people would turn from their foolishness and believe in the one God who is in Heaven."

The king said, "Just as you made my brother abandon his gods and believe in your god, I will make you abandon your god and sacrifice to my god."

The Apostle said, "The god to whom your brother sacrificed, I showed bound, and I made him smash his own graven image himself. If you can do that to my God, then you can make me sacrifice to your god. But if you cannot do that to my God, but I can destroy all your gods, then it is right that you should worship my God."

When the Apostle had said that, men came and told the king that his god Baldath had fallen down and broken into small pieces. The king was angry and tore his clothes. He had the Apostle of God beaten with staves and flayed alive, and then beheaded.[20]

Men came from twelve towns, along with King Polimius, and they took the Apostle's body with praise and all glory to God. They built him a large and splendid church, and there they buried the Apostle's body.

But when thirty days had passed, King Astriges was seized by an unclean spirit, and he came to the grave of the Apostle. All the high priests went mad because of demons, and they agreed to the holiness of the Apostle, and then they fell down dead at his grave. Then great fear and terror came over the heathen people, and they all accepted the faith and baptism from the priests that the Apostle had consecrated.

By divine revelation and the advice of all men, learned and unlearned, Polimius was made a bishop, and later, he began to work many miracles in God's name. Polimius was bishop for twenty years, and he was perfect in good works, and he greatly strengthened Christendom and all good customs. Then Polimius went to God in eternal glory, who lives and rules over all, from age to age. Amen.

CHAPTER IX[21]

Bartholomew taught doctrine in Furthest India, which lies at the edge of the world. As has been told, he was flayed alive for the sake of the name of God, and also terribly tortured. Then his head was cut off, by the command of the king named Astriges. The holy relics of the Apostle Bartholomew are now in Benevento, but formerly he was on the island called Lipari.

Shortly after the death of Bishop Polimius, there was a great invasion of wicked and infidel men. They were opposed to the donations and honors that men gave to the blessed Apostle Bartholomew, and they cared nothing for the miracles that he worked for sick people. When they had made a little progress in dulling the love in men's hearts for the Apostle, madness and folly claimed them, so that they made a chest of wood and had the holy relics of the Apostle placed inside, and they flung them all together out onto the ocean, along with holy relics of four other martyrs. These holy relics drifted out over the sea, and Bartholomew's chest was always in the lead, until it reached the island called Lipari, not far from Sicily. This was revealed to the holy bishop who lived and had his seat there, who was called Agathon. He investigated these great wonders, and he had the other relics that had arrived there sent to other bishoprics. He allowed a great many men to go and see the holy relics of the Apostle, with candles and censers and beautiful hymns. They wanted to bring the Apostle to the church, and they never could manage it. Their joy was turned to distress, and the people did not know what they should do. But God is near to all those who call upon Him, and He gave good counsel, as He always does, to those who sought Him with love and good will. They took two young bullocks, clean and handsome, and let them graze in front of the chest in which were the holy relics of the Apostle Bartholomew, and it freely followed them to the church. There it was put into place with all splendor, and many great miracles came to pass there. A volcanic eruption, from which men had suffered much, ceased to flow, and sick people recovered their health there, no matter what their trouble was.[22]

The holy relics of the Apostle were glorified there for a long time, until the time drew nigh when God willed to have his holy relics brought to an even more prominent place than where he had formerly been.[23] At the time when eight hundred and thirty-eight years had passed since the birth of Christ, the Saracens came and attacked the island of Lipari and pillaged everywhere, and they scattered every bone of the Apostle. When they had gone away, Bartholomew appeared to a Greek monk who was the churchwarden there, and said to him: "Get up and collect my bones, which are now scattered far and wide."

The monk answered, "Why should I gather your bones, or do you honors, when you weren't willing to offer us any help or protect your own people so that everything here might not be plundered and pillaged?"

The Apostle said, "God has spared these people for many years, for longer than they deserve, thanks to my prayers. Now their wickedness and shamefulness has begun to yield such fruit that I am declaring myself separated from this rabble. But you, do as I command. It may be that you'll find glory if you do as I say."

The monk answered, "How can I find your bones when I don't know where they are?"

The Apostle said, "Go outside at night, as soon as it is dark, and take everything that you see shining like a flame. Those are my bones."

The monk did as the Apostle ordered. He arose in the night and found the bones in the way that the Apostle had predicted. He was joyful. Then he placed them for safekeeping in a golden vessel, and left that place with the relics of the Apostle. Some men went with him, and they found a ship from Lombardy. They ventured on the ship and travelled all together.

When they had set out on their way with the relics of the Apostle, Saracen raiders attacked them, the same ones who had plundered Lipari earlier. (That nation is called the Saracens, but we[24] call them Serki.) When they had come so close that the men with the relics felt there was no hope of escape, they called on the Apostle. And there came up such a great darkness that the raiders couldn't see them anywhere, and they went freely wherever they wanted by the intercession of the blessed Apostle Bartholomew. They traveled on and had a good voyage until they reached the town called Benevento. As soon as the townspeople found out that the holy relics of the Apostle Bartholomew had arrived, they went out to meet them with rejoicing and hymns, and they enclosed them carefully in the high altar of the noblest cathedral in the town. And he is revered there now, and all manner of miracles occur at his holy shrine to this day.

The Saga of the Descent into Hell

Niðrstigningarsaga

The Gospel of Nicodemus is an apocryphal Christian text consisting of two parts that were originally separate: the Acts of Pilate, *describing the trial and crucifixion of Jesus and its aftermath; and the* Descensus ad Inferos *or* Descent into Hell, *an account of Jesus entering Hell after his death, overcoming Satan, and rescuing the Jewish prophets and patriarchs, who despite their great merit in life could not enter Heaven until after Jesus's death and resurrection. Although never part of the Biblical canon, the Gospel of Nicodemus was immensely popular in medieval Europe. The* Descensus ad Inferos *or "Harrowing of Hell" is retold in medieval English mystery plays and in Canto IV of Dante's Inferno, among other texts, and it is illustrated in medieval art from at least the 6th century onward.*[1] *A Norse translation of the* Descensus ad Inferos, *known as* Niðrstigningarsaga *or "The Saga of the Descent", survives in one complete text and three fragments.*

This saga is generally faithful to the Latin, but omits a number of doctrinal discussions and narrative digressions, and adds two passages about the trapping of Satan. Niðrstigningarsaga *has drawn attention for its creative use of words, concepts, and even scenes that seem to reflect pre-Christian Norse mythology. For example, Satan is explicitly called a* jötunn, *a mythological giant; and he is said to transform into* Miðgarðsormr, *the Midgard Serpent, only to be caught by the metaphorical baited hook that is Jesus on the Cross. The image is not original to Norse tradition—Gregory the Great had already described Jesus as the bait to catch the Satanic monster Behemoth or Leviathan, and his writings were well known in medieval Iceland.*[2] *Nonetheless, the translator's choice of just that image in that place is telling; to an audience that still remembered some of the old stories, it would have sounded very much like the myth of Thor fishing up the Midgard Serpent. The language is also more heroic than the original at key points; for example, the Latin* omnes sancti, *"all the saints", becomes* her miclum, *"a great army," while the devils who try to bar the Gates of Hell are called* kappar, *"champions". In short, this is not a slavish translation, but a thoughtful adaptation with an Icelandic audience in mind.*

Niðrstigningarsaga *may have been composed as early as the 11th century. My translation is based on a complete manuscript from the 13th century, AM 645, with some emendations from the closely related AM 623 and occasional references to two other manuscripts, all edited and published by Unger.*[3] *I have referred to Scheidweiler's translations of the oldest Greek and Latin texts,*[4] *but tried to let the Norse text speak for itself. The Norse text contains many quotations from the Latin Vulgate Bible, which I have rendered as quotations from the King James Version of the Bible in English and placed in italics.*

CHAPTER I

The brothers Carinus and Leucius,[5] the sons of Simeon the Old, tell of the descent of Christ into Hell in the book that they wrote about how Christ raised Adam and all the others together from Hell. Although what the book says about this matter is hardly as justified as other holy writings, it is not said that it is dubious. This book is called the *Act of the Savior*.[6] Men say that Nicodemus, the Lord's disciple, composed it.

"We were there," they said, "in a place which seemed like a field. Adam was there, and all the Patriarchs and Prophets. It was usually foggy and dark there.[7] Then it was extraordinary and remarkable when, with fearful suddenness, there shone a beautiful and bright light over us all, as if from the sun. Adam, father of all mankind, and all the Patriarchs and Prophets began to rejoice greatly and speak in this way: "This light must shine from God, who has promised to send us his own light."[8]

The Prophet Isaiah cried out and spoke: "This light is of God, just as I said when I was alive on Earth. I said this: 'the land of Zebulun and the land of Naphtali, beyond Jordan, in Galilee of the nations, the people that walked in darkness have seen a great light: they that dwell in the land of the shadow of death, upon them hath the light shined.' [9] Now that light, which I prophesied would come, has come over us. For truly we are sitting in the darkness of hell, but now we all may greatly welcome this light."

Then our father Simeon came walking to where the great multitude had all gathered together, and he spoke most joyfully with God's friends: "Glorify *our Lord Jesus Christ*, concerning whom, I took him in my arms when he was a baby, and I bore him into church. Then I was spoken to by the Holy Spirit, and I sang, '*Lord, now lettest thou thy servant depart in peace, according to thy word: for mine eyes have seen thy salvation, which thou hast prepared before the face of all people; a light to lighten the Gentiles, and the glory of thy people Israel*.'"[10] All of God's saints rejoiced greatly at this message.

A man came walking up whom they did not recognize. He was an able man, outfitted as if he had come from the wilderness. They asked the man what his name was, and what news he might tell. He said that he was called John. "I was a bold voice calling in the wilderness, and a forerunner of God's Son on Earth, telling men how to recognize that He is God's Son, who had come to them there in order to help those who were willing to accept him. And when I saw him coming to find me, the Holy Spirit compelled me, and I said this: '*Behold the lamb of God, that taketh away the sins of the world.*'[11] Then I baptized him in the river Jordan. And then I saw the Holy Spirit come over him in the shape of a dove, and I heard a voice from Heaven say, '*This is my beloved, in whom I am well pleased.*'[12] Now I can tell you this: I have brought this message from Him, to announce to you that it will be a very short while now until *The Son of God Himself* shall come down from Heaven to visit us, the men who sit here in hellish darkness."[13]

CHAPTER II

When our father Adam, the first man created, heard it said that Jesus was baptized in the Jordan, for which purpose this man John came from heaven, he was overjoyed to hear it. He turned to his son and spoke to him: "My son Seth! Tell the Patriarchs and Prophets about what you heard Michael the Archangel say to you, when I sent you to Paradise to seek out and beseech Our Lord if he might be willing to send his angel to bring you anointing oil from that place, which he might get there from the olive tree of mercy, so that he might anoint my body with it when I was sick, that I might receive healing."

Seth had come to where the Patriarchs and the Prophets were. He heard, and he spoke up in this way: "When I was going on my father's errand," he said, "in the end, I came to the Gates of Paradise. There were two different things before them: there was a burning fire, to bar every man from coming there, and angels to defend them from all devils and spirits of sinful men. When I undertook my mission, I stood there and prayed to God, and Michael the Archangel appeared to me. He spoke thus to me: 'I am sent unto you from the Lord. I am appointed to look after every man's soul. And I must tell you this, Seth: There is no reason for you to beg for this oil with tears on behalf of your father, though he be quite sick—since he will not have the oil from that place, not until five thousand and four hundred years have passed from now. Then God's only Son, Christ himself, will come to the earthly realm, and he will heal many sick men, and raise some from death. Christ himself will be baptized in the River Jordan. And when he steps out of the water, he will anoint all those who believe in him with the oil of mercy. That oil of mercy will become a second birth into eternal blessing for those who are born again by water and the Holy Spirit. It will also come to pass that the beloved Son of God, Jesus Christ, will descend below the earthly realm, and he will lead your father Adam into Paradise, to the tree of mercy.'"

All the patriarchs were most joyful at this journey that Seth had told to them.

CHAPTER III

Now as they were rejoicing greatly at this, it is said that the giant, Satan the prince of Hell—who sometimes appears with seven heads and sometimes with three, and sometimes in the shape of a dragon that is horrid and frightful and evil in every respect—had summoned giants and devils and all the mighty trolls that there were in Hell.[14] And he spoke: "Be prepared to seize and capture Jesus, who boasted that he was God's Son. Nonetheless he is a man, and I have observed that he is fearful of death.[15] That is the man who has opposed me much and has always been the fiercest enemy. Many men that I have made blind and crippled and leprous and mad, he has healed with his own words."

They spoke and answered him: "We do not know that he is as you say. But this we know and this we can see: My lord, you have never lured into our hands a man who has always smashed and ruined your power and might so much that he has spoken only one fearful word, like the man you now speak of. We think—and we fear the fate that awaits you where he is—that he must be almighty in his divine nature, so that no one in the world will prevail against him as he is in his human nature."

Then the Prince of Darkness said, "How can you have doubts and fears about seizing this man Jesus, who is both my enemy and yours—since I tempted him, and I stirred up the Jewish people to enmity against him, and I built a gallows for his crucifixion?[16] I have had a spear sharpened to stab him, and it will not be long at all now until he must die. Then I will lead him here, so that he may be subjugated both to you and to me."

They answered, "You did not mention that he had done anything by means of his words and healed the man that you had tormented and killed. But this we know: he has taken away from you many dead men who were held by us. Or who was the man of powerful speech who summoned Lazarus away from here? We had held him here in bondage for four days, and suddenly he was alive on Earth, snatched away from us."

Satan, the Prince of Death, answered, "That man was Jesus."

They answered him: "We swear this, by you and your power along with ours: you must not let him come here, because when we heard his command, it brought terror to us all. All our slaves and all our craftsmen trembled, and we were quite unable to hold onto Lazarus, because he vanished from here faster than anything, and walked on the Earth alive. We know that Almighty God is within this man, and he must have come here into this world to release men from sin and lead them to the life of his Godhead."[17]

There I will leave Satan and the devils conversing.

CHAPTER IV

But I am neglecting to say that even more great signs occurred. At that moment it became as bright as day, as the heavens opened, and first there came forth a white horse. The prince who rode that horse was in many respects more splendid than the greatest of all other men. His eyes were like a burning flame; he had a crown on his head, and there were many signs of victory to be seen. He had an outer garment that was soaked in blood. On his garment, over his thighs, these words were written: *King of Kings and Lord of Lords.*[18] He was brighter than the sun. He led behind him a great host. All those who followed him rode white horses, and they were all clad in white silk and were most bright. The mightiest ruler led them to Jerusalem and said, "Let the trap that is prepared at Jerusalem do harm to the Midgard Serpent." He hid the hook, which was concealed in the bait and couldn't be seen because it was laid in the trap. He was also able to hide the line so that it couldn't be seen. Then he ordered some of his holy men to go ahead of him and announce his arrival in Hell.[19]

CHAPTER V

Now I must return to where I left off. As Satan and his devils were conversing, they heard holy angels shouting so loudly that the noise seemed to surround them. They shouted, "*Lift up your heads, O ye gates; and be ye lift up, ye everlasting doors; and the King of Glory shall come in.*"[20]

Then the dwellers in Hell said to Satan, "Get away from our homes. Fight hard against the King of Glory, if you can. We don't want to deal with him." They drove their own prince out of Hell.

When Satan came out, he saw that a great host of angels had come to Hell. He didn't go and face them, and he slipped past. Then he turned himself into the form of a dragon and made himself so huge that he thought he could surround the entire world. He saw what was happening in Jerusalem, that Jesus Christ was dying, and he traveled there at once and meant to tear his soul away. But when he came there, thinking that he would swallow him and keep him, the hook of divinity pierced him, and the Cross fell down on him, and he was caught like a fish on a hook or a mouse under a mousetrap or a fox in a snare, as had already been foreseen. Then *Our Lord* came and bound him and told his angels to guard him.[21]

CHAPTER VI

But now I must begin to relate what the ones in Hell were doing after Satan left. The powerful devils in Hell said to their champions: "Take and hold all the gates and protect them, and bring iron bars and iron grates before them, and defend yourselves fiercely and stand against them firmly, so that you are not captured—or else that which you formerly held will be taken from you."

When God's holy ones heard that, they said to the evil beings: "*Lift up the gates*, so that the king of glory may enter." Then David, a king and prophet, began to speak loudly to God's people: "It was when I lived and was called the king of an Eastern realm, that I prophesied this to you: *O give thanks unto the Lord; call upon his name and his marvellous works that he hath done; for he hath broken the gates of brass, and cut the bars of iron in sunder. He took them out of the way of their iniquity.*"[22]

Then Isaiah the prophet said, "Do you not know that I once prophesied, when I was on the earth, that the dead would arise, and those who were in graves would rejoice,[23] and Death and Hell would lose their victory?"

When they heard the words of Isaiah, God's holy ones shouted fiercely at the folk of Hell, "Open the gates now, or else you will be overwhelmed." Then a second time they heard a voice so loud that all Hell seemed to shake: "*Lift up your heads, o ye gates.*"

When they heard the call to open the gates a second time, the chief devils were astonished and answered, "*Who is this King of Glory? The Lord strong and mighty, the Lord mighty in battle.*"[24]

Then David said, "I know those words that are spoken there, since I prophesied this by the Holy Spirit. Now I will tell you: The Lord strong and mighty, the Lord mighty in battle is the King of Glory, For he hath looked down from the height of his sanctuary; from heaven did the Lord behold the earth, to hear the groaning of the prisoner, to loose those that are appointed to death.[25] Hideous and filthy ones, open the gates, so that the King of Glory shall enter."

When David had said this, the King of Glory came to the ramparts of Hell. At once he broke down the fortress of Hell and made a great breach. He was revealed in the form of a man, with such great light that the darkness of Hell vanished. Every good man was then freed from the fetters with which he was bound. Such great shock and tumult had struck, when he rode through the breach in Hell so quickly, that all the devils began to falter and shiver. No sooner had they seen Christ the Lord walking there than they all stared and said this: "You have vanquished us; you have assaulted us most fiercely and sought to put us to shame. See this wonder and abomination! He appeared low and little, in the form of a slave, slain on a cross and buried. But now you have come here, released the bound ones and loosed everything." All the foul fiends of Hell began to say the same thing: "Where are you from, Jesus, man so strong, and such a mighty man, and so bright and so sinless? This earthly realm, which has been forced to pay us tribute for a long time, has never before paid us such a tribute of death. A mighty and brave man is this, who submited to our tortures and was not afraid, in order to help men. We remember now that this Jesus would come here. Our lord Satan said that he himself alone would rule the world, after Jesus's death."

Then the Lord Jesus Christ began to trample Death underfoot, but he bound the princes of darkness with eternal bonds of his own power. He led Adam to his own brightness.

CHAPTER VII

Then the dwellers in Hell made a dreadful accusation against their prince and chastised him. "Listen," they said, "prince of damnation, ruler of death, three-headed Beelzebub, laughingstock of the angels! Why did you promise us protection against his coming? You have planned this most unwisely. Now you may see that Christ has come here and driven away the darkness of death with the light of his Godhead, and broken down our ramparts. He is leading all the captives away from here, many who were accustomed to groan sorely under our torments. Everything is out of order, and his people will beware of coming here from now on.[26] Now it has come about that they are haughty towards us—they, who formerly could never be glad—and they are beginning to offer us threats. Listen, Satan, ruler of Hell and all evil! Why did you have to draw him here? Now we expect that there will be no weeping or groaning here. That great wealth of yours, which you defiled in dirt and filth, and the happiness that you had won by means of the Tree of Transgression, you have altogether lost by means of the Tree of the Cross. All your joy must be forfeit, since you wanted to challenge the King of Glory himself to face you. Your words are completely dim-witted. You have attacked the one who was so sinless and drawn him here, and now you must unwillingly let go of everything that you don't want to."

After that, it is said that the King of Glory spoke to all the dwellers in Hell together: "Now Satan must stay behind here, in the place of Adam and his sons of my righteousness."

CHAPTER VIII

Then God stretched out his hand and spoke: "Come to me now, all who have understanding of me. Know this: the Devil and Death are now overcome." Everyone came together and strove to run to the hands of *Our Lord.* Then *the Lord* took Adam by His right hand and spoke: "Peace be unto you, along with all your righteous children, my own."

Adam fell at the feet of the *Lord* and said, "*I will extol thee, O Lord; for thou hast lifted me up*"—he sang four more verses of this psalm.[27] All the holy ones sang the same thing and fell at the feet of the *Lord*. They said, "At this very moment, you have come and fulfilled that which you promised and which you foretold by means of the Law and the Prophets: to release us and bring us all home by means of your death on the Cross and your Descent to us, and to bring us out of Hell to glory by your power and the sign of your Cross, so that death may never rule us again."

Then the *Lord* made the Sign of the Cross over Adam and all the saints, and took Adam by the hand and ascended from Hell with a great host. All the holy ones followed the Lord. Then David shouted aloud and sang this: "*O sing unto the Lord a new song.*"[28] All sang with him and said "Amen."

After that, Habakkuk the Prophet called out: "You intended the salvation of your people, to free your chosen one."[29] All the holy ones answered and said, "Blessed is he who comes *in the name of the Lord*. God has freed us to eternal life."

And Micah the Prophet spoke thus: "Where is there a god like our god? You drove away our ills and overcame our sins; instead, your wrath bears witness against evil. You desire mercy for us; you have put to death all our ills and all our sins in memory of your death."[30]

All the holy ones answered, "He is our God in eternity, world without end." Then they all said "Amen." All the prophets began to sing their own words as they followed *Our Lord*.

CHAPTER IX

God ordered Michael the Archangel to lead Adam into Paradise.[31] Two men ran to meet them. The prophets asked, "Who are you, who are bodily in Paradise?" One of them answered, "My name is Enoch, and I was brought here by God's word. The one who is with me is named Elijah, called the Tishbite; he was driven here in a flaming chariot, and we two have still not died as yet. We must hide here until Antichrist has arisen, and then the two of us will go there and fight him by means of God's miracles and signs. He will have us killed in Jerusalem, but after three days and half of a fourth, we will be taken up among the clouds."

As Enoch and Elijah were talking with God's holy ones, a most wretched man came walking up. He carried a cross on his shoulders. They asked who he might be. He answered, "I was a criminal, and I did every kind of evil on Earth. The Jews crucified me along with Christ. It was then, when I saw the wonders that came about, that I realized that Christ must be the Creator of all creation. I began to ask him for mercy for myself, and I spoke thus: 'Remember me, Lord, when you come to your kingdom.' He received my words well, and he spoke thus: 'Truly I say to you, today you will be with me in Paradise.'[32] Then he gave me this cross and said, 'If the angel who is the guardian of Paradise bars you from going in, show him the cross and tell him that Jesus Christ, who is now crucified, has sent you there.' Now I did so; I said to the guardian of Paradise what I was told today. At once he opened up the gates of Paradise before me and led me inside to the right side and said, "Here we must wait a little while, because Adam the father of all mankind will soon come here with his righteous children of Christ the Lord, the crucified."

When the Patriarchs and Prophets heard what the criminal said, they all began to speak: "Praise be to you, Almighty God, who are so merciful that you offer mercy to the unworthy."

CHAPTER X

Carinus and Leucius were not found in their graves after the Resurrection of Christ from death. Instead, they were resurrected with him, and many others, as it says in the Gospels. Carinus and Leucius were sent at once to the town of Arimathea, to Joseph, and they wrote this tale of the Descent of Christ, since they did not wish to speak with men. They let the book pass into the hands of Nicodemus and Joseph, but they ascended.[33]

Many lifetimes later, the emperor Theodosius came across their book and sent it to Arcadius. He kept it with him in Constantinople and had it read out there, and there it was useful to men *forever and ever. Amen.*

Geography

Landafræði

Copied in 1387 by one Óláfr Ormsson, the codex now known as AM 194 is a virtual encyclopedia, containing texts on medicine, geography, and history. It begins with Landafræði *(literally "Lands'-Knowledge"), an overview of world geography compiled from several sources.*

Landafræði *opens with a description of the Earthly Paradise and the mythical Phoenix. The idea of an Earthly Paradise derives from classical descriptions of Elysium or the Isles of the Blessed,*[1] *reinterpreted and given new importance in Christian thought as the Garden of Eden. In an interpretation going back to St. Augustine, and propagated by scholars such as Isidore of Seville, Bede, and Honorius of Autun, the Garden of Eden is a real place, now inaccessible to sinful mankind, but still physically located at the farthest east of the world.*[2] *Its description in* Landafræði *is not completely consistent with* Eireks saga víðförla, *although both agree with the widely held concept that it was a bright place of beautiful flowers, abundant fruits, and pleasant climate.*

The section on the Earthly Paradise and the Phoenix is closely paralleled by a late Old English homily. Both the Norse and the Old English texts resemble the Old English poem The Phoenix, *which in turn is freely based on a 4th-century Latin poem attributed to Lactantius,*[3] *the first to link the Phoenix with the Earthly Paradise. Christian interpretations of the phoenix made the bird a symbol of human resurrection.*[4] *The rest of the text is a description of the inhabited lands of the world, closely following general medieval geographic thought, and much of it ultimately derived from the Book of Genesis.*

My translation is based on AM 194 as edited and published by Kristian Kålund; I have made a few emendations where the text is at fault. My authority for place names is the work of Rudolf Simek.[5]

In ancient times, God's friend in the land of the Jews was named Moses, the man who first began the beneficial task of writing sacred books about the wonders of God. There are five that he made: one from the beginning of the world[6] down to his own time, and four about the events that happened in his days. These books are the foundation of all Holy Scriptures, both in the Old Testament and the New. He begins the story when God created Heaven and Earth, and in his words is depicted all heavenly and earthly creations, just as God created all Creation in six days.

Here Moses speaks of Paradise[7]

Paradise is the name of a place that is not in Heaven and not on Earth. Rather, it is in midair, equally close to Heaven and Earth, just as it was established by God. Paradise is forty miles higher than Noah's flood reached.[8] Paradise is as long as it is broad. Neither mountain nor valley is there; neither frost nor snow is there. All the land there is the finest, and there are no evil creatures and no flaws. There is a good well; it is called the Well of Life.

There is a beautiful and admirable forest that is called Radion Saltus.[9] Its leaves never wither, and every tree there is as straight as an arrow and so tall that one cannot see over it. There are all kinds of tree there, which stand in all their beauty and bear all sorts of flowers and the brightness of apples and fruits. There not a leaf ever falls from a tree. This forest is in the center of Paradise. One fruit-bearing tree was forbidden to Adam; concealed inside it is the knowledge of good and evil.

There is neither hatred nor hunger, and never is there night or darkness. Rather, it is always day, and there the sun shines seven times brighter than in this world, because all the brightness of the heavenly bodies reaches there. Angels are stationed there to lift up their voices for joy. The souls of good men shall fare there and enjoy it until Judgment Day, ever since God opened it up when he led there the soul of the thief who lost his life on the cross.[10]

In Paradise there is a bird called Phoenix. It is quite large and wonderfully shaped, just as God created it, and it is the lord of all birds. It bathes in the Well of Life and flies up to the tallest tree in Paradise, facing the sun, and then beams of light shine from it, as from the sun. It glows all over like gold. Its feathers are more like those of God's angels; its breast is so fair, and its beak is like what we have said about the feathers. Its eyes are like crystal, and its feet are as red as blood. When the beautiful Phoenix flies up from Paradise to Egypt and stays there for fifteen weeks, it summons all kinds of birds, and they sing around it on all sides. Then the men who live there hear that, and they come to it from every direction and speak: "Welcome, Phoenix, to our land; you glow just like red gold; of all birds you are the king." The inhabitants make another Phoenix from wax and brass and shape it as much like the Phoenix as possible in every way. All birds fall at its feet and honor it with joyful voices. A red stripe lies along the length of its back, as fair as refined gold. When fifteen weeks have passed, the beautiful Phoenix flies back to Paradise. All birds fly with it, some below it, and some above it and on both sides. When they cannot travel any longer, then each goes to its own home.

John the Apostle says this of Paradise[11]

Four thousand years before the birth of Christ—when one thousand years had passed since Creation—the Phoenix had grown old, and it summoned a great host of birds to bring together a great pile of wood.[12] And by God's will it came about that the sun shone on the pile of wood, and from the heat of the sun, a flame was lit in the pile of wood. The Phoenix plunged into the middle of the flames and completely burned to ashes. But after the third day, it rose up from death, and then it was young again, and it went to the Well of Life and bathed there. Then feathers grew on it, the very fairest. It grows old every thousand years, and then it burns itself again and rises up young. But no man knows whether it is a male bird or female bird, save God alone.

Paradise is in the east of the world. Adam was meant to settle there, if he had held to what God commanded him. There stands a tree; if a man eats of the fruit, he feels no sickness or injury, and he does not grow feeble or old if he eats it, and it is called the Tree of Life. All the delights of water are in the spring that is there. From that spring, four rivers fall into this world.[13] One is called Phison, which is also called the Ganges; it springs up from underneath the mountains that are called Orcobaris. Phison falls into India and descends out into the surrounding sea, which is called Oceanus in book-language. Another river that falls from Paradise is called the Nile, also called the Geon; it separates two of the three parts of the world, Asia and Africa. It descends through Africa and across Egypt; it reaches the sea in seven places, and it is wide at each place. The third river that falls from Paradise is called Tigris; it descends through Serkland[14] and Greater Armenia. It springs up on the mountains that are called the Elding Mountains. The fourth river is called Euphrates; it springs up under the Elding Mountains. It descends through Armenia and Mesopotamia. There stands a city called Babylon; the Euphrates flows through it and comes out into the Mediterranean Sea a short distance from Antioch.

There are also mountains in Armenia; one is named Tabor, and the other is Hermon. Noah's Ark came to a rest there, between those mountains. There he stepped out of the ark, with his wife and his three sons and their wives. Then Noah divided the world among his sons, into three parts, and gave names to all the parts of the world that previously had been unnamed. He called one part of the world Asia, the second part Africa, and the third part Europe. Shem, Noah's son, was allotted to settle the portion of the earth called Asia, which is said to be one half of the world. Japheth, Noah's son, had to settle the northern portion of the world, which we call Europe. Ham, the third son of Noah, had to settle the southern portion of the world, which we call Africa.

Shem had five sons, and they settled the entire eastern portion of the world, as did their kinsmen after them. One of the sons of Shem was named Elam, the second was Assur, the third was Arphaxath, the fourth was Illudi, and the fifth was Aran.[15] These are the nations that they founded in that part of the world: India and Persia, where Elam settled; Assyria, where Assur settled; Media and Chaldea, where Arphaxath settled; Albania, where Illudi ruled; Bactria, Aramea, the Land of Amazons, and Great Scythia,[16] where Aran was. The number of all nations in that part of the world is four hundred and seven. When the languages were divided when the giants were building their tower, as is written[17], twenty-seven languages came into this part of the world that we have described.

Japheth had seven sons. These were their names: Gomer, Magoc, Madai, Juban, Tubal, Masok, and Tirak. These are the empires in that part of the world that is called Europe: part of Great Scythia, where Magoc ruled; the land of the Kylfings,[18] which we call Russia, where Madai was; Greece, where Juban ruled; Bulgaria, where Tirac was; in Hungary, Germany, France, and Spain, where Tubal was; the Romans' land, Denmark, Sweden, and Norway, where Gomer was;[19] Galatia and Cappadocia, where Masoc was. There are two hundred nations there in all, and twenty-three languages are spoken there.

In the part of the world that is called Africa, Ham, son of Noah, settled. He had four sons, and these are their names: Kaus, Mesraun, Phud, and

Canaan. These are the empires there: Ethiopia, where Kaus was; Egypt, where Mesraun was; Libya, where Phud was; and Arabia, the Saracens' Land[20], Gaetulia[21], Numidia[22], Mauretania[23], and the Land of Black Men[24], where Canaan ruled. There are three hundred and six nations there, and twenty-two languages. In all, there are seventy-two languages and a thousand nations in the entire world.[25]

It is said that the earth is divided into three named parts. One portion is called Asia; this extends out of the northeast and southwest and reaches the middle of the world. In that part of the earth, in the eastern half of the world, there are three Indias. In Furthest India, the Apostle Bartholomew preached Christianity, and there he lost his life. In the India that lies next to it, the Apostle Thomas preached, and also in the India that is nearest to here. He died there for the sake of God.

In the part of the world called Asia stands the city of Nineveh; it is the greatest of all cities in expanse. It is three days' journey long, and a day's journey broad. In that part of the world there is also Babylon, the ancient and great. Nebuchadnezzar once ruled in it, but it is now ruined, so that men cannot settle there on account of the serpents and all sorts of dangerous animals. In Asia, there are Jerusalem and Antioch, where the Apostle Peter established his own bishop's seat, and there he was the first of all men to celebrate Mass. Asia Minor is the name of a land within the greater Asia, where the Apostle John preached the faith, and his grave is there, in the city called Ephesus. In Egypt is New Babylon, and its capital, which is called Alexandria.

The second portion of the earth is called Africa, which extends from the southwest in both directions, west and northwest. In that part of the earth is the Land of the Saracens and the Land of Black Men. The Mediterranean Sea separates Africa and Europe.

Europe is the name of the third portion of the earth. It extends in both directions, west and northwest, and begins in the northeast. In the east of Europe is Russia; Kiev and Novgorod, Polotsk and Smolensk, are located there. Next to Russia, in the southwest, is the realm of the King of Greece. The capital of the kingdom is Constantinople, which we call Miklagard.[26] In Miklagard is the church that in their speech is called Hagia Sophia; Norsemen call it Egisif. This is the most glorious and splendid church in the world, in its finery and grandeur. Subject to the King of Greece are Bulgaria and a great many islands that are called the Islands of Greece. Crete and Cyprus are the most excellent of the Islands of Greece. Sicily is a large kingdom and belongs to the part of the world called Europe. Italy is the name of the realm that lies to the south of the mountain range that men call the Alps. On the east side of Italy is Apulia, which Norsemen call Pulsland. In the middle of Italy stands the city of Rome. To the north of Italy is Lombardy, which we call Langbardaland. To the north of the mountains eastward is Germany, and to the southwest is France. Spain, which we call Spanland, is a great kingdom in the south, towards the Mediterranean, between Lombardy and France.

The Rhine is the name of a great river that flows in the north, from the Alps, between Germany and France. Frisia lies on the branches of the Rhine, north to the sea. To the north of Germany is Denmark. The sea runs through Denmark into the eastern realms. Sweden lies to the east of Denmark, and Norway lies to the north. It is called Norway from Vegistaf[27] in the north, where Finnmark is located next to the White Sea, southwards to the Göta älv. These are the boundaries of this kingdom: the White Sea to the north, the Göta älv to the south, the Eid forest to the east, and Anglesey Sound[28] to the west. These are the chief cities in Norway: the market at Trondheim, where the sainted King Olaf lies; another in Bergen in Hordaland, where St. Sunniva[29] lies; a third is in Viken to the east, where King Olaf's kinsman St. Halvard[30] lies.

Götaland is east of the Göta älv, and next comes Sweden. Then next is Helsingaland, then Finland, which is said to border on Russia, as was said previously. Nearest to Gotland on the other side is Denmark, where the principal town in Skane is Lund. There is a bishop's seat there, and there lies St. Licius the bishop. There is another on Funen, in Odense, where the holy King Knut the Elder lies.[31] On Zealand lies King Knut the Younger[32], at Ringsted. In Roskilde, on Zealand, is the fair maid Margaret.[33]

Next to Denmark is Sweden. Then comes Öland, then Gotland, then Hälsingland, then Värmland, and then the two Kvenlands, and these are north of Bjarmaland. From Bjarmaland, uninhabited lands extend to the north until Greenland is reached. South of Greenland is Helluland; then there is Markland, and then it is not a long distance to Vinland the Good, which some men suppose extends from Africa—if so, then the outer sea flows in between Vinland and Markland.[34] It is said that Thorfinn Karlsefni cut down a tree for a weathervane[35] and then traveled to search for Vinland the Good, and reached where they thought that land was, but they didn't get to explore it and couldn't get any of the produce of the land. Leif the Lucky was first to find Vinland, and then he found merchants in a bad situation on the sea, and saved their lives by God's mercy. And he brought Christianity to Greenland, and it grew so much there that a bishop's seat was established at the place called Gardar.[36]

England and Scotland make up a single island, although each is ruled by a king. Ireland is a large island. Iceland is also a large island north of Ireland. These countries are all in the portion of the world called Europe.

The *Physiologus* and Related Texts

Physiologus

The Physiologus *("Student of Nature") is a set of descriptions of various animals and their ways, given Christian allegorical interpretations. The* Physiologus *was first compiled in Alexandria, possibly as early as the second century CE but perhaps more probably in the fourth century. Drawing on sources ranging from classical authorities such as Pliny's* Natural History, *to Egyptian myths and folklore, it became one of the most popular texts of Late Antiquity and the Middle Ages. It was translated from Greek into Syriac, Arabic, Ge'ez, Old Church Slavonic, Armenian, and Latin, and from Latin it was translated into most of the European vernacular languages. By the 12th century, many texts of the* Physiologus *had accreted much additional material from other sources; they came to be known as "bestiaries" and remained popular until the 16th century. Several of the "facts" transmitted by the* Physiologus *have survived in the popular imagination to this day, such as the "facts" that elephants are afraid of mice, or that the pelican wounds her own breast to feed her young on her blood.*[1]

Two fragments of Icelandic translations of the Physiologus, *apparently by separate translators, are preserved as manuscript AM 673A. Dating to about 1200, they are the earliest illustrated manuscripts from Iceland. The writer of Fragment A has stripped out almost all details except for the moral allegories, although the illustrations show that he was familiar with the descriptions of the animals. The writer of Fragment B has included a little more detail in his descriptions, but they are still sparse compared to the rather florid descriptions in other versions.*

Extracts containing animal lore from the Etymologies *of Isidore of Seville, one of the sources of the* Physiologus, *appear in several texts, notably the Bible translation and commentary now known as* Stjórn. *The encyclopedic compilation AM 194 contains one such extract, either taken directly from* Etymologies *or possibly by way of the* Physiologus, *simply titled* Ormar, *"Serpents".*

AM 673 also contains two allegories on ships (not included here), and a brief allegory on the rainbow, possibly intended as parts of sermons. Close parallel texts to the rainbow allegory exist in the manuscript Hauksbók *and in* Rímbegla, *a text on astronomy and calendrics.*

Finally, Fragment A of AM 673 includes two pages of drawings of strange humanoid beings: the "Plinian races", supposedly living at the fringes of the known world—giants, pygmies, one-legged men, headless men, dog-headed men, and many others. These drawings were done by the same hand that illustrated Fragment A of the Physiologus.[2] *Accounts of these "monstrous" peoples were originally compiled by the Roman author Pliny the Elder,*[3] *and widely copied by later scholars such as Isidore of Seville.*[4] *Most manuscripts of the* Physiologus *do not mention the "Plinian races" at all—but a group of early 13th-century English bestiaries does include them.*[5] *The Icelandic* Physiologus, *which may derive from an English original, may have once included a description of the "Plinian races." Even though this has not survived, assorted "Plinian races" were certainly known in medieval Iceland, and as a possible source I have translated a section of AM 194 known as* Risaþjóðir, *"Giant Nations".*

Beasts from the Physiologus *turn up now and again in the sagas, such as the elephant and the serpents mentioned in* Yngvars saga. *The later recension of* Örvar-Odds saga *includes encounters with two monsters based on the whale in* Physiologus*; and the native romance* Kirjalax saga *includes many appearances by fabulous monsters. Aside from direct borrowings, the* Physiologus *may have influenced animal symbolism in the Icelandic sagas, notably the appearance in dreams of animal-shaped* fylgjur *or "guardian spirits".*[6] *The "Plinian races" turn up in sagas as well: Cyclops turn up in* Yngvars saga víðförla, *and the race of short-lived women appears in* Samsons saga fagra. *Outside this book,* hundingjar *or "dog-men" appear in* Sturlaugs saga starfsama, *and* Eiríks saga rauða *depicts an encounter with an* einfætingr, *a "uniped" or sciapod.*

I have translated the AM 673a text of the Physiologus from Halldór Hermannson's 1938 edition.[7] *He did not include the treatise on the rainbow, which I have translated from the text published by Carla Cucina.*[8] *The* Physiologus *list of serpents and the account of the "Plinian races" are both taken from AM 194 as published by Kristian Kålund.*[9] *The illustrations are selected from Verner Dahlerup's 1889 lithographic facsimile,*[10] *made when the manuscript was in better condition than it is now, and redrawing damaged areas of the manuscript (for example, one page had been used as a flour sifter and is peppered with holes*[11]*).*

Fragment A

The phoenix signifies Our Lord in its nature, since it burns itself and revives. In this way, Jesus Christ took torment upon his body of his own free will, and arose on the third day and gave complete salvation to all. Thus the phoenix comes over the course of a year, when it dies and revives itself.

There are birds that pluck feathers from their own relatives, and burn them in order to put ashes into their relatives' eyes so that they may be clear-sighted and otherwise more healthy.[12] They signify those men who want to aid their kinsmen by their own labors, as much as they can here in this world.

The siren signifies, by the beauty of its voice, the sweetness of those delicacies that men have for their delight in this world. They pay attention to this alone, and they fall asleep with regard to good deeds. But the beast catches men and destroys them when they fall asleep from her beautiful voice. So many are destroyed by their life of pleasure, if that is all they want to do in this world.

There is a field in Babylon. When it bears crops, those flies called "horseflies" by the common people head into the field; they eat the seeds and spoil the crops.[13] They signify wicked men who behave as if they know what is right—yet it is wrong, and one needs to beware of them.

Honocentaurus is the name of the beast that we call the *finngálkan*.[14] It is a man in front and an animal behind, and by its shape it signifies insincere men. In learned speech it is said to be false and beastlike if a man flatters those who are near him, although he speaks falsely. A good man must always speak truthfully about every matter, whether he is rich or poor.

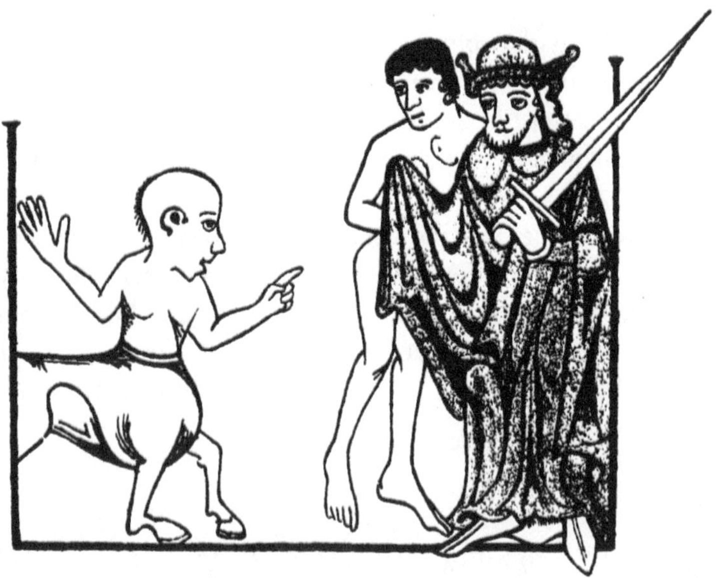

Fragment B

There is a bird in the river Nile, called the *hidrus*.[15] Solomon says of it that it kills the crocodile. It is its nature and its habit that when it sees a crocodile sleeping, it smears itself with mud and jumps in the crocodile's mouth as it sleeps on the riverbank, and it rips and tears it from the inside and bores through its belly to kill it. Thus does God snatch all his friends out of Hell, away from the devils.

The goat[16] is an animal that Greeks call *dorcas*, but it is *capra* in Latin. Solomon says that it loves the highest mountains and lives in mountain valleys, and it is so clear-sighted that it sees men walking in neighboring districts and knows whether they are wanderers or hunters. Thus does our Lord Jesus Christ love the highest mountains—that is, the patriarchs and prophets and all saints.

There is another animal called the onager. Solomon says of it that on the twenty-fifth day of March, it brays twelve times at night, and the same during the day, and thus one knows that it is the equinox, from reckoning the seasons and from the braying of the onager. In every season he brays for a while. The onager has a resemblance to the Devil. When he sees that the nights are equal to the days, it means that the Devil sees heathen folk who formerly walked in darkness turning towards God, and they become like the examples of the patriarchs and prophets, just as the night becomes like the day. In every season he brays, seeking his food, which he may devour. The onager does not bray except for when he is hungry. The Apostle Peter says of the Devil, "The Devil opposes us like a roaring lion, going about and seeking what he may rend."[17]

Apes have a resemblance to the Devil, because just as the ape has a head but no tail—though it is ugly all over, from behind it is much more filthy and hideous—so does the Devil have a head but no tail.[18] When he was in the forefront of the angels in heaven, he had a head; but since he was inwardly false, he ruined his own head, and he has no tail because he was ruined in the beginning, in heaven, and so it must be for eternity.

The heron is a huge bird, and it wins victories over eagles and eats them for food. It is not like other birds, which build nests and go to their nests in the evening. Wherever darkness overtakes it, there is where it sleeps. It signifies a monk with a cell; when he has gone inside, there he stays. And just as the heron wins victories over the eagle, thus does the monk win victory over the Devil who rules in this world.

There is a bird called the coot, and it is the wisest of all birds. It does not feed itself on carrion, and it does not fly from one place to another. Rather, it dwells in one place and stays there as long as it lives, and there it gets its food. Such is every man who believes rightly and follows God and does not wander astray hither and thither, but rather lives always in simple faith.

There is a beast called the panther, and it has beautiful variegated colors and is gentle. When it eats and is full, it lies down and sleeps. After three days it awakens and roars aloud, and with that roar comes a sweet scent from its mouth. Beasts near and far hear his voice and follow the scent—but the dragon creeps into a hole in the ground and lies there as if it were dead. But other animals follow the panther wherever it goes. Thus did our Lord Jesus Christ, who is a true panther, draw all people away from the Devil, who had formerly held him—because the panther signifies taking hold of all things.

There is a whale in the sea that is called *aspedo*, and its back resembles a forest. In the middle of the ocean it sticks out its back, and sailors think that it is an island and tie up their ship there, and then they kindle a fire. But the *aspedo* feels the heat and plunges down into the sea with all the sailors. Thus are those men betrayed, who place their hope in the Devil and take pleasure in his works, and they are plunged into eternal torment with demons.

It has another nature: when it is hungry, it opens up its mouth, and it allows a certain scent to go out. Little fish smell the scent and cluster together inside its mouth. But when its mouth is full, it closes its jaws and swallows them. Thus are faithless men defeated by the manifold temptations of the Devil, like little fishes. But better people are wary and do not come near him.

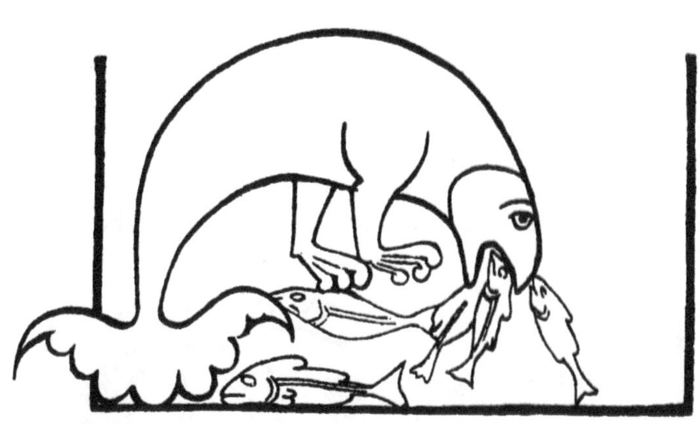

There is a bird called the partridge, and it is exceptionally cunning. It steals the eggs of all birds and hatches them. But when the young birds hear the voices of their kin, they abandon the partridge and fly to their families and go with them. The partridge is left behind, foolish and vain. The Devil is like this bird; he steals nations from their Creator and feeds them on lechery. But when they hear the voice of Christ, they turn and follow Him and commit themselves into His hands.

The honocentaurus has the shape of a man above, but an animal's shape below, and it has two voices and heads out into the meadows to speak to people. As the Apostle says, "Those having a promise of mercy, but denying its power."[19] And as the prophet David says, "Man, when he was in glory, had no understanding, and he is equal to foolish animals and has become like them."[20]

The Physiologus says that the weasel receives semen by the mouth and so becomes pregnant, and gives birth through the ear. Such are those men who eagerly hear the seed of God's word, and quickly forget it in their disobedience and behave as if they have not heard it.

The Physiologus says that asps have this nature: when the snake-charmer[21] comes to the cave in which the asps dwell, and calls them out with his song, they stop their ears with their tails, and some lay their ears against the ground, so that they do not hear it. Wealthy men in this world are like this: they thrust their ears into earthly desires and cover up their hearts and ears, so that they may not hear the commanding voice of the Word of God.[22]

There is a bird called the turtledove. Solomon says: "The turtledove loves her mate very much, and purely. If he dies, she will not take another mate." Listen, good men, what great chastity is to be found in a small bird, and make yourself like this bird.

There is an animal that is called the deer. David says, "As the hart yearns for springs of water, so does my spirit yearn for you, o God."[23] But when it drinks and realizes that a venomous serpent is in its mouth, it spits it out and tramples it underfoot until it is dead. Thus does our Lord Jesus Christ see the Devil, our enemy, and with the spring of divine wisdom, he drives him away from our hearts.

There is an animal that is called *salamandra* in Greek, but *stellio* in Latin. It is small, with variegated colors. Solomon says concerning it: "Like a *stellio* living in a king's house."[24] Solomon says, "If it falls into a fire, the fire goes out as if water were poured on it." Righteous men are like this, extraordinary to all people, just as the three young men—Ananias, Azarias, and Misael[25]—were in the glowing-hot furnace and did not feel the heat, just as the prophet Daniel said, and as the apostle Paul affirms: "We are tormented, and it does not harm us. We are driven away; we are not destroyed."[26]

In Hebrew, the house of the kite is mentioned. The kite seizes meat swiftly and tears it. Spiritually, it indicates those who hold fast to the kingdom of heaven like this: "The Kingdom of Heaven feels their strength."[27]

David says in a psalm, "A boar from the forest destroyed it." Some prefer to interpret this boar to be Vespasian, the ruler of Rome, who defeated the Jews in battle, or else his son Titus, who destroyed all of Jerusalem. But most prefer to interpret it as the Devil, who comes out of the forest of heathen peoples to destroy the Jewish folk.[28]

"I am like a night owl." We know that it is dark by day, but much darker at night. Thus do I see myself darkened on account of my sins.[29]

There is a beast called *elephas* in Latin, and *fill* in our language.[30] It is used in battle in foreign lands. It is so strong and powerful that it holds [thirty-two][31] men with all their weapons, and a stronghold built out of wood like a castle, which they need to have when they fight in battle, as is written in the Book of Maccabees.[32]

On Serpents

Draco is the name of the dragon. It is the largest of the serpents,[33] and has such great strength in its tail that there is no animal so strong that it is not killed if it gets the tail wrapped around itself. It can both fly and crawl. The noblest men in the Land of Black Men must carry off its head for food, if they catch it, and it is thought good for one's intellect.[34]

There is a serpent called *basiliskus.* It has venom in its glance, so that anything is killed if it feels the serpent's glance. Nothing kills it except for the weasel.

There is a serpent called *difsa.* A man dies of thirst if it bites him.

There is a serpent called *ipialis.* From its venom a man dies in this way: he sleeps to death.

There is a serpent called *emorvis.*[35] It bites so that blood runs from the entire body as if each wound were doubled, so that the bleeding is never stopped, and the man dies from this.

There is a serpent called *seps.* It is small, but so poisonous that as soon as it bites a man, his entire body flows away, like wax before a flame, and turns into nothing.

There is a serpent called *prestir.* From its hissing, the entire body swells up [*a few letters missing*]. . . it becomes much fatter than a human form [*a few letters missing*]. . .[36]

There is a serpent called *aspis,* and as soon as it stings a man, the man falls down dead.

There is a serpent called *iaculus.* It flies right through a man, just like an arrow shot with full force.

There is a serpent called *amphisbena,* which has a head on both ends. It turns its heads forward and back and forms a loop when it crawls. It has no power unless there is frost.[37] It has eyes as bright as the light of candles.

There is a serpent called *cerastes.* It is horned like a ram, and from anything that is made out of its horn, one may know if there is poison nearby, because then the horn becomes wet. This serpent has no venom; it bashes animals with its horns to feed itself.

There is a serpent called *scitalis.* It has the most beautiful colors of all serpents. It is a slow serpent, yet it often manages to kill people, when a man is amazed at its beauty. It is as hot as a glowing iron bar; it never cools down so that it does not glow.

There is a serpent called *rimotrix.* Every lake that it comes to, it mixes with poison.[38] This serpent has webs to house itself. Clothes are made from these webs, and these clothes may be smelted like metal. But they must never be allowed to enter the water, because the water that touches it becomes poison.[39]

On The Rainbow

There are three colors in the rainbow: the color of water, the color of burning brimstone, and the color of fire. That reminds us to fear the threefold wrath of God when it comes over the world. Water came in Noah's Flood; burning brimstone came over Sodom and Gomorrah; fire will cover all the world before Judgment Day.[40]

These same three colors in the rainbow denote the threefold forgiveness of sins: one is in baptism; the second is in repentance of sins; and the third is in laying down one's life for God's sake. The color of water symbolizes the forgiveness of sins in baptism; great joy accompanies it, with no trouble. Burning brimstone signifies the repentance of sins; great bitterness accompanies it. The color of fire signifies the forgiveness of sins in laying down one's life for God's sake; great dread and great brilliance accompany it.

This threefold fear of God's wrath is symbolized by the rainbow. It was not seen before Noah's Flood. Since then, it appears in remembrance of the oath that God swore to Noah, that a flood would never come again that would destroy the world, as had happened in his days.

The Nations of Giants

There were giants both before Noah's flood, and afterwards. These nations are huge. Some can be dealt with like other men, but some are hostile to men.

In Scythia are the Albani; they have yellow eyes, according to all the old accounts, and see better by night than by day. Cicopli are also there; they have one eye, and it is in the middle of the forehead, and they feed on animals' flesh. The headless Lamnies are in India; they have a mouth and eyes in their chests, and also eyebrows. Others have a neck, but have eyes on their shoulders. The Cenocefali in India have dogs' heads, and they bark. In Scythia are those men who have no noses, and the entire face is flat except for the mouth and eyes. Some have a lower lip so large that they throw it back over their heads and shade their faces from the sun when they sleep. There are also those there whose mouths are so small that they eat no food, except for drinking through a pipe. Some are tongueless and express everything with signs. Those who are called Panadios have ears so large that they cover their entire body with them. Those men are called Ardabadites who walk bent over, like livestock, and live to be no older than forty. Satiri have hooked noses and have horns on their foreheads and goat feet. The Greeks call one-footed men Skioppodas, since with their feet they shade themselves against the sun; they are as swift as animals. Antipedes live in Africa, twisted at the ankles so that the toes turn backwards; there are eight on each foot. Ippopedes in Sithia have horse feet. Acrobi live in India and are twelve ells tall.[41] There are also men one ell high, living on mountains in India; they are called Pigmei. There is also a race of women in India who have children at the age of five years and live to be no older than eight years.[42] Ermafrodites have the right breast like men and the left like women, and have both genitals and can be both fathers and mothers to their children.[43]

In Africa lives the tribe named Pagasi; they eat everything that they can sink their teeth into. There are also Trogodites there; they run faster than any animal. Antiofagi make use of no food but fish. Anthrofagi are cannibals. Magog eats nothing but raw meat, and eats both men and beasts.[44] There is also a tribe there where people fatten up their fathers and mothers as much as possible, once they are decrepit from old age, and then invite their friends and kinsmen when they are to be killed and eaten at their own funeral feasts—those who let their parents suffer and die from old age and infirmity are thought to do wrong. There is another tribe in Africa that is not harmed by venom, and babies in cradles play with venomous serpents. It is also the nature of certain women that they can bear only one child in their entire lives, and it has white hair when it is newborn, but the hair darkens when age comes on. They live for two hundred years, and they do not grow old or become decrepit.[45]

Beside the waterfall where the Ganges falls from the cliffs of Paradise, there is a tribe that has no mouths, but lives on the scent which comes from the apples and herbs that grow there. There are trees there which grow like wool on the outside, and these people only have clothing that comes from these.[46] These people die when they cannot smell on account of age. There are also men that are hairy like beasts and have no feet and are nine feet tall. Some spend no less time in water than on land, and have no food but raw fish and water to drink.[47]

In Siberia[48] are the Albani; they are as white as snow, in both their hair and their skin; when they are born, they have yellow eyes and see better by night than by day. The land called Women's Land[49] is there. These women and the Albani live nearest each other, and the women always fight among themselves, like men elsewhere, and these women are no more timid or weak than men elsewhere. There is also the tribe that is called the Horn-Finns: a horn grows on them out of the middle of the forehead, bending downwards, and they are cannibals.[50] There are also those whose chin is grown down to the chest; they are called Hundings, and they are as savage as dogs to men.

Top: Three men on a dragon, an attempt to represent the legendary three-headed King Geryon of Spain, a legend discussed by Isidore of Seville but not otherwise known in Iceland. (*Etymologies* XI.iii.28; transl. Barney, p. 245)

Middle: A giant (*Macrobii*); a dwarf (*Pygmei*); a dog-headed man (*Cynocephali*); possibly a family from the long-lived tribe whose women bear only one child.

Bottom: Two cyclops—the left one has an eye in the center of his forehead, while the right one is blind. (The two might be shown passing the eye around). A man with huge ears hanging down (*Panotii*); a man with horse feet (*Hippopedes*).

Top: A man who can only drink through a straw; possibly a "horned Finn"; a man with a long lower lip; a man whose chin is grown to his chest (*Hundingjar*).
Middle: a headless man with eyes on his shoulders; a headless man with his face on his torso (*Blemmyae*); a one-footed man (*Sciapodae*); a man handling a snake.
Bottom: a man handling a snake; a man on all fours eating raw food (*Artabatitae*); a man with feet turned backwards (*Antipodes*).

CHIVALRIC ROMANCES

The Saga of Parceval

Parcevals saga

Parcevals saga *is the Norse translation of Chrétien de Troyes's* Perceval, le conte du Graal. *The language suggests that it was translated in Norway; it may have been translated as part of King Hákon IV's "program", but we do not know. As usual for translated romances, the poetry has been rendered as prose, and descriptive and discursive passages have been shortened or deleted—the saga is about 40% the length of the original poem. The translator, or a later copyist, has also added a brief prologue and an ending; the ending brings Chrétien's unfinished story to a narrative conclusion, albeit with many plot points left hanging. One peculiarity of this saga is the insertion of moralizing maxims in the form of rhyming couplets, often but not always at the end of a chapter. These are not direct translations, although some are inspired by specific French verses. The translator has made several minor errors, and the words that he chose to render foreign chivalric concepts do not follow the conventions found in later sagas. This may indicate that* Parcevals saga *was one of the earliest translated* riddarasögur—*older than* Tristrams saga, *dated to 1226.*[1]

Chrétien's poem is the oldest literary work to introduce the Holy Grail, which originally seems to have been just a beautiful dish or vessel. Unfortunately, the translator does not seem to have understood what the Grail was, and his attempts to describe it are not helpful. Either the translator or later copyists have removed much of the mysticism of the original text, turning it into a straightforward account of the life and training of the young Parceval. The saga may have been received in Iceland as an edifying guide to how a child should grow into a mature adult, gaining both physical prowess and moral and ethical discernment.[2]

Le conte du Graal *begins with Parceval's story, but shifts to recounting adventures of Arthur's knight Gawain (Valver in Norse). The first part of Gawain's adventures is included in* Parcevals saga, *but Gawain's story continues as* Valvers þáttr, *the Tale of Gawain. For reasons of space, I have not included the sections of* Parcevals saga *that focus on Valver as the protagonist, nor have I included* Valvers þáttr.

I have translated from the normalized text as edited by Kirsten Wolf and Helen Maclaine, which is based primarily on the only complete surviving manuscript, Holm Perg. 6 4to, from the first quarter of the fifteenth century. This manuscript contains a sizable lacuna, part of which has been filled from another manuscript (NKS 1794b 4to). I have consulted both the French text and several English translations of the French,[3] *but I have tried to let the Norse text speak for itself.*

CHAPTER I
Here Begins the Saga of the Splendid Knight Parceval, Who Was Another of King Arthur's Champions

So begins this saga: There once lived an old man who was married to an old woman. They had only one son, who was named Parceval. This old man was a farmer by rank, but he had won knightly honors. He had been the greatest of all champions. He had captured a king's daughter as spoils of war and then settled down in the wilderness, because he didn't dare live among other men.[4]

When Parceval was twelve years old, his father had already taught him archery and fencing, and he could throw javelins so fast that three would be in the air at once.[5] Now that his father was dead, Parceval had taken up the habit of riding into the forest on his colt, carrying his javelins and spearing beasts and birds. And one day, he saw five knights riding. He rode into the forest. One of the knights saw that the boy was bashful, and he rode up to him and asked whether he had seen four knights riding with two ladies. But all that the boy could say was to ask the knight whether he was God. He said that his mother had told him that nothing was as beautiful as God. The knight answered, "I am not God."

The boy touched his shield and asked what that could be. The knight said that it was a shield. Then the boy asked about his helmet, mailcoat, lance, and sword. The knight told him that all of these were the arms that King Arthur had given him. The boy asked where that king was who was so open-handed, and whether he might be willing to give him arms. The knight answered, "You can try," and then they parted.

The boy went to his mother and said, "I think that I have seen God today, whom you said was more beautiful than anything. I was told that there is a king named Arthur, and he gives arms and clothing to men. I want to go there."

His mother answered, "Only those who are accomplished men with stout hearts, yet who know themselves to be wise, receive honors there. You are lacking in all that, and if you go there,

you'll be mocked and jeered,
not given gifts and cheered."[6]

The boy answered, "I certainly have to try."

When his mother saw that she could not dissuade him, she made clothes for him in farmers' style, as befitted a cottager's son. She got him a new canvas shirt, a vest and a hood, leg-wraps below, and rawhide shoes on his feet. Then she said, "My sweet son, you're making your mother sad now. I am afraid that your journey may be *all in vain, not a wise campaign*. Up to now, you have been the worst of laggards, and you haven't seen how good men behave. You want to ask for arms for yourself, but you don't know how to bear them; you'll be too weak at weapon-play."

The boy replied. "Mother," he said, "no one is born with such knowledge, and learning teaches more than nature. Practice also teaches much. And a man learns daring from another man."[7]

She said, "Your words are hardly spoken in cowardice, if it's true what's said that 'everything takes after its own kind' and 'he who can't walk, must crawl'—because your father was always reckoned among the best knights in this land, and he and I were considered to come from the best families. We were rich in landholdings and wealth, and many benefitted from this, and we came to be blessed with friends. But then our means of support were destroyed, and the two of us fled to this place, where we are now. Now, my good son, if God grants you good fortune, you'll be like your father. Be God-fearing, faithful, and gracious to the man whom you serve. Do not take part in reckless attacks. Be foremost wherever you may win praise, but not where you may win slander. Avoid all robbery, because theft rouses God's anger. Be forbearing with all people, and most of all with women. Even if you should desire a certain woman, take nothing more than a single kiss from her by force. But if you ravish a woman, promise recompense and hold firmly to your promise. Never take another man's lover unless your heart tells you so. If you vanquish a man in single combat, do not kill him, and if you find yourself in the company of good men, do not be too meddlesome in men's affairs. Always learn goodness from whomever is willing to teach it. Keep this in mind: every wise man asks questions. Get for yourself either a good friend or none. Among good men, be modest. Have nothing to do with prostitutes. Repay with good the one who does good to you."

The boy thanked her and swore to make good use of her advice. She accompanied him out of the yard, with a sad heart and sorrowful reluctance, and they parted beside a bridge. And when he looked back, he saw his mother lying in a swoon. But he paid no attention to it.

CHAPTER II
Parceval Comes to King Arthur

Next it happened that he came upon a tent, and he found no one there except for a beautiful woman, because her lover was not at home; he had gone hunting. He spoke pleasantries to her, but she told him to get away as fast as possible, and she said that it would do him no good if her lover were to come home. He asked for a kiss from her, but she refused. All the same, he kissed her against her will, and said, "I won't ask for more, because my mother forbade me to take a woman against her will."

He asked for food, but she said there was none. Then he searched the tent and found three loaves of bread,[8] along with wine, and he took them. He took a gold finger-ring from her, although he promised to repay her. She said that the trolls could have him and his repayment as well.[9]

Then he rode away—but her lover came home and asked what was causing her unhappiness. She said that a buffoon had come and kissed her against her will, and taken a gold ring from her, and eaten and drunk what he wanted.

"You wicked whore, you're hiding more of what he did to you! You will never have anything good from me. Your horse shall have no fodder, and you'll have poor care and little food, just enough for you to live on until I learn the truth from you. But if your horse dies, then you'll have to run on your feet. You'll never have any clothes other than these, and you'll go naked until I have the head of the man who disgraced you."

Now Parceval rode until he met a ploughman who was driving a donkey before him, laden with boxes of charcoal. He called out to him, "You, charcoal burner, show me the right road to the castle where King Arthur lives, he who makes knights. People say that he gives arms and clothes and honors and distinctions to knights."

"Lad," said the ploughman, "this road leads to a castle by the sea. There you may find King Arthur, cheerful or unhappy."

"Tell me," said the boy, "why do you say that he is cheerful or unhappy?"

The charcoal burner answered, "Well can I tell you. King Arthur fought against the stronghold of the Rim Islands[10] and won victory, so he is cheerful. But he is unhappy because many of his knights have departed for various towns where they feel most at ease. He does not know what they are doing, and that grieves him."

The boy rode along the road that the charcoal burner had showed him. When he had ridden for a long time, he saw a handsome castle standing beside the sea, and he saw a lone knight riding out of the castle gates. He held his lance and shield and bridle with his left hand, but in his right hand he bore a golden cup with a cover. The arms that he bore suited him exceptionally well; his weapons were colored entirely red, as was all his armor. And when the boy saw these arms shining brightly, they pleased him greatly, and he said, "I swear to God that I shall ask King Arthur for these weapons, and if he gives them to me, I will accept them gladly. I shall never ask for others from him; these please me perfectly."

He hurried towards the castle, for he was curious to see the king's court, and then he met the knight. The knight spoke to him. "Lad," he said, "where do you want to go?"

"I'm going to the king's court to ask him to give me the arms that you bear."

"You're doing well," said the knight. "Go quickly and come back, and tell that pitiful king that if he wants to keep his kingdom from me, let him send someone to defend it from me, because I claim it. If he does not believe it, tell him that I snatched this golden cup from his table as proof."

The boy answered, "Get yourself another messenger. I don't care what you say." And he hurried onward until he came to where the king was sitting at his dining table with all his court. He rode into the hall on the floor, which was tiled all over with marble stones of all colors. The king was sitting at the end of the table, sorrowful and anxious. The boy didn't know which man he should greet, because he didn't recognize the king, until Ionet[11] the king's page came to him, carrying a knife in his hand because he carved meat for the king. "You, man who has the knife," said the boy, "tell me where the king is."

Ionet was the most courteous of men and told him with gentle words where the king was sitting. He hurried over to that place and greeted the king, but the king was sitting there, filled with anxiety, and didn't answer. The boy addressed him a second time, and he remained silent. Then the boy said, "By my faith, this king will never make knights, if no man gets a word out of him."

The boy prepared to leave just as quickly as he'd come, and he turned his horse towards the hall doors. But he had ridden closer to the king than he realized, and at the moment that he turned his horse, he knocked the king's hat off his head and onto the table in front of him.

The king controlled his anxiety and turned to face the boy, and said, "Welcome, good man. I ask you to not blame me, although I was silent, because I could not answer on account of worry and anger. My worst enemy is troubling me out of malice, claiming my kingdom, and saying that he will have it whether I am willing or not. He is called the Red Knight. He lives in the forest called Quinquarie.[12] My queen had come here to comfort our knights who are wounded, and what the knight said would have caused me little grief, except for what he did to disgrace me over and above that: he took my goblet away and threw all the wine in the queen's face. She took to her bed, and I expect that I will not find her well."

The boy paid no attention to what the king said about either his disgrace or his grief, and he said, "Listen, king, make me a knight, because I want to leave right away."

Everyone who heard his words took him for a fool. Nonetheless, the king saw that he was both handsome and brave. "Good friend," said the king, "get down from your horse. Our pages shall take care of him, and I shall grant your request. Accept my offer, for I shall honor you as befits a man of rank."

The boy answered, "The man I met outside the fortress didn't get off his horse. Do quickly what you want done. I don't want to be a knight unless I have all my arms red. Give me the ones that the man I met had, the one who was carrying off the cup."

The king's seneschal[13] Kay said, "Friend, you speak rightly. Those arms are given to you. Go and take them from the knight, for you must have them. You did just what a wise man would do when you came here to ask for such a thing."

"Be silent, for God's sake, Kay," said the king. "Why do you talk like that? You are entirely too eager to make sport of strangers. Even though this lad may be young, it may be that he comes from a good family, because he has a handsome and valiant look. The only problem with his conduct is that he is not familiar with the customs of the court. Nonetheless he may become a fine man, and it is a disgrace and a failure of comradeship to mock such a man as he. It does not speak well of a valiant man to promise what he cannot give, or does not want to give, if he is not to gain the contempt of the one to whom he made the promise, who was formerly his friend. For if the promise does not work out, then the one who made the promise did so falsely, because he could not or would not do it. Thus it is better to promise nothing, or else to give what one has promised at once, rather than to earn dislike and disgrace for oneself because of false promises."

CHAPTER III
Parceval Kills the Red Knight

Now the boy turned to go, and he walked out through the hall. In the middle of the hall floor, he met a most beautiful and courteous maiden. He greeted her, and she him, and she spoke polite words to him. "Lad," she said, "as I live, I know that what my heart tells me is the truth: in all the world no bolder knight will be found than the knight that you will become."

She was older than twelve years. She spoke those words so loudly that everyone in the hall heard. Then Kay the seneschal rushed at her, and in his anger he struck her such a powerful blow on her cheek with his hand that she fell at once.

Once Kay had struck the maiden and turned away, there stood the king's fool in his way, beside the fire. When Kay came near the fool, in his anger he kicked him into the middle of the fire, because the fool had spoken much the same words as the maiden: that the boy would win the greatest renown in all of chivalry. Now the fool who was burned cried out, and the maiden who was struck wept. But the boy hurried after the Red Knight, since no one hindered him. Ionet, who knew all the roads, wanted to witness the truth about the boy's encounter with the knight, because he was always in the habit of bringing news. He left the castle by another route, with his companions.[14] They traveled on the way until they were a short distance from the spot where the Red Knight was sitting on his horse, waiting to see what would happen—whether anyone from the king's court would come to fight him and defend the king's realm, which he had claimed.

Just then the boy came riding up furiously. The knight had set down the goblet while he sat waiting, and as soon as the boy saw the knight and each one could hear the other's words, the boy said to him, "Lay down your arms and bear them no longer, because King Arthur gave me those arms."

The knight said, "Do you dare to come here and seek these arms that the king gave you? If there's someone else who's come here to defend the king's realm from me, don't hide it."

The boy said, "What are you saying, devil? Are you mocking me, since you still won't take off my armor? Take it off quickly! I forbid you to stay any longer."

"Boy," said the knight, "tell me if any knight is coming to fight me."

The boy answered, "Take my armor off, or else I'll take it off you. I'll surely beat you if you make me angry!"

The knight grew angry. He took his lance with both hands and struck the boy across his shoulders with the blunt end, so that the boy sank onto his horse's neck from the blow. Then the boy grew angry, and he sat up straight and brandished his javelin and flung it at the knight with all his strength. He pierced him through the eye so hard that his brain gushed out onto the back of his neck, and the knight instantly fell dead to the ground.

The boy dismounted and took the knight's lance and shield,[15] but he didn't know how to loosen his helmet from his head. He was also keen to unbuckle his sword from him, but he had no idea how he was going to do that. He grabbed the sword along with the shield and pulled and tugged at it. When Ionet saw that the boy didn't know how to do such a thing, he got down from his own horse and said, "What are you doing, my good lad?"

"I thought that your king had given me these arms. Now I will have to burn the dead man to cold ashes[16] before I can get them."

Ionet said, "Don't be troubled about that, because I will place all these weapons in your hands."

"Hurry up," said the boy.

Ionet flung off his own surcoat and stripped the knight of all his armor. But the boy was completely unwilling to exchange his own clothes for the knight's clothes, despite everything that Ionet could say to him. The knight was dressed in a tunic of the finest silk, with fine fabrics underneath his mailcoat, but Ionet could not make the boy take off his rawhide shoes. The boy said, "Are you making fun of me, you dolt? Do you think that I would exchange my clothes, which my mother made for me two days ago? A big new sackcloth shirt for this little shirt of his, which is worthless? My thick new tunic for this old and thin one, which is no good?"

It takes a long time to teach wisdom to a fool.[17]

The boy discarded all the knight's clothing except for his armor; it was no use trying to persuade him. Then Ionet armed him. He put mail leggings on him, and on the outside of his rawhide shoes he fastened golden spurs. He dressed him in the mailcoat and set the helmet on his head, and it suited him quite well. He girded the boy with the sword and showed him how to draw it and sheath it. Then he set the boy's foot in a stirrup, and the boy mounted the warhorse. His foot had never been in a stirrup before, and he was more used to horsewhips than spurs. Ionet gave him a banner and shield.

Before they parted, the boy said, "Friend, take my horse, and know this as truth: I have proved him to be a good horse, and you must accept him from me. I do not need him any longer. Also take the goblet and bring it to the king, and give him God's greeting from me. You shall also give my greetings to the maiden that Kay struck on the floor of the hall, and tell them all that I shall do such great deeds before I die that she shall say that she has been well avenged on the man who struck her."

CHAPTER IV
Ionet Tells the King About Parceval

Then they parted, and Parceval went on his way. Returning with the king's goblet to the king's hall where the entire court was sitting, Ionet said, "My lord, see your goblet here, which our knight has sent you."

The king said, "Which knight are you talking about?"

Ionet said, "The lad who came into the hall and asked for arms from you."

The king said, "How did he get the goblet? Was he such a good friend to the Red Knight that he gave it to him of his own free will?"

"No, my lord," said Ionet, "He sold it to him so dearly that he gave his own life for it, because the lad killed him."

"How did that happen?" said the king.

"I don't know for certain," said Ionet, "but at first, it happened that the knight struck the lad with his lance shaft and caused him great pain. But the lad immediately pierced him through his eye so that blood and brains gushed onto his neck, and at once he fell to the ground dead."

Then the king said to Kay the seneschal, "You have treated my retainers disgracefully, because thanks to your evil words, I have lost a good knight who did me a great honor today and killed my worst enemy, when I had done him no honor."

"My lord," said Ionet, "he also sent good greetings to the maiden whom Kay struck to disgrace him. And he said that he would certainly avenge her, if he lives and if he comes to a place where he might do that."

When the fool, who was sitting by the fire, realized what Ionet was saying, he jumped up and came before the king, and he said, "My lord, now your gifts are drawing near,[18] and now it can be seen what has become of those who are faithless and evil. I swear to you truly that Kay the seneschal need have no doubt that he used his hands and feet and his foolish tongue without cause, because the knight will avenge upon him this blow that he struck me with his feet, and the one that he struck the maiden, before half a year has passed. So dearly shall he pay for it that he shall carry his right arm broken by his side. This shall truly happen to him."

When Kay heard that, he was on the point of bursting from rage and fury. But he did not dare to attack the fool in front of the king, who was sitting so close to him. The king spoke: "Kay, you have done evil to me today. You drove the boy away from me before he had learned knightly arts, because without a doubt he will become the best of knights—if he can learn to bear arms, since he can't do it now, and he doesn't know how to wield a sword if the need were to come upon him. Now he sits on the best warhorse, but if some buffoon desires his horse and armor, he may manage to kill him quickly."

He who can't defend himself with arms
is ill-suited for war's alarms.
He who wants to learn the knightly art
needs courage and boldness in his heart.

CHAPTER V
Parceval Learns Skills from the Good Man

Now the boy rode on his way through the forest, until he came to where the land abruptly changed to a treeless plain, and there he saw a great river. He rode over the meadow to the river, and when he reached it, he found that it was very deep, with strong currents. He rode along the river, and then he saw a high cliff on the other side of the river. On it there were four towers, strongly and skillfully made, and between the towers he saw a fortified wall. This wall was so beautiful and well-crafted that he thought that he had never seen anything like it. In front of this castle was a strong bridge, stout and tall, and in front of the bridgehead he saw a tower, and in front of the tower there was a drawbridge, with huge iron chains on both ends so that it could be hauled up. It served as a bridge by day, but in the night it was raised so that no one could reach the towers. This was skillfully planned so that no hostility could harm those who were living there.

Now the boy rode towards the bridge. At that moment, there came a splendid man, richly clad in the finest brocade. He held in his hand a pliant staff to toy with. Two well-dressed young men followed him.

As the boy was arriving, he remembered how his mother had taught him to greet people politely, and he spoke: "My mother taught me that I should greet you politely. May God bless you!"

The good man realized at once that he must have been raised at home, and he said, "Where did you come from?"

"From where?" said the boy. "From the court of King Arthur."

"What did you do there?" he said.

"The king made me his knight," he said.

"God thank him for that!" said the good man. "But it's the last thing that would have occurred to me, that he would trouble himself over such a thing. I thought that he already had quite enough worries. But who gave you those arms?"

"The king gave them to me," he said.

"Under what circumstances?" the man said. The boy told him everything that had happened and that has already been told in the saga.

Then the good man asked, "What can you do with your horse?"

He answered, "I can make him gallop over smooth ground and rough ground, just as I used to make my previous horse gallop when I rode away from my home and my mother."

"Tell me," he said, "what can you do with your arms?"

"I know how to arm myself with them and take them off, just as the page took them off the man I killed and brought them to me, and I have borne them lightly ever since."

"God knows," said the good man, "you are to be highly praised. Now don't blame me when I ask you how it came about that you killed the knight."

"My lord," he said, "my mother taught me that I should follow good men and accept their counsel, and if I followed the counsels of good and wise men, that good fortune would result for me."

The good man said, "Blessings on your mother, if she taught you this wholesome and gracious counsel. But do you want to say something else?"

"Yes, my lord," he said, "I want to ask you to give me shelter tonight."

"Willingly," he said, "if you agree to what I ask you, and you'll profit well by it."

"What is it?" asked the boy.

"That you have faith in your mother, and in me."

"Willingly, my lord," said the boy.

"Dismount from your horse."

He did so. One of the young men took his horse, and the other took his arms, and he stood there in his outfit of the rawhide shoes and leather jerkin that his mother had made for him from an animal's hide, cut out badly and stitched worse. One of the boys put spurs on the feet of the good man, and he mounted his horse and reached through the handle of his shield and hung it at his shoulder. Then he took his lance and said to the boy, "Pay careful attention to how you must handle your weapons. Hold your lance, and spur your warhorse and rein him in."

Then he showed him how to hold the shield, letting the shield's base rest on his horse's neck. He took his lance and unfurled his banner and held it properly. Then he spurred on his good horse, worth more than a hundred marks of pure silver, for no horse was stronger or swifter than he. This doughty man was fully acquainted with all knightly skills and knew well how to ride and to bear shield and lance, because he had learned that in childhood. The boy was greatly pleased by his riding and by everything that he saw him do.

When the knight had ridden splendidly, he raised his lance and banner and rode up to the lad and said, "Friend, can you carry a lance and shield in this fashion, and guide your horse in this way?"

The boy answered, "I would willingly live to learn it so well. This knowledge seems better to me than great landholdings and stores of wealth."

"A man may learn everything," said the man, "if he tries hard and puts his mind to it. Since you have not seen such a thing done before, there is no shame for you in not knowing it. But now that you have seen it, you will suffer shame and harm if you refuse to learn."

Then he dismounted and had the boy mount up. The boy took up the lance and shield, and spurred the horse with all his might. Right away, he carried his shield so well, and held his lance so straight and true, that it was as if he had constantly been in charges and knightly combats ever since childhood; he bore his arms so well thanks to his family inheritance and his own nature. He was the boldest of men with weapons, and was eager to learn such things.

One with a good nature learns good ways
from those who do good works in their days.
Good fruit sprouts from a good tree's wood:
so do good habits come from a man who is good.

When the boy had ridden for a long time, he raised up his banner and rode up to the knight and said, "Tell me how my riding appears to you. I have never seen anything that I am as eager to do as that. Will this be of use to me, if I were to need it and put all my mind to it? I would be blessed if I were to learn knightly skills as well as you."

The good man answered, "Your heart will not fail you. Do not doubt that you will become a good knight."

The boy answered:

"My heart will never feel misgiving
when facing any man living;
I'll never flee from war demanding,
as long as on my feet I'm standing."

CHAPTER VI
Concerning the Good Man and Parceval

Now this good man mounted his horse again, and showed him all knightly tactics and ways of bearing weapons, three times, just as he had once learned them. And when the lad had carefully considered and observed everything that he had seen, and taken it to heart, he mounted the horse again and boldly did everything that he had seen, as perfectly as if he had always done it. That pleased the good man very well.

He said to the boy, "If you meet a knight and he strikes you, what will you do then?"

"Strike him," said the boy, "just as quickly."

"But if you break your lance," he said, "what will you do then?"

"I'll attack him at once and seize him with my hands," said the boy.

"No, friend," said the knight. "It won't do to try that."

"Then how?" said the boy.

"You must attack him with a sword," said the man, "and fight with it." He was eager to teach him swordfighting, and he stuck the butt of his lance fast in the earth, drew his sword and picked up his shield, and taught him swordfighting. Then the boy said, "I am a master of all those who know this skill. I learned this while living with my mother, so that no one is to be found who is better than me at fencing with sword and buckler."

The good man said, "Let's go home to rest for the night. You shall certainly receive the hospitality of St. Julian."[19] Then they took each other by the hand and walked towards the hall.

The boy said to the good man, "My lord, my mother taught me that if I attach myself to a good man, I should find out his name. And if she taught me well, I would like to know your name."

"My name is Gormanz of Groholi."[20]

There came a young man with a mantle to place over the lad, so that he should not get a chill after having become warm from riding. Then they went to dine, and the master of the house and the boy ate at the same table. The master of the house asked the boy to stay with him for twelve months, and he would teach him knightly skills. The boy refused. Then he asked the boy to stay there for a month. The boy answered, "For all I know, I may be near my mother's house. I pray to God that I may go home and see her, because she was lying in a swoon from grief at our parting, and for all I know she may be dead. So I must leave here early in the morning."

When the man of the house found that it was no use hindering him, they went to bed. In the morning, the master had knightly clothing brought to him, so rich and precious that a king might well wear them. There was a shirt and breeches of white silk, hose of red samite, and a tunic of the finest brocade. Then the knight said, "Now you shall dress yourself in these clothes, if you like."

The boy answered, "It would be better for you to tell me to put on the clothes that my mother made for me. Aren't they better than these?"

"No," said the man, "they are much worse. Good friend, when I took you into my home, you said that you would be attentive and obedient to me."

"I am willing to do that," said the boy, "and I shall never forsake your counsels."

The boy dressed, and gave up the clothes that his mother had made and exchanged them for better ones. Then the knight bound spurs on his right foot—such was the custom of knights then. Other knights armed him. Then the excellent man took a sword and girded him with it, kissed him and said, "Now by this service, I have done for you the consecration that God gave to knighthood, with all manner of courtesy and warriors' valor. Now you must remember what I tell you. If you fight with a knight and you are victorious over him, so that he asks for a truce, do not kill him at your will. Do not be too talkative or curious. If you find a man or a woman who is in need of your wise counsel, always advise them well with what you think is the most favorable advice. Pay good heed to Holy Church, and fear God. Pray to the One who created all things that He take care for your salvation, and guard yourself against sin and dishonor. May your life serve God for eternal bliss."

The boy said. "May God thank you for your good counsels. My mother taught me just the same ones."[21]

The master said, "Don't use that way of talking any longer, crediting your mother for your conduct, because that will make you be regarded as a fool."

The boy asked, "Then what shall I say?"

He answered, "Say that the lord who made you a knight taught you this."

The boy said that he would do so. The master gave him a lance with a beautiful banner. The boy thanked him and rode away, eager to find his mother.

He rode through a thick forest, and was more accustomed to riding there than on a plain, so he rode all day. In the evening he saw a strong castle. All around it he saw nothing but sea and water and wasteland. He rode over a drawbridge to the castle, and he pounded on the gates, which were shut. He saw a fair young maiden in a window, and as soon as she saw him, she ordered the gates to be opened for him. Four knights came and opened the gate and welcomed him cheerfully. They were thin and pale. He saw that the castle was completely empty of men, and all the houses were roofless. The maiden had him brought to a hall, where two aged men and a young woman already were. The woman was so fair that no living man had seen a more beautiful woman. They were all thin and pale from hunger. She was dressed in purple brocade. He was made welcome there. His outer clothes were taken off, and his horse was led to the stall, but there was nothing to feed him except a little grain.

This young maiden led him into a fine house and sat down there in a splendid bed. Then seven knights came walking in and sat down on another bed across from them, and they talked amongst themselves, saying that they had never seen two more handsome people, and they said that God must have meant for them to be together. The boy sat and was silent, remembering the counsel of his master that he should not be too talkative. When the maiden saw that he didn't want to talk, she said to him cheerfully, "Where have you come from, my lord?"

He answered, "Last night I was in a strong castle, where there was a courteous master named Gormanz of Groholi."

The maiden said, "You speak rightly when you call him a courteous man and a mighty king. He is my mother's brother, and his castle is full of all manner of grace, and he need not fear any enemy. But in our castle there are no provisions except for five monks' loaves,[22] which a friar brought me, and a cask of wine, and one red deer that our squires hunted today."

They went to dine, and then he was brought to his bed. The bed was so excellent that there never was an emperor who could not sleep well in it. He fell asleep quickly, because he had no worries.

Like a warrior, worry cuts deep,
and robs many of their sleep.
But this boy felt no alarm,
for he had no fear of harm.

CHAPTER VII
The Maiden's Lament

But the courtly maiden who gave him lodging had neither rest nor calm. Instead, she could not sleep, for she had no man who would take up her cause against the enemy who had offered single combat against her knights; not one of them dared to face him. All alone, she lamented her lot with terrible grief. She got up from her bed in her shift and covered herself with a purple mantle and faced her responsibilities herself, without flinching, for she was brave and strong-minded. And then it occurred to her to go to where to her guest was, and secretly plead her troubles before him.

Despite great fear and trembling, she entered the bower where the knight was sleeping. Weeping softly, she came to the sleeping knight, and she knelt before his bed and bowed down over his face, weeping so much that she wet his entire face with her tears. When she had been crying there for a long time, the knight awoke and found it quite strange that his face was wet. He looked at the maiden on her knees beside the bed, reached out to her and took her in his arms, and spoke courteously to her.

"Why have you come here, lovely maiden," he said, "and what do you wish? For God's sake, tell me why you are so grieved, troubled and sad?"

"Excellent knight," she said, "do not be displeased with me, and do not regard me as shameful for coming here. Neither sin nor shame ever entered my mind, though I come here nearly naked. But truly, I am the woman who lives with the greatest sorrow in all the world, and there is nothing that can comfort me. This shall be my last night in this world, because as soon as day comes, I shall kill myself. For this castle was splendidly manned by thirteen thousand bold knights, but now there are no more than sixty knights left.[23] Gingvarus, the seneschal of King Klamadius of the Hebrides,[24] has dealt with them this way: some he has killed, and some he has captured, and he has increased my sorrow that all my aid and strength has disappeared before my enemies. Their ferocity is the cause of my grief and affliction. Now so many men are dead or in distress on my account, and thus it is fitting that

I should be sorrowful. They have besieged this castle for twelve months, so that this Gingvarus never goes away, and his strength waxes daily, but ours wanes, and now our provisions are so completely used up that that there is no bread in my castle. If God does not grant us his mercy and aid now, we will have to surrender the castle, because it has no defenses. Then I will be surrendered along with the castle, more filled with grief and sorrow than all women that I should be born for such great evil for myself and others. Some are killed now, and some captured, but they shall never take me alive, because I have in my casket one knife which which I shall kill myself. Klamadius shall never embrace me alive, even though he has overcome me by force of arms. I care not what he does with me when I am dead. But I came here to make you aware of this. Now I want to go back and let you sleep in peace.

"May God send strength to your arms,
however he may ease our harms."

CHAPTER VIII
Parceval Speaks with the Maiden

Now Parceval understood that the maiden had no other errand, and her tears had fallen because she wanted him to take that single combat upon himself, and no knight had dared to defend her and her kingdom. Parceval said, "Beloved, forsake your sorrow and night-long grief. Be comforted, and weep no longer. I give you comfort in place of grief, for God is generous and merciful. May he grant you greater mercy in the morning. Get into this bed, because it will suffice for both of us. You shall not forsake me until the night is past."

She said, "If you prefer, I will go away."

But he touched her courteously and let her in under the bedclothes beside him, and she knew well that he kissed her. And so they lay all night, each in the other's arms, with kisses and embraces until dawn, without any sin. But when day broke, she went to her own sleeping quarters and dressed. No one was aware of this.

Next, a trumpet was blown to awaken the folk. The maiden came to Parceval and greeted him courteously, with kind words, and she said, "I would gladly invite you to stay with us. But because we have no supplies, we gladly give you permission to go wherever you like, and may God grant you another night with better cheer than the night you have spent with us."

Parceval answered, "My dear beloved, I will seek no other lodging for myself than this, not for a single night, before your kingdom is freed—if God lends me might and main for this. But if I find your enemy, and he invites me to where he is now, it will displease me if he holds his ground any longer, because he has done you great grief and harm. If it may come to pass that I kill him or triumph over him, then I will ask to have your love. No other wages will I accept."

Then the maiden said to him courteously. "You have asked little of me, my lord, and a poor portion, and it will not be denied you, because you will esteem me as haughty and arrogant if I refuse your love. But do not say that I am urging you to your death with the promise that I would be your lover, because that would be a grievous and criminal offense and irreparable harm to your beautiful body at a young age. . ."

[A page is missing from the main manuscript, Holm Perg. 6 4to. To summarize Chrétien de Troyes's narrative: Despite his lover's pleas, Parceval is armed and escorted out by the people of the castle. He encounters Gingvarus [Anguinguerrons]. After a brief bandying of words, they fight until Gingvarus falls and admits Parceval's superiority, noting that no one else would believe that Parceval could have beaten him. At this point, manuscript NKS 1794b picks up the narrative.]

". . . . believe that you would have been able to prevail over me, since you are unskilled. Now consider whether you have some powerful lord who has done some good to you, and whom you have not repaid. Send me there, and inform him how you have beaten me, and there I shall put myself into his power and do everything that he wants."

Parceval said, "I will claim nothing further for myself. You shall go to the castle and tell the lovely lady there, who is my lover, that you will not attack her for as long as you live, and surrender yourself completely into her power."

Gingvarus answered, "Kill me instead, because that is what she will do if I come to her, for there is nothing that she yearns for more than my death—because I killed her father, and I have done her such great injury that over the past twelve months I have destroyed all her knights—so I do not want to be sent to her. If you have another friend, send me to him, because I know that here I will be killed at once."

The knight said, "Then I shall send you to my best friend, the most courteous of men, who is called Gormanz of Groholi. He rules over a stronghold."

Then Gingvarus said, "Why would you want to send me there, where most of my enemies are? For if I come into his power, he will have me hanged at once, because[25] I killed his sister's son, who was defending that castle against me. Therefore I ask you to kill me yourself, rather than sending me there."

Parceval said, "Then you shall submit to King Arthur and give him my greetings and ask him to show you the maiden that Kay struck on my account. Tell her that I have sent you, vanquished by force of arms, into her power, and I shall avenge her on the one who struck her without cause on my account."

Gingvarus said that he would willingly go there, and he and all those who had surrounded the castle rode away. Parceval rode back home, and the knights of the castle rode to meet him and accompanied him into the place, and his armor was taken off. They asked, "Why were you not willing to kill Gingvarus, or bring him here with you?"

Parceval answered, "By my faith, I think that then I would have done wrong, because he has killed many of your kinsmen and friends. You would have killed him against my will, and then I would not have held to my truce with him. But since he asked me for mercy, I spared him and sent him to King Arthur."

At that moment, the maiden came walking up, and she welcomed him with joy. She led him into the sleeping quarters and comforted him with sweet kisses and embraces, and they amused themselves there, each in the other's arms, with tender and joyous speech. They had that instead of food and drink; it seemed just as good to them.

Love is the most precious thing of all,
to him who hearkens to true love's call.

CHAPTER IX
Concerning King Klamadius and His Men

King Klamadius thought that the castle would be surrendered to him that day, and there would be no defense. At that moment, a man came running and told the king of the mishaps of his seneschal Gingvarus, and that he had gone to King Arthur. The king asked where the knight who overthrew him came from, and how it could be that any living man could have overcome him. "I don't know where that knight came from," said the boy, "except that I saw him riding out of the castle with all his weapons and armor colored red, and I have never seen another knight so handsome."

The king asked the boy what would be advisable. The boy said, "Turn back, my lord, here you'll earn nothing but hurt."

Then the king's counsellor said, "Be silent, boy! I shall give the king much better advice. He shall persevere on his course and not believe your foolishness, because in Fair Fort[26] there is neither food nor ale now, and the entire force is hungry. They are starving and strengthless, and they can't make use of weapons. Now we should let no more than sixty knights ride to the castle. Our other fighters shall hide themselves. This new knight, who is now sporting with Blankifleur, will do something knightly, and as soon as he comes between our knights, he will be quickly captured and killed, because he will not be able to contend with them as one against many, since the knights of Fair Fort are starving and witless and will not offer him any help. But our knights shall flee at first, and then we shall get between them and the castle."

The king replied, "This is good advice, because we have fifteen thousand[27] knights, and we can capture nearly dead men."

Now Klamadius sent sixty knights to the gates of the fortress to attack the defenders. When Parceval saw that, he ordered the fortress to be opened up, and he rode out. Every man rode at his opponent, and Parceval killed everyone that he could reach with his lance, and he gave their horses to his own men who needed them. Just then, the entire main body of fighters that had been hiding in the forest advanced: four hundred knights and two thousand foot soldiers. But the defenders were waiting not far from the fortress gates that were standing open. The fighters that were coming saw the harm done to their own men, who were being killed and captured, and they advanced on the fortress in disorder and out of formation. The other side was riding in formed-up battle lines, and they began to defend themselves boldly. They shot the fighters that were attacking the fortress and killed a great many, until the attackers gained strength as they formed up their lines. Then the defenders could not withstand them, for they were few in number and hard-pressed. Some defenders climbed up into the towers and shot a great many men from above. The attackers managed to get inside the fortress with great difficulty, but those who guarded the fortress gates shut them with locks and latches.

Now King Klamadius was angry and distressed that he was shut out and his **men** were being killed inside the fortress. His counsellor said, "It is not surprising that harm should befall good men when it pleases God, and it may be seen by this that both good and evil may befall every man in this world. For the time being, it is truest to say that they have won a great victory and we have suffered great harm. But you may put out both my eyes if they withstand us for two days. The castle and the tower are yours, if you stay here. Then they will beg for mercy and surrender the castle. Also, the beautiful lady, who formerly refused you for a long time, will plead with you to deign to take her, for God's sake."

Then they pitched their tents and prepared their quarters, and they surrounded the castle. But those who were inside the fortress took off their armor and prepared the best resting-places that they could get. They allowed the knights whom they had captured to pledge their word that they would never offer resistance to the maiden and all her retainers.

Now when King Klamadius had arranged all his forces around the castle, that same day there blew up a great storm, and by God's will, it drove a large ocean-going ship up into the fjord, laden with wine and all sorts of provisions. Those inside the castle sent men to them and asked where they were from and what they had onboard. They answered that they were merchants and had loaded their ship with wine and flour and salted bacon, beef and mutton, beans and peas, and plenty of everything that one might need to buy.

The defenders welcomed them in God's name and said, "We will buy everything that you are willing to sell." They praised God for their arrival. Everything that they had in the ship was unloaded and brought into the fortress. And there was much rejoicing. Now they had enough provisions to last twelve months.

When Klamadius heard that they had enough provisions, he was quite vexed, and he challenged the knights to single combat against him on the field beside the castle. Parceval accepted, and when his beloved heard the news, she was deeply grieved. The messenger returned and told his lord Klamadius what he had seen.

CHAPTER X
Parceval Triumphs Over King Klamadius

As soon as the sun rose in the morning, Parceval quickly and boldly demanded his armor and weapons. His beloved had begged him all night not to set out to single combat with King Klamadius, for he had never before surrendered to anyone. Now she was filled with sorrow, as were all the knights in the fortress. He seemed resolved, and they bid him go in God's peace.

When Klamadius saw Parceval riding towards him, he was glad and thought that he had the matter completely in hand. As soon as they met, they rode at each other with such great strength and such utter ferocity that each knocked the other off his horse, and both of them lay fallen on the field. They sprang up boldly, and charged each other with great bravery, and they fought for a long time with swords. But the red knight was more agile and strong, and as Klamadius began to tire, the red knight struck as if he were maddened. In the end, it happened that Klamadius was forced to ask for a truce from the red knight. He offered all his possessions to save his own life, but he was not at all willing to go to Fair Fort, into the maiden's power. No more was he willing—not for all the kingdom of Rome—to go to the castle of the good man who had made Parceval a knight. In the end, it came about that he had to go to King Arthur, and to the maiden that Kay had struck on his account, and tell everything that had happened and say that Parceval would pay everyone back. Then Klamadius swore an oath that neither he nor his men would ever harm the maiden, nor her realm, nor her men. He had to release all her men willingly, along with their weapons and clothing. Then they parted.

Klamadius went home and ordered that all the maiden's men in his power were to be released, freely and without hindrance, with their weapons and clothing. Then King Klamadius went by himself to the castle where King Arthur sat, wearing the same outfit that he wore when Parceval overthrew him. He changed neither his weapons nor his clothes, because it was the custom at the time that a man who was sent to appear before a ruler should come just as he was when he was defeated. All the maiden's knights traveled home to her castle. They were all joyful and thanked God for their return. Now they needed fear no hostility. But Klamadius went on his way, just as his seneschal Gingvarus had gone, and he didn't swerve from his journey until he came to where King Arthur was staying with his splendid retinue.

When the knights outside saw Klamadius riding from afar, they told Gingvarus, who had come there and completed his mission and was then in great favor with the king. He noticed his lord at once, and he said, "Listen, my good lords, to a strange occurrence! At last I recognize my lord King Klamadius, and I believe and know to be true that the very same knight who came from here with red weapons and armor, and who sent me here defeated, has now overcome my lord King Klamadius—the one whom I thought no living man would overcome—and sent him here out of mercy."

At that moment, Klamadius arrived, and each rushed to meet the other with much rejoicing. This happened at Pentecost, when King Arthur always customarily held a great celebration, and there was a great multitude of nobles and dukes, earls and barons and powerful knights. Once the solemn mass was sung, and the king and all his retainers had returned to the royal court, Kay the seneschal came walking into the hall, in a splendid silken tunic and a coif on his head. Everyone in his path backed away, because no one wanted to get in his way on account of the sarcasm and ridicule that he had for everyone, with his spite, envy, and falsity. He came before the king and said, "If it be your will, it is time to dine."

"Kay," said the king, "that shall by no means happen, until some new tidings come to us."

Once the king had said that, Klamadius came riding into the hall and came before King Arthur and greeted him: "May God grant you peace and prosperity, noble king! It has truly befallen me, as it is said, that

many a man must reveal
what he would much rather conceal.

"One knight has sent me here into your power—the one who defeated and disarmed me. I surrender to your will because I could not have freed myself by any other means. Yet I do not know his name. He had weapons and armor that were entirely red, and you may have given them to him, as I think. He ordered me to bring greetings to the maiden that Kay your seneschal struck on his account, with great disgrace and malice. He said that he would truly avenge her, if God gives him life and good health."

Then Gerflet the king's fool, who had heard everything that he had said, leaped up and was so overjoyed that he shouted, so that all the king's court heard. He said, "God knows, my lord, that he will truly avenge this blow well that the maiden suffered for his sake. But Kay will bear a broken arm and suffer great disgrace from it, as he deserves."

When Kay heard that, he grew so infuriated that he would have attacked the fool if the king had not been so near. When the king had heard his speech, he shook his head and said to Kay, "You caused me much grief, Kay, when you sent that good knight away from me, because he departed thanks to your malice and your foolish tongue, and that has grieved me ever since."

Then the king called Gerflet and Sir Gawain, who by his courtesy and fellowship aided every doughty man who knew him. The king asked them to accompany King Klamadius to the loft where the queen and her handmaidens were. He bowed to the king and went with them. When they entered the loft, Sir Gawain showed him the maiden to whom he had been sent, and he told her his errand, just as she wanted to know, and said that her disgrace would be avenged. The pain from the blow that Kay struck had passed, but her shame and sorrow she could not forget. He who is fainthearted forgets his sorrow and lets it die with him, but a bold and stout-hearted man wins glory for himself, and casts off his disgrace by his valor.

Now Klamadius had completed his errand. He became a royal officer and stayed at court all the days of his life. He was esteemed highly by all knights, and well and worthily by the king's entire court, because he was rich in landholdings and bold in fighting, generous with gifts, thoughtful in counsels, kind in speech and proven in courage, renowned and perfected.[28]

The knight who won from him the realm of the maiden Blankiflur now stayed with her in great peace and joy. Now, if he wanted, he could marry her, like a strong and mighty ruler. But his mind was not on such things, because it occurred to him how sorrowfully his mother had behaved when she parted with him, falling down from grief and lying as if she were dead. This constantly interfered with his happiness, and therefore he was wholly bent on finding out what had become of her. Not for all the realm would he abandon her. He asked his beloved for leave to depart, but she refused and forbade him, and summoned all her retainers together to beg him to stay in the place that he had freed and made peaceful and joyful. It was no use for them—but he swore that if he found his mother alive, he would bring her there and stay there with them in the future. "But if she is dead, you may certainly expect that I shall return. Then I shall be the guardian and governance of the kingdom and the maiden's lands."

After that, he rode off on his way, and the beautiful and courteous Blankiflur was grieved, angry and sorrowful from the great love that she had for him. In the same way, all her knights and all the folk of the castle were grieved to see him depart, following him with great reverence and honor. Monks and nuns dressed themselves and followed him as if he were a saint, and they parted with him outside the fortress.

CHAPTER XI
Parceval Meets the King and the Fisherman

He rode all that day, meeting no one and no living being to show him the way. He prayed to God with all his heart that he might find his way straight and his mother alive. Just then he came into a valley, onto a fair and level field. There was a lake and a flowing river with swift currents, and he thought that he could not ride across the river, because he could not see the bottom anywhere. He spoke: "Lord God, if it be your will that I may cross this water, then I would find my mother, if she is alive, and give her to your service."

Now he rode all the way along the river, until he saw a huge crag, and the river ran alongside the crag so closely that he could not ride into the river anywhere, and he could not get over the crag. As he stood there, he saw a large boat floating down the river, and there were two men in it. He stood there and waited for them, because he thought that they would land there. They dropped anchor in the middle of the river and when they had anchored their boat, one of them dropped his hook in the water and pulled up a large fish. The man on land wasn't sure what he should try to do, because he couldn't get over the river. He called to them and asked them to tell him for God's sake if there were any bridge over the river. The man in the front of the boat said, "There is no bridge over this river, and no ship larger than the one we two have, and it will carry no more than five men. For five leagues up and down the river, no one can cross."

"Tell me, for God's sake, where I may have lodging for the night."

He replied, "I shall offer you lodging and the other things that you need for the night. Ride up on the crag and then you may see a great house in the valley beside a certain lake, with thick forest all around it."

Once he had said this, Parceval rode up onto the crag and saw no house. He said, "The man who directed me to come here has mocked me grievously, and may God give shame to the one who lied to me."

Then he looked down into the valley and saw a high tower, rising up fair and strong. A great lake surrounded tower. Beside the tower was a handsome hall, and he headed that way. Now he praised the fisherman whom he had blamed before. He came to the gates and saw there a bridge that could be hoisted up. When he had crossed the bridge, four handsome young men came and welcomed him and took his horse. One of them brought him a scarlet mantle, and he went with them, enjoying himself, to the place where the lord of the manor had come. Two pages led him into the hall, which was all decorated with the finest craftwork. When Parceval entered, he saw a noble ruler sitting in a bed; the bed was richly decorated, and the man was dressed in the finest silk, brocaded with gold.[29] He was elderly, and yet a most handsome man. He was reclining in the bed, and a fire had been built before him. The bed in which he was staying was in the middle of the floor of the hall. Four hundred men could sit comfortably in that hall.

When the great man saw the knight, he greeted him with kind words. "Friend," he said, "do not blame me because I did not stand up to greet you, because I am unable to do this on account of the sickness of my body."

"My lord," said the knight, "I do not reproach you for doing what is most comfortable for you."

Then the handsome man sat up and said, "Friend, come up into the bed and sit beside me."

He did so, and then the great man said to him, "Where have you come from, and what is your name?"

He answered, "I have come from the castle that people call Fair Castle, and it is truly fair, because I received a good welcome there."

"By my faith," he said, "you have traveled a long day's journey."

At that moment, a handsome page came and brought the mighty man a sword. He drew the sword halfway, and it seemed to be the finest of swords. The boy who brought the sword said, "My lord, a lovely maiden, your kinswoman, has sent you this sword, and she has asked you to bestow it well."

When he had said that, the master of the house girded the newly arrived knight with the sword, and he spoke: "Good friend," he said, "I give you this sword, and I think that it will never fail in dire straits."

He thanked the master with fair words. Then the sword was put into safe keeping, and he sat beside the master. In this great hall, everything was entertaining to look at.

As they were conversing enjoyably, a handsome boy came walking in. In his hand he bore a spear, with the butt end turned downwards, and he walked between the men sitting in the bed and the fire, so that the entire court saw the spear. Down from the iron point ran a single drop of blood, along the shaft to the boy's fist, and there it stopped. When Parceval saw that, he was astonished at how this could be, but he did not dare to ask how this could be happening, because he remembered what that excellent man who made him a knight had taught him: he shold not be too talkative if he came into an unknown place. Therefore, he was afraid to ask, not wanting to anger those who had offered him hospitality.[30]

Then two boys came in, young and handsome, and they carried in their hands candlesticks of refined gold, with two candles in each, and flames shining as brightly as mortal eyes could bear to see. Then a fair maiden came in, and she bore in her hands, just as if it were a Gospel book,[31] something that those who speak French call *graull*,[32] but that we may call "walking renewal."[33] From it, there shone such great light that the brightness of all the flames in the hall vanished like starlight before sunlight. It was made with great skill out of gold and all the most precious stones that existed in the world.

Behind this maiden walked another maiden, and she carried a tray[34] in her hands. They walked the same route that the boy who carried the spear had walked, from one end of the hall to the other, out of one side room and into another.

When Parceval saw that, he did not dare to ask, because he was afraid that that would harm him. But just as a man may harm himself by being overly talkative, he may also harm himself by being overly silent, because either excessive speech or excessive silence may do harm. But however it might turn out for him, he asked nothing about what he saw.

Then men went to dine. The master's table was made of ivory, and it was more than two ells wide. A great many dishes were set before them, along with the finest drink. When they were fed, herbs of all sorts were set before them, with good drink, and after that the clearest of sweetened wines.[35] Then the lord of the manor spoke to him: "Friend," he said, "it is time to go to bed now."

The lord was carried to bed, for he could not walk. The knight was also given a good bed, and he slept there until day came. Then he stood up and dressed himself, and he found it strange that he was alone. He walked outside and saw his horse and shield; he mounted up and rode around the fortress and found no one. It seemed strange to him that the entire fortress should be empty of people.

He rode away from the place and out into the forest. Then he saw fresh human tracks, and he followed them. When he had ridden a long way, he saw a maiden under an oak tree. She was wailing and lamenting bitterly, holding her dead husband in her arms. She spoke through her tears: "You are bitter, death, for not taking my life before my husband's life. It will be the worse for you, heart, if you do not burst from his death, because I want to die with him, just as my life was dear to him."

Love was different back then among folk,
As she showed in the words she spoke.
What now brings rue
Was once firm and true;
What now presses and binds
Was once gentle and kind.

CHAPTER XII
Parceval Hears of His Mother's Death

When Parceval heard her tale of woe, he greeted her, and she greeted him and said, "God grant thee welcome!"

Parceval asked, "Who killed your husband, and why are you so sorrowful?"

She said, "Early this morning, a knight killed him. But I am astonished that your horse is so well-fed, and you have had good lodging for the night, because there is no lodging closer to this place than forty miles."

He said, "I had such good hospitality last night that no one could wish for better. I have never had such good hospitality before."

"Surely you have been at the home of the good Fisher King," she said.

"That's how it was," he said, "and I met a mighty and courteous man. Yesterday evening, I saw two men in a boat when I rode up beside the river. One of them was fishing, and he showed me to his household and gave me splendid lodging."

The maiden said, "Good lord, he was shot through both thighs in a battle, and because of this he will never be well, nor able to ride a horse. And so when he wants to amuse himself, he goes out fishing, and he stays near the river because this is more convenient for him than at his other estates. Yet he is still the mightiest of kings."

"By my faith, you tell a wondrous thing," he said, "because yesterday evening, when I came there, many things appeared to me, wondrous beyond what I had seen before." And he began to tell her how matters had gone.

"Truly," she said, "he did you a noble honor when he seated you beside him. Tell me, did you see the spear whose point was bleeding, and there is no flesh nor sinew on it?"

"Yes," he said, "I certainly saw that."

"Didn't you ask why the spear was bleeding?"

"No," he said.

"May God protect me," she said, "you did evil and great folly. What is your name, friend?"

He wasn't certain of his own name, but he guessed at it. "I think," he said, "that I am called Pacuvaleis." But he wasn't sure if he was telling the truth or not.[36]

As soon as the maiden heard his name, she stood up to face him and spoke in an angry tone. "Friend," she said, "you've changed your name. It's gone badly for you, wretched Parceval, because you didn't ask about the spear or the 'walking renewal'—for that would have been best for the good Fisher King, and he would have become well and happy at once. But know this as truth now: Thanks to you, great misfortunes shall fall on you and others, because of your bad luck. And it's fitting that this should befall you, because you killed your mother with grief when you ran away from her against her will. I know you much better than you know me, because I was always with your mother since my childhood, and you are my close kinsman. Now know this as truth: your misfortune is no less grief to me than the death of your mother, and the death of this knight who loved me above all others."

"Alas, kinswoman!" said Parceval. "Is what you tell me true—the loss of my mother? Tell me, how did you find out about this?"

"I was standing right there beside her when she was laid in the earth."

"Then may God have mercy on her soul," said Parceval. "These tidings of my mother's death are grievous to me. Now that she is laid in earth, I need travel no longer, because my only reason for traveling was to see her. Now I must go another way than I had intended. And if you will come with me, I shall take care of you, because the man who lies dead cannot do so. It is great foolishness to sit up over him. Instead, let us go after the man who killed him, and I swear this to you truly: I shall triumph over him, or else he over me, if I have any chance of finding him."

But the maiden was full of grief and sorrow, and said that by no means would she part with her beloved before he was buried in the earth, so that neither beasts not birds might devour him. "But if you believe me," she said, "then follow this road. That mad and foolish knight who killed my beloved went that way. Yet I do not want to urge you to attack him, because I would never want harm to come to you on my account. Still, I wish him as much evil as if he had killed me myself. But from where was that sword taken, with which you are girded on the left side, which has never been tested in times of need? Do not put any trust in that sword. I know from where it came, and I know the one who forged it. Be wary of it, because without any doubt it will betray you and fail when you have greatest need of it; in battle it will shatter in two pieces. There is no one who can repair it, unless you come to the mighty man named Loth[37] under Mount Curvatus. The smith named Trehucer is there,[38] the best smith in the entire world now. But you will be betrayed if someone else does the work. It would grieve me if that sword fails, as likely as that is."

Then he wished her a good day and went off on his way. But she stayed behind and was not willing to part from her dead lover—

she who has true love for her man,
though never she'll call him her husband again.

CHAPTER XIII
Parceval and the Arrogant Knight

Now Parceval rode furiously along the great road, until he saw a knight's horse, terribly thin and as wretched as if enemies had been handling him. Never had he seen another animal as miserable and wretched. On his back was a maiden, wracked with misery and dressed in rags. She was beautiful and shapely. Her skin looked as if it had been gashed, and she was full of grief and tears, because she had suffered all manner of misery.

When Parceval saw her, he rushed after her, and as he drew near, she said, "Lord God, may it never please your goodness that I should have so many privations and troubles. Free me now, Lord, from the grasp of this merciless knight who has tortured me for so long."

When she had spoken thus, Parceval came and greeted her, but she returned his greeting in a low voice and said, "My lord, may God grant your wish for all the good that you desire; but I have not prayed for it rightly."

Parceval blushed for shame and asked why she was speaking that way. "Lovely maiden, I do not recall having seen you before, nor do I remember knowing or willing any harm done to you."

"You certainly have caused me to be tortured so wretchedly."

"God knows that this was not my doing," said Parceval. "But I am ever willing to find out what is the cause of your wretchedness."

"Woe, my lord!" she said. "Have mercy on yourself and flee, so that you do not suffer troubles because of me."

"I will not leave as long as I cannot see anything more to fear than I do now."

"My lord," she said, "do not spurn good counsel, for if the Arrogant Knight comes home, he will kill you."

"God knows that that he shall never boast of victory," he said. "I want to know why he torments you so fiercely."

She told him everything that had happened.

As they were talking, the Arrogant Knight came back from fishing. The moment that he saw Parceval, he screamed at him and said, "You knight, standing beside the maiden, you have no reason to come here! Now know this as truth: you're dead for sure, because you're interfering with this maiden's travels. Still, I won't do you any harm before I've told you what offenses I accuse her of, and why I torture her in such a shameful way. I had gone hunting in the summer, and I left this maiden behind in my tent, and I love her above all other things. But then something happened in such a strange way: a boy came to her. I never found out who he was. But this boy kissed her against her will, just as if she herself had agreed. No one would ever believe that he would kiss her, unless he did more, because a kiss entices a woman to marriage. Most of all, when a man and a woman find themselves together, the woman who makes her mouth kissable knows that whatever the man wants will follow. As soon as she enters the man's game and she finds that the man is eager to have her, she pretends not to like it at all that the man takes her by force. But when this is done, she gets neither thanks nor reward. I think that my beloved must have been taken in this way. And she allowed a golden finger-ring to be taken from her, and he carried off some of my choicest provisions, the food that I had intended for myself. Now she's received such a rich reward for her offense that what they say is proved true in her case, that 'hatred follows folly,' and 'he who does wrong and won't make it right strikes a criminal bargain.'"

When Parceval heard that, he said, "Now she has paid for your crime and completed her penance, so that God will be greatly pleased; for you have given her wrong and wicked punishments. Now I will inform you truly that I am the man who kissed her by force, completely against her will, and I did nothing more to her. As a matter of fact, I also drank, as I felt the need. But you are casting false accusations and making wicked guesses about her."

"I swear by my head", said the Arrogant Knight, "you have said the most astonishing things and confessed to this deed, and you have passed a death sentence on yourself."

"My death is not as close as you think," said Parceval. "Watch yourself, so that death does not come upon you instead."

They rode at each other with all their might, and when they met, each one stuck his lance fast into the other's shield. Both men fell to the ground, so that both lances snapped in two. Then they leaped up and fought with swords, and each one struck the other many mighty blows. Their battle was both hard and long, because both were strong, fierce, and bold fighters. But their encounter ended thus: Parceval was stronger, more skilled, and more valiant, and so he had the better of it, once they had fought for a long time and the Arrogant Knight grew exhausted. Then the Arrogant Knight asked for peace and mercy, and all his arrogance collapsed and he was forced to become humble. Parceval, who never forgot the good counsel of the good man who made him a knight and taught him the customs of single combat—that he should not kill the man who begs for peace and mercy—answered with these words: "Knight, by my faith, I shall show you no mercy unless you have mercy on your beloved, because never has she suffered such distress as has now been her lot because of you."

The knight answered, "My lord, I shall gladly compensate her for all that I have done wrong, according to your will. And I shall also do everything that you order me to. I am now truly informed that she is blameless, and I regret that I have done her wrong."

"Go to the nearest estate," said Parceval, "and stay there until she is completely healed. Then dress her well, and go to King Arthur and give him God's greeting and mine, and surrender yourself to his mercy. Say that the knight whom he knighted with red weapons has sent you. You shall also tell all the knights and ladies of his court about our encounter, and bring God's greeting and mine to the maiden whom Kay the seneschal struck on my account. Tell her that I will not enter King Arthur's court until I have avenged her disgrace on Kay, and she will say that she is avenged well."

The knight said that he would comply with everything that he ordered. They parted, and the knight went to heal his beloved, so that she became well and recovered all her beauty. He dressed her in the finest clothing, and they entered the castle where King Arthur sat with his court. When the knight entered, he came at once before the king, and in front of the entire court he gave himself up into the king's power, a defeated man. He offered to do everything that the king commanded him, and said that "those were the orders of the knight who asked for red armor from you, and you gave it to him."

When the king heard that, he said, "Good friend, take off your outer clothes. Blessed be the knight who sent me such a knight! For his sake, you will be welcome here and treated honorably."

"My lord," he said, "I must tell something more before I take off my armor—but I would like the queen to come, and her maidens, to hear the news that I have to tell you, along with the lovely maiden who was struck for the little laugh that she laughed."

The king immediately sent for the queen, and she came at once with all her handmaidens. Then the newly arrived knight said, "My lady, a certain knight sent you God's greetings—a knight whom I must praise highly, because he defeated me and gave my beloved, who now is here with me, into your care. The knight said that he would not enter the court of King Arthur before he had avenged the disgrace when Kay struck your maiden."

"May God reward him for that!" said the queen. "And I will gladly offer him and his friends honor and distinction along with friendship."

Then the king's fool jumped up and screamed out loud. "Kay, Kay, so help me God, now the time for your disgrace has come! You'll pay dearly for the dishonor that you did to the maiden and to me."

The king said, "Ho, Kay, how foolish you were when you mocked the boy! Your foolishness and mockery frightened him away from me, so that I think that I may never see him again."

Then the king spoke to the knight whom the boy had sent. "I give you your freedom, so that you are released from service to me."

Sir Gawain asked, "What knight is that, who has done such a great deed of bravery as to beat the knight whom we know is the best in this land?

The king answered, "He is unknown to me." And then the king told Sir Gawain how he had come to him, and how Kay had mocked him. "But he has always served me faithfully ever since, and I certainly would like to find him. In the morning, we must all go and search for him."

As soon as morning came, the king and all his court prepared to leave Korboel.[39] The queen and all her handmaidens went with him. The king rode all day. When evening came, he pitched a tent on a fine level field, and slept there for the night. The next morning there was a great snowfall, and it grew cold.

That day, Parceval had arisen early, and he rode out in his armor to seek adventures and knights who wanted to contend with him. He rode over the same fields where the king's host was; they were completely covered in snow. And when he came out onto the fields, he saw where a great flock of ducks was flying, pursued by a hawk, which had struck a duck so that it fell to earth. Parceval rode to where it had fallen down, wanting to catch it. The hawk was afraid of him and flew off quickly, and so did the duck, because it was not badly wounded. But the duck had bled onto the snow, and when Parceval saw this thing—newly-fallen snow and the reddest blood—it occurred to him that the same hues were in the face of Blankiflur, his beloved. He thought so much about this that he forgot everything else. He cared for nothing but to see her. He was pondering this so deeply,

and his love became so deep and true,
that there was nothing else he could do.

CHAPTER XIV
Kay Falls From His Horse

Now a pageboy from the king's tent saw Parceval, and he thought that the knight had fallen asleep on horseback. The king was not dressed, but the pages headed for the king's tent. They met the knight named Sigamor. He went to the king and told him that a knight was a short distance away, sleeping on the back of his horse. The king ordered Sigamor to summon him, and he rode, fully armed, to him and said, "Knight, you must ride to the king."

Parceval behaved as if he hadn't heard what he said.

Then Sigamor said, "You shall come with me to the king by force, if you won't do it willingly."

When Parceval saw the knight riding at him, he turned to face him, and when they met, each stabbed at the other, and Sigimor's lance broke in two. Parceval couched his lance so that the other rider fell down, but his mailcoat was trusty and protected him from wounds. But Sigimor's horse galloped to the king's tent. Sigimor's friends were vexed at his misfortune. But Kay the seneschal, who never could hold back from foolishness and folly, said, "My lord, now you may see how Sigimor is walking and leading his horse. But with his other hand he is leading the vanquished knight by force, and he has won a fine victory."

"Kay," said Arthur, "it's unworthy of you to mock brave men. Bring me the knight, and we'll see if you can win a better victory."

"My lord," said Kay, "I am happy if my going pleases you. I shall certainly have that knight brought to you by my strength. If he will not come willingly, then he must come unwillingly, and I shall press him to say his name."

Now he armed himself and rode to where Parceval sat on his horse, pondering just as before. When Kay came riding forth at Parceval, he said, "Knave, go to the king. By my faith, you shall go whether you want to or not."

When Parceval heard his words and his oath, he rode against him, and when they struck each other, Kay's lance-shaft broke in two. Parceval couched his lance so that Kay fell far from the horse. When he fell, his arm broke, because he landed on a rock, and what the king's fool had always prophesied for him came true. Kay lay unconscious, and his horse ran back. When the king's men saw the horse running with an empty saddle, many leaped on their horses, and when they reached Kay, they thought that he was dead. But Parceval was sitting in the same manner as before. The king was furious that his seneschal was so badly injured. When he found out that he was alive, he found a healer to treat him.

Then Sir Gawain said to the king, "God knows, my Lord, that I am convinced that it is not in the least right to anger a man while he is pondering some matter—which is just what these two men did to that knight. If you are willing, I will ride to him and invite him to come and join us."

When Kay heard that, he grew angry and said, "Sir Gawain, you may take his bridle and lead him here, because he will follow you, since you have captured and disarmed many knights."

"Ho, Kay!" said Gawain. "I tell you that if God wills, I shall bring that knight to the king in such a way that my arm will neither break nor be dislocated. You took a fitting reward for your labors. I will not take such a reward."

"Kinsman," said the king, "I am pleased that you are going, because you are a wise and even-tempered man. Bring him here in peace."

Sir Gawain armed himself and rode to where the knight was. He said, "Brother, I would gladly greet you if I knew that your mind was as well-disposed towards me as mine is towards you. Still, I shall speak to you with good will, because I am a messenger of my lord King Arthur."

Parceval answered, "Two knights came here, and they wanted to take my reverie from me, and they wanted to bring me to the king by force, as if they had captured and overthrown me. Now I am contemplating a reflection that pleased me well. But tell me, good friend, is the seneschal Kay with the king?"

"Yes," said Sir Gawain, "I tell you this truly, the king went to search for you and eagerly wishes to meet you. Tell me your name."

"My name is Parceval. But what is your name?"

"My name is Gawain."

"Yes," said Parceval, "now you tell me good news, because I am eager for fellowship with you, if you are willing."

"God knows that I am willing," said Gawain.

Then they rode to the king's tent. Sir Gawain spoke: "Take off your armor." And he had the finest brocade mantle brought to Parceval, along with the best suit of clothes. Now Parceval was well dressed, and he appeared to be the most handsome of knights. Then they went in to see the king. Sir Gawain said, "My lord King, now I have brought the knight Parceval, whom you have long yearned to see."

When the king heard that, he was so happy that he stood up at once to meet him, and bid him welcome in God's name, and swore that he never wanted to be parted from him. At that moment the queen entered. Parceval went to meet her and greeted her well and honorably, and she bade him be welcome. Then he spoke to the maiden who was walking closest to the queen, the one who had laughed at him: "I am the knight who shall never turn away from you, if necessity demands the help of a knight for you."

The maiden thanked him for his good will with courteous words. Parceval stayed there, highly honored, and he went to Korboel Castle with the king.

But at midday of the next day, a woman arrived there, so ugly and loathsome that never was a more hideous beast ever born. She greeted the king and all the court, except for Parceval: "Ho, Parceval! Woe to him who brings you greetings, because you rendered evil service when you were not willing to offer help to the good Fisher King with your questions—because he would be healed, if you had asked what it was that you saw. You are unlucky, since your silence drove your good fortune out of your grasp.

"Sir," she said, "I know a castle in which there are five hundred and sixty of the bravest knights, and each of them has his most courteous lover. Now I tell you this news: whoever wants to prove his knighthood may find bold fellows there, and they will gladly accept a challenge, without a doubt. But as for him who wants to own the highest fame in all the world? I can tell him where he might seek out the loveliest of all maidens in the world—if anyone might dare to ride out to defend her against the great siege which surrounds her on a high mountain. One might win plenty of honor and worth there, along with riches."

What they could make of what they now know
Is what this book will plainly show.

CHAPTER XV

Once the maiden had finished her speech, she rode away. Sir Gawain said that he would go there. Gerflet swore that he would travel to the splendid castle. Kinderin said that he would travel to where the maiden sat on the mountain. Parceval swore that he would not return until he found out what the "walking renewal" was. Then sixty knights leaped to their feet and made a pact that they would find out where that castle was.

[Summary of chapters 15-17: Gawain is accused by a knight named Grandilbrasil [Guinganbresil] of killing his lord. As he rides out, he comes to a tournament between the knights Meliander and Saibaz [Meliant and Tiebaut]. Though staying out of the tournament for a day, Gawain is ultimately persuaded to enter; he wins the tournament and triumphs over Meliander and Gandilbrasil. Traveling on, he takes lodging with a knight who has a beautiful sister, to whom he pledges his love; unfortunately, she is the daughter of the man Gawain is accused of killing, and when Gawain is recognized in a town, the townspeople attack him. Grandilbrasil stops the fight and challenges Gawain to fight him in one year's time. The story now returns to Parceval:]

CHAPTER XVIII
Parceval Confesses to the Hermit

Now as for Parceval, we must say that he lived for five years without ever coming to the cross nor to church, so much was his mind set on proving himself in knighthood. He sought out all the fiercest knights, and found none so bold that he could not beat him. These five years passed without God ever entering his thoughts.

It was on a Good Friday when he was riding through a wilderness. He met three knights and twenty women, and they were all walking barefoot, wearing woolen clothing. They asked why he was riding so richly—but he inquired why they were walking so wretchedly. They said, "Do you not know that today is the day when Christ suffered death to redeem all mankind? It is not the knightly custom to ride on this day."

"From where have you come now?" he said.

"From out of the forest, from a noble servant of God."

"What did you do there?" said Parceval.

"That which all Christians are obliged to do: confession of our sins. We received salvation from repentance."

When Parceval realized this, he was deeply touched in his heart, and it occurred to him how monstrously he had lived. He said to the knights, "I would like to go to this hermit, if I can find him."

They showed him the path they had ridden after leaving him. Then they parted, and Parceval rode on the path that they had shown him. When he had ridden a long way, he came to the house of this good man. He got down from his horse and took off all his armor and tied his horse, and then he went into the chapel to the good hermit. He saw one priest and one postulant, and they were conducting the most solemn divine office. Parceval prayed for mercy on himself, falling to his knees with tears and complete repentance. When the holy man saw his humility, he called Parceval to him. Parceval fell to his knees before the hermit and said that he was very much in need of his wise counsel to amend his sins. The hermit told him to confess his sins.

"My lord," said Parceval, "five years have passed now since I begged for God's mercy, and I have had no faith in him. I have done only what was wicked for five years." Then he told him all the events that he had seen with the Fisher King, and said that he had always felt the greatest grief because he did not ask about the spear or the "walking renewal". "And for this reason I have forgotten my faith."

"Friend," said the good man, "what is your name?"

"I am called Parceval," he said.

The good man said, "It is a great grief that you have gone so astray, first concerning your mother, whom you abandoned, which she did not want. It is also a great sin for you that you did not ask about the 'walking renewal' and about the spear that always bleeds from the point. You would have been lost for a long time if you had not benefited from the blessings that she prayed God to grant you. I am your mother's brother, and the Rich Fisher is the son of the king who has himself served with such a thing, and who welcomed you. It is a holy thing that the mighty man has carried before himself for the comfort and support of his soul and his life. But this holy thing is spiritual and not physical.[40] He has been there for seven years. But you, kinsman, take care of your soul from now on. Always go to church before you go to any other place, and hear Mass with humility before God.

Be humble and willing to serve all who are in need. Now you shall stay here with me for these two days."

He did so, and learned a good prayer in those two days, and lived as a good Christian ever after. He rode away and did not stop until he came to Fair Fortress. Blankiflur his beloved was overjoyed to see him, and so were all the others there. Then Parceval married Blankiflur and became an excellent ruler over all her realm, so noble and victorious that he never had a fight with a knight in which he did not win victory, and he faced all the bravest knights that there were in those days.

And here ends the saga of the knight Parceval.[41]

The Saga of Theodoric of Bern: Theodoric Claims His Kingdom

Þiðreks saga af Bern: Þiðrekr nær ríki sinu

Theodoric the Ostrogoth, the 5th-6th-century ruler of the western Roman Empire, became the hero of a medieval German cycle of tales, in which he is known as Dietrich af Bern, "Theodoric of Verona." There was active trade between Norway and the Rhineland from the late 1100s on, and these tales may have reached Scandinavia via those links.[1] *An unknown translator is responsible for* Þiðreks saga af Bern, *a compilation of tales of Dietrich and his heroes. It is unclear whether the translator compiled the saga from assorted tales that he had heard, or whether he translated an already compiled Middle Low German manuscript.*[2] *But whoever was responsible for the form of this saga probably drew on an epic about Dietrich; a lay of Siegfried's exploits; and a lost epic of the downfall of the Nibelungs, now referred to as the* Ältere Not *("Elder Trials") and thought to be a source for the* Nibelungenlied *as well.*[3] *To this core, he added episodes and details from many other sources, making many legendary heroes into Dietrich's champions to create a sort of "German Round Table".*[4]

The first half of the section of Þiðreks saga *known as* Þiðrekr nær ríki sinu *("Theodoric Claims His Kingdom") is translated here. Long before the start of this episode, Theodoric and his foster-father Hildibrand had been driven from their kingdom by King Ermanaric (who replaces the historical Theodoric's rival Odoacer in most of the legends), due to slander by Ermanaric's villainous counselor Sifka. They had taken refuge with Attila, king of the Huns. Both had tried to stop the fight between between the Huns and the visiting Burgundians—the same battle that concludes the* Nibelungenlied*—but in the end, both were drawn into the battle and fought on Attila's side.* Þiðrekr nær ríki sinu *begins immediately after the battle, and tells how Theodoric and Hildibrand won back their kingdom, Amelungland. This section includes a version of Hildibrand's conflict with his son. Unlike* Ásmundar saga kappabana *and the Old High German* Hildebrandslied, *but much like the 15th-16th century* Jüngeres Hildebrandslied, *it ends happily.*

I translated the text from Guðni Jónsson's normalized edition,[5] *but checked it against Bertelsen's diplomatic edition which gives variant readings.*[6]

CHAPTER CCCXCV

King Theodoric of Verona had lost many noble companions of the Amelungs in Hunland, and he was deeply grieved in his heart.[7]

King Theodoric and his foster-father[8] Hildibrand were speaking together. The king said, "Master Hildibrand, it is surely my greatest grief that I have been deprived of my kingdom and lived here in Hunland for so long. I have lost all my comrades and friends, and all my honor. See now, Master Hildibrand, how so many of our friends have been slain here. The good Margrave Rudiger is killed, and King Gunther of Nibelungland, and Hagen of Tronje, who were our dear friends. What shall we do here in Hunland? Why should we grow old here? God knows that I would rather die for my kingdom Amelungland,[9] and for my good city Verona, than grow decrepit with dishonor in Hunland. We have served King Attila long enough."

Master Hildibrand answered, "My lord, we have been away from our kingdom for a long time, and we have lost much, most of all because of Sifka's plots.[10] Because of King Ermanaric's might, we have to face overwhelming forces. But I am in agreement with the course that you speak of now: to die in Amelungland, rather than grow old with dishonor in Hunland."

Then King Theodoric said, "Master Hildibrand, what have you heard of my city of Verona? Who rules over it?"

Master Hildibrand answered, "My lord, I do not know who rules it, but I have heard something: the duke named Alibrand might be ruling over it, and he must be my son. It is said that he is the greatest of all warriors and champions, in every respect. It may be that my wife Oda was pregnant when I left Verona, and he would have been born later."

King Theodoric said, "If your son were duke over my city of Verona, it would be a great stroke of luck for us. He would welcome us warmly, if he were as true to us as you have been."

Hildibrand said, "My lord, how will you make this journey?"

The king answered, "We won't be able to return home to Amelungland with an army. With such losses of men as have come about in Hunland, King Attila cannot lend us his own commanders to win our kingdom. I will go to Amelungland in secret, and it would be best if no more than the two of us were to enter Amelungland together. I will swear that I will not leave Amelungland in disgrace a second time. There shall I die, or else win my kingdom."

Master Hildibrand said, "We will hardly seem to be embarking gloriously on this expedition if only the two of us go, my lord. But rather than not entering Amelungland, I am keen for us to make this journey."

CHAPTER CCCXCVI

Master Hildibrand spoke again: "Should we discuss this matter at all with King Attila?"

King Theodoric answered, "The plan is now made: I will go home to Amelungland whether King Attila likes it or not. And I shall conceal this from King Attila, and from everyone else, until we are ready to leave." Then King Theodoric said, "Lady Herrat[11] shall go with us, if she is willing. Go and tell her, and ask whether she will go or not."

Master Hildibrand came to Lady Herrat and told her in private what King Theodoric of Verona had in mind. Herrat answered thus: "If King Theodoric wants to leave Hunland, I will certainly go with him. But if this how it must be, I want to hear the plan from his own mouth."

Hildibrand went to King Theodoric and told him how she had answered. King Theodoric went to her and said, "Lady Herrat, will you come home to Amelungland with me, if I want to win my kingdom or die? So many of my dearest friends have I lost here that I cannot stay in Hunland any longer. Master Hildibrand shall go with me, my best friend. I have lived without my kingdom for thirty-two years."

Herrat answered, "My lord, I will gladly go home with you to your country. God must will that you win your kingdom, so long have you been without it. The day will never come when I will be as happy as the day when you regain your honor."

"Prepare yourself soon," said the king. "This evening we must leave Soest."[12]

She said that it would be done.

CHAPTER CCCXCVII

By evening of that day, Master Hildibrand had prepared for the journey and had readied three horses, and he had laden a fourth horse with gold and silver and their clothing. Now they lifted Herrat onto her horse and loaded it.

Master Hildibrand said, "My lord, you must not want to depart from King Attila in disgrace, without meeting him."

King Theodoric replied, "Go out to the city gates with Lady Herrat, and I will go to meet King Attila."

King Theodoric entered King Attila's hall, where he slept, and he told the guards that he wanted to go in and meet Attila. The guards let King Theoderic go wherever he wanted. They knew that he was such a great friend of King Attila that even if he were to go to him armed, he would do no harm.

King Theoderic entered the hall where King Attila was sleeping, and he woke him. When he saw that King Theoderic had come there by himself, King Attila said, "Welcome, King Theoderic, dear friend. What do you want? Why are you walking around by yourself, bearing weapons?"

Theoderic answered, "My lord, you must now hear what I will tell you: why it is that I bear my weapons. Come and speak with me by yourself, in private."

The king stood up and did so. King Theodoric said, "Mighty King Attila, I have news to tell you. I have abandoned my good city of Verona and all my kingdom, and my enemies possess them. That grieves me so much that matters cannot go on any longer as they are. I will go home to Amelungland, and I shall gain either my kingdom, or else my death."

King Attila answered, "Where are your soldiers? How can you win your kingdom? What sort of plans have you made?"

Theodoric answered, "I will travel in my kingdom in secret, because now I have no soldiers with whom I could invade my land in force."

King Attila said, "My good friend King Theodoric, stay for a while with us instead. If you're not willing to do that, then I will give you men, the Hunnish army, for you to win your kingdom. Do not depart from us in dishonor."

Theodoric said, "My lord, it is just as I would expect from you that you would get the better of me, as a warrior should. I thank you for your kind offer. But I want to go home alone and in secret, together with Master Hildibrand. I do not want to waste your glorious warriors again, to win my land."

King Attila went with him out to the city gates, and there they parted and kissed each other. King Attila wept, and he was deeply grieved that he had to dismiss King Theodoric with no better honors. But King Theodoric commended King Attila and his kingdom to God's care, and he said that they would meet again as friends. He leaped on his horse Falka, and they went on their way. Master Hildibrand rode in front with the packhorse, and Theodoric and Herrat followed. They turned along the western road to the Alps; King Theodoric wanted to travel that way. They traveled night and day, and they did not encounter people, nor did they enter towns.

CHAPTER CCCXCVIII

One night, they came to Pochlarn.[13] Then King Theodoric spoke, turning his horse towards the city: "Now, Pochlarn, I grieve for your lord, Margrave Rudiger, the most generous of all men, and the best comrade. When I had lost my kingdom because of my father's brother, I came here to Pochlarn. The margrave came to meet me with his queen Gotelind. She gave me a battle-standard of green—to many Huns it brought death keen—and a thick cloak of purple velvet stuff, which this foreign ruler dared to wear well enough.[14] Now I grieve deeply for my good friend the margrave. Were you now living, I would not pass this city in this way, without meeting you."

Master Hildibrand replied, "You certainly speak the truth. The margrave was a good comrade. We proved that in Russia, when I had lost my horse and he got me a horse. Had he not been there, I would have lost my life.[15] This I remember of him."

Now they went on their way and rode near the forest of Luruwald. By day they stayed in the forest, and they traveled at night.

CHAPTER CCCXCIX

Earl Elsung the Younger had crossed the Rhine with his men, thirty-two knights. He rode on his way, and news came to him that King Theodoric of Verona would ride that way. He remembered that Samson the Old[16] and his sons Ermanaric and Dietmar had killed his kinsman, the elder Earl Elsung Longbeard of Verona. It looked as though he had the best opportunity to take vengeance. He rode through the forest and searched for them.

As the sun was setting in the evening, King Theodoric said that they should ready themselves and ride on their way in the night. The king and Herrat rode ahead, and Hildibrand rode behind and led their packhorse.

Hildibrand looked behind him. He saw a cloud of dust stirred up by horses, and fair shields gleaming beneath it. He spurred his horse and rode after King Theodoric, and he told him, "I see a great cloud of dust where horses are passing, and beneath it, fair shields and bright mailcoats. They are riding swiftly after us."

Herrat replied, "Those must be our enemies. We must have to face overwhelming forces." And she wept.

King Theodoric turned his horse back and lifted up his helmet and said, "That is certainly a cloud of dust stirred up by horses, with armed men beneath it. Who would be riding there so splendidly? What do you suppose, foster-father?"

Hildibrand answered, "I don't know of any ruler we might expect to find here, unless Earl Elsung has crossed the Rhine. And I know that if it is he, and if he has heard about our journey, then it may be that he wants to find us."

Theodoric said, "These men are riding furiously, as if they want to find us. But how should we respond? Shall we escape into the forest and save ourselves? Or should we dismount and prepare to defend ourselves?"

Master Hildibrand turned his horse around and took the helm from his head and watched these men riding, and he said, "My lord, thirty-two men are riding there. Let us dismount as swiftly as possible and ready ourselves. We shall not flee before them. It shall be heard throughout Hunland that these men shall fall, some by our weapons, and some fleeing in terror." And he leaped from his horse, and so did King Theodoric. They tied their horses and helped Herrat down. They clasped their helmets on firmly and drew their swords.

King Theodoric said, "Certainly you are still a good comrade as always, Master Hildibrand. Wherever men must do battle, he who sees such a comrade at his side is blessed. Lady Herrat, weep no more. Be cheerful, unless you see us fall—but it will go better than that."

CHAPTER CCCC

Now Earl Elsung and his men came riding at them. Then the young lord Amelung spoke up—the son of Earl Elsung's sister, and the boldest of all men. He saw the woman and said, "If you're willing to leave this woman and let her come home with us, you shall keep your lives."

Hildibrand answered, "She has traveled from Soest with King Theodoric for another reason than coming home with you. We are certainly not willing."

One of Elsung's men replied, "I have never heard an old man answer more boldly and fearlessly, yet more arrogantly."

King Theodoric answered, "You must be much more childish in your wits and all your courtliness, though you may not be younger in age. For all his life, he has won victories with honor and valor, and thus has he grown old. Don't be so bold that you sneer at him again on account of his age."

Now Amelung said, "Give up your weapons quickly, and surrender yourselves into our power. If you won't do that, I'll seize your beard in my hand so that most of it will come away in my grip."

Hildibrand answered, "If your hand touches my beard, you'll regret it, because one of two things will happen: either my arm will break giving one blow, or your hand will quickly fall off. Who is your leader?"

Someone answered, "Your beard may be grey, but you're certainly half-witted. Don't you recognize Lord Elsung, our earl? How can you be so bold that you dare ask about our leader? We are certainly fools for standing here for so long in front of two men who are bandying words with us."

He drew his sword angrily and struck Master Hildibrand on the cowl over his helmet. The sword cut the cowl, but inside was Theodoric's helmet Hildigrim,[17] and the blow was blocked, as had happened before. King Theodoric himself now owned the helmet that young Siegfried had owned, the best of arms and the most richly ornamented with gold. But Hildibrand drew his sword Gram, which young Siegfried had owned, and struck at Ingram on his helmet. So mightily did he cleave the helmet and head and chest and mailcoat that sparks flew, and the sword came to rest in front of the saddle-bows, and Ingram fell from his horse, dead. Now King Theodoric drew his own sword Ekkisax[18] and struck the first blow at the shoulder of the lead rider, so that the rider's arm and side flew off and he fell dead from his horse. He aimed another blow under the right arm of Earl Elsung himself. The sword cut upwards through the shoulder and mailcoat, sheared off his arm, sliced up into his cheek, and split his jawbone and molars. He fell from the left side of his horse, dead.

CHAPTER CCCCI

Now there was great fear and trembling, and everyone wanted to be home in Babilonia.[19] All the same, a fierce battle broke out. In a short time, King Theodoric had killed seven knights on the other side, and Master Hildibrand had killed nine. The young Amelung attacked Hildibrand and fought against him, but all the survivors fled from King Theodoric. Hildibrand struck Amelung a blow on his shield and helmet, and Amelung fell from that mighty blow. Hildibrand leaped on him and ordered him to surrender his weapons and keep his life.

Amelung answered, "Surely it is not better for me to live, having been overcome by such an old man. Still, I will give up my weapons and live for now."

He surrendered his weapons. Hildibrand told him to stand up, and asked who he was and why those men had sought their lives. Amelung said that Earl Elsung wanted to avenge his kinsman, Earl Elsung the Elder, whom King Samson had killed—and King Theodoric was King Samson's kinsman.

King Theodoric spoke: "Amelung, good fellow, you shall now tell us what is happening southwards towards the mountains, if you know. And then you shall be granted your life and your arms and all your armor and all your retainers, and you shall keep that as compensation for your kinsman Earl Elsung."

Amelung said, "My good lord King Theodoric, I can tell you important news of your father's brother King Ermanaric. He has been sick for some time now, since his belly was cut open and his intestines and belly fat have slipped out. Sifka gave the advice to cut his belly and pull the fat out, and said that he would be better then. This was done, and now he's worse than before by half. We don't even know whether the king is alive or not."

Hildibrand and Theodoric laughed and thanked him very much for his news. Now all the knights who had fled came back home. Wherever they went, they said that Earl Elsung was dead, and few of his men had escaped, and two men were responsible: an old man, and another mighty man.

CHAPTER CCCCII

Now these men crossed the Rhine and traveled all the way to Babilon. And when they entered the city, they told of these event, as they had before.

The earl's counsellor asked who had done this. The knights answered, "Two men did it it. One of them was so old that it was a wonder. I don't know why that demon was so old—he certainly was a demon, and he had the Devil himself in his own hand. Not a soul could withstand him. His grey beard was so large that it covered up his chest."

The counsellor said, "I think it's most likely that that must have been King Theoderic of Verona and his foster-father Hildibrand, and they must have entered our lands. Wherever they are hiding, they will do harm to many men before they are killed."

At that moment, Amelung came riding up, and twelve men were riding with him. They were carrying all of Earl Elsung's weapons. When the men of the city saw that, they said that that must be Earl Elsung, and the surviving knights must have fled from him.

The counsellor himself stood up, and many knights went with him. They greeted Amelung warmly and said that it was a great stroke of luck that he had returned. They asked who these two men were who had fought him, and who the old man with the long beard was. Amelung answered, "That old man that you're asking about is a good warrior who spared my life when he had the choice to kill me. The other man was King Theodoric of Verona, and the old man is Master Hildibrand. It shows their prowess that they defended themselves so well. They had a pressing need to defend themselves; they were facing thirty-two men, and still we lost fourteen men to these two."

CHAPTER CCCCIII

King Theodoric told Hildibrand that they should ride south over the Alps. There was a forest before them. King Theodoric turned into the forest; there they dismounted and took off their horses' packs. King Theodoric and Lady Herrat stayed behind in the forest, and Master Hildibrand rode from the forest to a city. Another earl ruled this city; his name was Lothar,[20] and he was old now. His son was young, and his name was Conrad.

Hildibrand met a man in the woods. His home was in the town. Hildibrand asked this man, "Who rules this town that I see here?"

The man answered, "Duke Lothar and his son Conrad rule over it."

Hildibrand said, "What can you tell me of the man who rules Verona?"

He answered, "That is Alibrand, son of old Hildibrand."

Hildibrand laughed and said, "How good a warrior is Alibrand? How distinguished a man is he?"

The townsman answered, "Alibrand is the greatest of all champions, and superior to all men in generosity and courtesy. But he is fierce and hostile and wicked to his enemies, and he will not call any man his equal."

Hildibrand rode with him, and Hildibrand spoke again. "You are certainly a good comrade. What more news can you tell?"

The townsman answered, "Many important tidings are told. I think it must be true that King Ermanaric is dead."

Hildibrand replied, "That is important news, and his friends will not find it good."

CHAPTER CCCCIV

Now they came to the town. Hildibrand said, "Good fellow, will you carry out my errand in the town, since I do not want to travel farther for now? Ask the squire Conrad to come and see me, since he is quicker on his feet than his father."

The townsman said that he would carry out his errand. And when he entered the town, he found Conrad and said to him, "Squire Conrad, a tall man with a white beard is waiting by this town, and he asked me to call you. He gave me his own gold finger-ring."

Conrad was a humble man and was willing to go when the stranger sent word to him. He went out of the town by himself. Outside the town gates stood Hildibrand, who welcomed that man and asked who he was.

"My name is Conrad," he said, "and my father's name is Lothar. What is your name?"

"I am called Hildibrand the Wolfings' Champion,[21] if you have heard my name mentioned."

Conrad came to him and bid him be most welcome of any man. Conrad said, "Come with me to my father. You will certainly be welcome with us."

Hildibrand answered, "I cannot go with you for the time being. Can you tell me any news?"

"I can tell you important news," said Conrad. "King Ermanaric is dead."

Hildibrand answered, "Who wears his crown now?"

Conrad replied, "That's the bad news. It's that wicked dog, Sifka Balerad." Then he asked, "What news can you tell us? From where have you come?"

Hildibrand said, "It's more likely that I could tell you what you haven't heard—that Elsung has been killed in Babilon, and that King Theodoric has arrived in Amelungland."

"God be praised for that," said Conrad, "because your son Alibrand has sent men northward into Hunland after King Theodoric, so that he may return to his kingdom. Certainly Alibrand will not give up his city to Sifka, nor any other place in Amelungland. All the Amelungs would rather die than have Sifka rule Verona. Hildibrand, good comrade, come with me into the town to my father."

Hildibrand said, "First I have to ride out into the forest, because King Theodoric is waiting for me there."

Conrad said, "Good friend, wait for me. I want to tell the news to my father."

CHAPTER CCCCV

Conrad went to his father in the town and said, "My lord, I can tell you important and good news. King Theodoric of Verona has entered Amelungland, and our kinsman Hildibrand is with him. He is here outside the town, and he has summoned me there."

When the earl heard that, he stood up at once and went out, and many knights went with him. And when they came out of the town, they met Hildibrand. Duke Lothar came towards him and recognized him and said, "Master Hildibrand, you shall be welcome here to us and have all the honors that we can offer you. But where is King Theodoric?"

Hildibrand answered, "He is in this forest."

Then the duke sent for his horse; he wanted to ride out to find King Theodoric. At that moment, seven townsmen arrived with wagons, laden with honey and wine. The earl had these wagons taken and driven into the forest, along with the fine provisions. They all rode until they found King Theodoric. He had built a fire.

Duke Lothar and his son Conrad dismounted from their horses. They came before the king, and both of them fell on one knee and kissed his hand and welcomed their lord, King Theodoric of Verona. They offered themselves as his supporters in whatever he wanted done.

King Theodoric stood up and took them by the hands, and told them to rise and sit beside him. Each asked the other for news. King Theodoric had much to tell about his travels, and in the same way Duke Lothar told all the news that he knew. The earl invited King Theodoric to come home with him, but the king said that first he wanted to stay in the forest—"but Master Hildibrand shall ride to meet his son Alibrand," he said.

Now Hildibrand prepared to go. The reason why King Theodoric didn't want to go to the town was that he had sworn an oath that he would never enter any sort of shelter, until he entered his own city.

CHAPTER CCCCIV

Now Master Hildibrand was fully prepared, and the squire Conrad rode on the way with him. Conrad said to Hildibrand, "If you encounter your son Alibrand, speak courteously with him and say that you are his father. If you do not do so, that will be the death of you."

Hildibrand said, "Good friend, can you tell me how I may recognize my son, whether it is he or another man?"

"He has a white steed," said Conrad, "and the nails in its shoes are made of gold. His shield is as white as new-fallen snow, and his city is painted on it. No man in Amelungland is a match for him. You are old now, and you will not be able to withstand him."

Hildibrand laughed and said, "Though my son Alibrand thinks himself a great man, and his arrogance is so great that he will not call any man his equal, it may be that once again he will tell me his name before I tell him mine, even as old as I am."

CHAPTER CCCCVII

Now Hildibrand briskly rode on the way to Verona, and he reached the point where he could see the city. A man was riding to meet him. He had two hounds, and he carried a hawk on his left hand. This man was tall on horseback and rode his horse in courtly fashion. He had a white horse, and all his armor was white, and Verona was depicted on it, with golden towers. Hildibrand rode to meet the man, and he felt that this man seemed no less a man than he.

When Alibrand saw one armed man riding most boldly to meet him, and he could not see that the man would humble himself before him at all, Alibrand became angry and said that he would contend with this man.

He clasped his helmet firmly on his head and brought up his shield before his chest, and he aimed his lance forward and spurred his horse. When Hildibrand saw how Alibrand had readied himself, he held his shield up before his chest and aimed his lance forward and spurred his horse and rode towards him, no less boldly. They rode at each other, and each one struck the other's shield with his own lance, so hard that both lance shafts broke apart. The old man leaped from his horse's back at once and drew his sword, and so did the younger man. They came together and fought until both were weary. Now they set their shields down and leaned on them.

CHAPTER CCCCVIII

Alibrand said, "Who is this old man who has stood up to me for a while? Tell me your name quickly and give up your weapons, and then you will keep your life. But if you're not willing to do that, it may turn out to be your death."

Hildibrand answered, "If you want to know my name, then you have to say your name first, and you will have to give up your sword and arms before we part. If you don't want to do that willingly, then you'll have to do it by force."

Then Alibrand brought up his sword with full force and struck at the old man, and Hildibrand did the same. A hard fight broke out, and the second attack was fiercer than the first by half. Now both were weary, and Alibrand set down his shield and wanted to rest, as did Hildibrand.

Alibrand said, "If you will say your name and give up your weapons, then you will keep your life. If you won't do that, you will be killed."

"You would not say your name when we met, and that was no dishonor for you. But now you will have to say it when you are defeated."

Now the younger man grew most furious of all, and he certainly wanted to kill him. He struck at the old man with all his might, but the old man defended himself most bravely.

Now Hildibrand said, "If you are of the Wolfing lineage at all, then tell me, and I will grant you a truce.[22] If not, I will kill you."

Alibrand answered, "If you want to keep your life, give yourself up. I am no more a Wolfing than you. You are certainly foolish, even though you're old. Say your name quickly. But if you knew who I might be, you would not call my father a Wolfing."

They attacked each other more fiercely than ever. The old man got in close to Alibrand and struck his most powerful blow. Hildibrand struck such a blow to his thigh that his mailcoat split, and Alibrand suffered such a severe wound that he could hardly use his leg. He said, "See, here is my sword. I cannot withstand you any longer. You have the Devil in your hand." And he reached out his hand.

The old man turned his shield aside and reached out for the sword with his hand. Alibrand struck a surprise blow at the old man, meaning to cut off his hand. The old man brought his shield up high and quickly, and he said, "Your wife must have taught you that blow, not your father."[23] And the old man attacked so fiercely that the young man fell to the ground. The old man fell upon him and aimed his sword at the young man's chest and said, "Tell me your name and your lineage quickly, or else you'll lose your life."

Alibrand answered, "I will never tell, because from now on I don't care about my life, if such an old gray goose has beaten me."

Hildibrand said, "If you want to keep your life, then tell me quickly if you are my son Alibrand. Then I am Hildibrand, your father."

The young man said, "If you are Hildibrand, my father, then I am Alibrand, your son."

Then Hildibrand got up off him quickly, and Alibrand got to his feet. They kissed each other and recognized each other. Hildibrand was overjoyed to see his son Alibrand, and Alibrand felt the same way about his father Hildibrand. They mounted their horses and rode home to the city.

Alibrand asked, "Where did you part from King Theodoric?" Hildibrand told him all about how he parted from him in the forest, and also that Alibrand should ride out with all his men to meet him.

CHAPTER CCCCIX

In the evening, they rode to Alibrand's mother. She came to meet them and saw her son Alibrand, bloody and wounded. She wailed and wept and said, "My sweet son,[24] who gave you that wound?"

Alibrand answered, "My lady, I may endure this wound well, though it not be a small one. My father gave it to me. He is riding here with me now."

She was glad to see her son and her husband. She came to meet them, and each of them was glad to see the others. Alibrand's mother bandaged his wound, and they dined there that evening. Afterwards, they took their horses and rode to Verona. The watchman had come to the city gates and meant to lock them, but Alibrand rode up to the gates, and the watchman hardly recognized him. Hildibrand rode up to the gates and flung them open roughly. Now the watchman was angry and struck at Hildibrand with his sword, but Hildibrand ducked behind his shield and wasn't wounded. When Alibrand saw that, he drew his sword and swung at the watchman's neck, so that he cut off his head.

Hildibrand said, "Now you've done a wicked deed: you killed an innocent man, because that blow didn't hurt me."

Alibrand answered, "Your armor was the reason that it didn't hurt you. Had it not been in the way, I would have had to avenge my father. Then the watchman wouldn't have been innocent."

Then they rode into the city and were welcomed there.

CHAPTER CCCCX

Now Alibrand sent a message through all the city and had all the most powerful men in the city summoned. When a great multitude of men had assembled in the king's hall, Alibrand spoke: "I can tell you the good news that King Theodoric, son of Dietmar, has entered Amelungland and is asking for his kingdom. Now you must consider what answer you will give: whether you would rather serve King Theodoric or Sifka Balerad."

A nobleman answered his question and said, "If we were certain that King Theodoric had come to Amelungland, and that we might come out to meet him, then I know the will of all the people in this land. They have held the realm for a long time against Sifka and his men, waiting for King Theodoric. All of them would rather die with King Theodoric now, than fail to win his kingdom for him."

At this speech there was such a great uproar that for a long time that night everyone who was there shouted and thanked God that King Theodoric might appear before their eyes. Some said that King Theodoric would win his kingdom, which he had lacked for a long time—"and we will serve him, and never another man, as long as he lives." But others still said that it could not be true that King Theodoric had come to Amelungland.

Alibrand answered, "King Theodoric has certainly entered Amelungland. Hildibrand the Wolfings' Champion has come with him and is staying here with us now. He is my father."

Everyone shouted at once that Hildibrand was welcome. Alibrand said, "If you want to have King Theodoric as your king, all the best men must take their horses and arms and ride out to meet King Theodoric."

CHAPTER CCCCXI

Now all the knights readied themselves and rode out of the city, and seven hundred men rode with them. They all rode on their way until they entered the forest where King Theodoric and Duke Lothar were waiting. Master Hildibrand and Alibrand and all the knights dismounted from their horses and bowed to King Theodoric. The king stood up to face them and kissed Alibrand, and there was a joyful reunion. King Theodoric mounted his horse, and everyone rode together on the road that leads to Verona. When they approached the city and the townsmen saw the ride of King Theodoric, all the people came out to meet them, sporting and celebrating in every way. And when King Theodoric came before Verona, Hildibrand rode with his standard, and Alibrand was on his other side. Alibrand touched his hand to King Theodoric's hand, and he took a small golden finger-ring and handed it to him, and he said, "Mighty lord King Theodoric, ever since your kinsman King Ermanaric died, I have been appointed to govern this city and to guard all Amelungland as well. This realm never fell to Sifka. I wish to give you this little golden ring, my lord, and Verona with it, and all Amelungland, and myself and all my men to follow you."

King Theodoric answered and wished him God's reward for it, and said that he would reward the gift with good things for him. Now all the knights gave gifts to King Theodoric. Some gave large estates, and some gave good horses or other war-gear. All the noble men gave him the finest possessions, and there was much rejoicing. When this was done, King Theodoric rode into Verona to his estate. The dukes Alibrand and Hildibrand led him to his throne, and that day he had no fewer than a thousand men at his table.

The king sent a message through all his kingdom and summoned all those who governed cities or castles or shires. Many people came to King Theodoric every day to surrender their cities or castles or other realms to him.

CHAPTER CCCCXII

A few days later, King Theodoric rode out with a great army to the place called Ravenna. When he entered the city, he summoned an assembly, and at this assembly he told them important news: Sifka had assembled overwhelming forces and intended to ride into Amelungland and conquer the land. King Theodoric asked the townspeople whether they would rather have him or Sifka as king, and he said that he would not flee before Sifka's army. All the townsfolk who were there answered that they were willing to serve King Theodoric, and they would rather fall with King Theodoric than offer one penny to Sifka. Then King Theodoric said that all his men and all those who were willing to help him should arm themselves. He did not want to spend the night where he was, before facing Sifka.

CHAPTER CCCCXIII

King Theodoric rode out from the city of Ravenna, and he had eight thousand men. Sifka had reached the city called Gregenborg,[25] with his force of thirteen thousand men. Then King Theodoric came against them. Hildibrand rode forth with King Theodoric's banner, and just behind rode King Theodoric himself and all his men.

At that moment, an army of seven thousand knights arrived from Rome to aid Sifka, and they attacked the rear of King Theodoric's ranks. When the Amelungs became aware of this, Theodoric turned to face the Romans, with his banner, and Hildebrand and the Amelungs faced Sifka. Duke Alibrand rode forth against Sifka most boldly, beneath his banner. He struck the first blow at the arm of the man who bore Sifka's standard, so that he cut off the hand and split the banner shaft, and the banner fell to the ground. Then Sifka rode at him boldly, and each struck mighty blows at the other. Their combat lasted for a while, until Alibrand proved to be mightier and Sifka fell dead from his horse.

Once the King of the Romans had fallen, the Amelungs shouted a loud battle cry, and the Romans surrendered. When King Theodoric realized that Sifka had fallen and Alibrand was coming to him, he said that he had certainly received a great stroke of luck, and if he had done that nine years earlier, the kingdom of the Amelungs would be better off. The Romans did not grieve for their leader very much, and the entire army surrendered to Theodoric.

CHAPTER CCCCXIIII

Now King Theodoric rode with this army on the road that leads to Rome. Cities and castles were surrendered to him wherever he want. He rode into Rome with his entire army, and rode to the hall that King Ermanaric had owned, and sat in his high seat. There Hildibrand crowned him with King Ermanaric's crown. All the knights who had served King Ermanaric came to him and became his men, and everyone in the kingdom bowed to him, some in friendship, and some because they did not dare to do otherwise.

King Theodoric built many works that may still be seen, such as the baths that are called the Baths of Theodoric.[26] In Rome, he had a statue cast of his horse Falka and himself, which was made of bronze. He had another statue set up in the north of the city; there he stands, on a tower, and raises his sword Ekkisax towards the bridge that lies over the river.[27]

CHAPTER CCCCXV

Towards the end of King Theodoric's life, the heresy of Arius was condemned by Christian men, and all those who had followed this heresy turned back to the correct faith.[28]

A little while later, Hildibrand fell sick. The illness was serious, and King Theodoric stayed by his side. Hildibrand said, "My lord, this sickness has overcome me so much that I think it will bring my death. Now I want to ask this of you: Let my son Alibrand benefit from our friendship. I want him to be given my arms."

A little while later, Hildibrand died, and King Theodoric wept for his good friend. King Theodoric had his body richly laid out and held his funeral in noble style, and Hildibrand was mourned deeply. In all this saga, no man is praised as much as Master Hildibrand, most of all for the allegiance that he kept to King Theodoric. Besides that, he was the boldest of all men, the best fighter, and the most generous with money. German men say that he was a hundred and fifty years old when he died, but German ballads say that he lived for two hundred years.

A little while after the death of Master Hildibrand, King Theodoric's wife Lady Herrat fell ill, and this illness caused her death. She was a good woman, courteous and blessed with friends, as her kinswoman Queen

Helche, and Gotelind the wife of Margrave Rudiger, had been before. These three women were the kindest to all their friends, and the most generous with wealth, of all those that are mentioned in this saga.

The Saga of the Mantle

Möttuls saga

The French Le mantel mautaillié *(The Ill-Fitting Mantle), or* Le lai du cort mantel *(The Lay of the Short Mantle), presents a magic chastity test; a beautiful mantle or cloak will only fit a woman who has stayed perfectly faithful to her lover.*[1] *The mantle will not only fail to fit an unfaithful woman, it will reveal salacious details of the woman's infidelity by the parts of her body that it exposes. The anonymous parody, halfway between a chivalric* lai *and a* fabliau, *may have been influenced by a Byzantine tale in which a statue of Venus causes unfaithful women who walk past it to expose themselves inadvertently. Whatever its sources, it was popular enough to inspire German, English, Welsh, and French retellings, and it was also translated into Norse during the reign of Hákon Hákonarson of Norway.*[2] *This translation,* Möttuls saga, *was in turn the basis for a poetic retelling composed in Iceland in the 14th century, the* Skikkjurímur.

Möttuls saga *might have been the first translation made for King Hákon. The lengthy description of King Arthur does not correspond to the French original, and might have been deemed necessary for an audience that was not yet familiar with the Arthurian legend. In addition, several famous Arthurian names are garbled or replaced in* Möttuls saga, *as would not be expected if the translator knew the Arthurian corpus.*[3] *While some scholars have postulated that Hákon commissioned his translations of chivalric literature to instruct his court in the norms of knightly behavior,* Möttuls saga *parodies these norms, and it is hard to see it as anything other than humorous entertainment.*

I have translated from the text edited by Marianne Kalinke, which is based on the 17th century manuscript AM 179. This is in turn a copy of Stockholm 6 / AM 598 Iα, dating from around 1400; it is now fragmentary, but AM 179 was copied from it when it was still complete.

CHAPTER I

King Arthur was the most celebrated ruler for every sort of accomplishment and all manner of valor and courtesy, with perfect goodness of heart and the most beloved kindness, so that there was absolutely no ruler in the world in his day who was more famous or well-beloved. He was the most able with arms, the most generous with gifts, the gentlest in speech, the wisest in counsel, the most benevolent in mercy, the most prudent in good management, the most majestic in all royal governance; God-fearing in his works, kindly to the good, fierce to the wicked, merciful to the needy, hospitable to supplicants, and so perfect in all his rulership that no wickedness nor ill-will was to be found in him. None could tell the noble excellence and honor of his realm with a tongue more full of praise. This is confirmed for him by true stories and manifold good learning created by worthy clerics, concerning many of his deeds, and sometimes concerning the various splendid matters that took place within his court and far and wide throughout his kingdom in various ways, sometimes concerning valiant knighthood, sometimes concerning other wondrous matters.[4]

Now this book tells of a certain wondrous and amusing matter that took place in the court of the worthy and celebrated King Arthur, who held all England and Brittany under his absolute rule. Such truths as have been revealed to me in French,[5] I have translated into Norse for the enjoyment and entertainment of you listeners, since the worthy King Hakon, son of King Hakon, requested that my small wit create some amusement from the matter that follows.

CHAPTER II

On the holiday that Holy Church calls Pentecost, but that Norwegians call Whitsunday,[6] worthy rulers and kings of many lands came to King Arthur, with dukes and other noblemen, as this saga affirms, like many others that have been made about him. King Arthur was the most eager for knowledge of all men, and he wanted to find out about all events that occurred, in his realm and also in other lands about which he might inquire. For that reason, he announced everywhere, in the woods, on the roads, and at crossroads, that anyone who was traveling should come to his court and his feast. Along with that came the king's command that whoever had a beautiful beloved should bring her with him, and she would be as welcome to the king as her lover. Because of this, such a great multitide came there that one might scarcely make a count; and thus it was in vain for even the wisest to choose the most refined one from such a great multitude.

The queen rejoiced at their arrival and allowed the young maidens to stay in her upper chamber. The queen was the loveliest of women and held converse with them, along with all manner of amusements and games in courtly fashion. She herself wore a fine outfit, and she gave such precious clothes to each maiden, in all manner of colors and styles, that the meanest was made of velvet and trimmed with gray and white furs. Whoever might wish to examine their outfits carefully would be able to make a much longer tale of it, but I will not detain you longer, and I will say little about much: there were no finer clothes in the world than those that were given to them, and no merchant could afford to buy them or sell them. The queen was praised for every sort of excellence; she was the best-loved of women for her celebrated generosity. Next she had costly brooches and splendid belts brought forth, and golden finger-rings with all manner of gems, so precious that no man had seen such rare and noble treasures as the queen gave out of abundant good will—for she let each of the ladies take as many as she might wish to have.

But now it is time to speak of King Arthur the renowned, who gave to his court, and to the rulers and knights who had come there, rich outfits and trusty weapons, splendid trappings and the best of warhorses, which were sent to him from the west, from Spain, Lombardy, and Germany. No knight came there who was so wretched that he could not receive rich outfits and trusty weapons and splendid trappings and a good horse, for not one thing that he might need was lacking. In no royal court were such rich gifts given, nor so abundantly received, as those that were received there. The king himself was worthy of such great praise because he never regretted his gifts, and he yielded them up as if he valued all that he gave them at nothing.

The Saturday before Whitsunday, this great court was assembled, so well outfitted with horses and weapons and fine clothing that never in the world was there another court like it. There was much entertainment and all manner of amusement, with abundant good cheer for the many noble men who had come there. And when they had spent the entire day in happiness, and evening came on, each man went to his own lodging, and squires prepared their beds, and all that host went to sleep.

CHAPTER III

When day arrived and it began to grow light, everyone dressed. Then all the folk entered the king's court, and from there they followed the king to the principal church of the manor. The queen arrived with her chambermaids to hear the service. There one might see many courtly men and lovely women, quite well dressed, because all the most handsome folk in all the world had assembled there.

When the service had ended, the entire household entered the king's court, and the queen led her own retinue of women up to the loft with her. The stewards and servants at the king's court had the most plentiful supplies of fine provisions, and the best drink to be found in the world, to prepare in all manner of ways for the king's table. First they spread the whitest of linen cloths over the table, and laid silver spoons and golden spoons on it, with well-crafted knives and silver dishes laden with meat. Then the food was completely prepared for the king and all his court. But this was King Arthur's custom: he wasn't cheerful at all, and didn't want to go to the table on any day, until he had received new tidings of some occurrence that had taken place nearby or farther away, so that he might make merriment and amusement for himself from it.

The queen summoned Sir Gawain, the chief of all the king's stewards, and asked what could be be the reason that the king did not go to the table, where the food was completely prepared and his entire court was gathered and it was the ninth hour of the day. He went to the king and spoke thus to him: "My lord, why are you not eating? For the table has been laid for a very long time."

The king looked at hm and answered, "Steward, when did you see me assemble my court on a feast day, when I didn't receive new tidings of some occurrence before I went to the table?"

No sooner had the king said that, when there swiftly came a lad on a galloping horse, heading for the king's court, riding so swiftly that the horse was all lathered under him, for he was in a furious hurry. Sir Gawain saw him first and said to the courtiers, "If God wills it, we will eat soon, for I see a lad furiously galloping this way on his horse, and he will tell us some new tidings."

Just then, the lad came to the doors of the king's hall and dismounted, and servants took his horse. The lad was most courteous, and he took off his outer garments at once and tossed his mantle onto his horse's neck. When he had removed his outer garments, he appeared most handsome. White was the color of his hair; he was broad and sturdy in the shoulders; he had arms long and stout, hands white and powerful. He was entirely formed by Nature with such desirable beauty, arising from his strength and manliness, that no one could wish him to be otherwise than as God had shaped him. He was not lacking in eloquence, wisely arranging his words and gentle in his speech.

CHAPTER IV

When he had entered the king's hall where the court was, he addressed them with courtly speech. "May the sublime God who created us all," said he, "bless and keep your company and fellowship."

"Friend," they said, "may God bless you."

Then said Kay the Seneschal, "Your horse is lathered. Tell us some news about your journey."

"No, my lord," said he, "first you shall tell me where the good King Arthur us. And I swear by my faith that I shall tell the king news that shall not be to everyone's taste, although for one person it shall be welcome."

Everyone suddenly felt that it would take a long time for them to learn what the lad wanted to tell. A knight said to the lad, "Look, friend, there he sits on his throne."

The lad went there at once, and everyone in his way made room for him. When he came before the king, he greeted him with these words: "May the God who shaped Heaven and Earth and all creatures in the world," he said, "bless you and keep you, the highest crowned king, above all those who have been and shall be." He spoke again: "Now I am pleased that I have found you, as I have searched for you for so long. One of the loveliest of ladies, far from your land, sent me here to find you. She asks you to grant her one boon, as your duty. If you refuse her now, she will not ask again. But you may not know in advance what it is that she asks, nor who she is herself, until you grant the boon. She is so exceptionally lovely and glorious that there is no one like her in the world. I wish this to be known to you:

if I accept this boon on her behalf, I will ask for nothing that would be a disgrace to your honor, nor do harm to your kingdom."

The king agreed to what the lad asked for. The lad gave the king many thanks. And then, from his gold-embroidered purse, he took a silken mantle, so beautiful that never had mortal eyes seen one like it, nor one so fair. An elf-woman[7] had made it, with such incredible skill that among all the host of skillful and clever men that had assembled there, not one was to be found who could discern how the cloth had been made. It was brocaded all over with gold, with such beautiful embroidered figures of leaves that nothing like it was ever seen, for no one could find their end nor beginning. Above all that, what was most astonishing was that those who examined it most closely were least able to discover how this wonderful work of craft was woven together. I do not wish to dwell on this any further, for it was much more wonderful than might be comprehended. The elf-woman had woven a magic spell into the mantle: for any maiden who had been deflowered by her lover, the mantle would reveal her sin as soon as she dressed herself in it, so that it would be too long or too short for her—in such a wondrous way that it would shorten itself to the point where it would reveal to what degree each maiden had sinned. Thus it revealed all false women and false maidens, so that the one who dressed herself in it might conceal nothing.

The lad explained well and frankly, before all the court and the great multitude of rulers who were assembled there, in what fashion the mantle was woven, and what power it had to put women to the test. Then he said to the king, "My lord, I ask you that I let the women and maidens of the court dress themselves in the mantle, because I heard, far away from here, that the most magnificent of ladies and maidens were assembled here. Do this quickly, so that they may not find out about this happening. I have come here to offer you this gift, and no others—and I have no other mission."

All the courtiers and all the rulers who had assembled there were amazed and curious about this mantle. Then Gawain said, "This offer is willingly agreed to and accepted."

CHAPTER V

Now the king sent Sir Gawain and Kay the Seneschal and the pageboy Meon[8] to bring the queen, and he told them to say to the queen that she was to come to where he was, along with all the maidens and ladies with her.

"Have them all assemble, so that no one stays behind, because I certainly want to keep to the terms of the boon that I granted the lad."

They went and found the queen in her loft, all ready to go to the table, for she was hungry from having had to fast for so long. Then Sir Gawain revealed the king's message. "My lady," he said, "the king asks you above all to go now to the place where he is. For a young lad, most handsome, came to him and brought him a mantle, so splendid that no mortal eye has seen another one like it. The cloth is red within, and we have never before seen such a treasure, wrought with such wondrous and surpassing skill that it is not certain whether another one exists, or whether its like is to be found in all the world. Know this as truth: the king has promised this mantle to the one who is most justly suited for it. Choose now, my lady, and stay behind no longer, and bring with you all the ladies that have come here, for the king wishes to see their form and beauty. It is unknown to me who will be allotted this noble gift."

CHAPTER VI

Now the queen came to the king, and all the great multitude of beautiful ladies and splendid maidens followed her there, so that never before did the eye of man see in one place such a great assembly of such beautiful women and lovely maidens that there were ever any better clothes in the world than those with which they had decked out their bodies. For that reason, every man kept his eyes on them, and many fell in love with them. At the same time, the entire court entered the hall to wonder who the lady would be who would own the mantle.

Then the king took the mantle and unfolded it and showed to the queen, and he said that he would give it to the lady, or to those ladies, whom it might suit. But not a whit more did he say to them, for if they had known what powers the mantle had, not one of them would have put it on for all the gold in Arabia. It would have been as loathsome to them as a worm or a snake would be. Now it had come to the point that the mantle would tell how faithfully they had lived with their husbands, or kept faith with their lovers.

The queen was the first to take the mantle, and she laid it over herself. But it became so short on her that it did not reach her heels. As eager as she was to own the mantle, it would never have come around her neck if she had known with what magic it was woven. Her face turned red with shame, and then she turned pale from grief and anger that the mantle was not the right length.

Meon the page was standing beside her, and he saw that her expression changed, and he spoke to her. "My lady," said he, "it does not seem to me that the mantle is too long for you, but rather more than half an ell too short, and by no means will it fit you well. But this maiden," he said, "is standing here next to you and is almost the same height as you, neither taller nor shorter—she is the beloved of Aristes, son of King Artes.[9] Give her the mantle, and then you will see on her that the mantle was too short for you."

Then the queen took the mantle and gave it to the maiden next to her. She accepted the mantle eagerly and draped it over herself—and it was much shorter on her than on the queen. Meon the page said, "Now the mantle has shot up a great deal in a short time, and it hasn't been worn for long."

The queen asked all the nobles and rulers, "Tell me, my lords, wasn't the mantle longer than this?"

"My lady," said Gawain, "it appears to me that you are somewhat more faithful and have committed fewer deceits than she."

Then the queen said to Kay the Seneschal, "Tell me, what is this faithfulness that you speak of? What power goes with this mantle?"

Kay told her, from beginning to end, what the lad had said. The queen considered that if she were at all grieved or angered, the fact that she had sinned against such a ruler would be turned to her shame and disgrace. And so she turned it all to a joke and an amusement, to laughter and play and jesting. "Now," she said, "all maidens and ladies must certainly dress themselves in the mantle, since I was the first to put it on."

"My lady," said Kay the Seneschal, "today you and all your ladies' truthfulness and the faithfulness of your love shall be revealed, which your husbands and lovers expect when you say that you have long kept firm faithfulness—along with that love which knights have for your purity: they place themselves at risk of their lives and into manifold perils for your sake. In days past, you all said that you were so pure and true that if one man were to ask you all, and one brave man wanted to win you, each of you would quickly answer that she had never been with a man."

When they had all fully examined the skill with which the mantle was woven, and with what craft the elf-woman had drawn and embroidered the leaves on the mantle, there was not one to be found in all that great multitude who would not have eagerly wished to have stayed home with honor, rather than to have come there; for in all that multitude and mob there was not to be found one woman who dared to lay the mantle over herself or to dress herself in it, nor to hold it in her hands, nor to come near it.

CHAPTER VII
Fine Ladies Wear the Mantle

When everyone had rejected the mantle and no one had dared to clothe herself in it, the king said, "Now we may give the mantle to the lad, because it may not stay here with us for any of those maidens under our protection."

The lad answered, "That is not just or honorable, my lord, nor is it proper to your high station. I shall never accept the mantle until I see that all the women and maidens have dressed in it, because that which a king gives and agrees to must never be denied or taken back, not for the sake of any man's wishing or urging."

"You speak wisely, my lad," said the king, "and you say what is true and just. Nothing shall cause what I said and swore to you not to be upheld. Certainly every lady must take the mantle."

As everyone stood quietly, Kay the Seneschal called out to his lover with these words, before all the knights and nobles. "Beloved," said he, "come forward. You may accept the mantle, safe and unafraid. No one can be found here who is your equal in good faithfulness and other fitting and feminine endowments. We two shall bear off the victory this day, with honor and glory."

But the maiden answered, "If it be your will, I would rather someone else take the mantle, and I will see how it goes with her. For I see more than a hundred of them here who do not dare come near it, and not one of them wants to wear it."

"O ho!" said Kay. "It seems to me that you are somewhat fearful, and I do not know what that means."

"It is not that, my lord," she said. "Far more excellent and mighty women than I have already accepted the mantle. It is not that I am afraid of it. Rather, I am afraid of this: there is a great multitude of powerful women here, who are good and true and of the noblest lineages, and it will seem wrong if I excel over them. I might be in for a share of hatred and jeering."

"You don't need to fear their anger," said Kay, "for no one is in any hurry to put on the mantle. Yet I know this: you are faithful, and it will be an honor for you to own the mantle, but shame if you lose it."

Then the maiden placed the mantle over herself, before all the multitude of nobles and many other rulers. And the mantle was so short on her in back that it barely reached the backs of her knees—but in front, it didn't even reach her knees. Then the nobles mocked her and said, "Kay the Seneschal must be quite glad of your love, and he will distinguish himself in knighthood for your sake, for now your faithfulness is revealed, so that all of us may know that your like is not to be found in the realm of the King of England."

When Kay saw how his beloved had failed, he wished that she had never come there, rather than suffering such shame and disgrace. Ideus[10] said to Kay the Seneschal, "It is just as well that the mockery and disgrace turns from her to you yourself, since you mock every man. But what do you have to say? Doesn't the mantle fit your beloved well—the one whom you've praised so much for her faithfulness?"

The maiden was greatly grieved that she could not defend herself against their words, because the entire court had seen how the mantle had fit her. Then Kay said to another knight, "Don't be too impatient—we will see how beautifully the mantle will fit your beloved." But Kay's beloved threw off the mantle and went to her seat, shamed and disgraced.

CHAPTER VIII

Now when the entire company of ladies saw how matters had gone wrong for this maiden, they all cursed the lad who had brought the mantle there, because now they were certain that it would be no use to object to taking the mante, even though they might find plenty of reasons to be excused.

The courteous page Bodendur[11] spoke to the king. "My lord," he said, "it seems to me as though we do not have the proper order for taking the mantle. Sir Gawain's beloved is so desirably beautiful that she should have taken the mantle right after the queen."

Gawain the steward was sorry that she should take the mantle, because he suspected that she would gain no greater honor than the women who had already taken it. The king said that Bodendur, the courteous page, should call her, and she stood up at once, for she dared not do otherwise. The king had the mantle brought to her, and she took it and draped it over herself, as the king had ordered. And as soon as she was dressed with it, it was so long on her in the back that she dragged it behind her for four and a half ells. But in the front, it shot up to her knees—and on the left side, it raised itself up to her back.

Kay the Seneschal was glad when he saw that the mantle was so short on her, because men had thought that she would be more faithful than all the maidens and ladies in the king's court. "By my faith," said Kay the Seneschal, "God be praised! I will not be the only one today disgraced on account of my beloved. I can discern well what this means. This beautiful maiden lifted up her right leg, but laid her left leg down quietly, while she was giving what she wanted to give to the man who pleased her."

Sir Gawain was sorry that the infidelity of his beloved should be brought to light so openly, but he could do nothing about it. Kay said to her, "Come here, beautiful. I shall lead you to a seat next to my beloved, because you two are as alike as two humps."[12]

Then the king took the daughter of King Uriens by the hand; she was the loveliest of maidens. Her father the king was the mightiest of men, and he often went hunting with hounds and hawks. "You, lovely one," said the generous King Arthur, "you will be tested and found true by this mantle, because no one finds fault with you."

"My lord," said Geres[13] the Little, "do not say much of this before you have fully seen how the mantle fits her."

The maiden realized that it was no use to speak against what the king had commanded, and so she took the mantle. But once she was dressed in it, it became so long on her right side that one and a half ells lay on the ground around her, but on the left side it jumped up to her knee.

"My lord," said Geres the Little, "foolish is he who trusts in any woman, because they all deceive their own lovers, and not one of them can be relied upon. Those who behave and speak most fairly are the least trustworthy, and betrayal strikes those who are least aware. Not one is good once tested. They all deceive their husbands and want a new man as soon as the old one has become tiresome. Their curiosity is so eager that no one can trust what they do. Now I want to say openly what I think about the behavior of that maiden. The mantle is so long on her right side—that shows us that she eagerly let herself tumble down on that side by her own good will. But the left side, where the mantle has shot up—shows us that she is not upset when her clothes are hiked up there."

The maiden was so angry that she didn't know what to say. She seized the straps and flung the mantle far from her and frequently cursed the man who had brought it there. Kay the Seneschal said, "Do not be angry, lovely maiden—you shall sit next to my beloved. The three of you are equal in this distinction, and not one of you can blame the others."

CHAPTER IX

Then the king commanded the beloved of Paternas[14] to come forward, and he addressed her with kind words. "Lovely lady," said the king, "undoubtedly you shall have the mantle, for you have perfect and faithful affection for your lover."

Gerflet, the king's fool, could not stay silent. "My lord," he said, "for God's sake, do not press the matter so firmly before you know or can see how it will turn out, for the day is praised at evening, and many things may turn out otherwise than men suppose."[15]

The maiden took the mantle, for she knew that it would be futile to refuse. And when she had to dress herself in it, the mantle's straps broke and fell to the ground—and so did the entire mantle, so completely that it never stuck to her. The maiden trembled all over and didn't know what to do, because a great many noble ladies and handsome pages and many other mighty men were standing around her. They all cursed the mantle and the one who made it and the one who brought it to the court. They all affirmed that no one could be found among the great multitude of ladies of the court whom the mantle would fit. Neither lady nor maiden would get it to fit, and there was not a woman so fair or fine that the mantle would fit her figure, not for weeping nor for sorrow. Nonetheless, each of them wanted to own the mantle.

Then Gawain went to his beloved and said, "Here I bring you this lovely maiden, so that she may keep company with you." There was no woman among them who thanked her for coming, but he made a joke of it and turned back laughing. Then the lad picked the mantle up off the ground as fast as he could. He put the straps on it, taking them from his purse, and he brought it to the men at once—because he didn't want his business and his mission to fail.

The king took the mantle and said, very angry: "We've been fasting for too long. What is the matter with these women? Why are we delaying in having them dress in the mantle?"

Gerflet, the king's fool, replied, "For God's sake, my lord, you might as well pardon the ones that are left. Or do you wish to disgrace them still further? Now that they've seen the mantle, they all agree, before their husbands and rulers and friends, that they have somewhat strayed." The fool spoke to him again: "What more will you demand of them all?"

The king wanted to let the matter rest. The lad rushed before the king and said, so that the entire court might hear: "My lord, keep your word to me, and keep the oath that you swore to me. These knights will not know what to say about their beloved ladies at this point, if some have been tested and some have not been tested and get off scot-free."

Ideus replied, calling out to his beloved. "You, my lovely one," he said, "I thought earlier today that no one in this court would be more faithful that you. But Kay the Seneschal answered me when I accused his beloved, and I was rash and said that I had so much trust in your faithfulness that I was completely unafraid for you. I regret this very much now, because I see that you are afraid. Take the mantle and dress yourself in it."

The king had the mantle brought to her, and she took it and laid it over herself. And when it came over her, it fit her perfectly in the front, so that everything thought that nothing but goodness would be found in her. But at her back, it was so short that it didn't come down to her loins; it just barely concealed her girdle. Gerflet the fool, who saw this first, said in a loud voice, "My lady, your mantle is too short in the back, and it will never become so long in front that it will fit you well."

Kay could not keep silent longer, because Ideus had mocked his beloved, and he quickly said to Ideus with scoffing and mockery, "See, Ideus! How do you think it's going? Your beloved has gone somewhat astray. That's what I think about the state she's in, since you could mock all of us, and yet we can all truly see that your beloved is not well covered up, where her loins are bare. Now I say, to all who can hear, that she is accustomed to let herself be shamelessly served from behind, just as the mantle clearly shows."

Ideus didn't know what to say; he just seized the mantle in grief and anger and flung it at the king's feet. Kay took Ideus's beloved by the hand and led her to where the others who had previously worn the mantle were sitting, and he said, "By my faith, soon there will be a great and goodly company here."

CHAPTER X

Now there was nothing else to be done but to have all the women who had come, both ladies and maidens, older and younger, dress themselves in the mantle as quickly as possible, one after another. It fit none of them—with all their lovers watching. Kay took each of them by the hand and led her to a seat in the great circle of women on the floor of the hall. There was not one in all the multitude of rulers and knights there who did not have a beloved lady there, and whoever saw his face might quickly find grief and sorrow on it. But there was this for comfort: no one could mock anyone else without finding himself in the same situation.

Kay the Seneschal spoke: "Good rulers," he said, "do not be angry or aggrieved at this, for we are all in rather the same condition. Our beloved ladies have been much honored and renowned, far above all other court ladies near and far, wherever they may be. Today they have won great fame for themselves. But this may be the greatest comfort for them: no one can blame another."

Sir Gawain answered, "I do not find that you are looking at this matter correctly, because it would be abhorrent and monstrous in every way if I were to take comfort from this disgrace. We will never agree that a good warrior becomes worthless because his beloved has committed adultery with another man. Rather, let her bear the blame of her own deeds and lusts herself, along with the man who consented to her wicked schemes."

At that moment, the lad rushed in before the king and said, "I am afraid, my lord, that I must take back the mantle, although I don't see how it is possible that one woman who may wear the mantle cannot be found, out of such a large company. Have your upper chambers searched, where the women are accustomed to sleep or to sit, so that no one is hidden or concealed there, because the folk of your court have praise and fame above all people in the world. But if I have to leave with matters left as they now stand, fewer tidings will come to you from now on than before, if I must part from you with my errand unfinished."

"By my faith," said Sir Gawain, "the lad speaks truly. Let the upper chambers be searched as quickly as possible, so that no one may be hidden there."

The king ordered that all the upper chambers be searched. And when he had so commanded, Gerflet the Fool rushed into the upper chamber as quickly as possible and found a young lady there. She had not hidden herself; rather, she was feeling a certain heaviness, and she had lain down in a bed. Gerflet the Fool spoke to her at once. "My lady," said he, "never did a man see a more beautiful event than the one that is taking place in the king's hall. You must certainly take your part, as all the others have taken part."

"Certainly I will get up," said the maiden, and she dressed herself in the best fashion and in the most beautiful clothes that she had—and they were very good, for she was descended from a rich family—and then she entered the hall. Her lover was there already, happy and cheerful before she entered. But he grew grieved and angry when he saw her arriving, because he never wanted her to take the mantle, since he loved her so much. Even though he would know the truth about her infidelity, he did not care about that, because he never wanted to forsake her, on account of the great love that he had for her.

Just then, the lad brought her the mantle and told her with what power it was woven. Karadin, her lover, called out in a loud voice to those who could hear. "Sweet beloved," he said, "if you have done anything wrong, never come near the mantle. I would certainly not lose your love for all the world's gold, even if I knew you to be unfaithful, because I love you with all my heart."

Kay the Seneschal said, "Why are you talking like this? He who loses a faithless lover may be glad and cheerful."

But the maiden answered with a cheerful expression. "My lord," she said, "if a good man's lover is proved to be untrue to him, it may truly bring him lasting grief. But if my lover does not object, I will accept the mantle."

"By my faith," said the knight,[16] "you may not get out of this in any way, nor refuse it, because all the other ladies have put it on."

Yet she was not willing to take the mantle until her lover gave her permission. As soon as he gave her leave, she accepted the mantle and dressed herself in it before all the court. And it fitted her so perfectly that it was nowhere too short, nor too long; rather, it touched the ground in all directions around her.

Then the lad said, "By my faith, well and truly may one ask for the hand of this maiden. My lady, it seems to me that your lover may be happier than the others that are here. Now you shall know as truth that I have brought this mantle into a great many courts, so that more than a thousand of those who were called maidens have shown themselves to be false under this mantle. It has never before revealed anyone like you in the purity of maidenhood. And now I agree to give you this precious mantle, so excellent that there is not its like in the world, for no man can value it rightly. You alone may rightly wear it, keep it and have it and give it to your heirs."

Thus the lad ended his speech. Then the king spoke up and said that she alone might rightly own the mantle, and that she alone was worthy to own it.

CHAPTER XI
The Messenger's Departure

Although all the women sitting there in the circle were envious, for they all wanted to own the mantle, not one of them could get it, and not one of them dared to speak against it. Then Sir Gawain spoke. "I take this in hand on your behalf, lovely maiden," he said. "You do not owe anyone anything for the mantle, except the purity of your maidenhood, so that all men and women who see your goodness now agree that you should have it. The ladies would certainly speak out against you if they could find true cause. But now it has been established that their envy and sorrow is your joy, their grief is your comfort, their dishonor is your honor, and their faithlessness will be your praise, growing in every land."

Then the lad took his leave of the king. He did not wish to stay there at all, and he did not want to eat. Rather, he wanted to hurry back to his lady and bring her the news of his errand. The king sat down at the table with all his court, and truly it may be said that many a good knight sat there grieved on account of his beloved. But King Arthur feasted his court with such lavishness that there has never been another feast given or received like it.

When the court was fed, Karadin came before the king and received permission from him to go away. He left with his beloved, happy and cheerful. They placed the mantle in a certain monastery for safekeeping.

Now there is curiosity about it again. The man who owns it says that he shall bring it everywhere to test lovely maidens and beautiful women. We expect that few ladies will be found who may own it, so it will stay new for a long time. He who has the mantle intends to send it to all courts, so that all the ladies and maidens of the court shall dress themselves in it. But

I don't want to be the messenger who brings the mantle, to be treated badly by powerful men for such an offer. Now let no one say anything about ladies but good, because it is more honorable to conceal transgressions than to speak openly about them, even if a man knows them to be true.[17] For each lady who puts on the mantle, it shows what sort of person she is who dresses herself in it. And so we may praise good women according to their merits—because they have become famous and celebrated.

Now here ends the Saga of the Mantle, and may you live well for many good days. Amen.

Lais of Marie de France

Strengleikar

In the late 12th century, an author now known as Marie de France[1] composed a set of lais—chivalric tales in verse, celebrating courtly love and warning of its dangers. Although Marie's lais are in Norman French, and she herself may have lived in England, she claimed that they are retellings of lays by Breton poets; many are set in or near Brittany and contain Breton terms or personal names.

Eleven of Marie's lais, plus ten more lais by unknown authors,[2] were translated into Norse, forming a collection called Strengleikar, literally "Stringed Instruments." The translator's prologue states that "King Hákon" had them translated—presumably Hákon IV of Norway, who is credited with sponsoring other translations (including Parcevals saga and Möttuls saga in this book). The unknown translator was possibly a Norwegian student, cleric, or envoy who found the lais in England and translated them at some time between 1220 and 1260.[3] The translations follow the French text fairly closely, although the verse is turned into prose, some descriptive passages are left out, and the translator adds occasional explanations of matters that may not have been familiar to his audience.[4]

Almost all of the Strengleikar are known from only one manuscript: Uppsala DG 4-7, dated to approximately 1270 and probably written in southwestern Norway, in or near Bergen. The manuscript unfortunately has lost several leaves, and several of the lais are incomplete.[5] An 18th-century Icelandic manuscript containing a lai[6], as well as allusions in other sagas and folktales, hint that at least some of the Strengleikar were more widely known in Iceland than the surviving evidence would suggest.[7]

Four of Marie's lais have been selected for this anthology, in the order in which they appear in the manuscript. Bisclaret (Bisclavret) presents a version of the werewolf legend. The brief Laustik (Laustic) is a tragic depiction of idealized courtly love; the equally brief Geitarlauf (Chevrefeuil) deals with the doomed love of Tristram and Iseult. Janual (Lanval), set at King Arthur's court, presents a variant of a widespread motif in Celtic myth, the "Offended Fée" who must leave her mortal lover if he speaks her name, tells anyone about her, or performs *some other forbidden action.*[8] *Unfortunately the manuscript is missing the beginning, which has been supplied here from Marie's French text.*

My translation has been made from the electronic critical edition published by MENOTA, the Medieval Norse Text Archive. I have also consulted Aðalheiður Guðmundsdóttir's normalized text, Robert Cook and Matthias Tveitane's edition and translation, and Alfred Ewert's edition of the French text.

Preface by the Norse Translator

It has pleased us to seek out and investigate the ways of those men who lived in ancient times, because they were skillful in their crafts, clear-sighted in their discernment, intelligent in counsels, bold with weapons, conversant with courtly custom, generous with gifts, and most famous for all kinds of valor. And because many wondrous things happened in olden times, events unheard of in our days, it occurred to us to teach, to those present and those yet to come, these stories which highly learned men made about those events that happened in olden times and wrote down in books as everlasting reminders, as entertainment, and as great instruction for peoples yet to come—so that each man might improve and enlighten his own life from the knowledge of these past matters; so that that which took place in the beginning may not be concealed in these latter days; and so that each man may thus consider with all his mind, and strive with all his might, and achieve and fulfill with all his means, to prepare and improve himself for the Kingdom of God by respectable habits and good deeds and a holy death. Because bold deeds and bravery and all manner of goodness are the ornaments and splendor of the lives of those who are pleasing to God, and of those who became most celebrated and beloved in all the world in ancient times, these things vanish all the more thoroughly as the world of these days slips away more and more.

This book, which the worthy lord King Hakon had translated into Norse from the French language, may be called the Book of Songs, because poets in Brittany[9]—which lies in France—made songs from these tales that this book discloses, which were played on harps, viols, hurdy-gurdies, lyres, dulcimers, psalteries, zithers, and all other sorts of stringed instruments which men make during their lives to have pleasure for themselves and others.

Here ends this preface, and the beginning of these songs comes next.

Marie de France's Preface

For all those to whom God has granted wisdom and knowledge and the eloquence to reveal them, it is not fitting to hide or conceal God's gift inside themselves. Rather, it is fitting for them to show others, with good will, what it has pleased God to lend them. Then they will bear leaves and flowers like the finest of trees, and as their goodness becomes known through the improvement of others, their fruit ripens and nourishes others.

It was the custom of the wise and courteous men of old that they should express their learning, so to speak, with obscure words and deep meanings for the sake of those who were yet to come—so that those men might explain in illuminating discourse what the others had said before, and search their own wits for whatever pertained to the explanations and correct interpretations of the teachings that the wise men of old, the *philosophi*, have created.

As the world and the lives of men have continued, skill and heedfulness and attention to detail have increased in many ways, so that the most knowledgeable men in every country came to speak in their native language. And it befits those who want to keep their own lives blameless always to ponder and labor over something that will make them well beloved, and which will make others wise from their own art. For that reason, I considered making some good tale and translating it from French into Latin, so that what most could understand, most would find comforting.[10] But the songs that I have heard were made in Brittany, concerning wondrous events that took place in that land. It has pleased me to translate them and tell them to others, because I have heard a great deal that I am certainly willing to reveal, concealing nothing of what I can call to mind, for a certain courteous king,[11] to whom God grants wisdom and power over us, good fortune, and manifold abundance of the most celebrated excellence. Therefore, I have often considered collecting all the lais into one book to bring to you, my lord, the courteous king. If they please you, I am happy that my labors bring pleasure and ease to such a wise king and the courteous clerks and mannerly men[12] of his court.

Bisclaret

Here is the Lay of Bisclaret

Now since I am endeavoring to create and tell you songs and lays, I do not wish to forget Bisclaret. Bisclaret was a knight, brave and courteous, bold with his weapons, never one to flee. His name was *Bisclaret* in the Breton tongue,[13] but Norsemen called him *Vargulf*.[14]

In olden times, one might hear about something that could frequently happen: many men changed their shape and became wolves and lived in woods and forests. There they had homes and rich households. But a werewolf was only an animal while he was in wolf-shape; then he tore men in his fury if he caught them, and he did great evil. He rushed through the forests and through the woods and lived there while he was in that shape.[15] Now I will set that aside, because I want to tell you about Bisclaret.

In Brittany there lived an excellent man, the most honorable and the most praiseworthy of all his peers. The splendid knight maintained himself well and richly, and was the dearest of men to his lord, blessed with friends and benevolent to all his neighbors. This man married a beautiful wife, wise and well-mannered, and they loved each other. Now there was one matter that distressed her the most: she found him absent for three whole days in each week, so that she did not know where he went, nor what became of him. None of his men could tell her anything about him.

One day, when he had come home and was in his hall, cheerful and glad, she asked him about it. "My lord," she said, "most handsome beloved, I yearn to ask you about one matter, if only I dared. Don't be angry."

As soon as he heard her words, he placed his arms around her neck and drew her close and kissed her, and he spoke to her. "Beloved," he said, "Ask what you wish. There is nothing that you want to know, and that is known to me, that I will not tell you with honest good will."

"By my faith, my lord," she said, "you comfort me greatly. My lord, I am constantly distressed and frightened and grieving deeply by day, and I am completely sick at heart and sorrowful, when I am parted from you. I am very much afraid that I will lose you. Unless you comfort me quickly, I will suffer death from this grief. Now, dearest beloved," she said, "I beg of you, as you value my life—tell me where you go and where you are and in what place you stay, because I fear that you love some woman besides me. If it is so, then you are cold and cruel, and I am disgraced and will surely die from this grief."

"My lady," he said, "have mercy on me with your words! For it will end in suffering and harm for me if I tell you. I would lose your love and destroy myself."

When she had heard his words, she was not willing to let matters rest there, by any means. Rather, she coaxed him and wearied him with her pleadings and entreaties for such a long time that he explained his entire situation to her. "My lady," said he, "I am a shapeshifter. All by myself I rush through the woods where they are thickest, and I live on the flesh of the beasts that I kill."

When he had told her the whole story, she asked him at once whether he went clothed or naked. "My lady," he said, "I run naked."

"My lord," she said, "where are your clothes then?"

"My lady," he said, "I will not tell anyone, because if my clothes were taken from me, and someone were to find out where they were lying, I would be in that shape forever, and never have rest or calm, nor return to human form, until my clothes were returned to me. I will tell no one where I keep them."

Then she answered, "My lord, I love you above anything in the world. It is unworthy of you to conceal anything from me, because it is unworthy of you to have evil suspicions or any mistrust of me. If I wanted to deceive you, there would truly be no love for you within me. Tell me, and don't be afraid of anything. Tell me, and profit and good fortune will come about for you."

So long and so much did she entice him with her entreaties, and so well was he pleased with her pleadings, that she drove him aground. He could not resist her entreaties and enticements, and he told her everything. "My lady," he said, "in the forest, beside a path where I am accustomed to go, there is an old chapel that has done me much good, and where you have often received aid and help. There is a stone carved with a hollow inside, beside a bush. There I place my clothes while I am outdoors, until I return home."

When this lady had heard these strange tidings, she screamed, terrified of what had happened. She pondered carefully how she might be separated from him, so that she would not lie beside him again. Now there was one knight in the shire who had loved her for a long time, and who had long entreated her and often tried to turn her will to his own lust. He had given her many gifts and rendered her much service, but still she had not loved him at all and had not agreed to any of his entreaties. But now she sent her messenger to him, turning to him with all her heart. She told him in a letter: "Dearest, be happy now, cheerful and glad, because that which you have long been pining for, I grant you now: my love and my body. You shall make me your lover." He thanked her with many thanks and accepted her trust and her pledge. Then he took an oath from her, so that he would be secure and live without fear.

When their oath and partnership were pledged, she confessed everything and told him all that her husband had told her: how he shifted his shape, and where he went, and where he was while he was in wolf's shape. She revealed all these things to him. Then she directed him to the woods and told him where her husband's clothes were lying, and said that he should bring them home with him. In this way, Lord Bisclaret was betrayed and mistreated by the wickedness of his own wife. And because he disappeared so often, everyone thought that he was completely lost now. He was inquired about and searched for everywhere, but no one had any news of him, and he wasn't found anywhere. For that reason he was quickly forgotten, like a man who has died. The man who had loved Bisclaret's wife for a long time settled down with her.

So matters stood for twelve months, until the king went out hunting in the same woods where Bisclaret was. As soon as the hounds were loosed, they found Bisclaret, and all the hounds and huntsmen chased him all day, so that they had nearly captured and cut and killed him when he recognized the king. He rushed to him at once to beg for mercy. When he reached him, he laid both feet on the king's knee and kissed his legs and feet.

When the king saw him, he was very afraid, and he called out to his men. "Lords," he said, "come quickly and see what a wonder is here. This beast has human reason. It humbles itself and begs for mercy. Drive all the hounds away and take care that no one strikes or hurts it, because this beast has sense and discernment, and it certainly recognizes me, as I think. I grant my peace and truce to this beast, and I will not hunt here all day."

Then the king turned and headed for home. Bisclaret followed him as closely as he could, and would not be parted from him by any means. The king kept him with him in his castle and cared for him, and he was delighted with the beast. He ordered all his courtiers that no one who wanted to have his friendship should injure or strike his beast, because he had never before seen such a beast, and therefore he thought it was wondrous. He cared for it with great affection, with good victuals and the choicest drink, and everyone heeded the king's orders to treat the beast well. It was always among the best knights, those dearest to the king, and it slept every night beside the king's bed. This beast was dear to every man in the king's court. And every time that the king left home, the beast followed the king, and the king found that the beast loved him. It was so courteous and gentle and mild and full of good will; it never got angry with people, and it harmed no one. For that reason, it was liked well by all men.

Now it is time to tell of what happened next: The king held a lavish feast in honor of a royal holiday, and he summoned all the knights and powerful men and friends of his, who held their estates and rulership and honors in fief from him, to come and celebrate his holiday and receive his hospitality. But among the crowd and company, there came the knight who had married Bisclaret's wife, richly clad in style befitting a knight. It did not enter his mind that he might find Bisclaret so nigh and near to himself. When he came into the king's hall and Bisclaret recognized him, he leaped at him and seized him with his teeth and flung him to the ground. He would have bitten him and torn him and done him irreparable harm right then, were it not for the king, who shouted at him and threatened him. On that same day, he made a second attack on him, and had he not been fettered, he would have avenged himself so properly that not a thing would have been lacking. Everyone found this strange, and everyone in the king's hall and household was quite astonished. Most of them discussed what this could mean, because he had never acted this way to anyone in the court before, nor to anyone who had visited, and they decided that he must not have done this without cause. They said, "Surely this knight must have done him some harm and mistreated him, for him to show more ferocity to that knight than to any other man who has come. He was eager to avenge himself if he could." Thus matters stood for the time being.

Now when the king had offered his lavish feast and held it honorably, the great host of earls and landholders and knights received leave from the king to travel to their homes. First of all those departing was that knight whom Bisclaret wanted to bite, glad that he had gotten away. It was not surprising that Bisclaret wanted to avenge himself on the man who had taken his clothes so that he could not change his shape back.

Now it was a little while later when the noble king went hunting a second time in the same woods in which he had found the beast. Bisclaret went with him. Late in the evening, when the king came out of the woods, splendid lodgings were obtained for him in that same district. When Bisclaret's wife found out that the king had arrived, she dressed herself in her finest clothes. In the morning she came to the king to meet him, and she had many valuable and fine offerings brought for him. But as soon as Bisclaret saw her coming there, no one could hold him, and nothing restrained him. He charged at her as if he were mad, and all could see how well he avenged himself. He reared up and tore off her clothes—he could do no worse disgrace to her.[16] Everyone threatened him and would have beaten him if there had not been one wise man there who spoke to the king. "My lord," he said, "listen to what I wish to tell you. This beast has been with us for a long time, and every one of our men has often seen it and gone near it, both night and day. It has never shown fierceness nor hostility towards any man, except this woman whom we see has come here. By God and my faith, he has some reason above all to be angry at her and also her husband. This woman married the knight who was your dearest friend, but now it has been such a long time since men have seen him that no one knows what has become of him, and we have heard no news of him. Take this woman and have her tortured until she confesses why this beast hates her. She will reveal to us what she knows. Many strange happenings have we seen here in Brittany."

The king hearkened and agreed to his advice and counsel at once, because he was the most intelligent of his counsellors. He had the knight who had married her imprisoned there, but he had her kept all by herself, and he pressed her so much that, for love of her husband[17] and fear of the king, she confessed everything that had had happened: how they had taken the clothes from her first husband, and how he had told her everything about his condition, how he changed shape and where he went. She said that ever since she had his clothes taken from him, he had never been seen in the district. She thought it certain, and truly believed, that this beast was her husband and her lord, without a doubt.

The king demanded his clothes and garments from her, and he said that he would surely have them, whether she liked it or not. He had her bring back his outfit. The king had them brought to Bisclaret, but he didn't want to look at them when they were placed before him. Then the king's chief counsellor, who had previously advised him concerning Bisclaret, spoke with him privately. "My lord," he said, "you are not doing things correctly. He will never accept his clothes here before our eyes, nor change his shape before so many men. You see what is happening: he finds his condition a shame and disgrace. Have him brought into your sleeping quarters alone, along with his outfit, and leave him alone for a very long time."

The king himself led Bisclaret into his sleeping loft; he closed it himself and locked all the doors. When some time had passed, the king went back, and two earls went with him. When they came into the sleeping loft, they found the knight, dressed in his full outfit, sleeping in the king's own bed. When the king saw him, he hurried to him and threw his arms around his neck and kissed him many times, so glad was he to find him.

In the end, the king gave him much more than he had had before, more than we are able to tell you. The king drove Bisclaret's wife out of the district and made her an outlaw for all the days of her life. The man who had married her went with her, because she had betrayed her husband for his sake. Later on, they had many children, and they were all easily recognized. Many women are descended from her and her offspring, and all of them had no noses—they were noseless.[18]

Now there's nothing to be found that is more true than this event that we have related to you, because many strange things happened in olden times that no one hears of now. The man who translated this book into Norse saw, in his childhood, a prominent farmer who shape-shifted. At times he was a man, at times he was in wolf-shape, and he told everything that wolves got up to. There's nothing more to tell about him.[19] But the Bretons made the Lay of Bisclaret from this story which you have now heard.

Laustik

CHAPTER I

Now I want to tell you of an occurrence about which the Bretons made a lay, and they call this lay *Laustik.* Such is its name in the Breton speech,[20] but in French it is *Russinol*, and in English *Nictigal*: the nightingale. This is a little bird. As soon as summer begins, it sings and calls through the night, with a voice so beautiful and soft that it is lovely and delightful to listen to.[21]

CHAPTER II

In the shire of Brittany where Saint Malo sleeps, there is a strong and famous town.[22] In this town there lived two knights, and each of them had his own stronghold. One of them was married to a fair and fine lady, clever and courtly. The other was known to all, gracious and helpful to worthy men and to his peers. This young knight loved his neighbor's wife. So much and so long did he plead with her, and such goodness did she find in him, that she loved him above all others.[23] From the loft where she slept, she could speak with her beloved when she stood or sat in her loft, and he could speak with her from his loft in the same way. This did not displease them, for they both lived in contentment—except for one thing: they could not meet, as they yearned to do. In this fashion they loved each other for a long time.

Now on one occasion, when summer began, the nightingale began to sing the most beautiful song, and he called his mate to renewed love beneath the broad leaves and flowers. One who was in love might think deeply about whatever he desired to love, because of the bird's songs. Because the knight was in love, he set his heart on the songs of the birds, as if all that he yearned for might be there, and he listened with rapt attention to the birds' songs which urged him on to love. The lady whom he loved so much saw what her beloved was up to. In the moonlight, when her lord was asleep, she got up from his bed and dressed in her cloak and went to stand by the window, because she knew that her beloved was standing on the other side in the other window and lived such a life that he stayed awake almost all night.

It came to pass that her lord and husband became angry at her getting up so often, and he accused her with many harsh words and demanded to know why she got up and where she went. She replied, "My lord, there is no man living in this world, if he hears the *laustik*, the little bird and its voice—with how fair a voice does it sing all night long!—who cannot be comforted and cheered from such fair songs as it sings. That is why I went to the window: I stand there to listen to its beautiful sweet songs. By no means will I conceal this from you any longer."

CHAPTER III

When her lord had heard this, he fell silent from grief and anger, and he decided that he must certainly catch the nightingale in a trap. He told his servants, and at once they made plans and traps to catch the nightingale. They smeared birdlime and attached traps on every branch of all the trees there were in the stronghold, so that at last they caught the nightingale and brought it alive to their lord and master. He cheered up at once and rejoiced that he had caught the bird, and he went into the sleeping quarters. "My lady," he said, "come here and talk to us. I've trapped your nightingale now, since you've been tossing and turning every night and staying awake for so long."

When the lady heard his words, she grew angry and sorrowful, and she begged her lord to give the bird to her. But in his anger he threw it at her breast, dead, so that he stained her linen shift with blood from the slain bird.[24]

The lady took up the bird's body and wept bitterly, and she cursed all those who had chosen to catch the nightingale and all those who had made snares to entrap the nightingale and capture it. She took cloth of gold and wrapped the body of the nightingale in it, and all around she embroidered her sorrow and sadness at its death, in golden letters. Then she called the most trustworthy of her pageboys, and she told him to carry the bird to her beloved, laid out in this way, and for him to tell him how her lord trapped the bird, and for him to tell her beloved her sorrow and sadness over what had happened.

When the page came to him, he brought him the bird and told him everything that his lady had bade him. He, the most courteous knight, was deeply grieved that the nightingale had been trapped out of such envy and spite. He had a golden vessel made for it, sealed with a golden lid, and he had precious gems set all around, beautifully arranged with great skill. And he laid the nightingale in this vessel.

This news spread throughout Brittany, and the Bretons made this lay about these events, which they call the Lay of Laustik.

Geitarlauf

The English call this Gotulæf, but we call it Geitarlauf

I am most pleased and eager to show you the *lai* that is called *Chefrefuillinn* in French, or *Geitarlauf* in Norse,[25] and where this lay was made and recited, and in what fashion. I have read in a book what many people say and affirm about Tristram and the queen and the most faithful love between them, from which they suffered much grievous woe. In the end, they both died on the same day.

King Marhes was angry at his kinsman Tristram and banished him from his kingdom, for the reason that Tristram loved the queen. Tristram traveled to his homeland, South Wales, where he was born and raised, and he stayed there for a full twelve months, since he did not get permission to return. Then he risked his life—do not let yourselves find this strange, because he who loves faithfully is most grieved when he cannot have his will and his desire. Tristram was very sad, and so he left his homeland and sailed to Cornwall, where the queen ruled, and he hid in the forest all alone. When evening came, he left the woods and found lodgings, and asked what news there was of the king. Those who had heard told him that all gentry and nobles were to assemble at Tintagel, because the king wanted to hold a festival there and entertain all his courtiers and nobles. All had to be there on Pentecost, and there would be no lack of entertainment and lavish celebration, and the queen had to attend. When Tristram had heard this, he was much comforted, because she could not travel along that road without him seeing her.

Now on the day when he knew that the king had to travel that way, Tristan entered the forest beside the roads that he knew the queen had to ride. He cut down a hazel sapling and shaped it with his knife to have four sides, and he carved his own name on the staff. If it so happens that the queen sees the staff, she will think of her lover, because this has happened to her on other occasions. Now it was carved on the staff[26] that Tristram had awaited her there for a long time, and was listening for news of her and find out how he might see her, because he could not live without her by any means. "So it is with us," he said, "as with the honeysuckle that is twined around the hazel. While these two trees both live together, they live and bear their leaves. But should someone separate these trees from each other, the hazel dies, and then the honeysuckle; it bears no leaves, and both wither and perish. Beautiful beloved of mine, we two are just the same. I cannot live without you, and you cannot live without me."

The queen came riding up, and she saw the staff that was standing in the road. She picked it up and read what was carved on it. She had the knights who accompanied her stay where they were, and she ordered them to wait for her. She said that she wanted to dismount from her horse and rest there for a while. They did as she commanded. But she walked very far from her men, and she called her maidservant, who was named Brengvein, always gracious and true to her. Then she left the path—and she found the one whom she loved so much above all living creatures, and there was a most joyous reunion for the two of them. She told him everything that she wanted to tell, at her leisure; and he spoke the same way to her. Then she told him how he could reach a settlement and gain the confidence of her lord the king—and that the king deeply repented that he had driven him away and believed the false counsels of wicked men. And then she parted from her lover. When their parting came, they both wept.

Tristram stayed in Wales until the king, his mother's brother, sent for him and put aside his anger at him. Now, from the joy that he had in the forest from the queen's comfort, and from seeing and meeting her, and in order to remember the words that she spoke, Tristram, who was a master of all manner of songs made upon the harp, composed a new lay. The Britons call it *Gotulæf*, French men call it *Chefrefuill*, and we may call it *Geitarlauf*. And now I have told you what I know to be truest, concerning this entertainment.

This is Geitarlauf.

Janual

[I will tell you the story of another lay, as it happened. It was made concerning a certain noble knight, who bore the name *Lanval* in Breton.[27]

Arthur, the worthy and courteous king, was staying at Carlisle on account of the Scots and Picts who were destroying the land, invading the country of Logres and causing much damage. The king stayed there, at the summer feast of Pentecost, to give out plenty of rich gifts to his counts and barons and to the knights of the Round Table—they had no peers in all the world! He distributed wives and lands to all, except to one man who had served him. That was Janual; he did not remember him, nor did he care for him. The majority envied him for his valor, his generosity, his handsomeness, his bravery. Those who pretended to show him love would not have wept once if the knight had suffered misfortune. He was the son of a king, of high birth, but far from his native country; he was of the king's household. He had spent all he had, for the king gave him nothing, nor did Janual ask for anything. Now Janual was deeply troubled, very sad and very anxious. My lords, do not be astonished: whoever is a stranger, with no resources, is terribly sad in another land, when he does not know where to go for help.

This knight of whom I have told you, who had served the king so much, mounted his steed one day and went to amuse himself. He rode out of town; all alone, he came to a meadow. He dismounted beside a flowing stream, but his horse began to tremble very much; he unsaddled him and let him roll in the meadow. He folded his cloak under his head when he lay down. He was deeply troubled over his hardships, and he saw nothing that could please him.

He lay there in this manner, observing the valley beside the stream, when he saw two maidens arriving. He had never seen maidens more lovely. They were dressed richly in two tunics of fine purple cloth, laced up tightly, and quite beautiful were their faces. The older one was carrying basins of refined gold, well made and fine—I tell you the truth without deceit—and the other carried a towel. They were coming straight to where the knight was lying. Lanval, who was very well-bred, rose to his feet to meet them. These ladies first greeted him, and then told him their message: "Sir Lanval! My lady, who is exceptionally courtly and beautiful, has sent us for you, so come with us! We will conduct you there in safety. See, her pavilion is close by!"

The knight went with them. He took no notice of his horse, which was grazing in the meadow before him. They brought him to a tent, which was most beautiful and finely bedecked. Not even Queen Semiramis[28] at the very height of her wealth and power and wisdom, nor the Emperor Octavian,[29] could have afforded the right-hand flap. An eagle of gold was placed on top; I can't tell the price of it, nor of the cords or the stakes which held up the panels of that tent. Not a king under the heavens could have bought it at any price he might pay.

Within this tent was the maiden. In beauty she surpassed a lily or a new rose when it appears in the season of summer. She lay upon a most beautiful bed—the sheet was worth as much as a castle—in nothing but her chemise. Her body was most shapely and fair. A costly cloak of white ermine fur, lined with purple cloth from Alexandria, she had thrown off on account of the heat, completely exposing her side, her face, her neck and breast, whiter than hawthorn flowers.

The knight stepped forward, and the maiden beckoned to him. He sat down beside the bed. "Lanval," she said, "dear friend, I have come from my homeland for you; I have come a long way to search for you. If you are worthy and courteous, no emperor or count or king will ever have as much joy or good fortune, for I love you above all else."

He looked at her; he saw that she was beautiful. Love struck the spark that lit his heart and set it ablaze. He replied to her respectfully. "Beautiful one," he said, "if it pleases you to love me, and if this joy befalls me, you will not be able to command anything that I will not do to the best of my ability, whether wise or foolish. I will carry out your commands, and for you I will forsake all others. I never wish to leave you; there is nothing that I desire more."

When the maiden heard him say that he could love her so much, she granted him her love and her heart. Now Lanval is set right! Afterwards, she gave him a gift: never more would he wish for anything that he could not have. When he gives and spends lavishly, she will find the means for him. Now Lanval is well provided for! The more lavishly he spends, the more gold and silver he will have.

"Dear friend," she said, "I warn you, I command you, I entreat you: do not reveal yourself to any man! I will tell you exactly what will happen: on the day that this love is discovered, you will have lost me. You will not be able to see me, nor have any right to my body."

He answered that he would keep well what she had commanded. He lay down beside her in bed. Now Lanval is lodged well! Lying beside her, he put off getting up until the evening. . . .][30]

. . . . and he would have stayed there longer, if it had pleased her. She spoke to him. "Beloved," she said, "stand up. You may not stay here longer.

It is best for you to go away now, and I will stay behind. But I will tell you one thing: every time that you wish to speak with me, think of a place that you see where it is suitable for a man to speak with and meet his beloved, free from scandal and blame, away from the sight of men. Then you shall see me beside you, and do what you wish."

As soon as he had heard that, he was most glad, and he thanked her with many thanks, kissing her and embracing her neck. The maidens who led him into the tent dressed him in a fine suit of clothes. When he was so richly clad, he looked like the most handsome of men. He took supper there with his beloved, which he could hardly refuse. There was no lack of all sorts of dishes, but the knight felt satisfied with kisses and embraces from his beloved. When they got up from the supper table, they led his horse to him, and he took his leave and mounted his horse and rode to the castle, thinking deeply on what had happened. He was uncertain in his mind how this matter would turn out.

When he came to his house, he found his men well dressed. That night he held a lavish feast, and no one knew from where those provisions had come to him. He sent word all through the town that all knights who were in need of help should come to him, and he assisted them well and worthily, with abundant good cheer. Janual gave them many rich gifts. He redeemed those who had been captured in wars. Janual gave clothing to those who were minstrels. There was no foreigner, nor mute person,[31] to whom Janual did not give gifts. Janual had great joy by night and by day, because he often spoke with his lover, and she was everything that he might wish for.

Now as I was told, in the summer of that same year, after St. John's Eve,[32] thirty knights of the king's household all went together to amuse themselves in the garden below the castle towers. All sorts of sweet herbs scented the air. In their company was Sir Gawain, and his handsome kinsman and fellow Sir Ywain.[33]

Sir Gawain spoke, the good and courteous knight who befriended every man. "My lords," he said, "we have poorly treated our comrade Janual, who is so generous and courteous, and the son of a king. We have not invited him to come with us." They turned back to his home, and after their entreaties and invitations, he went with them to share in their fellowship.

But at the same time, on that same day, the queen was sitting in her upper room and peering through a carved window, with three lovely ladies beside her. She recognized the household troops of the king, and Janual with them. She told one of the ladies with her that she was to summon all the loveliest of her maidens, because she wanted to go down into the garden to amuse herself alongside the king's knights. More than thirty maidens went with her, those who were the most beautiful and courteous. She went down the steps. The knights all went to meet them and welcomed them with great good will and courtly manners. Each of them led his own lady, and when they had sat down they held refined conversation and enjoyed more courtly amusements.

Sir Janual went off by himself, and he did not care to make the acquaintance of the queen or her maidens. He sat down far away from them, and he longed for his beloved, to kiss her and embrace her and sport with her in well-mannered play. But because he did not have what pleased him, he cared nothing when he saw them amuse themselves.

Now when the queen saw that he was sitting by himself, far from the others, she went straight to him and sat down beside him and called him, and made all her intentions clear to him. "Sir Janual," she said, "long have I loved you deeply, praised you and extolled you above many. Often have I yearned for you with great desire. You may have all my affection. Tell me quickly what you wish."

"My lady," he said, "do not speak so. Truly, neither your love nor your desire pleases me. Neither for your sake, or for the sake of your love, will I be a betrayer or a disgrace to my lord."

Then the queen became angry, and in her anger she slandered him. "Janual," she said, "I am sure that you have little liking for women's love or for dealings with them, because it pleases you better to carry on with young boys and work your sinful will on them. Such is the amusement that pleases you."

When Janual heard that, he suffered great anguish and sorrow from her words, and he was too quick to give her an answer that he would often repent. In his grief, he spoke: "Lady," he said, "I have never taken up that sort of business, and never entered into that wickedness. Rather, I am the lover of the only lady, of all those whom I know to be living, who is worthy of praise and celebration. Know this as well, my lady," he said. "I tell you plainly that the lowliest of her servants is lovelier than you, lady queen."

The queen stood up, and in her anger she went away into the king's chamber, weeping. She lay down on her bed and declared that she was sick. She said openly that she would never get up until the king did justice for her, because Janual had disdained her and slandered her.

The king came from hunting in the forest, where he went to catch game. When he came into the queen's chamber and the queen saw him, she complained to him about Janual, who had disdained her. She told him that Janual had begged for her affections. But since she had refused him, he had shamed her with his words and boasted that he had a lover who was so glorious and wealthy and powerful, that he said that his lover's lowliest serving-maid was finer than the queen.

At once the king grew very angry, and he swore a great oath: if Janual could not justly defend himself against the king's accusations, the king would have him burned at the stake, or else would hang him on a gallows like a thief. The king left his chamber and summoned three of his friends, and he sent them after Janual, who had quite enough grief and trouble. He was then at home in his house, and he found out that he had truly lost his lover, because he had violated her affections and revealed them. He was all alone in his bedroom, with his mind filled with anguish and great distress. Very often he called to his beloved, but that did him no good at all. He could never cry out nor express his grief in such a way that she would take pity on him. How must he look now?

At that moment, the king's messengers arrived and told him that he was to come to the king, as the king had ordered him, with the slanderous words that the queen had spoken of him. Janual would have killed himself if he could, in the terrible grief that he suffered then.

When he came before the king, he appeared just as he was: sick at heart and sorrowful, listless and sad. The king spoke to him in great anger. "You dolt," he said, "you have disgraced me terribly and acted shamefully towards me. This day you have begun a wicked and worthless business. You have disgraced me and mocked the queen. You have made a most foolish boast. Your beloved is too lovely and too glorious, if her serving-maid is finer and wiser than our queen."

Janual defended himself with many avowals that he had never disgraced his own lord. "But now I have lost my beloved," he said, "because I boasted of her affection. That is why I am filled with grief." But he was willing to submit to those accusations with which the king charged him—those that the king's court could see were true. The king was very angry, and he sent at once for all his courtiers to judge what was right, so that the king would not be blamed. They did as he had ordered, whether they liked it or not. Once everyone had arrived, they all judged that Janual should have one appointed day to answer for himself. In the meantime, Janual should get men to pledge that he would abide by his sentence to appear before the king. By that time, the king's court would have more people, because few men were at home except for those nearest and dearest to the king. They sent word to the king and explained to him how the state of the case looked to them. The king demanded that they provide someone to provide surety. But Janual was still all alone, far from his kinsmen and friends.

At that moment, Sir Gawain and all his companions came and pledged surety for him. Then the king spoke: "I place Janual in your keeping," he said, "on pain of surrendering everything that you have received from me, estates and castles and rich towns and all manner of other rich gifts that are given and received for the honor of noble men."

Once they had pledged surety, they went to their own lodgings. The knights accompanied Janual and reprimanded him sharply. They admonished him not to suffer such terrible grief from his love, and they cursed such extravagant love.

Now when the day came that they had appointed for ruling on the charges that the king had laid against Janual, all the vassals of the king were assembled. The king made his accusations against Janual, as did the queen. Then the king's knights who had stood as surety for Janual came, and they brought him before the king. All who were sitting in judgment were terribly sad, and they grieved deeply that they should have to judge such a splendid man, so generous and courteous, tried and found true, and a foreigner without help or comfort from all his kinsmen. But there were many who wanted to ruin him to please the king and queen.[34] The king ordered them to hurry with their judgment, for the sake of the queen who asked for their verdict.

Just as they were about to render their verdict, they saw two maidens arriving on two handsome mounts. They were the loveliest of ladies. Everyone who was there observed them carefully and said that he had never before seen maidens so lovely. Sir Gawain came to Janual with three other knights, and told him about the maidens and showed him, and he was greatly comforted. Then Sir Gawain made a humble request of him: to show him which of the two maidens was his lover. "I don't know who they are," he replied, "nor from where they come, nor what they want, nor where they wish to go."

The ladies rode forth and did not halt until they came before the king. Then they dismounted from their horses. They were the loveliest of ladies, and they spoke courteously. "Lord King," they said, "let chambers be cleared for the coming of our lady, for she wishes to dismount and lodge with you."

The king readily consented to what they asked, and he summoned two knights. They accompanied the maidens up into the chambers and did what the maidens asked. The maidens said nothing more for the time being.

Then the king demanded a response and a rendering of the verdict from his nobles who were sitting in judgment. He said that they had grieved him very much, since they had delayed so long in telling him what they had judged. "My lord," they said, "our assembly broke up when we saw the maidens, and we had not completed our judgment at the time. Now we will seat ourselves to render judgment a second time."

Once they were assembled a second time, they debated and argued loudly. But in the middle of the arguments among them, they saw two maidens coming, richly appareled on the finest horses.[35] Everyone seated in court was glad for Sir Janual, and they all said that these maidens had come to help Janual, who was so brave and bold in combat, courteous and generous, and as noble as a king. Sir Ywain and his companions went to him,[36] and at that moment the maidens came to the king and dismounted from their horses. The elder was clever and courteous and eloquently explained her mission. "My lord king," she said, "have lodging readied for my lady. She is coming here to speak with you."

The king said that knights should lead these maidens to the chamber that he had provided for the earlier maidens. Everyone found these maidens much lovelier than the first pair, and everyone praised the second pair much more highly.

Once they had left, the king demanded from the nobles the judgment that they had to render. He said that their sentence had been delayed for too long, an entire day, and they had to render it in full, right then. But just then, there came riding from one end of the estate to the other a maiden so lovely, on such a good horse, that in all the world there was no one as lovely as her, nor any other horse as good as hers. Her steed was as white as snow and so steady, swift, bold, and distinguished above all mortal horses, that no one had seen any horse like it.[37] The maiden bore a sparrow-hawk on her right hand, and a hound followed her. There is no need to describe her beauty and refinement beyond what has already been said, but she rode at a rather swift pace,[38] and there was no man in all the town, young or old, who didn't rush to see her as she rode through the town. Those who were sitting in judgment were astonished and amazed when they saw her. There was no man among them who didn't stare at her, and most felt warmed by the sight of her.

Those who were friends of the knight came to him and told him. He who had sat with his head bowed, grieving and fearing the king's knights' judgment of his charges, lifted up his head, for they told him that if God so willed, this maiden would release him and free him. When he had heard their words and looked around to see her, he fully recognized her, and he answered them. "By my faith," he said, "this is my beloved. If she will not take mercy on me, then I do not care who kills me. I am helped by the sight of her now."

The maiden rode straight into the king's courtyard. No one had seen another lady so lovely. She dismounted from her horse when she came before the king, and everyone stared at her in order to see her clearly. She let her mantle fall so that she might be seen clearly. The king, the most courteous man, stood up to greet her. Everyone showed honor and respect to her, and everyone eagerly sought to serve her.

When everyone had fully seen her and highly praised her beauty, she spoke in such a way as if she did not want to remain there longer. "My lord king," she said, "I love a knight of your household, Sir Janual. Accusations were made against him in this court. But I do not want my words to cause harm to anyone,[39] and I want everyone to know that the lady queen has wrongfully accused him, because he never asked her for anything. As for the boasting and praise when he spoke, I have come to redeem him, so that your nobles may rule that he is a free man, as they were discussing in their deliberations."

The king consented to what she asked for, and everyone ruled that Janual was a free man. He was free of calumny and fully released from their custody. The maiden went away. As long as she was in the king's court, everyone honored her and eagerly served her with good will—but the king was quite unable to make her stay any longer.

Outside, before the hall doors, there stood a marble stone. Janual leaped up onto the stone as she rode out through the hall doors. He jumped onto the horse's back, and she rode with him to the island called Avalon. The most truthfully informed men have said that this is the most beautiful island in the world; thither was this young man taken. No man ever heard news of him afterwards, and so I can tell you nothing further about him.

Here ends this saga. Thanks to those who listened.[40]

ICELANDIC ROMANCE

The Saga of Halfdan the Son of Eystein

Hálfdanar saga Eysteinssonar

Hálfdans saga Eysteinssonar *is a rollicking adventure tale that sweeps across Scandinavia, Russia, and more distant lands. As is typical for a "classic"* fornaldarsaga, *there are plenty of monsters and treasures pulled from the grab-bag of* fornaldarsögur *stock motifs. As is also fairly common, the saga heroes are related genealogically to the heroes of other* fornaldarsögur, *as well as to families in the* Íslendingasögur *or "sagas of Icelanders." Especially noteworthy is the independent, resourceful, and strong-willed princess Ingigerd, who uses disguise and deception to steer the plot towards a favorable resolution. Whereas in many sagas, women play the role of the inciter of conflict and violence among the men—the* Hetzerin, *in German scholarship—Ingigerd helps to avenge her father, and yet turns Halfdan's vengeance into an alliance against the true villains of the saga.*

Hálfdans saga Eysteinssonar *survives in sixty-six manuscripts written between the 15th and 19th centuries, attesting to its popularity.*[1] *I have translated from the text published by Guðni Jónsson and Bjarni Vilhjálmsson in* Fornaldarsögur Norðurlanda, *based on the text published in 1917 by F. R. Schröder, which in turn was based on the late 15th-century manuscript AM 343a. This manuscript contains a total of fifteen legendary and chivalric sagas, including* Samsons saga, Yngvars saga, *and* Vilmundar saga *in this book.*

CHAPTER I

There was a king named Thrand. Trondheim in Norway is named for him. He was a son of King Saeming the son of Odin, who ruled over Halogaland.[2] Saeming married Nauma, for whom Namdalen is named.

Thrand was a mighty ruler. His wife was named Dagmaer, the sister of Svanhvit whom Hromund Gripsson married.[3] They had one son named Eystein. Another son was Eirek the Far-Traveler, who discovered the Fields of the Undying; his mother isn't named.[4] Eystein was betrothed and married to the daughter of Sigurd Hart, who was named Asa. Her mother was Aslaug, daughter of Sigurd Snake-in-the-Eye.[5] Eystein received Finnmark, Valdres, Toten, and Hadeland along with her. He was powerful and a strong ruler.

Eystein and his wife had a son named Halfdan. He was also a good ruler, even-tempered and handsome. From an early age, he was trained in all the skills on which a man might pride himself, which it was better to have than to lack. He was careful in choosing friends, but faithful and trusty to them, and a very cheerful man, so that everyone could share good cheer with him. If someone displeased him, he was gloomy and resentful, but he did not act rashly. He grew up with his father until he was fifteen years old. Then his mother fell ill and died. The king and everyone else felt that to be a terrible blow, and she was given a worthy funeral. From that time on, the king didn't stay in his kingdom very much; he went out raiding every summer.

There was a man named Svip. He was a rich farmer, and fairly popular. He had three sons. One was named Ulfkel, called the Hero. He was a most overbearing man and not very smart. He went on raids with King Eystein and had five ships of his own. The king held him in high esteem. The second son of Svip was named Ulfar. He was a counsellor of the king. He was a well-liked and trustworthy man, and he tried to improve matters for both the king and other people. Svip's youngest son was named Ulf. He was called Ulf the Wicked. He raided throughout the eastern Baltic and Bjarmaland.[6] He led a large band of raiders and was not well liked at all.

One summer, King Eystein was raiding in the Eastern realms. Ulfkel the Hero was with him, along with the king's son Halfdan. They had thirty ships, well equipped. Ulfar, Ulfkel's brother, was in charge of King Eystein's kingdom while he was away raiding.

CHAPTER II

At that time, a king named Hergeir was ruling over Ladoga. He was elderly. His wife was named Isgerd; she was the daughter of King Hlodvir of Gautland. Her brothers were Sigmund, the forecastleman of King Harald Fairhair, and Odd the Showy, father of Gold-Thorir who is mentioned in the *Book of the Settlement of Iceland*.[7] They had one daughter, who was named Ingigerd. She was the loveliest of all maidens, as tall as a man, and quite gifted in most respects. She was fostered by the jarl named Skuli, who ruled over Alaborg and the jarldom that went with it.[8] He was said to be the brother of Heimir, the foster-father of Budli's daughter Brynhild, who is mentioned in the saga of King Ragnar Shaggy-Breeches. Skuli was a great champion, and the wisest of men.

There was a man named Kol, who was Skuli's thrall. He was a tall man and so strong that he had the strength of twelve men in any task that he set out to do. It might be said that he was the jarl's closest adviser, and he was faithful to him. He had a daughter; she was named Ingigerd and was the loveliest of all maidens, much like the king's daughter Ingigerd in both height and appearance. But their characters were not alike, because Ingigerd the king's daughter was well-mannered, but her namesake was the greatest hussy—yet she was highly accomplished, because the king's daughter had taught her needlework, and she was often in the king's daughter's bower.

Jarl Skuli loved his foster-daughter very much. Skuli wasn't married. He was such an accomplished man at sports and skills that no one could quite equal him.

CHAPTER III

King Eystein arrived at Ladoga town with his forces. King Hergeir had few men to oppose him. King Eystein advanced on the town with his men. King Hergeir faced him well and bravely, but he wasn't prepared for a battle, and the matter ended when King Hergeir fell along with the greater part of his forces. As soon as the king had fallen, King Eystein offered a truce to all those who survived. The survivors gave up the fight and accepted the truce. The king ordered the town to be cleansed. Then he had the queen brought before him, but she was in a foul mood.

The king faced her and looked at her for a while, and then spoke. "It's a pity," he said, "that the events which have all taken place together here should have caused you terrible distress. But 'there's compensation for everything,'[9] and I want to take your husband's place now. I am not an unworthy man to compare with him, because he was old."

"His old age was no disgrace to him," said the queen, "and I am not certain whether I will be faithful to the man who killed him."

"You have two choices," said the king. "One is for me to take you as a concubine, and that will last for as long as fate will have it. The other is for you to marry me and surrender the entire kingdom into my power, and I will do you great honor. I have no fear that betrayal from you would cause my death, when I die."

The queen said, "The old saying must be true, that 'dire choices are hard ones.' I choose to marry you."

The king said that that was what he would prefer. The matter was concluded, and this plan, and everything that will be told later, began to unfold.

CHAPTER IV

Immediately afterwards, the king summoned all his men. He spoke to Ulfkel the Hero and to his own son Halfdan. "Here's how the matter stands," he said. "Jarl Skuli rules Alaborg to the north. King Hergeir's daughter Ingigerd is being fostered with him there. Skuli is a mighty warrior, and we can expect him to move against us in force. For that reason, you two must move east against him and subjugate the land, but bring me the king's daughter. If you manage to win the land, Ulfkel will rule it as a jarl on account of the warrior service that he has rendered me, and I will grant him a suitable marriage. But Halfdan shall marry Ingigerd, if he likes the idea."

Ulfkel and Halfdan readied their forces, and they didn't stop until they came to Alaborg.

CHAPTER V

Jarl Skuli had heard the news of what had happened in Ladoga town, and so he summoned large forces. But when the forces had assembled, Skuli fell very ill. By that time, he had heard the truth about Ulfkel and Halfdan's forces. He spoke with Kol. "What I want," said Skuli, "is for you to become the commander of these men. Take up my banner and my clothes. I shall give you the title of jarl, and I shall betroth my foster-daughter Ingigerd to you, if you win victory."

Kol said that he was quite prepared. "Skuli" then spoke in front of the men, telling them what to do. The men thought only that the man who was Kol must be Skuli. He set out with his forces to face Halfdan and Ulfkel. Jarl Skuli hid in a village. By that time he was on the mend.

Ingigerd the king's daughter called on her namesake, Ingigerd Kol's daughter, and spoke with her. "I want you to make a pact with me," she said, "and let no one know for as long as you live. You are to take my clothes, because we two are very much alike. You shall be called King Hergeir's daughter, and I will take your clothes and go away with the other serving-wenches. You must never give up this pact as long as we both live. And if those who have come here win victory, then Halfdan the king's son will ask for your hand in marriage, or else Ulfkel will. Then you will be married well, and whatever comes of it will turn out for the best."

She said that she was quite willing, and they carried out the plan.

Now Halfdan and Ulfkel came on with their forces. Kol opened up the town gates and came out with his entire host. A battle broke out, and he stood there, risking his life. Kol was both strong and a powerful striker. Everyone thought that he was Jarl Skuli, and he broke through their ranks.

Herbjorn was the name of a kinsman of Jarl Skuli. His ranks faced Halfdan, and their fight was most valiant, but in the end Herbjorn fell. His men broke ranks and fled, and Halfdan pursued the fleeing men all the way to the forest.

Now we must tell of the encounter between Ulfkel and Kol. Kol had killed many a man. Snaeulf was the name of Ulfkel's standard-bearer. He bore the standard forward boldly and fought like a true warrior. Kol and Ulfkel found each other, and their fight was most valiant. They fought for a long time, and no one intervened in the fight. All their armor was cut off from their bodies. Then Kol struck a tremendous blow at Ulfkel. It landed on the outside of his helmet and cut off everything it could reach, which was a quarter of the helmet and the left ear along with it. The blow was so mighty that Ulfkel fell—but just then Snaeulf came up and struck at Kol, and that blow landed on his face and cut off his nose and both his lips and his chin, and his teeth fell down into the grass. Kol didn't sit quietly even though he had suffered that wound. He struck at Snaeulf's neck so that he cut off his head. But by that time Ulfkel had gotten to his feet, and he stabbed Kol through the chest so that the point came out between his shoulders. Kol fell down dead, and his men broke ranks and fled.

Ulfkel pursued the fleeing men, but Halfdan turned back. He saw two people walking, an old man and an old woman. His men struck up a conversation with them, and they asked how the battle had gone. The people told them quite clearly, and then they parted. The old man was so stiff that he was lying across the old woman's shoulders, and that's how they dragged themselves to the forest.

Halfdan asked his men whom they had talked with, and they said it was a wretched old beggar. “You can’t be too careful,” he said. “There is the man who will bring me grief, and it would be better if he were killed.” They called that a cowardly deed. By that time, the old man had gone into the forest, and it was no use searching for him.

Now Halfdan rode home to the town. Ulfkel had entered the town and gone to the bower where Ingigerd was, and she was led before him. She said to Ulfkel, “You have won a great victory and killed the ruler of the town. If you are fair-minded warriors, you will not treat me shamefully now, nor the other people here who have no ruler, and let me meet my mother.”

Ulfkel said, “That will be fitting, because for what we have done we will compensate both you and your mother well, if you will be faithful and gracious to us, obedient and compliant and not stubborn with us.”

“My affairs have come to this,” she said, “I think that pride would have little purpose.”

They promised that this would turn out well for her. Then the treasuries were unlocked. They took gold and silver and anything else that they wanted, but they offered a truce to all the people. The dead were given burial, and a worthy tomb was built for “Jarl Skuli,” who was really Kol. Then they subjugated all the land and prepared to meet King Eystein, and Ingigerd went on the journey with them.

CHAPTER VI

King Eystein heard about their arrival and what a great victory they had won. He welcomed them with honor, and they entertained him with the tale of their expedition. The king thanked them very much, and asked Halfdan how he liked the king’s daughter. He said that he didn’t have much of an eye for women, but he said that she was beautiful. Ingigerd was brought into the queen’s hall, and the queen welcomed her well, but with less cheerfulness than many were expecting. Then the king had the mother and daughter sent for. And when they came before him, he spoke to Queen Isgerd. “Now your daughter has come here,” he said, “and I want to do all honor both to you and to her, with your consent. I would like Halfdan to take my advice, and it would please me for him to marry her, if she is willing and you are as well, o queen.”

"She was born with enough wits," said the queen, "that she can well answer such a proposal for herself."

Halfdan said, "I'm not very keen on getting married, as it is. And I haven't seen many kings' daughters. But whoever had Ingigerd would seem well married to me, and I'd encourage you all to see to a good match for her."

Then Ulfkel said, "Long have I served you, my lord, and I expect good from you. I would find it a great honor if you would betroth me to this maiden. I have spoken somewhat with her before, and she has not flatly refused my proposal."

The king now asked Ingigerd how she felt about it, and she said that it was mostly up to him, if her mother had no objections—"and then, o king, you might be willing to grant Ulfkel some increase in rank."

The king asked the queen how she felt about it, and she said it would please her best for him to arrange it as he liked.

After that, the king betrothed Ingigerd to Ulfkel, and he gave him the title of jarl and Alaborg and the lands that went with it to rule. Their wedding-feast was held, and Ulfkel went to Alaborg and took over the realm. He became its ruler and paid the king tribute. So it went for a long time. Love began to grow between him and Ingigerd.

CHAPTER VII

Now King Eystein stayed in his own kingdom. He loved Queen Isgerd very much. She behaved like a lady towards him in all respects. And so three winters passed.

It happened on one occasion that a large trading ship came sailing out of the east in a gale, off the coast of Finland.[10] The ship disappeared, and not one mother's son was found. People thought that the gale must have smashed this ship.

Later, on a day in autumn, two men came to King Eystein's household. They were very tall, but not well dressed. People couldn't see their faces clearly, because they wore long hoods. They went before the king and greeted him worthily, because he was merry in his way of talking, as usual. He asked who they might be. They said that they were both named Grim[11] and came of Russian stock, and they had lost their money in a shipwreck. They asked the king for lodging over the winter.

The king asked the queen what she thought best. She said that he should decide such things himself, but she said that many unknown men could turn out to be either good or bad: "I can't be blamed for anything, if I say nothing about it."

The king said that she was always unwilling to take part in giving advice. "But I don't intend to refuse them food, as far as they've come."

Seats were arranged for them between the guests' seats and the seats for the men of the household. They didn't mingle with people much, but were pleasant to everyone. The elder Grim was so tall that few were like him. He was strong and agile in all games, and he was often playing with the king's men, shooting at targets or playing ball games. With his strength, he did well, and he never tricked anyone, but he wasn't short of strength if others went after him. The younger Grim was agile in games and skilled at archery, but he rarely put his strength to the test. But he was the best of all men at shooting the longbow and crossbow, and he played board games so well that no one could equal him. Halfdan the king's son often competed with him, both in boardgames and in archery. But he kept such a close watch on the Grims that they didn't sleep a night without him staying awake and keeping track of them. So the winter passed until Yule.

CHAPTER VIII

One day during Yule, men were playing ball[12] in front of the king. He was sitting on a chair, and the queen sat on another chair. The Grims were playing, and no one could play as well as the elder Grim, except for the king's son Halfdan. The Grims had never spoken a word to the queen that winter.

On one occasion, the elder Grim hit the ball out of bounds, and the younger Grim had to fetch it. The ball rolled all the way up underneath the queen's chair. Grim crawled after the ball, and when he straightened up, he spoke some words in the queen's ear, and she blushed.

When it was time for morning drinking, the game was given up, and the men started to drink. The king had plenty of drink served out, all day long, and every man passed out in his own seat if he couldn't get himself to bed. The king drank for a long time that evening, and the queen sat beside him. The king asked her what Grim had said to her, but she said that she hadn't paid attention to it. The king said that she wanted to keep most of what was said to herself, without giving him much information. The queen told him to watch out for himself, and then she went away. The Grims were already asleep.

The king went to his bed, and his son Halfdan went with him. When they came to the bower, the queen was not there. The king lay down in bed, fully dressed, and laid his sword in front of him. The bedservants put out the lanterns, but Halfdan went into the hall, and the Grims were lying there asleep.

Halfdan saw that the younger Grim had taken off his glove, and his hand was bare. He though he had never seen anyone's hand that was so beautiful. On it was a gold ring, so handsome that he thought he had never seen another one like it, most of all because of the stone that was on it. He couldn't make out what sort of stone it was. He slipped the ring from the finger and dropped it in the glove. Then he ordered the light to be put out, and he sat down by the Grims. It was dark in the lower part of the hall. He held the glove in his hand. Sleep quickly came upon him.

When he awoke, the lights were extinguished, but the younger Grim was holding up a light in front of his eyes, so bright that he couldn't stand to look at it. He seized the glove from him, and he said, "For this hand, ring, and glove you shall search and yearn, and you'll never manage to get them, until the one who now takes them away puts them back in your hands just as willingly."[13]

Then he aimed the light towards the nearer doors, but he himself ran for the farther doors and escaped.

CHAPTER IX

Halfdan leaped to his feet and rushed to the doors where the light was aimed, but they were locked. Then he turned and ran to the other doors and shouted to the men inside that they should wake up. The doors were locked, and he had to break them down before the men could get out. Halfdan ran to the bower, and there was the king, run through with a sword and dead. Three pageboys had also been killed; the fourth had escaped up onto a rafter, and he said that the elder Grim had come there and killed the king and all those who were dead. Then he had shouted, "Tell Halfdan that Vigfus and Ofeig[14] have avenged King Hergeir," and left.

At that moment the queen entered the bower, and the news struck her so terribly that she collapsed in a faint, and it seemed as if she were about to die. There was a commotion in the town. Men went out to search for the Grims, both on sea and on land, but they were not to be found anywhere. The search lasted for a month and extended a long way down the roads. And yet, eventually, it began to be forgotten. By then, it was the will of most people that Halfdan should be taken as king.

CHAPTER X

A little while later, Halfdan had the assembly summoned. And when the chieftains had come, people made entreaties to him to be their king. But he answered: "Given the events that have happened here recently, it's not right for me to bear the title of king as long as matters remain thus, because I am not an heir to this kingdom. Many will find it more honorable for me to avenge my father and seek out those who have killed him. No matter what we do, I think it best for the queen to send for her brother Sigmund to come here. But I will leave and not return until I have found my father's killers, whatever revenge I may be destined to take."

The queen said that she felt that her kingdom would never be better off than with him. But whatever was said, it was decided that Halfdan should sail away from the land with five ships, in command of good warriors. He first sailed into the eastern Baltic and was successful at winning both wealth and fame, but he never lay awake without seeing before his eyes that beautiful hand and the fair gold ring which he had lost at Ladoga town.

Let's let him sail for all of five years, as he wishes.

CHAPTER XI

Now we'll begin with how Ulfkel and his wife Ingigerd lived at Alaborg in the north. They heard about the death of King Eystein and how it had happened. Ingigerd discussed with Ulfkel whether he might want to be raised to the kingship, inheriting it through her father King Hergeir. He said that he was quite ready.

At once they prepared for their expedition, and they didn't stop until they had arrived at Ladoga town. Sigmund was there with the queen. Ulfkel demanded the kingdom from the queen, but she said that he and his wife had enough of a kingdom if they didn't covet more than they already had, and she said that she was pleased for them to keep it. The meeting ended with mutual threats.

Ulfkel went home and summoned his forces. Sigmund followed him northwards, and they encountered each other at a place called Krakunes.[15] A battle broke out between them, and it ended with Ulfkel and his wife fleeing in a single ship.

Ulfkel first sailed northwards to Norway and met his brother Ulfar there. He told him how he and Sigmund had parted and everything that had happened in the Eastern realms. He ordered Ulfar to surrender the kingdom to him, and said that Halfdan still had a larger kingdom in the East. Ulfar told him not to speak to him of such an unmanly thing as to betray his lord. He told him to build up his strength in his own kingdom and invade the eastern realm if he wanted to own it, and said that he was willing to support him in this. Ulfkel said that that wasn't enough for him. An argument broke out between them, and their meeting ended thus: Ulfkel killed his brother Ulfar, and subjected all his land to his rule and made himself lord over it. Everyone felt that this was the most wicked of deeds, and it caused him to become altogether detested.

CHAPTER XII

When Ulfkel had claimed the kingdom, he summoned men and ships and set out with them to the eastern realms. He had thirty longships, and one dragon-ship with seventy oars on each side. He had Vikings and outlaws with him, and every sort of wicked men that he could get. Ivar Little Bag was the name of the man who steered the dragon-ship; he was a berserk and the wickedest of men.[16] His brother was named Hrafnkel; he was Ulfkel's standard-bearer and the strongest of men. Ulfkel had many other large and strong men with him. They didn't travel in peace; they raided every land that they reached, and they pillaged mercilessly along the shores. They traveled eastward to Hlynskog, to the place called Klyfandanes.[17] From there is isn't far to Bjarmaland.

Ten ships sailed out against them there, all crewed with brave warriors. It was Halfdan, the son of King Eystein, who had arrived; he had found out everything about Ulfkel's journey. As soon as they recognized each other, Halfdan asked why Ulfkel had dealt shamefully with his own brother and taken his kingdom. Ulfkel said that Halfdan had taken an even larger kingdom in the Eastern realms, which he himself had held. Halfdan said that he wasn't so sure that Ulfkel was worthy of any good kingdom. At once they went for their weapons, and a battle broke out. But because the forces on two sides weren't evenly matched, soon there was a terrible slaughter among Halfdan's men.

Svidi was the name of Halfdan's closest adviser. He was a strong man. He explained how the ships should be tied together, and he sailed them all together so skilfully that Ulfkel couldn't attack with all of his own ships, some of which lay in shooting range. Fierce fighting broke out, and Halfdan cut a swath around himself. He saw that it wouldn't do them any good to fight until they were exhausted, so he and Svidi both decided to board the dragon-ship and attack Ulfkel. First to oppose them was Ivar Little Bag, and they traded heavy blows with him. Ivar struck at Halfdan, and the blow landed on the outside of his helmet and cut off what it touched—that was the helmet crown above the head, and Halfdan's head was shaved. Halfdan struck at Ivar in return and cut off his arm at the shoulder and chopped the banner-staff in two. Svidi killed Ulfkel's steersman, whose name was Egil. Then Ulfkel stabbed at Halfdan, and the blow caught him unawares and pierced his shield and mailcoat and came out under his arm. He suffered a wound in the side, and three of his ribs broke. Svidi stabbed at Ivar Little Bag and pierced his eye, and that was the death of him. Halfdan struck at Ulfkel, but he spun on his heel and dodged; the sword struck the deck planking and chopped off Ulfkel's big toe on his right foot. Ulfkel then stabbed at Halfdan with a great spear. Halfdan leaped up over the windlass. The great spear stuck in the latch-hole, and Halfdan jumped down on the shaft and snapped it in two. Then Svidi struck at Ulfkel between his shoulders, and the blow was so great that Ulfkel fell to his knees.

Just then, a stone struck Svidi in the chest so that he fell off the dragon-ship and landed in a boat that was floating alongside. At that moment, Hrafnkel struck Halfdan such a huge blow with a club that he went flying overboard. Svidi was nearby, and he seized the boat-hook and hooked Halfdan up out of the ocean. By then, Halfdan had suffered six wounds; he was unconscious and in no condition to fight.

CHAPTER XIII

Now many things happened all at once. Men saw twenty-five ships sailing before the headland. They were all large ships, with armored men on all of them. On one ship, a very tall man, well armored and wearing a sleeveless silk surcoat, was standing beside the sail. He asked who was fighting such an unequal battle. Svidi told him the truth, and explained how the battle had gone.

"Will Halfdan accept our help?"

Svidi asked who he might be. The man said that that was none of his business. Svadi said that he would gladly accept help from them.

The battle broke out a second time, more fiercely than before. Ulfkel's men were badly wounded. The tall man on the dragon-ship sailed right for Ulfkel's dragon-ship, and Svidi headed for the smaller ships, and they swiftly cleared their way. Now the losses were on Ulfkel's side.

The tall man boarded the dragon-ship. Ulfkel faced him first, and their fight was fierce and long. The tall man struck a huge blow at him, completely splitting the shield before him, and the sword landed on his foot and took off his three outer toes. Ulfkel struck in return, and the sword landed on his helmet and broke at the hilt. Then Ulfkel saw no other choice than to save his life. He leaped into the ship that was closest to him and fled. Hrafnkel flung two great spears at once at the tall man, but he caught both in mid-air and flung them back and hit a man with each one. Then he thrust at Hrafnkel with a spear through his shield and both arms, and he heaved him up and flung him out into the sea. He and Svidi attacked Ulfkel's men so fiercely that they were eager to beg for a truce. A truce was given to those who asked, but the tall man didn't want to have their service, and they were marooned on land with no possessions. Ulfkel fled in a single ship, and his wife was with him, but the others took all the ships and booty. Halfdan's surviving men submitted to the tall man.

CHAPTER XIV

The tall man came to where Halfdan was lying, and his wounds were gaping. He said to Svidi, "Halfdan's wounds look to me as if they might heal if a good healer touches them, but I don't think vagabonds and seafarers will do for him, so I will send him up onto land to my friend Hrifling. His wife is named Arghyrna.[18] They are good healers, but suffer great poverty and live from hand to mouth, and it's what you'd call a rag-tag existence.[19] If they can't save Halfdan, he's not fated to live. Then he will come to us."

He got his trusted retainers to bring Halfdan up onto land, and gave them a hundred marks of silver. He ordered them to tell the old man and woman that they were to take as much care with healing Halfdan as with himself if he were to come to them, and they should tell him exactly where he might be found, once he had been healed. They went and found the old man and woman and told them what they'd been ordered to, and gave them the money, but the old couple said that this was only their duty.

The messengers went away, and the couple began to heal him. That was hard to do, because Halfdan's wounds were badly swollen, and he lay wounded for eighteen weeks. But he was restored to health. He had to stay there for twelve months before he recovered his strength. That seemed like a long time him, because the beautiful hand and the gold ring and glove that he had lost were always on his mind.

CHAPTER XV

We now return to Ulfkel the Hero's flight from battle. He escaped to land with fifty men, but had lost the rest of his forces. He listened for news of where his brother Ulf might be, and he was informed that he was in Bjarmaland. He went to find him.

Harek was the name of the king who ruled there. His daughter was named Edny. Ulf had asked for her hand, but the king didn't want to betroth her. Then Ulf raided in his lands.

Once the brothers had found each other, they devised a plan together that they would go to find King Harek. They had sixty ships. When they sailed into the anchorages in front of the king's hall, Ulfkel the Hero went to meet the king and greeted him fittingly. The king asked who he might be. He told the truth. The king asked who was in command of the huge host that had arrived there, and Ulfkel said that Ulf the Wicked was in command—"and we are brothers. I came to find you because we want to offer ourselves to be your men. If you will betroth your daughter to Ulf, I will contribute Alaborg and Ladoga town and all the realms that go with them, because those are my property. I expect that you'll get great support from us brothers. But if we were to try to do evil, many would find it crowded in front of the doors."[20]

The king asked him to wait until he could hold a council with his men, and Ulfkel granted him that. The king asked his daughter what she thought, and she said that she felt that the brothers' raiding would cause problems—"but if the kingdom could be secure, I would think it was worth considering." Yet she said that if the brothers were denied, she wouldn't put any evil past them. In the end, Ulf married Edny, and the brothers took over the defenses of Bjarmaland.

Ulfkel listened for news of who could have been fighting against him when he and Halfdan had fought. King Harek told him that the man was called Grim. "He rules in the east, on the Gulf of Finland, and has forced his way to the rulership, and people don't know where his family comes from. His foster-daughter came with him—such a lovely maiden that people have never heard of another one as beautiful."

"That's the man," said Ulfkel, "to whom I would row on the path of vengeance, if I had the choice. I want help and support from you."

The king said, "We can agree on that, because that's the maiden that I intend to ask for."

They both said that they would stand by him, and said that it was a good decision. They swore that they would go there as soon as summer came and would not leave until Grim was in Hel and the king had married the young maiden. They stayed at home quietly for the time being.

When springtime came, they readied their ships. They had an enormous host. Two Finnish kings were with them; one was named Finn, and the other was Floki, and they were sorcerors.[21] Now they sailed eastward until they reached the Gulf of Finland and encountered Grim. There was no need to ask for a reason; they offered to fight Grim, or else for him to surrender to them and give the king all the realm and his foster-daughter. Grim said that it would go worse for them. "This king has no quarrel with us, but you, Ulfkel, will have a harder road to travel than before."

They slept quietly that night, but in the morning Grim left the castle with all his forces. The fiercest fighting broke out, and the battle lasted until evening. By that time, Grim had lost many men. He went back into the castle, and in the morning they resumed the battle, and no able-bodied man was left behind in the castle.

CHAPTER XVI

Now it is time to tell about Halfdan the king's son: he was healed of his wounds and had recovered all his strength. He came to speak with the old man and old woman, and he said that he felt like going away. He asked who the man who had sent him there to be healed could be, and how he would have to repay the gift of life.

Hrifling answered, "Since I trust your valor, I can give you directions to where he is. Grim is the name of the man who rules on the Gulf of Finland to the east. He is a great champion. He sent you here to me. Now you can repay him for the gift of your life, because he is in need of good warriors. King Harek of Bjarmaland has gone there, along with Ulf the Wicked and Ulfkel the Hero. He wants to avenge the disgrace that he suffered in his encounter with you. They have now headed that way with their forces, and I'm told that King Harek wants to marry Grim's foster-daughter, who is named Ingigerd and is the loveliest of all maidens."

"Well said, my fosterer," said Halfdan, "Yet there's something else that I think is no less important: for you to tell me who killed my father."

"I can tell you that clearly," said the old man. "The man's name is Skuli, and if I shall tell you the truth and not lie to you, this man is the same as Grim who saved your life. Much will depend on your nature as a warrior when you two meet. But Skuli is such a great champion that he's completely ready for every man who fights him in single combat."

"Can you tell me anything about the shortest way?" said Halfdan. "Because I want to go there as fast as possible."

"Most of the paths are difficult here," said Hrifling. "You can't make it by ship in fewer than five weeks, and that's the greatest risk to your life, on account of Vikings and fighters. Another way lies to the east, and you have to travel across mountains and wastelands. That's a long and difficult way, and it's not certain whether you could make it. The third way is shortest if all goes well, because you can travel it in three weeks, but there are many obstacles. First there is a forest twenty leagues[22] wide, which is called Kolsskog. The robber named Kol lives there with his daughter, who is named Gullkula.[23] No one whom they find has any hope of surviving. Another forest, called Klifskog, is a short distance from there, and it's twenty-four leagues wide. The robber named Hallgeir lives there. There's a wild boar that lives with him, and it's harder to handle than twelve men. Next, you come to the forest called Kalfarskog, thirty-six leagues wide. There's nothing to eat there but berries and tree sap. The robber named Sel lives there, and with him is a dog the size of a calf. He has human intelligence and is a better fighter than twelve men. When you come out of the forests, there's a river flowing from the east, out of the Kjolen Mountains. No one knows its source. Only the best swimmers can get across, but from there it's not far to the castle that Skuli rules. If nothing slows you down, you should get there just about in time for the battle to happen." Halfdan asked him to make preparations for his journey.

In the morning, Halfdan prepared to travel. He went to the old woman and bid her farewell. The old woman spoke many fair words over him. Then she took her ragbag out from under the head of her bed. She took a knife out of it, as shiny as a mirror. It looked to him as if venom were dripping from the edges. She told him that he who bore it would always have victory, and it would never be blocked in its stroke if it were wielded well. She took a necklace of stones and tied it around his neck and told him that it should never be moved out of its place. Then he kissed the old woman.

The old man went with him and told him how to navigate. He gave him his own lapdog, and told him to follow wherever the dog went and never take roads that the dog didn't want to take. He said that the dog knew how to avoid the dwellings of the evildoers.

Halfdan said that no robber would be the death of him. "And if you become short of money, then visit their huts, because I won't carry off their money, even if I manage to beat one of them to a pulp."

Then he parted from the old man, and each one wished the other well.

CHAPTER XVII

Halfdan turned and entered the forest. When he had walked for two days, he saw a hidden path. The dog wanted to take the path, but Halfdan kept going on the main road until he found a hut. The door was closed; Halfdan flung it open, and just as he walked in, there was Gullkula in front of him, the daughter of Kol. She struck at his neck with a sharp blade, but the old woman's stone necklace was in the way. The necklace made a loud clashing sound, and the blade snapped in two. Halfdan seized her and slammed her down hard, and then gripped her by each foot and ripped her apart lengthwise and flung her out in front of the door. Kol came home at nightfall, and when he looked through the doors, Halfdan sliced his neck with the knife, and that was the death of him.

But in the night, when Halfdan was asleep, Kol and his daughter came inside, and they both attacked Halfdan.[24] The dog jumped up and tore Gullkula in the groin and pulled out her intestines. Halfdan rushed in under the hut-dweller's grasp, and they wrestled for a long time, but it ended when Halfdan threw him down and broke his neck. Then he took fire and burned them both up. He stayed there for two nights.

Then he went on his way and didn't stop until he came to Klifskog. There he found a large hut, and the door was so heavy that he had to exert all his strength before it opened up. He saw a room there, two ells longer than he was tall, and a sleeping place as large as a cow stall. By then it was growing dark. He heard a loud racket outside: the boar was grunting and acting hostile. Halfdan stepped out of the hut. The dog rushed at the boar barking, and the boar turned to get away. Halfdan struck at it and cut off its tail. The boar spun around and stuck its snout between Halfdan's legs and tossed him in the air so that he dropped the knife, but he landed on his feet. Then the hut's occupant came and struck at Halfdan with a spiked club. He dodged the blow, but couldn't manage to get the knife. He seized the boar's leg and pulled it towards him. The blow landed right between the boar's ears and shattered its skull. Halfdan tore a leg from the boar and drove it against the robber's ear so that he fell to his knees. Then Halfdan rushed at him and kicked him on the head. The robber gripped Halfdan, and they wrestled fiercely, and first one and then the other was underneath. Then the dog Old Man's Gift rushed in and bit the hut-dweller's nose and tore it off. Halfdan managed to get the knife and cut off the hut-dweller's head, and then he burned him on a pyre. By that time, he was stiff and exhausted. He stayed there for the night.

Then he came to Kalfarskog and arrived at Sel's hut. The door was halfway open. He charged at the door three times before it opened up. Halfdan sat down in the hut-dweller's room. He had an oak stick in his hand, and he whittled it to a sharp point on both ends and scorched it in the fire. He saw the inhabitant of the hut walking outdoors, and the dog was dashing ahead of him. Halfdan's dog was frightened and leaped up onto the crossbeam. Halfdan went outside to face the inhabitant, but as soon as the dog saw him, he charged at him with gaping jaws, howling most savagely. Halfdan stuck his hand between the dog's jaws and turned the stick so that one end pointed upwards, into the palate, and the other pointed down, and the dog couldn't bring his jaws together.

At this moment, Sel arrived. He carried a bear on his shoulders and a whale calf in front of him.

CHAPTER XVIII

Sel flung down his burden and stabbed at Halfdan with his bear-knife. Halfdan struck in return with his knife and chopped Sel's knife-shaft in two, cutting off all of his fingers on one hand. Sel picked up a stone and turned to face Halfdan. Halfdan slipped out of the way and came so close to Sel that he grabbed the tooth which projected out of his snout. Sel jerked back so hard that the tooth came out. Halfdan struck Sel's nose with the tooth and broke his nose and his entire row of teeth. By then, the giant didn't look like anyone—except himself. He gripped Halfdan and squeezed his sides so hard that blood poured from his ears and nose. Then Halfdan tried a heel-throw on Sel, who fell on his back. His tooth hit the stone necklace, and one stone broke. Halfdan couldn't manage to move anywhere. Old Man's Gift, the dog, rushed into Sel's nostrils and clawed both of his eyes out. Then Halfdan got free, and he cut off Sel's head and flung it out into the great river that flowed nearby.

Halfdan went to Sel's dog and said to him, "Never shall that stick leave your jaws, unless you be as loyal to me as you once were to Sel." The dog crept up to him and rolled over, exposing his belly. Halfdan took the stick out of his jaws. The dog was so happy that tears ran down over his muzzle.[25]

Halfdan got himself food and went straight to sleep, but in the morning he prepared to leave and traveled until he reached the river. The dog Sel's Gift ran forward along the shore until he found a heap of moss. He pawed the heap apart, and there was a boat inside. Halfdan took it and sailed over the water, and then he walked all day until evening.

CHAPTER XIX

In the morning, Halfdan saw the castle to which he'd been directed. That morning, Jarl Skuli had gone to battle against King Harek and the brothers, a long way from the castle. Jarl Skuli's forces were much smaller. The castle was empty of fighting men, but women were standing on the ramparts when Halfdan came there. He saw a young maiden there whom he found attractive. She went down to the gate and greeted Halfdan by name. He received her greeting warmly. Then she said to him, "You must think it's time to see the glove and gold ring that you lost in Ladoga town."

"Will you be able to make that happen?" said Halfdan.

"That's mostly up to you," she said. "My foster-father is now in battle, and he must have need of help and strong support. I must do as much as I can so that he may win victory."

"I don't have anything good to contribute to your foster-father," said Halfdan, "but if you will promise me your loyalty, I will go to battle by his side."

She tossed the glove out to him and told him to keep it as a token of their agreement. "The gold ring must stay with me, from now until our next meeting. But the castle will never be taken by men, even if no one is left to defend it but women."

CHAPTER XX

Now Halfdan went into battle, and it was a dreadful slaughter. Svidi carried Jarl Skuli's standard and advanced so boldly that he killed King Harek's standard-bearer, who was named Krabbi. Halfdan didn't waver. He first attacked the Finnish king Floki's position. The king was shooting three arrows at once from his bow, and each arrow hit a man. Halfdan attacked him and chopped at the bow with his knife, so that the bow broke. He chopped off Floki's hand, and it flew up into the air. The king reached up towards it with the stump, and the hand landed on it and was healed.

Finn the other Finnish king saw this, and he turned into a walrus and charged up at those who were fighting against him.[26] Fifteen men were trapped underneath him, and all of them were killed. Sel's Gift rushed at him and tore him apart with his teeth. The walrus gaped his jaws open, but Old Man's Gift rushed into the walrus's jaws, all the way down into the belly, and he tore him from the inside and ripped out his heart. Then he ran out and dropped dead.[27]

Halfdan brandished the knife and struck at Floki a second time, but Floki blew at him so hard that the knife flew out of Halfdan's hand and landed far away.[28] Floki struck at Halfdan, but the blow landed on the stone necklace and the blade broke. Halfdan suffered a wound on his neck where the stone had broken away—but he would have lost his head if the stone necklace hadn't protected him. Halfdan grappled Floki and slammed him down hard. At that moment Ulfkel the Hero came at him, and Halfdan had all he could handle. The dog ran up and ripped Floki's entire face off, but Floki grappled the dog and broke every one of his bones, and there they lay, both dead. Halfdan saw nothing else to do. He charged Ulfkel and grabbed his sword and struck him in the nose with the flat of the sword and told him to defend himself—and then Halfdan managed to get the knife. They charged each other and fought, and in the end, Ulfkel the Hero got his death.

By that time, Jarl Skuli had killed Ulf the Wicked. Then King Harek of Bjarmaland came and attacked Skuli, and they had a fierce exchange of blows. Harek struck at Skuli and hewed off his entire shield, and gave him a wound on the finger, but not a serious one. Skuli struck in return and cut off the king's ear and his cheek, flaying the skin down to the shoulder. Then Harek turned into a flying dragon and struck Skuli with his claws so that he was knocked unconscious. A warrior named Grubs came at the dragon and cut a leg out from under him, but the dragon hooked Grubs with his other claws and tore him open at the groin. Then Halfdan came at him and struck at his neck, and that was the death of him.

Men broke ranks and fled, and the invaders rushed to their ships and escaped in three ships. The ship that Kol's daughter Ingigerd was on crashed into a rock and every mother's son on it drowned. Halfdan turned back to where the battle had been, and there was a huge plunder to divide up. They didn't find Jarl Skuli, so they went home to the castle. The men's wounds were bound and the store of wealth was brought home. Ingigerd welcomed them warmly. When three nights had passed, she summoned an assembly, and everyone in the castle came. Ingigerd also came to the assembly. She sat on Halfdan's knee and gave herself and all her landholdings into his power, and she gave him the gold ring that was mentioned before.

"We two are now reconciled," said Halfdan, "if you'll tell me what you said to your mother, before my father was killed."

"I asked her to leave the bower open that night. Now I will now compensate you for everything concerning that and everything else, as you see fit—although according to higher laws, both sides have something of a case."

CHAPTER XXI

Just then they saw a man walking, and the people recognized Jarl Skuli. He was well armored. He came before Halfdan and took off his helmet, and he said, "Now here's how it is, Halfdan: I will offer you a settlement and let you name the compensation for the matters in which I have wronged you. Along with that, I want to offer you sworn brotherhood and also betroth you to my foster-daughter Ingigerd. But if you don't want that choice, I will not risk any further encounters with you, and each of us will go on with his own affairs as he is able."

"Looking back while running does no good," said Halfdan. "I wouldn't be speaking to you of everything that happened when we had to fight Ulfkel the Hero, if you had not shown your boldness to me."

"You've repaid me for it," said Skuli.

Then Ingigerd suggested that they should be reconciled, and that was easy. Most men felt that both of them were worthy, and people were glad of their settlement.

Now the plunder was divided right away, and there was so much wealth that many a man who'd formerly been poor was now quite rich. Halfdan then ordered his wedding feast to be prepared. While that was being done, he sent out a search for the money that the robbers had had. That was such great wealth that fifteen large ships were laden with all sorts of treasures. He also had old man Hrifling and all his household sought out, and he made him quite wealthy. Halfdan held his wedding feast and invited all the chieftains. Jarl Skuli supervised everything, and the feast proceeded in splendid style. All the men were sent home with fine gifts, and Halfdan became so popular from this that everyone wanted to serve him.

CHAPTER XXII

Afterwards, Halfdan held an assembly with the men of the land, and he made it known that they should invade Bjarmaland within a month. The men were pleased with that, and they all prepared quickly and came to Bjarmaland. Jarl Skuli was on the expedition with them. There was not much resistance, and they subjugated all the land. Halfdan took King Harek's daughter Edny into his wardship. Grundi was the name of the son of King Harek; he was three years old at the time. He was fostered by Jarl

Bjartman, the son of King Raknar who had the ship *Raknar's Sledge* built. He became one of Halfdan's men.

After that, Halfdan sailed away and came home to Ladoga town. He had been away for five winters. The men were happy to see him. The queen welcomed her daughter and thanked both Halfdan and Jarl Skuli for how well they had treated her.

CHAPTER XXIII

Sigmund, the son of Hlodvir and brother of Queen Isgerd, had been in charge of defending Russia. He came to meet Halfdan with a great host of men, and he was well received. Halfdan had an assembly summoned. He spoke up: "I have been here in the Eastern realms for sixteen years now, and there are two points: we came here by force and suffered great loss of life, and we've taken turns falling off the horse. Now we must let that go, if we are to have friendship together. Know that reports have been going around that Ulfkel the Hero had married Ingigerd, the daughter of King Hergeir—but Ulfkel and his wife are now dead. So I want to know the truth of this matter from Queen Isgerd and her brother Sigmund, and from my sworn brother Jarl Skuli, whether this Ingigerd whom I have brought here is Kol's daughter, or King Hergeir's daughter, because I had intended a better match for mysef than to marry Kol's daughter, if I'd had the choice."

Queen Isgerd said, "Though we've dealt with each other harshly for a long time, I won't cheat you in any way, Halfdan, because in all our dealings you have taken the high road. So I tell you that this Ingigerd whom you have brought here is my daughter and King Hergeir's, and she alone is the rightful heir to this land. I hereby make it known that I give myself and my daughter and this realm into Halfdan's full ownership and thus compensate him for each of his losses. And I would very much like to know that Jarl Skuli has had honorable terms which have pleased him."

CHAPTER XXIV

Jarl Skuli now began his story, and he told of how he had made Kol the leader of his forces, and how they had traded names, and how he and Ingigerd had been the old man and woman who had fled from Halfdan at

Alaborg and whom Halfdan had wanted caught. He now said that he and his kingdom were in Halfdan's keeping.

Halfdan said, "Now it's come to this: all these lands have bowed to me. So now I want to show you what I want to have done: I will give Queen Isgerd to Jarl Skuli, along with the realm that she has here in Russia. I now have Bjarmaland and King Harek's daughter Edny in my power. That kingdom I will give to Sigmund, and the maiden along with it, if both of them are willing."

Sigmund said that he was pleased with that, if the maiden agreed, and Edny said that she could expect no better proposal: "I'm well pleased with this."

Halfdan said that he would go to the kingdom that he had in Norway. "It's for the best for everyone to live where he's born."

Matters went forward, and these wedding feasts were held with great splendor, and when they were over, each of the chieftains went to his own land. Halfdan stayed there over the winter, and he and Ingigerd loved each other well. They sent Svidi Bold-Attacker[29] east to the Gulf of Finland, and he was to be chieftain there and hold the realm of Jarl Skuli.

In the spring, as soon as the ice broke up, Halfdan mustered both ships and men, and he and Sigmund and Jarl Skuli prepared to go to Bjarmaland. Their journey went well, and the land submitted to them. Sigmund became the ruler of Bjarmaland, but he stayed with Halfdan. Jarl Skuli traveled home to Alaborg, and he and Queen Isgerd loved each other much. Their son was Hreggvid, the father of Ingigerd whom Hrolf the Walker married.[30]

CHAPTER XXV

Now it is time to tell how Halfdan set out for Norway, and Sigmund went with him, along with his brother Odd the Showy and a splendid host. When Halfdan came to Norway, his kinsmen welcomed him warmly, and he was raised to the kingship over Trondheim and all the realm that his father King Eystein had ruled, and he was a very popular man with his subjects. He and Ingigerd had two sons. One was named Thorir Hart, and the other was Eystein Rattler.[31] Odd the Showy became the guardian of Halfdan's lands and was the most valiant of men. He traveled to Iceland in his old age, and a great family is descended from him.[32]

Later, Sigmund's men came from Bjarmaland in the east and said that Vikings were raiding in Bjarmaland and Novgorod. They had killed Svidi Bold-Attacker and subjugated the Gulf of Finland and a large part of Russia. When Halfdan and Sigmund heard the news, they summoned their forces and traveled east to Bjarmaland.

CHAPTER XXVI

At that time, the king named Agnar ruled over Gestrekaland and all the realms east of the Kjolen Mountains. He married Hildigunn, the sister of that Harek who was called the King of the Bjarmians. They had two sons: one was named Raknar and the other was Val. They were Vikings and sailed out into the Arctic Ocean and raided the giants. Raknar owned the ship called *Raknar's Sledge*, with space for a hundred oarsmen. That was the largest longship ever built in Norway, aside from the *Long Serpent*,[33] and it was crewed with all manner of evildoers. There were fifteen sons of whores at every oar. Raknar took over uninhabited Slab-Land[34] and cleared out all the giants. His brother Val lurked in the Arctic Ocean, and there is a great saga about him.[35] The brothers thought they were rightfully entitled to Bjarmaland after the death of their mother's brother Harek. Val had two sons, one named Kott and the other named Kisi.[36] They were tall strong men. Val had killed Svidi and subjugated the Gulf of Finland. He had gotten so much gold that no one knew how much it was, and he had taken it from the giant Svadi who lived on the mountain called Blesanerg. That's north of the Arctic Ocean. Svadi was a son of the god Thor.[37] Val owned the sword that was named Hornhjalti;[38] it was richly ornamented with gold and it was never checked in its stroke.

Halfdan and Sigmund came east to Bjarmaland and got news of where Val was. They found him north of the White Sea, and a battle broke out at once. Two of the men with Sigmund are named: one was named Hauk, and the other was Gauk.[39] They were steersmen on his ship. Raknar's son Agnar sailed his ship against Halfdan, and their encounter was most dreadful. Hauk and Gauk sailed free; they attacked the outermost ships and cleared them all.

Val leapt up onto Sigmund's ship, and Kott and Kisi went with him, and they cleared a swath. Val struck at Sigmund and split his entire shield. The sword landed on the outside of his foot and cut off two toes. Sigmund struck back. Val had a gilded helmet, and the sword hit it and broke in two at the hilt. Val was ready for the blow and leaned back. Sigmund rushed him and pushed him backwards and overboard, and he went down to the bottom. When he came up out of the sea, his men pulled him up into a ship.

Kott and Kisi now retreated from the ship. When they boarded their own ship, Odd the Showy and Gauk and Hauk sailed at them, and there was a fierce fight between them. Since Val was out of the fight, Kott and Kisi fled in one ship, but Odd sailed after them and chased them to land, where a great river fell down from the cliffs into the sea. Val was on the ship with them. He picked up two chests of gold. They were so heavy that it was all two men could do to carry them. Odd rushed after him, but when they came to the waterfall, Val plunged down into it, and that's how they parted.[40] Then Kott and Kisi and Gauk and Hauk arrived, and when they got to the waterfall, Kott seized Hauk and Kisi seized Gauk, and they plunged down into the waterfall with them and killed them both. A huge cave was under the falls, and the father and sons dived into it. They lay down on the gold and turned into flying dragons, wearing helmets on their heads and swords under their flippers. They lay there until Gold-Thorir conquered the waterfall. Odd turned back alone.

By then, Halfdan and Sigmund had killed all the Vikings, and Agnar fled in a single ship. He came to Halogaland and became the most wicked robber. He accumulated great wealth, and in the end he built a great burial mound for himself and went in it alive, as his father had done, with all his ship's crew, and he turned into a troll on the hoard.[41]

CHAPTER XXVII

Halfdan and Sigmund now went home to Bjarmaland, and Sigmund settled down in his own kingdom. Halfdan went to Norway, and there is a great saga about him. He died of illness, and so did Queen Ingigerd. Many mighty men in Norway and the Orkneys are descended from them.

And here we end this story. Go in peace.

The Saga of Samson the Fair

Samsons saga fagra

Samsons saga *was once thought to be a translation of a lost Arthurian romance, but the "King Arthur" whom Samson serves is not the famous King Arthur of legend. On closer examination,* Samsons saga *turns out to be a patchwork of motifs drawn from a remarkable range of sources. Personal names seem to be borrowed from both French and German tales of chivalry. The underwater battle in Chapter VII between Samson and a troll-woman has drawn attention as an analogue of Beowulf's fight with Grendel's mother. Æsop's fable "Venus and the Cat", the Otherworldly Stag motif from Celtic legends, and a cart-driving dwarf who may come from medieval tales of Lancelot (but who lives inside a stone like a typical Norse dwarf) all rub shoulders in the first half. The second half of* Samsons saga *veers off into a much more Norse world, dominated by the mighty Godmund of Glæsisvellir, but mixed with "learned lore" such as the race of short-lived women, one of the "Plinian races". The magic mantle that tests a woman's chastity is derived from the Arthurian romance* Le lai du court mantel, *known in Norse translation as* Möttuls saga; *in fact, Samsons saga turns out to be a "prequel" to Möttuls saga that provides an origin for the magic mantle. And yet the author has managed to assemble this hodgepodge into an entertaining story.*

This translation is based on Bjarni Vilhjálmsson's edition in Volume III of his 1951 compilation Riddarasögur, *which is based on Björner's 1737 edition of heroic sagas,* Nordiska kämpa dater. *Some readings are taken from the late manuscript Lbs 203, dated 1720–1750. I have checked Vilhjálmsson's text against the text edited by John Wilson and published in 1953, which is based primarily on AM 343a (1450–1475) but includes variants from other early manuscripts, including the mid-17th-century manuscript AM 181b, which seems closer to Lbs 203. Vilhjálmsson's text usually varies from Wilson's edition only in fairly minor details, which have been footnoted where they seemed to be relevant.*

CHAPTER I

There was a king named Arthur who ruled over England. He was a mighty king with a large following, and a powerful ruler. He had a queen of noble descent, as well befitted him. She was named Silvia,[1] the daughter of the king of Hungary. Their son was named Samson. He was tall and strong, handsome to look at, courteous and mannerly, well-beloved and fond of fine clothing, zealous by nature and cheerful each day, so that everyone loved him wholeheartedly. He was called Samson the Fair, and he was well and truly named, for there was not a blemish to be seen on his body.

The king and queen had another child, a daughter named Grega. She was both fair and courteous, and she was well versed and instructed in most of the arts that were customary for young ladies in those days.

King Arthur had been a great warrior while he was young. But when he began to grow old, he settled down quietly and ruled his kingdom with great renown and splendor.

The prince was given in fosterage to a knight named Salmon. He was wise and well-beloved and insightful in his counsels. His wife was named Olympia. She was a native of Brittany, and there she had many large estates. She understood many things well; she was wise and insightful in her plans, as will be told later. She was a most loving foster-mother to Samson. There he grew up until he was eleven years old, and he learned sports and knightly skills from Salmon. He was so accomplished at sports and skills that no one in all England could equal him.

Then his foster-father fell ill and breathed his last. Everyone felt this to be a terrible loss. Samson went to his father and stayed by his side. Olympia no longer cared to stay in England, and she traveled to Brittany and settled down on her estates. She owned a castle that stood in a certain forested district, far off the beaten path, and she usually stayed there without many retainers.

CHAPTER II

At that time, the king named Garlant ruled over Ireland. He was powerful and a great ruler. He had had a queen, but she had died by the time that this saga takes place. He had one daughter, whose name was Valentina. She was both wise and well-beloved, and well-mannered. She had learned all the accomplishments of ladies.

In those days there had been great strife between King Arthur of England and King Garlant. They had fought many perilous battles, and sometimes one and sometimes the other had come out on top. In the end, the rulers reached a settlement and exchanged hostages: King Garlant sent his own daughter Valentina into King Arthur's power and keeping, and in return King Arthur sent his own sister's son to King Garlant. They kept their agreement firmly ever afterwards, as courtly men should. Some time passed.

CHAPTER III

On one occasion, a dance was held in the queen's court, for both men and women.[2] Samson the Fair held Valentina's hand and spoke thus with her: "My lady," he said, "how do you feel about serving here in England, with no greater wealth nor retinue than you now have? It would do you greater honor to get for yourself a goodly lover of noble descent."

She replied, "Mock me not, good sir, for it is honor enough for me to serve the king and queen, but it is not easy for me to choose a lover."

"My lady," Samson said, "how would you receive it, if I were to request that you might be my lover?"

"My lord," said the maiden, "if this pure desire were yours, I would choose no one before you, and I would desire no other love."

They ended their conversation for the time being.

Somewhat later, Samson came to speak with his father. "Father," he said, "the daughter of King Garlant is here in our court. She is a lady who is much to my liking. And if you are willing to grant me marriage with her, it would please me well."

The king said, "That match is not entirely mine to grant, for she is my hostage—but her father, and she herself, will decide her betrothal. In no way will I act against their will in this matter. And I might support you in getting a betrothal that will not lessen your honor. You have not traveled widely to meet noble ladies who will seem no less worthy to you. I am also not willing for her to suffer any dishonor at my court."

A little later, King Arthur spoke with the lady. "You have now been at our court for three years," he said, "with honor and glory. I am now fully assured that your father will be our firm ally. Therefore, I wish to send you home. Tell your father that our alliance is certain. I am also not willing for you to suffer any disgrace in my court, since your father placed you in my trust. Has any man made proposals to you since you came here?"

"Not that I have taken much notice of," she said, "yet I'll not deny that your son Samson has made certain hints. But I will not aim for a match with him or anyone else, if it displeases you."

"It does not displease me," said the king. "If he is sincerely bent on it, he may seek it in your father's court, and I shall grant him my full support."

With that said, they parted.

CHAPTER IV

A short time later, King Arthur outfitted Lady Valentina's expedition home to Ireland, with great store of riches and a suitable retinue, and he sent worthy gifts to her father. The queen prepared her well to leave the court, with beautiful clothing and worthy gifts. She thanked the king and queen fittingly for their hospitality, and gave fine gifts to her friends. Lord Samson turned to speak with her, and he said, "My lady, remember what I have said when you come to your father, because I will find you there."

"I will not forget your words," she said, "but I cannot make my promise any firmer without my father's supervision. But accept this gold ring from me."

She bid him farewell, and then she boarded the ship and sailed away, voyaging home to Ireland on a favorable wind. King Garlant welcomed his daughter warmly, and at once sent his hostage to King Arthur with fitting gifts and trustworthy offers of friendship. He and Arthur kept their pledge and their alliance.

A little while later, Samson the Fair came to speak with his father, and he said, "My lord father, I want you to get me ships and crewmen. I want to travel away from this land and make the acquaintance of unknown rulers, and find out if I might gain something that might increase my renown or power, and learn how to increase my honor, so that I do not sit at home like a maiden awaiting her marriage."

"My dear son," said the king, "everything shall be made ready that we are able to offer and that you wish to ask for, so that you and your men shall be self-sufficient in every land that you reach. Choose both ships and men yourself."

Samson thanked his father.

Now his expedition was ready. He sailed away from his land in five ships, crewed with good companions who were endowed with great prowess and courtly manners. He set out raiding and won great wealth. He kept on with this for some time, and accomplished many glorious deeds, although they are not described here.

CHAPTER V

In those days, a jarl named Finnlaug ruled Brittany. He was married and had one daughter, whose name was Ingina.[3] She was lovely and accomplished in all respects. Many noble men were under the jarl's command, who gave him faithful service.

One man who served the jarl was named Galinn.[4] He was a miller, and he was always plying that trade. His son was named Kvintalin; he was a thief and skulked out in the woods. He knew many cunning tricks and had learned many skills. He was a great master of playing the harp. With his playing, he had lured many noble women to him in the woods and kept them with him for as long as he liked, and then sent them back home, pregnant, to their fathers or husbands. For that reason, he had an evil reputation among men. No one knew his mother's lineage, but most men suspected that Galinn must have fathered him on the ogress[5] who lurked under the millrace.

CHAPTER VI

King Garlant of Ireland ruled a large realm in Brittany, and he often stayed there. It is said that he traveled there on one occasion, and his daughter went with him along with many other folk. The king stayed there for a long time. Garlant asked his daughter whether anyone had proposed to her in England. She told her father the entire conversation between Samson and herself. The king approved of it, and said that it would be a great stroke of luck if she could make such an excellent marriage.

When King Garlant had stayed in Brittany for as long as he liked, he prepared to travel home to Ireland with his retinue. But when the king had not gone far, the winds turned unfavorable. He sailed into an anchorage next to a grove of nut trees. His daughter was on this journey with him. With her went a little maid who had come to her in Brittany and befriended her there. She told the princess many things that she wished to know.

Now the two of them went into the forest together. There they heard harping so fair that they had never heard such music before. The princess said that they would find out who might be walking with the harp. Whenever they came under one tree, they heard the playing coming from another tree. They ran for such a long time that the princess grew weary. She took off her diadem and mantle and gave them to the maid to carry, and in the end she took off her long gown. Now the maid grew weary and couldn't keep up with her, and they separated.

The princess couldn't manage to get near the harper, and she kept going until the sun was setting. By that time, she had come to a brook. She stepped over the brook—and then she didn't hear the harping. She stepped backwards over the brook, and she heard the harping. She continued to follow her hearing until she saw the harper in a level field. She felt that matters were taking a hopeful turn.

Just then, a beautiful and well-dressed woman came up to her and greeted her and asked her name. The princess told her her name.

"But why are you traveling alone?" said the woman, "and where do you want to go?"

"I am eager to listen to this harp music which keeps escaping from me," replied the princess. "But what is your name?"

"I am called Olympia," said the woman, "and I have a home not far away from here. I came to find you because you've fallen under a spell. So heed my advice and get that thief out of your mind. We'll send him a message he'll take notice of."

There was a greyhound bitch running with Olympia. Olympia took a thread and tied it around its neck, and it took on the appearance of a lady. She showed the bitch the way to the thief, and spread her mantle over the princess.

Now the master harper went home to his hut. When he looked back, he saw the lady coming. He welcomed her warmly and thought that he'd had a stroke of luck. He took her hand and kissed her in every way. Then he led her into his hut and closed the door. Olympia and the princess followed, and Olympia said that they should watch their encounter. They climbed up onto the hut. Olympia told the princess that the man was Kvintalin the thief, and that he was in the habit of seducing many noble ladies in that way.

The thief sat at the table, and his lady sat next to him. She didn't want to eat anything except for the food that he placed into her mouth. The mealtime passed in this way, and she didn't say anything to him, even though she was most cheerful with him in every respect. Then he went to bed and invited his lady to lie down. She did—she lay down at his feet and wanted to scratch his toes. He swept her up onto the bed beside him, but she growled at him and sank her teeth into his chest. He pushed her away, and she leaped up onto the bedpost[6] and then onto the crossbeam and out the window, and he didn't have her any more.

Olympia went home to her castle. The princess went with her, and she explained to the princess what sort of woman she was. The princess asked her to bring her to the ships, but she said that she didn't dare to—"because I know that the king would leave before we could get there," she said. "I expect that Kvintalin will remember you. That's why you should stay here, for the sake of my foster-son Samson. I don't want that thief of women to do you harm."

And so it was that she stayed there.

Now there is this to tell of Kvintalin: He was not pleased with his lot, and he was eager to take his revenge. It so happened on one occasion that the princess had gotten up early. She went to the brook that was mentioned earlier, and she washed her hair. Then she heard the harp-playing as before, and she dashed after the wicked music and forgot the advice of her foster-mother. A little while later, Olympia found her foster-daughter running, and scolded her soundly for roaming outside alone. "Take care that such a thing doesn't happen to you again," she said. "Once again he'll get what's coming to him."

This time she had a cat with her, and she sent it to him in the same way as she had sent the bitch to him earlier. He welcomed the young maiden. She mewed in reply, and he thought that she must be speaking Irish. He went into his hut and sat down at the table, and his lady sat beside him and kept yowling. She looked at him rather squint-eyed, but he didn't notice that. Then they got into his bed, and he embraced his bride most tenderly. But as soon as they were undressed, a mouse came running out from under the timber wall. The young maiden leaped up at once and ran after the mouse. Kvintalin grabbed for her and got hold of her tail and pulled her down into bed with him, but she hissed horribly and sank her claws into his cheeks. He grabbed at her, and at that moment the cat escaped. Ever since then, her tail has been striped, because it was bruised where his fingers had been.[7]

Olympia and the princess went back home to the castle.

CHAPTER VII

As for King Garlant, we must say that he grieved the loss of his daughter. She was searched for far and wide, but she was not found, and neither was the young maid who disappeared with her. The king stayed there for a long time. But when men gave up the search, King Garlant sailed home to Ireland. He felt this was a terrible loss, and so did all those who heard the news. Yet eventually people stopped talking about it. King Garlant stayed at home in his own kingdom, and some time passed.

At that time, Samson the Fair was out raiding, and he accomplished many glorious deeds and won much plunder. After three winters had passed, he came to Ireland with his men. King Garlant invited him to a worthy feast, and he stayed there and received a warm reception. Once when they were drinking, Samson said to King Garlant, "Where is Lady Valentina, your daughter? She is the maiden for whom I have great love. Why is she not here to adorn our feast?"

"Lord Samson," said the king, "do not remind us of our grief. She disappeared from us in Brittany, in the wilderness, where we were hunting. We have heard nothing of her ever since, and our grief will never be soothed."

"I did not know that," said Samson, "What do people think is the cause?"

"Some suppose," said the king, "that evil spirits must have bewitched her. Some think that a beast must have killed her, or that she must have unwittingly fallen into a lake— along with a little maid who disappeared with her, the one who came to her in that land."

"That may be," said Samson, "but for the sake of love for her, I shall go to Brittany and find out whether I may get news of her."

The king said that he was grateful for that. And as soon as the winds were right, Samson sailed from Ireland with all his men, endowed with fine gifts from the king. There's nothing to say about his journey, until he came to Brittany and reached the harbor that was under Jarl Finnlaug's rule. When the jarl heard the news, he went to meet him in suitable fashion and invited him to a noble feast. Samson accepted, and he stayed with the jarl for some time.

On one occasion, Samson asked the jarl how Princess Valentina's disappearance had happened, andwhat guesses there might be as to what could have become of her. The jarl said that no one knew. Samson asked the jarl to advise him on how news of her might be found. The jarl said that he had no advice to give—"but it seems most advisable to me to find those who live in the wilderness and take them with you on the search. They will be most familiar with all the hiding places in the wilderness. I know one man in the forest there; his name is Galinn. He is a miller, and a stout man who knows many things, but he is not to be trusted. And if you take him into service with you, it will not go smoothly if he does not get something out of the business."

The prince took this advice. He got lodging for his men, but he himself went into the forest and found men whom he felt would be likeliest to know something. But they were not able to tell him anything.

Finally, he met Galinn the miller by his mill beside a waterfall. The stream flowed easily through his mill, and under the waterfall was a deep hole with a great whirlpool. Galinn greeted him and asked who he might be. Samson told him the truth. "I've come here because I have been told that you are knowledgeable about many things. I am on a quest for Valentina, the daughter of King Garlant, if she can be found dead or alive. I would like to have your help in this matter and for you to come with me on the search. I shall give you gold and silver, and my friendship."

Galinn answered, "Friendship with you seems like a good bargain, but I don't think it's likely that she'll be found. Everyone thinks that a wild beast has killed her. But in this matter, I will only ally myself to a man like you, since you may be of some importance. If she is alive, then I expect that news will come of her."

Then Samson took a purse, and there were ten marks of gold in it.[8] He said to Galinn, "I will give you this money for your friendship. And if we can manage to find the princess, I will make you a great man."

Galinn answered, "Your money seems quite valuable to me, but your friendship seems even more valuable. But even if we strive hard, I don't know what it will amount to. Still, if I am on this search with you, then if we don't find her, she isn't in this forest."

As they were talking, Samson was standing on the bridge over the millstream. They shook hands, and at that moment, Samson was grabbed by both legs and pulled down into the stream unawares. A troll-woman had come, and he had no strength to resist her, but as soon as he got his hands on her, they began to wrestle. They landed on the bottom, and he realized that she must be intending to push him against the bottom. He struggled desperately and managed to reach a knife that Princess Valentina had given him. He aimed it at her chest and sliced her entire belly open, so that her bowels burst out and the river looked like blood.

Samson was now on the point of drowning. He freed himself and swam underneath the whirlpool. There he found the mouth of a cave and crawled up under the overhanging rock. By now he was so weak with exhaustion that he had to lie there for a long time before he could move. When he got up, he wrung out his clothes. Then he searched the cave, and he thought that he would never reach the end of it. He found a side cave, and there he saw a great pile of goods and many fine treasures of gold and silver. There was a splendid bed there, with hangings and fine linens. There was a taut rope line with gold knobs on the ends, and many clothes hanging on the line. There he saw Princess Valentina's gown and cloak, and he also saw her diadem, sash, and brooch. He took down such things as he wanted and then went to the end of the cave. There he found a stone door. It was shut, but not locked, and he went outside. He didn't know which way to turn.[9]

On the fourth day afterwards, he came to some broad roads. He walked to a settlement, and then he was then shown the way to find Jarl Finnlaug. The jarl welcomed him warmly and asked how it had gone with him. He told him quite plainly and showed him the treasures, and they felt that she was most probably dead.

A little while later, Samson sailed to Ireland and met King Garlant. He told him of his journeys and showed him the treasures, and they decided that she must be dead. Samson stayed there for a while. When he left, he sailed to England. His father welcomed him warmly, and he told him about his journeys. He had won great fame on this journey. Now he stayed with his father.

CHAPTER VIII

On one occasion, King Arthur and his son were talking. The prince said to his father, "It has come to this, father: I desire to be married, and I would have your counsel in this matter."

"That is well," said the king. "You must have seen many noble ladies, and you must clearly know where you wish to seek."

"Many maidens have I seen," said the prince, "but none of them I esteem more highly than Valentina. But there is also Ingina, the daughter of Jarl Finnlaug of Brittany."

The king said that he had heard good report of her—"but I will hardly make a grand expedition if you seek no greater match than the daughter of a jarl. You will have no need of my strength, wealth, or supporters."

They ended their conversation for the time being.

In the spring, Samson readied his ships and his men. He sailed away from England and went out raiding through the summer. As summer was passing, he sailed to Brittany and pitched his tents on land. The jarl gave him a warm welcome and invited him to stay, but Samson said that it would mean a great deal if he were willing to betroth his daughter, the lady Ingina, to him.

"I expect that she could hope for no better marriage," said the jarl. The jarl was easily convinced, but he said that he wanted to hear her answer. The jarl had his daughter summoned and told her how the proposal stood, and he asked what answer she would give to it. She was silent for a while, and then she said, "You should not be concerned that I would respond to this suit with reluctance, because I would choose no other man, even if the choice were entirely mine. But my heart tells me that this betrothal will not turn out to be fortunate for me. Are you quite certain that Princess Valentina is dead?"

The prince said that he didn't believe that she could be alive.

"I also don't want to stand in the way," said the maiden, "either of your happiness, or of her fortune and honor. But I must not break with my father's decision."

To make a long story short, Samson was engaged to Ingina in the end, and the time for the wedding was fixed for the coming summer. The prince stayed there for a little while before sailing to Ireland, and he spent the winter with King Garlant. But in spring he prepared to go to England, and he invited King Garlant to his wedding and told him where to meet. The king promised to come. Now Samson sailed to England and met his father and told him of his betrothal, and invited him to come to his wedding. The king promised to come.

Now the men made great preparations, and they took the greatest care with their ships and suitable weapons and disciplined men and fine clothing.

When they were ready, they sailed to Brittany, but they didn't reach the harbor that they intended. It was two days' journey to the fortress where Jarl Finnlaug lived. King Garlant joined them with all his men, and there was a joyful reunion between them. Jarl Finnlaug found out that they had come, and he rode to meet them with his men, driving many riding horses for their use. Each man was glad to see the others. And since it was a week till the appointed time of the wedding, they were willing to stay in their tents, and the jarl was pleased with this. During that time, they had all manner of entertainments: board games and jousting, archery and fencing. Sometimes they rode into the forest to amuse themselves.

CHAPTER IX

Now there is this to tell about Kvintalin Women-Thief: he was displeased with his situation, and felt that he had suffered a great disgrace. He met his father and told him that he wanted to take his revenge. But Galinn told him in reply what he and Samson had said, and he said that he supposed that Kvintalin's mother must have killed him—"we should go and visit her, and she will advise us."

They went into the cave, but they didn't find their friend, and they realized that she must be dead and Samson must have killed her.

"What is your plan now?" said Kvintalin.

Galinn said, "There's a stone standing in the forest, not too far from here. A wily dwarf named Grelant rules it.[10] If you can manage to defeat him, he will give you some advice on capturing Princess Valentina."

Galinn went to his mill, and Kvintalin lay in wait for the dwarf. Just once, Kvintalin was able to spot the dwarf outside the stone. He seized him with his hands and swore to kill him. The dwarf said, "There's little glory for you in breaking the stumpy bones in my body. I would rather redeem my life and do something with some bravery in it that will benefit you."

Kvintalin answered, "You must bring Lady Valentina into my power. And tell me if Samson the Fair killed my mother, and if he is alive."

The dwarf said, "He is certainly alive, and he killed your mother. He has betrothed the daughter of Jarl Finnlaug and fixed the wedding. But even if I were to do all I can, it is not certain whether I could beat Olympia, and I will need to lie in wait for them for a long time. Still, I'd rather agree to this than lose my stone."

The dwarf swore to uphold this agreement, and then they parted. Now the dwarf built a cart with wondrous skill. It ran on wheels,[11] and he could pull the cart behind himself. There was a bed and some food inside the cart. Now he waited to catch the princess.

Kvintalin met with his father and told him what had happened, and said that Samson could be expected to arrive. They conspired to betray Samson as soon as he should come to their land. They built a large pit trap where they thought he would ride, with caltrops scattered all around.[12]

When there were four days remaining till the wedding, all the nobles rode to the woods with a great many retainers. They sent a great many of the beasts that they hunted to the fortress that day. Samson saw a single stag in a clearing, so fair that he had never seen the like before. It looked to him as if sunbeams were shining from his horns. He was most eager to catch the stag and rode off a long way from his men, and they did not know what had become of him. But this stag was so swift that it was a wonder.[13] They came to a level plain. Samson spurred his horse. But before he reached the clearing, the horse ran right into the pit trap and broke its neck. Samson leaped up out of the pit, but he landed on the caltrops, and they stuck fast in the soles of his feet.

Just then, he saw a hideous dwarf coming out of the woods, pulling a golden cart behind him.[14] Samson couldn't tell what was in it. And now the stag disappeared right before his eyes. The dwarf acted as if he didn't hear when Samson called, and then he vanished into the forest. But the caltrops were so thick on the ground that Samson got stuck by one as soon as he freed himself from another.

Just then, a little boy came forward into the clearing, riding on a donkey colt. The boy called out and said, "My good man, did anyone leave this place just now?"

Samson answered, "A little while ago a dwarf was here, driving a cart on wheels. But I don't know what was in it."

"Well," said the boy, "that was my master, and he was traveling with Lady Valentina, the daughter of King Garlant. She was searching for her lover, and she said his name was Samson the Fair."

"Good friend," said the prince, "I am that very same man, but my feet are so pierced with spikes that I cannot walk anywhere. Ride after them and ask her to come here quickly, and for that I will give you my shield."

"Give me something by which she may recognize you," said the boy.

The prince took a gold ring and gave it to him. "Go now," said Samson, "and come back soon."

The boy rode into the forest. Samson didn't take the donkey colt because it was too little.

Now the story turns to Valentina. It so happened one morning that she arose early and went out into the courtyard, and she saw the cart. She had never seen such a sight before. She went up to the cart and sat down in in, and suddenly a sleep fell upon her. The dwarf drove off on his way. Olympia was still asleep. This all happened at the same time and on the same day that Samson was lured away from his own men by the tricks that the father and son had prepared for him, which were described earlier.

Now we return to Samson, who thought that the boy was dawdling. He saw a man coming out into the clearing. He recognized Galinn, and each greeted the other cheerfully. "Good friend," said Galinn, "why are you sitting there so alone?"

"I'm in a bad way now, because my feet have been injured by spikes," said Samson.

"This is no time to rest," said Galinn, "because an ugly, nasty dwarf was driving your beloved into the forest, and there's no better time than now to catch her."

"Good friend," said Samson, "much depends on the help you are willing to offer me."

Galinn answered, "I meant to offer you help that will last you forever. Give me your sword. I shall kill the wicked dwarf. Wait for me here."

"I'm placing great trust in you," said Samson, "if give you my sword."

"I don't dare go after that dwarf without a weapon," said Galinn, "and I recall what we said to each other. But we'll never manage to find her if the dwarf brings her inside the stone."

Now Samson gave him his sword and begged him to hurry. He promised to do his best and ran into the forest, and Samson was left behind without a weapon.

A little while later, Samson saw two men riding forth into the clearing, fully armed. He recognized Galinn, and the other one was Kvintalin Women-Thief. He called out to Samson and said, "You have brought misfortune on yourself in this place. You have killed my mother and stolen my wealth. And now I shall kill you and take your beloved."

They both dismounted and drew their swords. Samson had no shield. He said, "Galinn, good friend, give me my sword."

Galinn said, "This sword won't go any farther from you than your shirt." Both of them struck at him at the same time, but Galinn was faster. Samson dodged the blow and suffered a wound on the shoulder blade, but the sword was knocked out of Galinn's hands. At once Samson seized Galinn and thrust him in front of the blow that Kvintalin struck. That blow landed on his helmet and cut off the noseguard and Galinn's entire face, so that he fell dead in the grass. Samson tore himself from the caltrops and seized his sword and struck at Kvintalin, and he split his shield from end to end and knocked out three of his teeth. The woman-thief turned to run, and he leaped onto the back of his horse. Samson ran along the path that Kvintalin had ridden, and he pursued him until they came to a field. At the end of this field was the cave that Samson had entered when he killed the ogress. The thief dashed into the cave, but Samson struck at him, and he was wounded on both buttocks[15] and his horse was chopped in two just behind him and his saddle. And so they parted for the time being.

CHAPTER X

Samson turned back onto the field. Now he saw where the golden cart was standing, which he had seen before. In another place he saw the dwarf and a woman having a hard struggle, each wanting to overcome the other. Samson charged there with his sword drawn. As soon as the dwarf saw that, he shouted in a loud voice, "Lord Samson, do not kill me! I will gladly serve you faithfully, and I transgressed against you unwillingly, and I shall make amends for everything. Oh you good woman, help me!"[16]

Samson recognized his foster-mother, and he went to her. They were glad to see each other. She led the dwarf to Samson and said, "Spare the dwarf's life, and put him in my power, and he may be of use to us."

"Whether he lives is up to you," said Samson, and they went to the cart. Valentina was asleep in it, and she didn't know what had happened. Olympia woke her and said, "Now see how little effort it takes to track you down."

She replied, "Where am I? I saw this cart in the morning, and I sat down in it and fell asleep at once."

"Look around," said Olympia.

Valentina stood up from the cart and saw where Samson was standing. As he recognized her, they embraced each other, with loving words and tenderness. For a long hour their mouths lay gently together, and each must have given the other more than a thousand kisses.

Olympia said, "Lord Samson, what about your journeys? And why have you come here, so exhausted?"

Samson began to tell the whole story. He told how the boy tricked him out of his shield and Galinn had tricked him out of his sword, and how their encounter had gone, and how thickly the caltrops lay throughout the forest by the clearing—"and not all of them are loose from my feet."

"I know that the wicked thief Kvintalin has deceived you," said Olympia, "just as his mother deceived your beloved, and he has cheated her out of all her things. Yet she would have been more terribly shamed if she had been alone. He thought that it was she, when the bitch and the cat came to him.[17] Even since then, this wicked thief has been plotting to entice her, and he has cowed that dwarf into joining forces with him."

Samson asked whether the dwarf was willing to make amends for the wrongs that he had done. He said that he was eager to pay. "Follow me to Kvintalin's cave and deliver him into my hands," said Samson.

"I cannot do that," said the dwarf, "because no one may enter, on account of a powerful incantation." And now the dwarf swore an oath to be loyal to Samson.

Olympia said, "I think it's best for us to go to our castle." And so they did, and Olympia healed Samson.

Now it is time to turn to how King Arthur and his men missed Samson and searched for him. When they entered the clearing, they thought they saw him lying dead in his clothing, but they could not recognize his face because it had been cut off. They found this to be a dreadful shock. No one knew who could have caused it. Then Jarl Finnlaug arrived, and he felt that this was the hardest blow. He said that Kvintalin the thief and his father Galinn must be responsible. They brought the body home and prepared it honorably and wept over his grave—but the bride had little to say, and many found that strange. Then the feast became an inheritance feast, and pomp and merriment began. And when the feasting had lasted for five days, King Garlant called for a hearing and said, "Jarl Finnlaug, I wish to hear how you would answer me if I asked for the hand of your daughter Lady Ingina, who lost her beloved a short while ago—whom we would buy back with gold, if that were possible. Here in return I will give myself and my realm."

The jarl said, "That is well said"— but he said that he still wanted to hear her answer. Then she was asked and the suit was brought before her. She said, "I find it incredible that Samson should be so short-lived, and my heart suspects that something else has happened. But you should not interpret my words to mean that I am asking for this marriage for myself. My heart has long told me that my destiny would turn out to be greater in Ireland than in England. But I must have the counsel of my father concerning my betrothal."

Whatever was said there, it came to pass in the end that King Garlant was married to Ingina. The inheritance-feast was now turned into a wedding feast, and there was no lack of merriment and happiness and all manner of good cheer. This went on for a week. King Garlant went to bed with his beloved Ingina, and the rulers were honored with worthy gifts.

CHAPTER XI

One morning, Olympia said to Samson: "The time has come for us to find out what has become of the kings. They must be grieved at your disappearance."

Samson said that it was up to her. They left, taking Grelant the dwarf with them.

That same morning, Jarl Finnlaug and the kings were on the playing field. Samson the Fair and Lady Valentina arrived, with Olympia and the dwarf. Everyone was astonished. King Arthur welcomed his son warmly and asked how this could have happened. Samson told them all the circumstances that had delayed them.

Now King Garlant came up to Samson and said, "Many things turn out otherwise than men expected. We would not have done what we've done, if we had known that you were alive. If you feel wronged in this matter, I want you to leave my honor uninjured."

"Well do I believe," said Samson, "that you have done this unwittingly. I will not diminish your honor in any way if you will betroth to me Lady Valentina, your daughter."

King Garlant said that he was quite willing, and so did Lady Valentina. Samson betrothed himself to Valentina, for her to be his only wife. Their wedding had to wait for the next summer. They drank until the feast was over. Worthy gifts were given to everyone, and they parted as good friends. King Garlant went home to Ireland with his wife.

CHAPTER XII

Samson stayed behind and spoke with Grelant the dwarf. "I want your support," he said, "to avenge my disgrace on Kvintalin the thief."

The dwarf said, "If you bring him out of the cave, then I can capture him, but I cannot enter the cave."

Samson went to the waterfall next to where the mill stood. The others had to go with the dwarf. Samson dived under the waterfall and reached the entrance to the cave. He armed himself and found the thief, but he fled. Samson chased him to the cave doors and couldn't catch him. Kvintalin slammed the doors shut. But when he tried to run away, he was caught on the caltrops that the dwarf had thrown down there. Now Olympia and the dwarf came with their men, and they manhandled him and took him to Jarl Finnlaug. Samson took all the wealth from the cave. They were all astonished at how much wealth Kvintalin had stolen.

Kvintalin begged Olympia for his life, but she said that it would be a bad thing to trust him. Samson said to Kvintalin, "Now that you are in my power, the old saying proves true, that 'the digger sees the pit that he's dug'". Now, Kvintalin, I shall torture you in many ways, and then kill you."

Kvintalin said, "That won't increase your honor much, even if you kill me. But I might do an honorable deed that would bring you greater glory."

"I will not negotiate for your life so that you can steal from me," said Samson.

Olympia replied, "Lord Samson, it would be a good idea to send him on a certain quest, so that he may win one fine treasure and risk his life there."

"Where shall we send him?" said Samson.

She said to Kvintalin, "You must swear an oath not to steal from us." He swore the oath at once.

Olympia said, "You must go and seek the precious cloth that four elf-women have been weaving for eighteen winters, where the sun shines from underneath the Earth when it reaches its highest in the summer, and they never sleep at that time. Besides that, you must get two other treasures of the same value."

"I find this to be a terribly difficult task," said Kvintalin. "Yet I shall accomplish it, if you will allow the dwarf to go with me."

Let us leave off for the time being.

CHAPTER XIII

Here we begin the second part of the saga, and it begins with a king named Godmund. He ruled over Glaesisvellir[18] in the east; that is east of Risaland. Risaland lies east and north of the Baltic realms, and extends northeastwards from there. Then there lies the land that is called Jotunheim, and there live trolls and monsters.[19] From there all the way to uninhabited Greenland lies the land called Svalbard, and various tribes live there.[20] There are those who live to be two hundred winters old, but seldom have many children. There is another tribe that must be considered human, but they have a foolish nature, and what they have is called "mountain man's wits."

A low-lying cape extends out into the sea, and there lives the tribe called Little Girls. They never grow older than fifteen years, and they have children when they are seven years old.[21] Ogres wield such power in Jotunheim that if men say out loud that "trolls should take something," they come and take it.[22]

CHAPTER XIV

It is said that on one occasion, King Godmund of Glaesisvellir traveled north to Jotunheim and raided the giants and did many warlike deeds among them. The giants came against him with a great force, and the king sailed out to sea.

One day, they sailed past the Land of Little Girls and headed for harbor. The cooks went onto land to prepare some food. They found three women by the sea, and one of them was loveliest. "Look here," said one of the cooks, "I've never seen a lovelier maiden. Let's bring her to the king."

She answered, "Wherever you grew up must be poorly off for maidens, if you're calling me a maiden—a widow, eight years old, and I've had two husbands! But what sort of person is this that you call 'king'?"

"He is a man like us," said the cook, "and you must go with us."[23]

They came before the king and showed him the woman. The king was well pleased with her, and laid her beside himself in bed. The king stayed in the Land of Little Girls over the winter, but in spring he sailed away and took the woman with him, and she was pregnant. They had not been sailing for long when she went into labor, and she gave birth to a baby boy, large and handsome—but she died in childbirth.

Now the king thought about what to do, because at the time there were laws that if the king or another man should have a child outlive his wife, he had to forfeit his wealth and his realm, and his eldest son had to take them and also the title of king—but the child and all its descendants were condemned to slavery. King Godmund hit upon a plan: he had thralls bring the child to land, and he ordered them to see to it that the child never become a source of shame to him. They brought the baby to a mountainous district and wrapped it in linen and left a gold ring nearby. They laid the baby between stones and left a cake in its mouth to suck on, and then they laid a slab of rock over the stones. After that they returned to the ships. King Godmund sailed home to his kingdom and knew nothing about this.[24]

A short while after the thralls had left the baby, a certain old man who lived nearby came there. He was called Krok, and his old wife was Krekla.[25] They were strong[26] and stupid and had "mountain man's wits." One day Krok went into the forest to hunt ptarmigans. He heard a baby crying, and he found the baby with the clothes and items that the thralls had left with it. He picked it up and brought it to his old wife. They were happy, because they had no children. They named the boy Sigurd, from the sucking-cake,[27] and they called him their son. He grew up there and soon became incredibly tall. They couldn't manage him, because the old man was half afraid of him.

The family had one prized possession that they felt was better than anything else. It was a ram. His fleece was so long that it dragged, and it was of all colors: the colors of gold and silk, cloth and dyes. He shed his fleece three times each year.

CHAPTER XV

At that time, a king named Skrimnir ruled Jotunheim.[28] He was a giant, and all giants and many other people served him and were obligated to pay tribute to him. Krok and Krekla rendered him the fleece of their ram every year as tribute.

There was a giant named Krapi. He had four daughters. They were skilled at weaving, but they didn't have much work to do. They were in the habit of stealing the wool from King Skrimnir. He didn't know what was going on.

One night, the king heard a noise in the attic where the wool was kept. He went there and saw four troll-women[29]; they had packed up bundles of the tribute for themselves. The king seized them and asked why they were stealing his tribute, and they pled poverty. Their settlement was that they should keep what they had taken, and make a mantle out of it for the king, with many colors and many powers, and not sleep until it was finished.

Sigurd grew up with Krok and Krekla. He was poorly clothed. A cassock was made for him out of camel hair, woven like a bedcover. He wore ankle-high shoes of shaggy fox-skin on his feet, and he carried a club. So matters went until he was fifteen years old.

CHAPTER XVI

It happened one day that the old woman had to water the ram. He was in a bad temper and knocked the old woman down. She cursed him and said the trolls could have him.

Sigurd said, "You've blundered now, if you're giving your most prized possession to the trolls."

"I'll never take him back," she said.

"It's not fitting for petty trolls to have such a fine treasure," said Sigurd, "and I would rather take him to the king."

"Then you'll never come back," said the old woman.

"Fate must decide that," he said.

He took the ram and traveled for a long time. Many trolls came to find him and demanded the ram. But he said that the king had to have it, and he bashed them in return.

He traveled until he found an old woman who was weeping sorely. Sigurd asked what the matter might be. She answered, "I was quarrelling with my husband, and I said that all trolls could have him, and they took him away at once. I will reward you well if you can manage to get him back."

Sigurd said, "Will you take the responsibility of caring for the ram?"

She said that she would try.

He hurried on his way and came to a cave. There were four troll-women inside. They had tied the man up by the feet to a beam and were swinging him among them, and they said, "You filthy devil, you aren't one of us!"[30]

Sigurd killed the troll-women with his club and brought the old woman her husband, half dead. He left many treasures with them, which he had taken from the cave. He took the ram and went on his way, and they asked him to meet them when he came back.

On Christmas Eve, Sigurd arrived at King Skrimnir's royal seat. He entered the cave and sat down outside the chamber. Just then he saw a man walk into the cave and came before the king and greeted him, and he held up a chest wrought with gold. He took a mantle out of the chest. It was such a splendid treasure that none finer was to be had. He handed it to the king and said that his daughters had sent him. The king accepted it, and asked why they had not come themselves. He said that they had a new victim. "But they mean to meet you on the eighth day of Yule. I must go home for now, and come later with my daughters, and take my share of the ram that Krekla gave me and all trolls."

"I firmly agree with her," said King Skrimnir. "That's no possession for a petty troll."

"That's true," said Krapi. He turned and left. And when he came to the outer edge of the cave, there was Sigurd before him with the ram. Krapi said, "It's a good thing for you, Sigurd, that you've shortened my trip. I'd meant to fetch the ram that the old woman gave me."

"She would hardly give him to you," said Sigurd, "because he's a possession for a king."

"Shut up, beggar," said Krapi, and grabbed the ram. But Sigurd struck him so hard with his staff that his skull broke and both his eyes went flying. He fell dead to the floor with a dreadful crunching sound. The giants in the cave went to the doors and saw that Sigurd had entered the cave. Skrimnir asked what that racket might be in the outer parts of the cave. They told him that it must be a child who had come—"and he's coming with a great treasure. But we have never seen a monster like him, and we think that he's killed Krapi."

Skrimnir ordered Sigurd to be summoned, and it was done. Sigurd came before the king, and there weren't many pleasantries between them. He said to the king, "Here is the ram that my foster-mother gave to all trolls, but I think it's better that he come to you. At the cave doors, a wicked ruffian came at me and wanted to take the ram from me, but I struck him with my staff. I suppose that did him some harm, because he's not standing up. Now you should take care of the ram."

The king said, "Have thanks for it! It's likely that you'll be a fortunate man. And you're no disgrace to your family line, because King Godmund of Glaesisvellir is your father."

Then Skrimnir had fine clothing brought to him and had his hair combed, and he seated him by his side on the high seat, and he looked like a completely different man. He stayed there over Yule and quickly learned the giants' customs.

CHAPTER XVII

On the eighth day of Yule, the king asked Sigurd what task he wanted to take up, and Sigurd said that he wanted his advice about that. "Since you're the son of King Godmund," said the king, "I think it's best for you to go and find him and find out whether he's willing to acknowledge you. I will give you a ship and men."

Sigurd said that he was quite eager—"but first I must find my foster-mother. I will return at midwinter."

Sigurd left, and they parted in friendship. Sigurd came to the old crone whose husband he had brought back. She was called Gnod, and her husband was Kritur. They welcomed him warmly and asked how it had gone with him. He said that he was pleased, and said that he would like to have her advice. Gnod said that that would do him good. "There is a good harbor here, and you should come here when you leave Krok and Krekla,[31] and find out whether I can manage to get you a reward for your assistance."

Then Sigurd found his foster-mother, and she welcomed him warmly. He told her what had come of his journey, and said that he wanted to visit his father. She said that she was quite willing to help. When Sigurd prepared to leave, the old man and woman went down to the sea with him, and they found a heap of woodchips. The old woman took out of it a ship that would accommodate one man, as fair to see as gold. "I will give you this ship, Sigurd," said the old woman. "No matter where you want to sail, it gets a favorable wind when the sail is raised. It can never be overloaded."

She hauled up the rigging, and she and Krok raised the mast. She took a cask of good wine and gave it to Sigurd and told him never to drink it dry, and it would fill again. Then she gave him the gold ring that had been found with him.

Sigurd sailed until he met Gnod and received his reward. At their parting, Gnod gave him a staff, and said that whoever carried the staff would never be poor or weak. Now Sigurd sailed until he met King Skrimnir, and Skrimnir invited him to stay. Sigurd said that he wanted to find his father and find out whether they might reach an agreement, and what honors his father might be willing to grant him. Skrimnir said that the choice was his. He went to the ship with him and gave him riches and men, and at their parting he gave him a sword ornamented with gold, and the fine mantle that the troll-women had woven. The mantle had many powers. It revealed the falsity of wives, if they had been untrue to their husbands, or of maidens who had not dutifully stayed at home, as will be told later. Sigurd and Skrimnir parted in friendship, and Skrimnir told Sigurd to call his name if he needed any help.

CHAPTER XVIII

Now Sigurd sailed away from Jotunheim with these treasures. He set out raiding in the summer and accomplished many brave deeds. When he came into any difficulties or dangers, he always called out the name of King Skrimnir, and Skrimnir always came to help him, and everything went smoothly.

In the autumn, he came to Glaesisvellir, to King Godmund. He came before the king and greeted him. The king accepted his greeting and asked who he might be. He said that his name was Sigurd—"and I am obliged to bring you this message." Then he gave the king the gold ring that he was found with, and he said, "Do you remember where you parted with this ring?"

The king blushed deeply at that, and said when he looked at Sigurd, "I think that I can resolve this question. But you can't have managed this by yourself."

"My foster-mother Krekla told me this," said Sigurd. "Now I want to know what arrangements you will make."

The king said, "Everything here shall be at your disposal. You are welcome to stay with us. I shall treat you well."

Sigurd accepted, and he stayed with the king over the winter. The king treated him well and seated him beside himself. Many were amazed that the king was paying so much attention to a foreigner and making so much of him, and they envied Sigurd. But this was not discussed much, because Sigurd was popular.

In the spring, the king asked what he meant to do, or what task he meant to take up. "I want you to give me support," said Sigurd, "and I want to go out raiding."

The king said that that would be a good plan, and he gave him ships and men. Sigurd set out raiding and harried in Bjarmaland, Karelia, and Smaland,[32] and he subjugated those lands.

Harek was the name of the king of Bjarmaland. He had a daughter who was named Oddny. Sigurd asked for her hand, and she was given in marriage to him. He stayed there most often.

CHAPTER XIX

One summer, Sigurd readied his forces, meaning to meet his father King Godmund. But before he sailed away from Bjarmaland, Oddny fell ill, and the sickness brought about her death. They had one son, who was named Ulfhedin. He grew up with King Harek and became a mighty champion; he was later called Ulfhedin One-Hand. He is mentioned in the saga of Sigurd Hring, the father of Ragnar Shaggy-Breeches.[33]

Sigurd came to Glaesisvellir. Godmund welcomed him warmly and asked what he meant to do. Sigurd said that he wanted to travel to Risaland and meet his foster-father Skrimnir. He said that he no longer had a wife—"but Skrimnir has a daughter named Gerd, by the daughter of Jarl Agdi of Gniparland.[34] She is a beautiful maiden, and she takes more after her mother's side than her father." He asked his father whether he found that a good decision.

Godmund said that it was not a bad plan. "Although you may think that Skrimnir will begrudge you being king over Jotunheim, he will still betroth the woman to you. But do not put any trust in him, because giants are jealous."

Now Sigurd sailed to Jotunheim and met the king at mealtime, and he brought his proposal before him. He received it favorably, and said that his son Geirrod would inherit his realm and kingdom, after himself—"but I will give my daughter the Land of Little Girls and the realm that belongs to it."

Sigurd paid the bride-price for Gerd and married her. Geirrod, Skrimnir's son, was out raiding. When he heard of this, he was not pleased, and he went to the Land of Little Girls and raided in King Sigurd's realm. When King Sigurd heard that news, he moved against him with his forces, and they encountered each other at the landmark called Gardar. There was a battle, and in the end Geirrod fell. The place has been called Geirrodargardar ever since.[35]

When the battle was over, Skrimnir came with a host of giants, but Sigurd wasn't prepared. His men were few, and their weapons were broken. He offered Skrimnir a settlement and the right to set his own conditions. Skrimnir wasn't willing to settle unless Sigurd were to swear an oath that he should never come to Risaland for as long as Skrimnir lived, and give back the Land of Little Girls and the fine mantle. Sigurd didn't hestitate to swear the oath. He went to Skrimnir and took his hand, and Skrimnir was to pronounce the truce. But Sigurd never went anywhere without the staff that Kritur and his wife had given him. When Sigurd took his father-in-law's hand, he picked up the staff and drove it into his ear, so that his skull shattered and his eyes flew out of his head. And with that, the friendship between the father-in-law and his son-in-law came to an end.

Sigurd claimed Jotunheim and became king over it, and no man spoke against him. He ruled it for a long time afterwards. Sigurd had a son with his wife, who was named Ulf; he was a handsome and courteous man, and well skilled in sports and achievements. Sigurd ruled his realm for more than a hundred years. By that time his wife had died.

CHAPTER XX

At that time, a jarl named Asper[36] ruled over Risaland. He was a mighty ruler. His wife had died. He had a daughter who was named Hrafnborg. She was a lovely and well-mannered woman. She was thought to be the best marital prospect in the Eastern lands.

On one occasion, King Sigurd set out for Risaland. He had a large and splendid force with him. And as soon as he came before Jarl Asper, he made his proposal to him and asked for the hand of his daughter Hrafnborg. They felt he was elderly, yet there was such fear of King Sigurd that the jarl did not dare to refuse him the maiden. It was resolved that Hrafnborg was to be betrothed to Sigurd, and the wedding was to take place at once. Sigurd's son Ulf was out raiding at the time. People thought it would have been better for him to have married Hrafnborg.

Now the wedding was arranged, and many preparations were made. Oxen were killed and ale was mulled. There was no lack of food and drink, yet more provisions were searched for in all directions. Men went to the forest to hunt beasts and shoot birds, and women went to the groves to pick pears and plums and all kinds of fruits.[37] The jarl's daughter was in the forest. Sometimes she was alone, and sometimes there was a little maid with her.

CHAPTER XXI
Kvintalin Gets the Fine Mantle

Now we must begin the story of how Kvintalin Women-Thief and Grelant the dwarf had traveled to fulfill their sworn oath and the task that had been set before them. By now they had arrived in Russia in their cart, and they entered the same forest as the jarl's daughter, whom we mentioned earlier. They came up to the jarl's daughter and set the cart near her, and then left. The jarl's daughter saw where the cart was standing, and she sat down in it. Right then and there, she fell into a sleep. Kvintalin arrived, and he took off her clothes and put them on himself. With his magic and sorcery he exchanged appearances with her. Then he ordered the dwarf to watch the cart, and he went to the jarl's daughter's chambermaid and went home with her. No one suspected that he was not Lady Hrafnborg.

Now the wedding was begun and the people were seated. There was no lack of good cheer, and the people drank with great joy. In the morning, the brides were led in. They brought great radiance into the hall. King Sigurd had the fine mantle brought forth. It had many magical powers. It revealed the falsity of wives, if they had deceived their husbands; on each wife, it shortened itself to show everything that she had revealed when she laid herself down.[38] It worked in the same way for unfaithful maidens. But if a thief dressed in it, it fell to the ground.[39] The maidens were dressed in the mantle, and they were shown to be very unfaithful. Next it was given to Lady Hrafnborg. She asked to be given space while she threw the mantle over himself, and it was done.

King Sigurd was standing nearby, because this concerned him the most. He was supporting himself with the fine staff; he was quite decrepit, because he had lived a hundred and fifty years. The bride seized the staff and made the king stumble, and she struck the staff against his ear and told the trolls to take him. At once Kvintalin dashed out with the staff and the mantle, and not a hand could touch him.[40] He found the dwarf and they seated themselves in the cart, and it quickly disappeared.

A panic broke out among those who were inside and standing beside the king when he fell, because he died instantly. Men rushed outside and saw nothing of the bride, and no one could follow her tracks.

The people began to build a burial mound, and they wanted to bring King Sigurd there. But trolls came and said that he had been given to them at his death. They took him and brought him to Risaland, and there is no more to tell of him.

CHAPTER XXII

As for Kvintalin, we must report that he and the dwarf came home with the treasures that they had won. This happened at the same time that Samson the Fair held his wedding, at Ruduborg in Ireland.[41] King Garland held this feast. King Arthur was there, the father of Samson the Fair, along with Jarl Finnlaug and many other rulers.

On the morning that the brides were led in, Kvintalin and the dwarf arrived. They greeted the rulers in suitable fashion. The rulers welcomed them well and asked whether their journey had been successful. Quickly they took the treasures and showed them off, and everyone was quite amazed and felt that these were splendid goods. The special nature of the mantle was tried out, and it was quickly shown that few were completely pure—it fit Lady Valentina well, but no one else. Then they led forth Lady Hrafnborg, and Kvintalin told how he had acquired her and the treasures. Everyone found her most lovely. Kvintalin gave Samson the mantle, and Samson gave it to his lady as a bridal gift. He gave the staff to King Garlant, and the lady to Jarl Finnlaug.

Samson said, "Now you have proven to be better than many would suppose. And if you're willing to be a mature man from now on, Kvintalin, you'll be worthy of fine rewards."

The rulers agreed to give Kvintalin the title of jarl and the island called Anglesey; it was to be under his rule forever. And now the feast ended with great honor. Jarl Finnlaug betrothed himself to Lady Hrafnborg and invited the rulers to his own wedding. Each man traveled to his own realm.

CHAPTER XXIII

Now we must tell about Ulf the son of Sigurd: he came home from his raiding and heard of the loss of his father and the disappearance of Lady Hrafnborg. He went to find Jarl Asper. Ulf told him that he had heard that Kvintalin the thief had stolen Asper's daughter and killed Ulf's own father. He asked what support the jarl was willing to give him so that he might avenge their disgrace. He added that Jarl Finnlaug had married Asper's daughter. The jarl said that he would lend his full support.

Then they summoned their forces and sailed west over the sea, and they came to the land that Kvintalin ruled. He was not at home, but that evening he sailed into the harbor where Ulf already was. When Ulf found out, he ordered his men to arm themselves, and they boarded the ship and captured Jarl Kvintalin, but they knocked his men overboard. Then they went to the forests with Jarl Kvintalin and hanged him. So ended his wicked life.

CHAPTER XXIV

Now they meant to find Jarl Finnlaug. They set sail for Ireland and landed there. King Garlant moved against them, because they were ravaging the land. Their encounter was at the place called Myrkjol.[42] King Garlant fell there, and Ulf subjugated the country.

Jarl Finnlaug heard about this, and he summoned his forces and sent word to Samson the Fair. Samson was out raiding at the time; he had conquered the land called Westphalia, a part of Germany. Lady Hrafnborg came to speak with Olympia and said, "Let us now make use of your wisdom and bring about a settlement between Jarl Finnlaug and Ulf."

Hrafnborg begged Finnlaug to reach a settlement with Ulf and Jarl Asper. Finnlaug loved her very much and said that Olympia should have the most power to decide it. Then men were found to serve as intermediaries. By the terms of the settlement, Ulf was to marry Lady Ingina, whom King Garlant had been married to, and she should have the landholdings that Hrafnborg had held in Russia. Jarl Asper married Olympia and took the stewardship of Ireland, and Lady Hrafnborg was to own it in exchange for her own holdings.

Ulf went home with his wife. They had a son who was named Sigurd. He was a handsome man. And as soon as he came of age, he set out raiding and became a worthy man. He raided in Germany. By that time, Samson the Fair was very old. He and Valentina had a daughter whose name was Herborg. Ulf's son Sigurd asked for her hand, and she was married to him. He became a jarl in France.

When Samson the Fair heard of the loss of his father, he traveled to England and accepted the realm and became king over that land. He and Lady Valentina had a son named Walter, and Samson gave him the realm that he owned in Westphalia. He married a woman named Gertrude, the daughter of the Duke of Brunswick. Walter became the Duke of Holstein.[43] As for Sigurd, we can say that he had a son with his wife Herborg, who was named Ulf. Ulf's son was Sigurd who fought against Harald the Sacrificer and defeated him. Then he married Cecilia, the daughter of the King of Sicily, and there is a long saga to tell concerning him.[44]

The fine mantle that Samson the Fair owned, he gave to Lady Ingina. A long time afterwards, it was stolen by Grimar[45] the Viking. He carried it west into Africa. A powerful and jealous woman named Elida sent it to England, to King Arthur, and that's how the *Saga of the Mantle* originated.

The Saga of Vilmund the Outsider

Vilmundar saga viðutan

Vilmundar saga viðutan *is usually classified as an "original* riddarasaga*", a romance composed in Iceland in imitation of foreign romances. However, it shares a style, setting, outlook, and many motifs with the* fornaldarsögur. *The bumpkin hero Vilmund, coarse Ruddi, and urbane Hjarrandi mirror the roles of Parceval, Kay, and Gawain in* Parcevals saga.[1] *However, Vilmund is the grandson of Bósi, the hero of* Bósa saga ok Herrauðs, *which is usually classified with the* fornaldarsögur. *Other plot elements, notably the princess exchanging her identity with a servant, may have been borrowed from* Hálfdanar saga Eysteinssonar. *The plot as a whole shows a pattern seen in myths and sagas about Thor and Thor-like heroes: the incredibly strong hero, associated with goats, is helped by a friendly giantess-figure (Silven), and fights both a male and a female ogre using crude weapons or hand-to-hand combat.*[2] *The resulting adventures lack the elevated mysticism of Perceval's quest for the Grail, but they include many of the stock elements of Icelandic romances: evil suitors for a princess's hand, a conflict between evenly matched adversaries which ends with their swearing brotherhood, a few outrageously bloody battles, and in the end, splendid weddings for the heroes and their beautiful brides. This could all seem hackneyed, but the tale is told well, with frequent flashes of wit and a plot that moves* allegro con brio *from scene to scene.*

The Norse text published by Agnete Loth is based primarily on manuscript AM 586 4°, a vellum manuscript dated to 1450–1500.[3] *The manuscript includes several other romances, including* Bósa saga *about the hero's grandfather, as well as* Hálfdanar saga *and* Ásmundar saga *in this volume.*

CHAPTER I

There once was a king named Vissevald[4] who ruled over the realm of Russia. He was married, having been betrothed to the daughter of the king of Hungary, but her name isn't known. The king had succeeded to his father's throne at a young age. He was valiant and well-mannered, and well-liked by everyone. Before he had married, he had had a son with the daughter of a certain jarl. This son was named Hjarrandi. He was a strong and handsome man, and so accomplished at sports and skills that few men could compare with him. He was daring and bold-spirited, a steadfast friend, and so keen in every situation, whether he was in battle or in a joust, that wherever he charged forward was just like the coming of a whirlwind. For that reason he was called Hjarrandi Gale. He was always out raiding, but stayed with his father in winter.

On one occasion, King Vissevald had to go to a council of kings, and it was expected that he would be away for more than twelve months. The queen was pregnant, and far advanced in her pregnancy when the king left home. At that time, there were many wise men in Russia. There was one woman who was the most highly honored of all soothsayers, and noble women always sought her out to speak prophecy over their babies, because what she predicted always happened later. The queen had this done, inviting her and preparing a splendid feast for her. While the wise woman was there, the queen went into labor, and the seeress attended to her. She gave birth to twin girls, both healthy and beautiful. The seeress picked up the baby girls and laid them on one blanket on which all sorts of stories were depicted. She had gold and treasures, flowers and fruits of the earth, brought and placed on the blanket. The baby girls laid their hands on whatever lay close to them, and the firstborn girl picked up a hawkbit flower[5] and put it in her mouth. The second girl picked up a gold ring, and it slipped onto her finger.

The seeress brought the babies to the queen and spoke many promising words over them. She told the queen that the girl who took the gold ring would be blessed with descendants and would be betrothed to a noble prince, "because gold signifies royal honor. But the girl who took the plant will be blessed with wealth and good harvests, and will be betrothed to a farmer's son of berserker stock, because the produce of the earth signifies the common folk. And this man will be outstanding, because no plant is as strong or as bitter as the hawkbit." She gave names to the baby girls, and the one who took the plant was named Soley,[6] while Gullbra[7] was the one who picked up the gold ring. The queen thanked her with fine words, and she was sent away with rich gifts.

A little later, the queen fell ill and died. This was considered a terrible blow, and her funeral was held with splendor, in the style that was customary at the time. The king came home from the kings' council when he had completed his mission. He had already heard everything before he came home. His daughters were shown to him, and he liked them very much. He felt that Gullbra was much more beautiful, but Soley was fond of finery and bold-spirited, and he felt that she would be haughty and clever.

The king had Soley fostered in the town by an elderly woman named Silven. She had a pretty daughter, but her husband was dead, and the mother and daughter were all alone. That's where Soley grew up, until the girls were old enough that one could tell what character each girl would have by the actions she chose. Gullbra was gentle and sweet and kind to all, and everyone loved her wholeheartedly. She grew up in the king's hall, and everyone played with her. Soley was somewhat more reserved; she had great stores of wealth and was generous with it, withholding nothing from her friends—but she also wanted to get what she claimed as her due from everyone. The king didn't love her as much. All the same, both sisters had many friends.

So time passed, until they were both twelve years old.

CHAPTER II

Hjarrandi set out raiding on the Western Sea and won renown. His raids went well, and he was blessed with victory.

It is said that on one occasion he was raiding in Ireland and subjugated a great part of it. The King of Ireland was in Gunnvaldsborg,[8] the most populous and strongest of the towns there. Hjarrandi surrounded the town, but the king and a few men crept out of the town one night. The next morning, Hjarrandi broke into the town and plundered a great deal of wealth, and then he set the town on fire. As it was burning, a man came out of a cookhouse. He was tall and very ugly. His hair was burned off, along with his shoes and stockings up to his knees. His neck was bowed, and he was carrying a large chest on his shoulders. He had evil eyes, and his teeth were worse. They spared his life and asked him his name. He said that he was called Kol the Crooked[9] and that he was a slave in the town.

Just then, they heard that the king was gathering his troops. The inhabitants' forces were so large that Hjarrandi could not match them. He sailed away from Ireland[10] and back east to Russia. He gave his father the slave, and the king made him major-domo over twelve slaves. The slave was so powerful that he had the strength of twelve men for every task that he did.

There was a serving-wench on the estate named Oskubuska, much bigger and stronger than the other serving-women.[11] She and Kol got along very well.

CHAPTER III

Hjarrandi Gale had an estate in the town, and it was strongly fortified. He kept his men there, providing for all their needs, but he stayed at the king's estate. Hjarrandi swore an oath that he would only betroth his sister Gullbra to the man who was equal to him in all knightly achievements. Then he had a strong castle built in the town, and brought his sister there, and he got the daughters of dukes and earls to serve her, along with courteous manservants. No man might be so bold as to go and speak with the maiden without Hjarrandi's permission, and anyone who might dare to do so had his head cut off and tied to a fencepost. And if men came who wanted to ask for the maiden's hand, they would surely have to joust with Hjarrandi; he knocked them all off their horses' backs, and they lost both honor and wealth. But if men came forward to joust whom Hjarrandi felt were of no account, even if they came from good family, he had their heads cut off and set on fenceposts.

When Hjarrandi was not at home, he set a man named Ruddi to guard the castle. He was big and strong and hard to deal with, and so merciless that no one could expect good treatment from him. The royal estate got a nickname, and was called Castle Disgust[12], because most men shunned coming there. A bower was built in the castle for Soley, and the daughters of noblemen served her, but everything was less splendid there than in Gullbra's home. But Soley was ambitious, and was unwilling to maintain herself in lesser style than her sister.

CHAPTER IV

There was a man named Ulf the Strong, a powerful farmer from the east of Russia. He was said to be rather malicious, although a mighty man. He was married and had a son named Ulf Pure Evil,[13] a mighty warrior, cruel and stubborn and greedy and boastful, yet the bravest of men. On one occasion, he went to Novgorod with his men, intending to ask for Soley's hand in marriage. Soley's foster-mother Silven found out about this and told her foster-daughter. Soley asked whether the match seemed like a good idea to her. Silven said that she wasn't pleased with it, but that the king would betroth her, whatever she said.

"Can I trust you?" said Soley.

"Might and main must go together here," said Silven.

Ulf came to meet with the king and made his proposal of marriage. The king received him well and held a splendid feast for him, and said that they would speak with Soley in the morning, but added that he was quite willing as long as she did not object. That evening, Ulf went to his tents.

That night, Soley summoned Kol the Crooked and said, "It's come to this, Kol: I have to place my trust in you. Ulf Pure Evil has come here, the son of Ulf the Strong. He wants to ask for my hand in marriage, and I'm told that the king will betroth me whether I'm willing or not. But I know that he will not shrink from doing anything wicked, and I don't want to marry him if I can avoid it. So I want you to kill him on my account, and you shall have my complete friendship and choose for yourself whatever reward you want."

Kol said, "I won't do it, because then I'd suffer the king's anger and the anger of many other good men. I would be called a betrayer of my lord, and surely I wouldn't be able to get out of that trouble by myself."

"Everything looks too difficult to a miserable coward," she said, "Maybe if I promise myself as the pledge, somebody else will try."

"There's no need to question my courage," said Kol. "If you want to stake yourself as a pledge, then I'll dare to try. But it's not clear how I'll be able to enjoy you if the king finds out."

"As long as we're in agreement, it will happen," she said. "You must arrange it so that no one knows of it, except the two of us. And you must build a castle in the woods, and we will go there as soon as we're found out. I know that no farmer's son would be better for me to marry than you, if that is my fate."

They made a firm pact, and she gave him a gold ring as a sign of her good faith.

CHAPTER V

In the night, Kol prepared to go to Ulf's tents. Ulf had no one keeping watch; his men had passed out drunk, and no one was expecting any danger. When Kol went into the tent, Ulf was asleep in bed. Kol had a slender iron rod in his hand, pointed on either end.[14] He slipped the sleeping furs out from under Ulf's hands and jabbed the iron rod into him so that it stuck in his heart. Kol held the furs together from the outside, so that all the blood stayed inside, and he lay down on top of Ulf's head so that he couldn't get any sound out. Now Kol left, having murdered Ulf in his sleep, and no one was aware of what had happened in the tent.

While that was going on, Soley had summoned the wench Oskubuska and spoken to her. "I want to strike a deal with you," she said.

"What's the matter?" said the wench.

"I want to exchange appearances and clothes," said Soley.[15] "You are to go into my bower and say that you're the princess, and do everything the way that I usually do. And if Kol the Crooked comes there and claims some sweet promises from you on my account, you must make them all come true and do everything that he wants. And you must never let him think that you're anything but a princess. I must go to the cookhouse and take over your labors. For this I'll give you my gold ring."

Oskubuska approved of this bargain, and they sealed it. The princess went to the cookhouse, where she was so mean and harsh to deal with that no one could put up with her. Oskubuska went to the bower, and the maidens accepted her and served her well. She wasn't picky, and the cooks found that she liked her food.

CHAPTER VI

In the morning, Ulf's men awoke and found him dead. They searched and never found any weapon-marks on him, and they agreed that he must have been given poison to drink. Rumors of this spread, and the news came to the king's attention. He was not pleased, mostly because he thought that others would blame him for it. But since the king was well-liked, no man wanted to consider the possibility. Ulf's men went home, and his death was not mourned, because no one liked him.

Now we must tell how Kol the Crooked came into the princess's bower and claimed the promises that she had made to him. She wasn't shy about it at all, and she gave herself to him. They carried on like that in secret.

Some time passed. Kol was living in the lap of luxury, and he wasn't exactly innocent of fooling around with the handmaidens. He got six of them pregnant. The princess was also pregnant. Each one concealed it from the others.

CHAPTER VII

Asgaut was the name of a jarl who ruled over Ladoga town. He went to meet King Vissevald and asked for Soley's hand in marriage. The king received his proposal favorably, and said that he wanted to discuss it with his daughter.

When the princess heard about this, she told Kol. He said that there was no time for resting. "Now we must go into the castle that I have built, because we can't dally here any longer." Kol had built the castle in deep woods so that it was surrounded by cliffs and could never be taken. He rode there with Princess Soley to the place he had planned. Twelve slaves who were in on the scheme went with him. They lacked nothing that they needed.

In the morning, the king came to his daughter's bower, and she had vanished. By now, he had found out the truth of how Kol had killed Ulf and impregnated all the handmaidens and carried off his daughter. The king was quite displeased, as were the others who had suffered shame and injury from the slave. And thus they outlawed Kol and all his followers, and a price was placed on his head.

When Kol heard of the sentence passed on him, he stayed in the forest, often rushing into the settled areas to steal many cows and kill men, and he made himself very unpopular. He offered sacrifices to a swine, and she became such a huge and dangerous beast that she killed both men and livestock and ruined fields, both for the king and for others.[16] This went on for a long time. Many expeditions set out against Kol, but he was never beaten, because he was gifted both in sorcery and in strength.

At the time, Hjarrandi was out raiding, and sometimes he spent winters in foreign lands.

CHAPTER VIII

An old man lived in a hidden valley, far away from other men. He was called Svidi Bold-Attacker, the son of Crooked-Bosi.[17] His wife was named Herbord. They had a son named Vilmund. He was tall and strong and handsome, with the finest hair of any man, and keen eyes. He was fine-looking in every way, although there were men with more handsome faces. All the same, many men would rather look like him than like those who were called more handsome. His father had been the greatest of warriors, and so he taught his son skills: swimming and board games and archery and fencing with shield and sword. He learned these skills so well that his father couldn't even compare with him. His mother taught him book-learning. He asked the old man and woman where all the saga heroes were. They told him that the men were all dead, but that trolls were left in some parts of the world, and they would kill men if they saw them. "Elves are alive, and they're down in the earth."

The old man had many livestock animals: nanny goats and billy goats, oxen and wethers. Vilmund always took care of the livestock. He often shot animals and birds. So he lived until he was twenty years old.

Now it is said that on one occasion, Vilmund went to the forest to search for his goats. He climbed up out of the valley, farther than he usually went, and he came to a flat sandy place, with a wide forest on the other side. He walked across the sand and found some stones piled together in one place, with steaming hot water inside.[18] Then he saw human tracks, which he had never seen before. He found a shoe, ornamented with gold. He picked it up and kept it. He saw one huge boulder a short distance from the pool, and he walked to it because the tracks led to it. He walked up to the boulder, and there was a window in it. There he saw three women inside. One was old, but the other two were younger.

The old woman said, "What was the news, my foster-daughter, when you left your home?"

"There was no news," she said, "but the latest happening was that Kol the Crooked was outlawed."

"What crime had he committed?" said the old woman.

"Hardly a minor offense," she said. "He had debauched all the handmaidens and gotten the princess pregnant."

"That princess is a good match for him," said the[19] old woman. Then she said to her daughter, "Where are my foster-daughter's shoes?"

Her daughter looked around, and then said, "This hasn't turned out well. One of them was left behind by the pool. As it happens, we can't go there now because of the trolls coming and going."

"This is a great misfortune," said the old woman, "because those shoes were made by dwarves, and their nature is that they can never wear out. But she won't be able to wear any other shoes. Now she'll have to walk with one bare foot."

"Let's not quarrel over that, foster-mother," she said. "But I will only marry the man who brings me back the shoe."

Then they went to bed, but Vilmund left and came home late. He was astonished by what had happened, and he didn't tell either the old man or the old woman about it. But afterwards, he couldn't sleep as well as before.

CHAPTER IX

The old man had one treasure that he thought was better than any other. It was a nanny-goat. He named her Fortune. She was as big as a calf and had four teats like a cow. She never failed to have three kids every year, which greatly increased his herds.

On one occasion, Vilmund couldn't find the goat, and his father ordered him to search more widely. Vilmund readied himself for a journey. He wore a tunic of shaggy red bearskin, sewed with great skill. He had a heavy silver belt around his waist, with a large knife hanging from it, worked with silver. He wore a hood of otter skin on his head, and a silver headband. His hair was as golden as silk, and it hung down to his shoulders, as curly as wood shavings.[20] He carried in his hand a great silver-inlaid broadaxe that his father had given him. His mother came out and spoke to him. "Where are you planning to go, Vilmund?" she said.

"I intend to search for Fortune," he said.

"You've seldom taken so much trouble over your clothes," she said.

"I won't come home until I find Fortune," said Vilmund.

"That would be a good thing, if it were to happen," she said.

He bid farewell to his father and mother, and walked off into the forest. By the time he had searched in all the usual places, it was very late. He lay down to sleep in the mouth of a cave and slept there through the night.

In the morning, when he awoke, such a thick mist had descended that he couldn't see in any direction. He walked through the forest and lost his way, and he didn't know where he was going. He kept going all that day, and the next day until evening, and the mist kept getting thicker. By that time he had reached a cliff face, and he thought he heard human voices and the cries of all sorts of animals all around him. The cliff was multicolored, white and blue, red and gold, and it was as smooth as if it had been planed. He couldn't see how high it was, because of the mist, but he also heard human voices coming from up in the air, among other places.

Just then he came to where they were great doors in the cliff. They were open, set into a huge gate with iron bolts. He was astounded at this, but he went through the gateway and saw a broad path. He followed it until he reached a great courtyard with a gateway, which was unlocked. He pushed open the gate and went into the courtyard. Four men came up to him, and one of them said to him, "You wicked ruffian! Who gave you permission to come in here with weapons at night? Give me the axe!"

Vilmund didn't know what to answer, but he gave him the axe. The man swung the axe, meaning to drive it into Vilmund's head. Vilmund rushed under his grip and knocked him down so hard that the axe fell out of his hand. One of the men struck at Vilmund's shoulders with a very large stake. But Vilmund seized the legs of the man whom he had knocked down and struck the other two men so that they fell, and one of them never got up again. The man he seized got a raw deal.

CHAPTER X

Now Vilmund saw a grand and beautiful house, and he went there. There he saw twelve men walking, carrying silver dishes in their hands. Vilmund followed them. He flung the door open faster than the man inside could react, and the man fell over backwards onto the floor. Vilmund went in and saw more than sixty maidens sitting inside, all with bright hair and golden headbands. One of them was far lovelier than the rest, and she was sitting in the middle. Vilmund didn't know what pretext he had for coming in.

Most of the maidens inside were frightened by Vilmund, and the servants asked whether they should call for men to spread warning of this huge man. The princess answered, "He's harmless to us, and we will not deal with him that way. But if he means anything other than good, then there'll be an opportunity." They said that was a terrible risk.

Then the princess said, "You huge man, sit down and have some food, or else get out of our bower, and don't cause us any trouble while you're staying here."

He went to where the princess was sitting, and he sat on a chair before the table and began eating. Although he had been starving for a long time, he ate in a most mannerly fashion.

When the meal was over, the princess said, "You huge man, either go to sleep, or get out of the bower." He saw a bed in the middle of the hall floor. He went over and lay down on it. The princess wanted to have his clothes taken off, but he wasn't willing. The maidens talked among themselves about how this man must be either a fool or some sort of villain. The princess said that she thought[21] that he must not be used to having people around, and ordered them to leave him alone. He lay there through the night and soon fell asleep.

In the morning, the princess came to the bed and awakened him, and told him to stand up and go away from there, "because it will mean your death if people see you here."

"First tell me something that I feel is important," he said. "Are you a human being or a troll or an elf-woman? Where am I, and what's your name?"

She smiled at that, and said, "Do I look trollish to you?"

"I don't know," he said. "I've never seen a troll, or an elf."

"My name is Gullbra," she said, "and I am the daughter of the king who rules this land. I know that he won't be pleased if he finds out that you've been here."

"I've heard of a king," he said, "but I don't know what that is, because I've never seen any people except for my father and mother."

"What's your father's name?" she said. "And where do you live?"

"My father lives in a valley a long way from here," he said. "His name is Svidi."

"Where do you have to go?" said the young maiden.

"I'm seeking my Fortune," he said.

The lady smiled and said, "Do you think you'll find it here? What is it?"

"It's my father's goat, with three kids," he said.[22]

"She hasn't come here," she said. "You must flee this place and not be found here."

"That's what I'll do," he said. "Still, I want to tell you the dream I just had. I seemed to be here, right where I am now, and I seemed to see many ships sailing to land. From one of them, a boar waded ashore. He was huge and looked wicked. He had a snout and rooted up everything. Many swine came running after him, and they all squealed horribly. But a red-cheeked bear came running down from the land to face him, such a handsome animal that I've never seen one more beautiful. It charged the boar and they had a terrible fight, and in the end the boar beat the bear. The people were all terrified and fled. Then you seemed to come to me, and I thought I picked you up and put you under my fur coat. Then I attacked the boar, and then I woke up."[23]

"Your dream seems significant to me," she said, "and I think it not unlikely that you'll be useful to me. If you take service with my father, call on me for the things that you need."

Then Vilmund dressed and bid all the ladies farewell. He went out of the tower. The weather was fine with bright sunshine.

CHAPTER XI

Now Vilmund looked around. He saw how the sun was shining on the city's towers, and they looked like glowing gold to him. He didn't know what sort of place he had entered that evening.

He saw a house with smoke coming out, and he headed for it. Inside there were many people, with meat boiling in kettles. He went inside past the fires. No one noticed him. He sat down on a seat.

Just then a woman came forward, dressed all in tattered clothes. She grabbed at him with great strength and flung him out of his seat, so that he lay fallen in the ashes. Now he seized her hand and squeezed it so hard that blood gushed from under every nail. He grabbed her neck and squeezed it until water gushed from both her eyes. And then he noticed her face, and it looked very much like the one that he had seen inside the stone.[24] He let her slip out of his grasp and stood up and left the cookhouse.

Then he saw many men entering a house, and he followed. He came into a splendid abode and saw many men sitting there, and he realized from the princess's instructions that it must be the king that everyone was bowing to. There was food on tables all through the hall. He took a place inside on the hall floor. No one noticed him. The king told the serving-page to give him something to drink, and invited him to get food from any place in the hall. The page did as the king ordered. Vilmund saw where there was a chair not very far from the king's seat. He sat down there, and food was set before him. He enjoyed the food very much, and ate as much as four knights. Many people laughed at him.

The king addressed him: "What is your name, large man," he said, "and where did you come from?"

"I'm called Vilmund," he said. "And I came from my father and mother."

"So did most people," said the king. "But where do you want to go? You're a promising man."

"I'm seeking my Fortune," said Vilmund.

"Men who are no more promising than you have found fortune," said the king. "But do you see it here?"

"I haven't," said Vilmund. "Or else it hasn't come here so that you'd recognize it."

"I don't know what you call fortune," said the king.

"It's my father's goat with three kids," he said.

Then everyone in the hall laughed and said that he must be a fool. But the king said that he didn't think that. "It may be that he's not much used to other people."

Just then, a man came into the hall, very tall and very ugly. It was Ruddi. He said to the king, "This oaf who's come here has done you a great shame. He slept last night in the castle next to your daughter, and I suspect that he's done more ignoble deeds there. And he's killed two of the men who had to defend the courtyard. I know he'd soon lose his head if Hjarrandi were home."

"So you kept a poor watch on the courtyard," said the king.

"It's my duty to punish him for his audacity," said Ruddi.

"It would be good sport for the two of you to wrestle," said the king, "but we will let revenge wait for Hjarrandi."

"This is going just the way I want it," said Ruddi.

"You'll get what you want," said Vilmund, "and I'm ready."

The king said that they should wrestle out in the courtyard, as soon as the tables were taken away, "because there we can have better sport." They shook hands on the deal, and Ruddi left.

Just then, Hjarrandi came home with eleven other men, and he came before the king and greeted him. The king gave him a warm welcome and invited him to sit next to him on the high seat. He asked for news, and Hjarrandi told what there was to tell. Hjarrandi asked who that huge man was who was sitting in his seat. "That man is quite a mystery to us," said the king, "because he came here today, but we've been told that he slept next to your sister in the castle last night."

"I daresay it's a good thing that he's taken up residence here," said Hjarrandi. "That will protect him well."

"That mostly depends on you now," said he king. "But he and Ruddi have agreed to wrestle, and we'll have to watch the bout first."

Hjarrandi said that he would be there, "because it will be an even match."

"I don't know about that," said the king. "Either this man is a fool, or he's not used to being around other men. But I think that he has enough strength to fall back on."

Hjarrandi said that this would have to be put to the test.

CHAPTER XII

Then the tables were taken away. The king and all his household left the hall. Vilmund came last, and when he walked outside, he saw where the king was sitting on a chair with Hjarrandi beside him, and his retainers were standing in a ring around him. There was a field, very stony. Ruddi was standing on the field, wearing a wrestling jacket that reached to his knees. He asked who this bumpkin might be who had agreed to compete against him.

Vilmund came into the enclosure. The king said that Ruddi thought he'd been waiting for him for a long time. Vilmund said that he had arrived now, and asked the king to take care of his axe. The men laughed, but the king asked if they knew anyone who` would be more appropriate. They said that they didn't, and talked a lot about his modesty.

Vilmund threw off his clothes and came forth onto the field. Ruddi charged at him, driving both his fists ahead of his chest with all his strength. Vilmund made a strong counter; he laid his hands on the outside of Ruddi's arms and powerfully hoisted him up into the air. There was a fierce exchange of blows between them, and almost everything was knocked out of place. Any place that Ruddi touched turned black and blue, because he had sharp nails. The wrestling jacket was so tough that Vilmund couldn't get a grip on him. The king and all his household followed the contest and were impressed by Vilmund's strength.

They fought all over the field until they came to a stone into which a sword blade was set. Vilmund said to Ruddi, "Should we play this game any longer?"

"Until one or the other of us falls," said Ruddi.

"Then make a better attack," said Vilmund.

Ruddi stamped so powerfully with his feet that he sank into the earth up to his knees,[25] but he gripped Vilmund so hard around his back that the flesh was torn off. Vilmund lifted him up to his chest and moved towards the stone, gripping him. He flung him down onto the sword's edge so hard that Ruddi was split in two at the middle.[26] Vilmund came before the king, holding Ruddi's lower half, and most people thought that he looked savage.

Hjarrandi wanted to stand up and avenge Ruddi right then, but the king said, "We shall not mistreat this man, because Ruddi was no great loss. I don't want you to send this man down to Hel. First, let's find out what skills he has."

Vilmund threw Ruddi down and asked the king to give him back his axe—

"because you don't seem trustworthy to me."

The king said, "Are you as gifted in other skills as you are in strength?"

Vilmund said, "In any sport that I know, it doesn't matter to me whom I strive against. But if you want to take my life, you can find out how I'll respond."

Hjarrandi sked whether he knew how to throw stones. Vilmund asked him to pick up a stone and try a throw. Hjarrandi picked up a stone that weighed three hundred and fifty pounds.[27] First he threw it twenty paces, and invited Vilmund to throw after him. Vilmund did so, and he threw it two yards[28] farther. Hjarrandi picked up the stone a second time, and threw it thirty-two paces. Then Vilmund took the stone and threw it three yards farther.

The king said, "It's just as I expected: this man is more accomplished than we thought."

Hjarrandi grew angry and gripped the stone and held nothing back, and he threw it forty paces and told Vilmund to throw after him. He did so, and threw it five yards farther. Then Hjarrandi didn't want to keep going any longer.

CHAPTER XIII

The king asked Vilmund to throw as far as he could. Vilmund took the stone and set it on his foot, and kicked it as high as a man's height, up into the wall of the hall so hard that it stuck there. And it may be seen there to this day.

Hjarrandi now took a great spear and threw it at a stone pillar so that it sank up to the socket. That throw was ninety yards long and ninety yards high. A very tall tower stood upon that pillar, with a dove sitting on it. Vilmund threw the same spear at the bird and skewered it, so that both bird and spear came tumbling down. Vilmund then ran around the hall and caught the spear and the bird in the air. Then he threw the spear through the stone pillar so hard that it is stuck there to this day, and anyone who goes there may see it.

Hjarrandi now asked him how he was at swimming. Vilmund said that swimming was the best of all his skills. They went to a lake and took off their clothes. Hjarrandi swam out into the water, and Vilmund was right behind. First they had a race, and people thought it was close. Then they competed in many feats of agility, and the people felt they'd never seen better sport. Hjarrandi now swam at Vilmund and dunked him in the water, and they were down for a long time.[29] In the end they came up, and both were quite weary. Now Vilmund gripped Hjarrandi and dunked him in the water, and they were down for so long that everyone thought they were probably dead, but the water was churning from their thrashing. As the day was ending, Hjarrandi came to land, and he was so stiff that men had to support him so that he could walk. They didn't see Vilmund—but much later, they saw a huge wave arise on the lake, and then Vilmund came up. He hauled up a tall stone and sat down on it and rested.

Thanks to the advice of wicked men, the king released a polar bear that was kept by the town gates. They drove it to the lake. The bear swam out into the lake, shaking itself and growling. Vilmund saw that this was no time for sitting down. He leaped from the stone and swam at the bear and reached out and grabbed it by the muzzle, and they wrestled hard. Vilmund got the bear under him, and by this time he was terribly weary. He took his belt-knife and stabbed the beast under the shoulder, in the heart. That was a bold deed, to triumph over such a huge animal! As soon as the bear had suffered its death-blow, it dropped dead, because its nature is that it does not struggle as it dies. The lake was filled with blood.[30]

The people didn't see any sign of Vilmund, but a little later, they saw where he was floating on the gush of blood. When Hjarrandi saw that, he swam out into the lake to Vilmund. Vilmund was so weak from exhaustion that he couldn't do a thing on his own, and Hjarrandi swam to land with him. There he was tended and brought good clothes. Vilmund soon began to feel better. Afterwards, he and Hjarrandi swore brotherhood with each other. Everyone said that never before had a more valiant man than Vilmund come into that country. But while he was a newcomer, he wasn't very sociable with other men, because when men went to feast, or left the feast, they always had to call to Vilmund, as he was always alone and didn't mingle much with other men. Thus he was called Vilmund the Outsider.

CHAPTER XIV

The next thing to relate is that Hjarrandi and Vilmund went to the forest to hunt animals, and many men went with them. They stayed out in the forest for weeks. Vilmund kept to himself and wandered far and wide, as he often did. He came to the same sandy place where he had been before, and reached the same boulder. He climbed up onto the boulder and saw the same women as before. He heard them talking among themselves. The old woman spoke: "What was the news when you left the town, my foster-daughter?"

"Much had happened," she said. "A man named Vilmund had arrived. He is a huge and powerful man, and people think that he must be one of those fools who sits around in the cookhouse.[31] But he has beaten Hjarrandi Gale, and they have become sworn brothers. When I left, people saw ships sailing for land. There were thirty-two ships all together, most of them dragon-ships and galleons. People thought that someone must be coming to ask for Gullbra's hand, but Hjarrandi is in the forest with Vilmund. They felt that berserkers must have landed, because black men[32] have been seen in their ranks. Everyone thinks that Hjarrandi will be put to the test."

Then the stone closed up, and Vilmund went away.

CHAPTER XV

One day, people were standing outside by the king's palace. They saw ships sailing in; they were huge, with black sails. They soon made landfall, and their crews brought out tents from the ships. Men were sent from the beach, and they came before the king. Their leader was named Skjold. He greeted the king and said, "The prince who has sent me to you is named Buris, the son of King Rodian of the Land of Black Men.[33] He has arrived in your harbor on this errand: he wants to marry your daughter who is called Gullbra, because her magnificence has been told far and wide throughout the world. He has ordered you to do the right thing and bring your daughter down to the sea to him, and you can negotiate the terms there, because he doesn't want to bother his people with coming up to the hall. But if you're not willing to do that, he'll take your daughter as plunder and kill you and lay your kingdom waste."

The king said, "This isn't my business, because her brother Hjarrandi is in charge of her betrothal. I expect that he will have something to say about it."

Skjold said that the prince wasn't willing to seek her hand in vain any longer. "You may assume that you will face our hostility in the morning, if you refuse the woman. Be well." And he went to the ships.

Hjarrandi came home from the forest, and he was told the news. He ordered trumpets to be blown at once, and a host of men was summoned from the nearby settlements. There was no time to lose, and there was commotion in the town. Every man armed himself with his own weapons.

In the morning, trumpets sounded in Buris's camp, and he had his standards raised. The field was covered far and wide with his host, and most of them were black men and berserks. Hjarrandi moved against them with his host; compared to Buris's host, it was small. Vilmund had not returned from the forest, and men felt that he had proved the truth of his name and was an outsider. Skjold bore Buris's standard, and he was both strong and hard-hitting. Hjarrandi broke through Buris's lines, and no one could stand against him. Skjold turned to face him and thrust at him with a spear. Hjarrandi leaped into the air, and Skjold stabbed the ground with his spear and bent over. Hjarrandi struck him in the backbone with his sword and chopped him completely through, and the sword sank into the ground up to the hilt.

Then Buris came at Hjarrandi and they fought in single combat, with such mighty blows that whoever struck first had the advantage. Buris was enchanted so that iron could not cut him, but Hjarrandi's armor was cut off, and so he suffered wounds. He now gripped his sword with two hands and struck at Buris. The blow landed across the prince's face and broke his nose and his upper jaw, and all his teeth fell onto the grass. By that time Hjarrandi was exhausted from loss of blood, and he collapsed, severely wounded. A dreadful panic seized his men.

CHAPTER XVI

At that moment, Vilmund came home from the forest to the town. The princess was about to flee, and she intended to hide. Vilmund asked what was going on. People said that they thought that Hjarrandi must be dead. Vilmund went to the battle, and every man was on the point of fleeing. But when men saw Vilmund, every man who had been frightened became filled with courage.

Fighting broke out a second time, and Vilmund was foremost in the ranks. Buris attacked him and struck at him. Vilmund brought up his shield, and the sword split it down to the hand-grip; the sword's tip scratched his forehead and gave him a slight wound. Vilmund twisted his shield so hard that Buris dropped his sword. Vilmund swung his axe with both hands at Buris's chest, and that was such a mighty blow that Buris sank to his knees, but the axe didn't cut. Vilmund turned the axe and struck between Buris's ears with the blunt end, and Buris's skull was shattered in pieces. His men were filled with panic and their ranks broke and fled, but Vilmund and the men of the town pursued them to their ships. Some plunged into the water, and some were killed on land, but no one surrendered until all that rabble was killed; not one man of Buris's forces was left. The plunder that they took in gold and silver, weapons and clothing, ships and tents, was of such great worth that no one could set a price on it.

Vilmund searched among the fallen and found Hjarrandi, alive but badly wounded. He was brought home, and his sister began to treat him, and soon he began to recover. Vilmund had the town cleansed, and he took the corpses out to sea and sank them to the bottom.

Some time now passed until Hjarrandi was healed.

CHAPTER XVII

Vilmund now told Hjarrandi that he wanted to visit his father. Hjarrandi told him to do so. Vilmund found Svidi and told him what had befallen him since they parted, and invited him to come with him and not live so far away from people any longer. Svidi accepted and said that he was tired of living alone. He went with Vilmund to the king, and he was appointed as chieftain over a large district. The people soon saw that he knew how to set both the land and the laws in order.

Now the story turns to Kol the Crooked in the forest. He did many wicked deeds and pillaged the king's land, burning both castles and market-towns, and he killed men and plundered livestock. The king came to speak with Hjarrandi and ordered him to go after Kol. He and Vilmund prepared to enter the forest. They searched for Kol with sixty men in all.

At that time, Kol had ridden to a settled district and burned a castle and taken much wealth, and now he was riding back to the forest with his slaves. Hjarrandi and Vilmund came against him, and a battle broke out. Kol and his men attacked fiercely, and they were so skilled in sorcery that Hjarrandi's men's weapons could scarcely cut them, except for Vilmund. When the fighting was at its fiercest, fifty swine came out of the forest and attacked Hjarrandi's men and tore them to death. Even though the men struck at them, their swords bounced off. This attack was both daring and deadly. Yet in the end all of Kol's slaves fell, but so did all of the sworn brothers' men. Ten swine were left. Kol ran off into the forest. Both Vilmund and Hjarrandi were wounded, but they still chased him to his castle, and there they parted from him. They went home, and they were very stiff, but soon recovered.

Now Kol summoned his forces a second time, and he got twenty men. He behaved just as he had before, and even worse. The sworn brothers went to the forest after Kol a second time, and they had a hundred men. They found out that Kol had gone to the district. They rode towards him, and another battle broke out between them. As before, Kol struck mighty blows, and he blunted the blades of Hjarrandi's men. Then the swine rushed out and attacked them. The encounter ended when all of Hjarrandi's men and all of Kol's men fell.

Vilmund began to fight the swine, and Hjarrandi fought Kol. He struck down onto Kol's skull, which was easiest for him—but the sword broke in two and didn't cut. Kol shook his head and struck at Hjarrandi, but he turned and dodged. The sword hit his calf and cut all the way down, and that was a serious wound. Hjarrandi gripped one of Kol's ears and tore off the flesh of his cheek, so that his exposed teeth shone.[34] Kol rushed into the forest and fled. By then, Vilmund had killed all the swine, except for the sow. She escaped to the forest, having bitten off one of Vilmund's fingers, and that's how they parted. They told the king what had happened, and he felt that it all came from the same source: the wickedness of Kol. As soon as Hjarrandi had recovered, he was intent on avenging himself on Kol.

CHAPTER XVIII

One night, Vilmund awoke, and Hjarrandi had left. Vilmund leaped to his feet and seized his weapons. He went to the forest, and when he came close to Kol's castle, he saw that Hjarrandi and Kol were fighting in a swamp. The sow had entered the fight on Kol's side, and Hjarrandi had suffered three wounds and broken his sword. Now he picked up a stone so huge that four men would hardly have been able to lift it. Hjarrandi flung it at Kol, and it struck him right in the teeth, so that Kol fell backwards. The back of his head struck a rock, and his skull shattered into pieces. That's how Kol ended his days.

The sow charged at Hjarrandi so fiercely that he fell to the ground. At that moment, Vilmund came up and stabbed at the sow with a spear, but she blocked it with her thick skin and the spear broke in two. Vilmund seized her hind leg and pulled it towards him so hard that her belly ripped open and her intestines fell out. She had fastened her teeth in the armor on Hjarrandi's chest, so close to the bone that she tore off his nipple so that his breastbone was exposed. Vilmund pulled so sharply that Hjarrandi and the sow both went flying into the air at once. The sow died, but Hjarrandi was unable to keep fighting.

At that moment, Vilmund suffered such a mighty blow between his shoulders that he fell to both knees. He turned around and saw that Kol's girlfriend Soley had come, and she attacked Vilmund in such a fury that for a long time he could do nothing but defend himself. He saw that he couldn't deal with her in that way. He gripped her by her hair and wound it around his hand. With his other hand he took his knife and struck her on the neck so that her head flew off. By now he was stiff and weary. He laid Hjarrandi on his shield and carried him from the forest into Castle Disgust, and he asked Gullbra to heal him. But he entered the hall and set Soley's bloody head on the table before the king. He said, "Now your son-in-law Kol the Crooked is dead, the worst evildoer that there has ever been. Take the head of his concubine, and these evildoers won't harm your kingdom any longer."

The king was so enraged at his words that he ordered his men to stand up and kill this fool who had done him such a grievous disgrace as to set that head, treated that way, on the table before him. "Although I wanted my daughter dead on account of her wicked schemes, I cannot suffer the shame that her blood should run over my table, for it calls to me to avenge it. Vilmund shall not come before my eyes while my mood is like this."

The men were in no hurry to attack Vilmund. He turned and left the hall, and ordered his squire to get his horse. Vilmund rode to his father and told him what had happened. Svidi said that the king had right on his side, and to set such a head on the table before the king was going too far.

Vilmund stayed with his father. Later, he took his horse and many men to go with him, and they traveled to the castle that Kol had held. There were all kinds of food and wine there, along with gold and treasures. Vilmund stayed there for some time.

Hjarrandi was soon healed of his wounds. When he met his father, Hjarrandi rebuked him for how he had parted with Vilmund. The king said that Vilmund had put him through such a terrible ordeal that it was quite intolerable. But Hjarrandi said that Vilmund would become a dangerous outlaw, if he chose to become other than good. With that said, father and son parted.

CHAPTER XIX

On one occasion, Vilmund left his castle, because he found life dull since he and Hjarrandi had parted. He went to the pool where he had been before, and this time he saw where three women had walked from the pool to the boulder. He climbed up on the boulder to hear their conversation.

The old woman spoke up. "What's the news now, foster-daughter?" she said. "It's been a long time since you visited me."

"Much news has happened," said the other woman. "First of all, Kol the Crooked is dead, and also his woman Oskubuska. That's what I call a necessary deed."

"Who did that?" said the old woman.

"Hjarrandi and Vilmund," said the other. "Hjarrandi was Kol's killer, and Hjarrandi nearly would have lost his own life if Vilmund hadn't helped him. Vilmund killed Lady Oskubuska, and he killed the ferocious sow that people thought would never be beaten. I am certain that a more valiant man than Vilmund is not to be found. But he didn't get the rewards that I would think he'd earned, because the king made him an outlaw."

"What happened there?" asked the old woman. The other woman told her how things had gone with them.

"Vilmund would certainly seem to have pushed the king too far," said the old woman, "if it had been as the king supposed, but it's just as well that that's not so. But how long will you keep yourself concealed, foster-daughter?"

"I'm in no hurry to reveal myself," she said. "I've heard some promising news, foster-mother. We saw twenty ships sailing towards land. They were splendidly decorated and well fitted out, with one dragon-ship so handsome that I have never seen one like it before. Everyone thought that they must have come from far away, but I left the city before I could find out who they were."

"It's obvious that someone has come to ask for Gullbra's hand in marriage," said the old woman.

"Then Hjarrandi and his skills will be put to the test," said the other woman, "and he stands alone, now that Vilmund isn't with him."

"Where Hjarrandi's pride is concerned, I don't know what to expect," said the old woman, "nor do I know how Gullbra's betrothal will turn out. But I would think it more important to be sure that your betrothal is a good one. I would think it better for Vilmund to marry you than Kol, whom people thought it would be."

"I would find the woman whom Vilmund married to be married well," said the maiden, "but I think it would first need to be arranged between him and my father, when they seal the arrangement.[35] I would not want that to happen, even if I had the chance to live with Vilmund in the castle, if he behaved like Kol did when he proposed marriage. But first we must find out what is happening at home."

The window shut, and Vilmund went to his castle. He had spies in town to find out what was happening there.

CHAPTER XX

There was a king named Baldvini who ruled over Galicia.[36] He was married, and he had wedded a queen of noble descent. He had two children with her: a valiant son, and a beautiful daughter. His son was named

Gudifrey; he was a bold and well-mannered man, ahead of most men in all accomplishments. He was so well-liked that everyone loved him with all their hearts. His sister was named Rikiza; she was the loveliest of all women, and more accomplished than any maiden in the land. The king loved his children deeply.

Gudifrey set out raiding with a great host, and he did well on his raids. He harried in the Eastern realms. He had heard of Gullbra, and much was said to him about her beauty. He had also heard about Hjarrandi's oath concerning her betrothal, and so he made an expedition to Russia. The king's men were outside when the ships sailed into the harbor, and people were impressed by their sailing. They had twenty longships and a dragon-ship that was ornamented all over with gold above the waterline. People thought that they had never seen a more handsome fleet of ships, or more elaborate rigging, because all the ropes looked as if they were made of pure gold, and the sails were striped with every kind of fine cloth, brocade and silk and velvet. These men made for the harbor, and set up tents on land. The people were no less impressed with how neatly they took in their sails, than with how brilliant a light appeared when they pitched their tents, because light shone in all directions from the garnets set in the golden knobs that stood atop their tents. The people told the king that noble men must have arrived from a foreign land. He ordered inquiries to be made as to who these men were, and he sent Hjarrandi to the seashore.

When Hjarrandi approached the tents, many men came to meet him, and he saw one man who far surpassed them all. Hjarrandi greeted them politely, and they returned the greeting. He asked who their leader was. The handsome man said, "I am called Gudifrey, and I am the son of King Baldvini of Galicia."

"We are curious," said Hjarrandi, "what business you have in our lands, with such a great host."

Gudifrey said, "We think it's good to be prepared if someone wishes us ill. But no harm shall come to you from our host of men, for we want to have peaceful relations with you and to have leave from your king, so that he may hold a market for us to purchase food."

Hjarrandi said, "You shall have your market right away. The king has asked me to come to you and tell you that he invites you to a feast, if you are willing to accept, for three nights, with as many men as you wish."

"We will gladly accept," said Gudifrey, "and we will go there in the morning. But is Prince Hjarrandi in the land, who is much praised for his valor?"

"Certainly he is in the land," said Hjarrandi, "for he is speaking with you now."

"Not only are you highly praised," said Gudifrey, "but I think it likely that every good report of you must be true. Come into our tent and drink with us."

Hjarrandi did so, and they drank from nothing less than golden goblets. Hjarrandi admired the manners of these men, and everything about them. When he felt it was time, he took his leave to go home. He told the king that a prince from Galicia had arrived. "We think they must have some important mission, although they have not told it to us. They will come here in the morning."

The king asked him what he thought of these men. Hjarrandi said that he had never seen a more handsome man, or more courteous servants.

Now the night passed, and in the morning, Prince Gudifrey came to the hall with sixty men. They were all handsome and well dressed. Hjarrandi came to meet them, and he brought them before the king. The king welcomed his guests well, and he sat in his high seat with Gudifrey beside him. Many excellent men sat at the king's table. Hjarrandi sat on a golden chair. Everyone said that never had a more handsome man than Gudifrey come there. They drank cheerfully.

CHAPTER XXI

The king addressed Gudifrey and asked him about his lineage and native land, and where he wished to travel. Gudifrey said, "I am the son of King Baldvini of Galicia. Since we live far away in the west of the world, we desired to explore the Eastern realms, and see the customs of unknown men, and make the acquaintance of rulers. We have heard that you have a beautiful daughter, and we were curious to see her, if you or her brother are not opposed. We have also heard that your son Hjarrandi is a highly accomplished man. We two are the same age, but there may be a great difference between our skills. We are told that his sister will not be betrothed except to the man who can compete against him. Even if we cannot equal such a man, we would find no shame in that."

Hjarrandi said, "Do not praise yourself too much. As for Gullbra, I have not said anything that I do not mean."

"I would enjoy trying all sports with you", said Gudifrey, "whether archery or fencing. I know that your sister cannot be betrothed well until we put each of our skills to the test, but you should not assume that my purpose is hostile or ambitious."

"So be it," said Hjarrandi, "and I think it's a good thing that we're showing each other our skills for entertainment."

The next day, they went out onto a broad field, and a very tall stake was set up there. Hjarrandi set an apple on top of it, and then he took his spear, the one that he and Vilmund had thrown in their contest earlier. He threw it and knocked the apple down from the stake. Everyone felt that his throw was amazing. Now the apple was set up again. Gudifrey came up and set a boardgame piece up on the apple, and backed up as far as Hjarrandi had. He threw and hit the butt-end of the game piece so that it fell down, and the apple stayed there undisturbed. Everyone praised this throw. Then they tried shooting crossbows and other abilities, and they were so close in skill that no one could tell the difference.

Vilmund's spy came to find him, and he told him what had happened with the princes, and said that he had never seen such a man. Vilmund told him to go back and tell Hjarrandi that he should compete with him in all sports except for fighting.

The next morning, jousting horses were prepared for them, with splendid trappings, and the men were excellently armed. They took their lances and mounted their horses and rode out onto the field. Hjarrandi entered the field first. He took a thick gold ring and rolled it ahead of him on the path. Then he spurred his horse after it as fast as he could, and when he drew level with the ring, he stabbed his spear into the ring and picked it up without checking his horse's pace. The ring stuck on the point of the spear, but he swung the spear all around himself, and when the ring went flying off the spear, he caught it on the spear so that it never touched the ground.

Now Gudifrey entered the field, and he had a crystal goblet in his hand, full of wine. In his other hand he held a golden bowl. He rode his horse as fast as he could go, with his lance couched in the shield-hook. The horse ran as fast as he could, while Gudifrey poured wine into the bowl until it was full. Then he rode at Hjarrandi and reached out to him without stopping his horse. Hjarrandi took the bowl and drank from it, and threw the ring to Gudifrey, and he caught it in mid-air. Neither man checked his horse. They rode to the ends of the course, swiftly turned their horses around, and charged at each other, and each passed the ring and the bowl to the other. Then each one struck the other's shield so hard that the broken spear-shafts went flying a long way over their heads. Thus did they end their tournament, for the king did not want them to compete any more.

Hjarrandi told Vilmund's messenger that he wanted to arrange a settlement between his father and Vilmund. The boy told him that Vilmund didn't want that—but that he had asked Hjarrandi to support him when he came before the king. Hjarrandi said that he would do that.

Then Hjarrandi and Gudifrey went to the hall and competed in chess, and in every respect they were so close that no one could distinguish between them. And so they went to the celebrations on the last day of feasting. Gudifrey asked to see the king's daughter. Hjarrandi said that he was willing to do that on account of their friendship. She was sent for, and she was led in, to the beautiful music of stringed instruments. Although it had been bright and radiant in the hall, it shone even more brightly when she came in. Gudifrey brought forth his suit before the king and Hjarrandi, asking whether they were willing to betroth the maiden to him. Hjarrandi said that her will must take precedence. But she said that she would not go against their wishes.

Hjarrandi sent a messenger to Vilmund and asked what seemed best to him. Vilmund said that he felt it was the best course not to reject this man, and he added that Hjarrandi could not protect her for her entire life. He ordered the messenger to tell Hjarrandi that he would come to the wedding, no matter how he and the king would settle matters when they met.

CHAPTER XXII

The next morning, Gudifrey said that he wanted to know how his errand had been received, without waiting there for anything. They entered the princess's castle and discussed the matter with her. She answered everything courteously, yet she said that she found it daunting to travel into an unknown land, far from her kinsmen. "We wish to know," she said, "what you are willing to do on our account."

"What are you asking for yourself, lady?" said Gudifrey.

"We have been told," she said, "that you have a sister named Rikiza. If you were willing to allow our brother to marry her, we would think that much good would be gained."

The prince answered, "We would not object in any way. But we think that your brother himself is best suited to ask for this woman."

Now whether it was settled with many words or in few, their agreement in the end was that the maiden Gullbra was betrothed to Prince Gudifrey, and their wedding was to be held right away. Great preparations were made in the castle. The king invited his friends and many powerful men, and for an entire month, people came from all directions and gathered in the castle. People were quite surprised that the servant Oskubuska had disappeared, and no one knew what had become of her. Time passed until the day of the wedding came. There was no lack of music from all sorts of instruments in the king's hall, and rulers were shown to their seats. Hjarrandi was in charge of everything.

CHAPTER XXIII

Now the story returns to Vilmund staying in the castle. He rambled off into the forest. He told his men to go back to the castle and wait for him there, so that no one should find out where they were. But he went to the same sandy spot that we mentioned earlier. He climbed up onto the boulder, and it was shut. Then he came down from the boulder and went to the spot where he thought the doors must be, and he struck the boulder a mighty blow and ordered anyone alive inside to open up, "or I'll smash the entire boulder."

The stone opened up, and a rather elderly woman came out. "Who are you," she asked, "who's pounding on the door like that?"

"My name is Vilmund," he said, "and what is your name?"

"Silven," she said. "Are you Vilmund the Outsider?"

"I've been called that," he said.

"I've been informed," she said, "that you've accomplished greater deeds than smashing up my boulder."

"Who else is here?" he said.

"There are three of us here," she said, "and I'm in charge. You must let us have our freedom, if we let you in."

"We're agreed," he said.

They went into the boulder and greeted the people inside. Vilmund sat down and found it pleasing to the eye. They asked what news he had to tell. He said, "You don't need to ask for news from me, because clearly you know what is going on in the town, better than I do."

Silven answered, "You have often been in the habit of coming to our boulder, and I think that you have been informed here of many matters that you've been curious about."

"There's only one thing left," he said, "that I'm most curious about."

"What is it?" she said.

"What kind of women are you?" he said. "And why do you live here?"

"I won't hide it," said Silven. "This is my daughter standing here, and this is my foster-daughter sitting on the dais. Her name is Soley, daughter of King Vissevald."

"People are quite in the dark about the truth," said Vilmund, "because for a long time everyone has been saying that she was with Kol the Crooked in his castle and consented to his wicked deeds."

"It was better for that not to happen," said Silven, "so she changed appearances with the wench Oskubuska, and has done her work ever since. She also has proof that you came near her once in the cookhouse." She picked up a gold finger-ring and asked him, "Do you remember where you last saw this gold ring?"

"I recognize that hand," said Vilmund, "and the eyes that go with it."

Then Silven held out her foster-daughter's right hand, and he saw the marks where the flesh had been squeezed by his fingers. The flesh had turned white. Vilmund said, "I recognize both that ring and the hand, and also those eyes which I first saw here, inside the stone. And as a sign, I found a shoe decorated with gold, beside the lake a short distance from here. Do you remember, young lady, any of the words that you said when you found that it was missing?"

Soley blushed, but Silven said, "You don't need to blush, foster-daughter, because it's not at all certain whether a more valiant man could ask for your hand. And you've said that you'd consider the woman that Vilmund married to be married well."

Vilmund said, "Get ready at once. We must go to the king's hall. The king has been ignorant of the truth about his daughter for too long."

Silven said that it was his decision. They dressed in their finest outfits and traveled to the town, at the same time when Gullbra was being led into the hall with her retinue. Vilmund's men came to meet him. Once the people had sat down and the drinking had begun, Vilmund walked into the hall, carrying Soley on his arm, leading sixty men all together. Vilmund came before the king, and he said, "O king, think about whether your daughter Soley has come here, or whether she has been hiding out with Kol the Crooked, whom you thought was your son-in-law. A son-in-law like that suited you. Take good care of your daughter. I won't cause you any grief by staying here—this time. But when next we meet, you'll find out who it is that you've accused."

Vilmund turned away, very angry.

CHAPTER XXIV

Hjarrandi said to his father, "It's not good for us for Vilmund to leave without a reconciliation between the two of you, because as an outlaw he will be a thorn in your flesh. You know yourself that we all wanted him dead when he first came to us, but he has saved our lives and undergone many trials for us, and never received a good reward from us."

"What do you want to do for him?" said the king.

"You should offer him your daughter," said Hjarrandi, "and a third of Russia, and whatever rank he chooses."

"That hardly saves us from being humiliated," said the king.

"It's no worse than the disgrace that was done to him when he was outlawed," said Hjarrandi. "And he has already saved your kingdom."

"Do as you wish," said the king.

"Stand up and follow me," said Hjarrandi. The king didn't delay; everyone inside the hall leaped to their feet and went outside with him. By that time, Vilmund had reached his horse. Hjarrandi grabbed the reins and said, "For the sake of our friendship, please accept a settlement with my father, because he will make you a good offer."

"I'll do this on account of my debt to you," said Vilmund, "but he'd be dead now if it weren't for you."

Then the king spoke up. "Vilmund," he said, "do not leave, for we are willing to compensate you with gold and fine treasures for the wrong that we have done you. Also, I want to give you the hand of my daughter Soley, and a third of Russia, and whatever rank you wish to choose for yourself."

Vilmund answered, "Soley is the one that I want most, out of all women, and Hjarrandi is the one for whom I will do most, out of all men. Therefore I am willing to accept this settlement, if he agrees."

Vilmund dismounted from his horse and was led into the hall. Soley was summoned, and it was easy to get her consent. Vilmund was betrothed to Soley and received a third of Russia along with her, and the title of duke along with that. Now both weddings had to be held together, and they proceeded with the greatest splendor. When the feasting was ended, everyone was dismissed with fine gifts, and the king paid out the dowry for his daughters.

Gudifrey set out for Galicia. His father was dead when he reached home, and he became king over the realm. Vilmund took up the dukedom that he felt was the richest in Russia, and there he built a strong fortress for himself.

Hjarrandi stayed with his father for a while, until King Vissevald suffered the illness that led to his death. Hjarrandi held a worthy funeral for his father, and invited his kinsman Vilmund, and the funeral feast proceeded well. When it was over, they prepared to travel to Galicia. When King Gudifrey found out, he and Gullbra traveled more than sixty miles from their castle to meet them, and they conducted them to the castle with great honor and held a worthy feast for them. They stayed there for six whole months, and their friendship was so great that no one felt he could bear to part with the others. Before they departed, King Gudifrey betrothed his sister Rikiza to Hjarrandi, and she accepted as her dowry the realm that Gullbra had owned in Russia. In return, King Gudifrey took the realm that Rikiza had owned in Galicia.

At the conclusion of the feast, Hjarrandi and Vilmund set out for their home in Russia, with many great treasures and splendid gifts that King Gudifrey had given them. At their parting, there was no man so hard-hearted that he could hold back tears when he saw how saddened these affectionate friends were by their parting. Vilmund and Hjarrandi came home to their lands and settled down in their kingdoms, and ruled them for as long as they were destined to live.

Here we end the saga of Vilmund the Outsider, with these concluding words from the man who wrote it: He who has read it, and those who have listened to it, and all those who are not rich enough to pay taxes to our king, can go kiss Oskubuska's arse. Take for yourselves everything that happened when Kol the Crooked fucked her, and enjoy whatever peace you get from her. Farewell![37]

The Saga of Yngvar the Far-Traveler

Yngvars saga víðförla

*Despite its atmosphere of unreality—a voyage to the fabulous Orient, with monsters and savages and treasure enough for Indiana Jones—*Yngvars saga víðförla *has a historical basis. A group of about 26 runestones, clustered in southern Sweden, commemorate men who "fell wth Yngvar" in "Serkland", a rather nebulous term used for the Middle East and central Asia.*[1] *The historical Yngvar led a large expedition, probably to Russia and down one of the great Russian rivers to an unknown destination, where he died in 1041. There were Viking raids at Baku on the Caspian Sea coast in 1030-1033, and Varangians (Vikings based in Russia and Byzantium) fought for King Bagrat IV of Georgia at the Battle of Sasireti in 1046-7. It is still up for debate whether any of these expeditions might be identified with Yngvar's expedition. Many details in the saga cannot be made to correspond with real geography; at best, the account we have has been garbled, and we may never be able to know what parts of it are historically accurate. By the time it was written down, the story had been retold in poetry and reshaped to fit well-known narratives, such as myths and tales about gods or heroes traveling to the lands of giants.*[2] *Still, at the very least, it is clear that Viking bands were operating as far as the Caspian Sea, and making contact with local rulers, at about the same time that Yngvar made his expedition.*[3] *Even a few of the "fantastic" elements in the saga can be correlated with historical fact; for example, the warships armed with flamethrowers are clearly based on Byzantine "Greek fire".*

Yngvars saga *boosts its claims to fact by giving its own textual history; "Brother Odd", probably the Icelandic monk Oddr Snorrason, composed the saga from orally transmitted accounts of three different men.* Yngvars saga *begins much like a* konungasaga, *a biography of Norse kings, and events related in the opening of the saga can sometimes be corroborated in other sources. Yngvar's expedition moves into* fornaldarsaga *territory, although Odd added considerable Christian lore to the traditional motifs; monsters like the jaculus, elephant, and cyclops all appear in texts like the* Physiologus *and Isidore of Seville's* Etymologies, *and Yngvar's relationship with Silkisif may have been influenced by the apocryphal legend of Joseph and Aseneth.*[4] *Odd also seems to have added the story of Yngvar's son Svein,*[5] *and generally shifted the story from an adventure tale to a crusade, in which Yngvar's foes must be fought not only with weapons, but with prayer, hymns, and consecrated fire.*[6] *By the end, the saga has become a hagiography, treating Yngvar as a saint even though he has worked no miracles. It is noteworthy that Oddr Snorrason is also known to have composed a Latin life of King Olaf Tryggvason—whom, like Yngvar, he also praises as a saintlike figure and an outstanding warrior of royal blood, who converted a pagan land, but who unfortunately cannot be considered a saint because he has worked no miracles.*[7]

Odd's saga of Yngvar was probably in Latin, but none of his text has survived. The Norse saga, however, was fairly popular in medieval and early modern Iceland, with 26 known manuscripts.[8] *The text is translated from Jónsson and Vilhjálmsson's edition but checked against Emil Olson's 1912 edition, which in turn was based primarily on AM 343a, dated between 1450 and 1475 and containing several other fornaldarsögur and indigenous romances (including* Hálfdanar saga, Samsons saga, *and* Vilmundar saga*).*

Replica of the Gripsholm Stone from Södermanland, Sweden (Sö 179), one of the "Ingvar stones." The inscription begins at the head of the snake and reads **tula : lit : raisa : stain : þinsat : sun : sin : haralt : bruþur : inkuars : þaiR furu : trikila : fiari : at : kuli : auk : a:ustarlar:ni : kafu : tuu : sunar:la : a sirk:lan:ti.** "Tola had this stone raised for her son Harald, Ingvar's brother. They traveled boldly for gold, and in the east gave the eagle [food]. They died in the south, in Serkland." Original image © 2017, Swedish Historical Museum; released under license CC BY 2.5 SV. http://kulturarvsdata.se/shm/media/html/227107

CHAPTER I

There was a king named Eirek who ruled Sweden; he was called Eirek the Victorious. He married Sigrid the Strong-Willed, but he divorced her on account of her difficult frame of mind, because she was the most obstinate woman about everything that concerned her.[9] He gave her Gautland. Their son was Olaf of Sweden.[10]

In those days, Jarl Hakon ruled over Norway, and he had many children. We must say something concerning one of his daughters, named Aud. King Eirek also had a daughter, who isn't named. The Swedish chieftain Aki asked for Eirek's daughter's hand, but the king didn't think it worthwhile to betroth his daughter to an undustinguished man.

Some time later, a petty king from Russia asked for her hand. The king agreed to give him the girl, and she went eastward to Russia with him. Some time later, Aki went there in secret, and he killed the king and carried Eirek's daughter off with him. He went home to Sweden and married her. At this wedding, eight chieftains swore to support Aki. They stayed there for a while, risking the king's anger, because the king was not willing to fight them and cause such a terrible slaughter of his own men within his lands. Aki and his wife had a son, who was named Eymund.

Afterwards, Aki offered the king compensation for this rash act. King Eirek accepted it, and once it was done, he asked for the hand of Aud, the daughter of Jarl Hakon from Norway. His proposal was favorably answered—yet the jarl said that he would prefer that King Eirik not allow the man who had become his son-in-law by force to rank as highly in Sweden as the jarl himself. Aud was betrothed and the wedding day was set, and new messages went back and forth between Aki and the king. Aki offered the king the right to settle their dispute on his own terms, except for outlawry, and this was accepted.[11]

The king prepared for his wedding and invited the chieftains from his lands. He invited his son-in-law Aki first, along with the eight chieftains who followed him.

CHAPTER II

On the appointed day, Jarl Hakon came from Norway to Sweden. There was a great crowd at Uppsala, because all the best men from Sweden were there. There were many large cabins, because many chieftains with large followings had assembled there, although Aki had the most retainers except for King Eirek and Jarl Hakon. And so the second largest cabin was prepared for Aki. King Eirik's daughter was not there, and neither was her son, because they thought that the king's invitation was not to be trusted.

Now men sat down and feasted for some time, with great gladness and good cheer. As the feast began, Aki watched out for himself carefully, but less so as the wedding feast went on—until one night after the feasting, King Eirek caught them all unawares and killed all eight of the chieftains who had been at odds with the king, and he killed Aki in the same way. After that the feast broke up. Jarl Hakon returned to Norway, and every man returned to his own home. Some men blame Jarl Hakon for this plan. Some say that he himself was in on the killing.

Now the king claimed as his own all the lands and wealth that the eight chieftains had owned. He brought Eymund and his mother home to live with him. Eymund grew up in the king's household, honored highly, until King Eirek breathed his last. Then Olaf took the kingdom and held Eymund in the same honor as his father had done. When Eymund was grown, he remembered his grief, because every day he saw his own estates with his own eyes and felt stripped of all honor, because the king claimed all the tribute from his estates.

King Olaf had a daughter named Ingigerd. She and Eymund loved each other very much on account of their kinship, because she was an excellent woman in all respects. Eymund was a tall man, physically powerful, and the best knight.

Eymund now considered his position, and felt that it was taking too long to set his losses right. He felt it was better to suffer sudden death than to live with shame. This was his plan: when he found out that twelve men of the king's household had gone to collect the tribute from the shires and lands that his father had held, he went with eleven more men into the forest where the king's men's route lay. There they fought, and there was a fierce battle between them.

That same day, Ingigerd followed them into the woods and found them all lifeless except for Eymund, and even he was badly wounded. She had him laid in her wagon and drove off with him, and she had him healed in secret.

When King Olaf heard the news, he summoned the assembly and made Eymund an outlaw, condemned throughout his kingdom. But once

Eymund recovered, Ingigerd secretly gave him a ship. He set out raiding and gained much wealth and many men.

CHAPTER III

Several years later, the king who ruled Russia, whose name was Yaroslav, asked for Ingigerd's hand.[12] She was betrothed to him, and she traveled east with him. When Eymund heard the news, he traveled east to Russia. Yaroslav welcomed him, as did Ingigerd, because at the time there was great unrest in Russia, for King Yaroslav's brother Burislav had invaded the realm. Eymund fought five battles against him, and in the last one Burislav was captured and blinded and brought to the king.[13] Eymund won great wealth in gold and silver there, along with many kinds of treasures and fine possessions.

Ingigerd sent men to meet King Olaf her father. She asked him to give up the lands that Eymund had owned and be reconciled with him, rather than fearing an invasion from him. One might say that permission was given.

At that time, Eymund was in Novgorod; he often fought battles and was victorious in all of them, and he won back a large tribute-paying land for the king. Eymund was eager to visit his estates. He had large and well-equipped forces, because he was short of neither wealth nor weapons. Eymund left Russia with great honor and esteem from all the people. He came to Sweden and settled in his realm and estates. Soon he contracted a marriage and married the daughter of a powerful man, and with her he had a son who was named Yngvar.

Olaf the King of Sweden heard that Eymund had entered the land with a mighty host and plenty of wealth, and that he had settled in the realm that his father and the eight chieftains had held. He felt that this was a serious matter, but he did not trust himself to do anything, because every day he heard tell of Eymund's many mighty deeds. Now each man lived quietly, because neither wanted to bow to the other.

Eymund stayed in his realm. He governed it and ruled it as kings customarily do, and he built up his power, because he came to have a large following. He had a great hall built for himself and fitted out splendidly, and he held a feast there every day with a great multitude of men, for he had many knights and plenty of crewmen for his ships. He lived peaceably for the time being.

Yngvar grew up at home with his father until he was nine years old. Then Yngvar asked his father to allow him to go to meet the king and other chieftains in Sweden. Eymund gave him his permission to go, and outfitted his expedition worthily. Yngvar took the best helmet that his father owned, gilded and set with gemstones, and a sword ornamented with gold, and many other treasures. Yngvar went with fifty of his father's men. All their horses were armored, and they themselves had armor and shields, with gilded helmets and all their weapons ornamented with gold and silver. With his men thus equipped, he traveled to Sweden from the east. The news of his journey was heard far and wide, and chieftains from far and near sought him out and invited him to feasts. He accepted, and they gave him fine gifts, and he gave fine gifts to them.

Yngvar's fame spread far and wide throughout Sweden, and it reached King Olaf's ears. King Olaf had a son named Onund,[14] the most promising young man, nearly the same age as Yngvar. Onund asked his father to go and meet his kinsman Yngvar and welcome him with honor. He got what he asked for, and he went to meet Yngvar with great honor, and their meeting was quite friendly. Then they went to meet the king, and the king came to meet them and greeted his son and Yngvar warmly. He led Yngvar into his hall and welcomed him and all his retainers. Yngvar said that they would stay there for a while. Then he brought forth the treasures that were mentioned before, the helmet and the sword, and he said, "These gifts my father has sent you, to strengthen the peace and firm friendship."

The king gratefully accepted the treasures, but said that it wasn't Eymund who had sent them to him. Yngvar stayed there all that winter and was the most highly honored of all men by the king. In the spring, Yngvar prepared to go home, and Onund went with him. The king gave Yngvar a good horse and a gilded saddle and a handsome ship.

Now Yngvar and Onund left, highly honored by King Olaf, and traveled to Eymund. When they came to Eymund's estate, Eymund was informed who had arrived, but he acted as if he hadn't heard. They came to the hall, and Onund wanted to dismount, but Yngvar ordered them to ride into the hall. They did so; they rode all the way into the hall, before Eymund's high seat. He greeted them well and asked for news, and asked how they dared to make such a commotion, riding into his hall. Yngvar answered, "When I came to King Olaf, he came to meet me with all his household, and he welcomed me well and worthily. But you don't want to do his son any honor when he visits you at home. Now you know why I rode into your hall."

Eymund jumped up and lifted Onund off the horse in his arms, kissed him and set him down, and ordered everyone within the hall to serve him. Then Yngvar brought the gifts to his father, those that he said that King Olaf had sent him to strengthen the peace; they were the horse and saddle and ship. Eymund said that he wasn't the one that King Olaf had sent them to, but he praised him highly for giving such worthy gifts to Yngvar. Onund stayed there that winter.

In the spring, Onund prepared to go home, and Yngvar went with him. Eymund gave Onund a hawk with golden hues on its feathers. With that, they left and went to meet King Olaf, and he welcomed them warmly and was glad that they had come back. Onund brought him the hawk and said that Eymund had sent it to him. The king blushed and said that Eymund might have mentioned his name when he gave the hawk—"maybe he intended that."

A little later, he called on Onund and Yngvar and said, "Now you must go back and take Eymund what I am giving him. It's a banner, because I have no other gifts as precious as this to give him. It has this nature: the man before whom it is carried will always have a sure victory. That shall be the sign of the settlement between us."

They went back and brought Eymund the banner, along with the king's words of friendship. Eymund gratefully accepted the king's gift and told them that they had to go back quickly and invite King Olaf to his home. They had to say this: "Eymund your servant invites you to a feast with good will, and is grateful to you for coming."

They traveled and met King Olaf and told him Eymund's message. King Olaf was overjoyed and traveled with a large company. Eymund welcomed him warmly and with great honor. They agreed to a firm friendship between them, and they kept it well. Then the king traveled home with fine gifts. Yngvar always stayed with the king, because the king loved him no less than his own son.

Yngvar was a tall man, handsome and strong and fair-skinned, wise and eloquent, generous to his friends but fierce to his enemies, courteous and the quickest to react, so that wise men have compared him in achievements with his kinsman Styrbjorn,[15] or with King Olaf Tryggvason, who was and will be the most famous man in the Northlands for ever and ever, in the eyes of both God and men.

CHAPTER IV

When the kinsmen Onund and Yngvar were fully grown, the folk called the Semigallians had a dispute with King Olaf.[16] They had not paid tribute for some time. King Olaf sent Onund and Yngvar with three ships, to fetch the tribute. They landed and summoned an assembly of the inhabitants and claimed the tribute from the Semigallian king. Yngvar showed such accomplished eloquence that the only thing that the king and many other chieftains felt was right to pay the tribute that was demanded—except for three chieftains who did not want to follow the king's advice. They refused to pay tribute and summoned their forces. When the king heard of what they were planning, he told Onund and Yngvar to fight them, and he lent them support. They fought, and there was a terrible slaughter before the chieftains fled. As they fled, the chieftain who had been most strongly opposed to paying tribute was captured, and they hanged him, but two of them escaped. Onund and Yngvar took many possessions as plunder and collected all the tribute. With that done, they returned to meet King Olaf, and they brought him a great store of wealth in gold and silver and fine treasures. Yngvar's worth had greatly increased on this journey, so much that the king set him above other chieftains in Sweden. Yngvar took a concubine and fathered a son on her; he was named Svein.

With these honors, Yngvar stayed with King Olaf until he was twenty. Then he grew so sad that he never spoke a word. The king felt that this was a serious problem, and he asked what was the cause. Yngvar answered, "If you think my sadness is a serious problem, and you wish me as well as you say you do, then give me the title and honors of a king."

The king replied, "Anything else you ask for, honors or wealth, I will grant you. But I cannot do this, because I am not wiser than our ancestors. I do not know any more than our kinsmen who have gone before."

This matter drove them apart, because Yngvar always asked for the title of king and never received it.

CHAPTER V

Yngvar prepared to leave the country to search for a foreign kingdom for himself. He commanded a force of men from his land and thirty ships, all fully crewed. King Olaf heard that Yngvar was ready to leave, and he sent men to meet Yngvar, asking him to stay and accept the title of king. Yngvar said that he would have accepted it if it had been offered before, but he said that now he was ready to sail as soon as the wind turned favorable.

A little later, Yngvar sailed away from Sweden with thirty ships, and they did not lower their sails until they came to Russia. King Yaroslav received him with great honor. Yngvar stayed there for three winters, and there he learned to speak many languages.[17] He heard it said that three rivers flowed from the east beyond Russia, and the one in the middle was the largest.[18] Yngvar traveled widely through Russia and asked whether someone might know from where that river flowed, but no one could tell him.

Yngvar prepared to depart from Russia, meaning to explore and search out the length of this river. He had the bishop consecrate a flint and steel for him. Four men are named who went with Yngvar on the journey: Hjalmvigi and Soti, Ketil who was called Garda-Ketil—he was an Icelander—and Valdimar.[19] After that, they set sail on the river with thirty ships, and Yngvar steered their prows eastwards. He laid down the law that no one was to go onto land without his permission. If anyone were to go, that man was to lose a hand or a foot. A man had to stand watch through the night on each ship.

When they had traveled for some time along the river which was mentioned before, Ketil had to stand watch one night. He felt that his watch was a long one, while most people were sleeping. He grew curious to go onto land to look around, and he was gone longer than he intended. He stopped and listened. He saw a tall house right in front of him, and he walked up and entered the house. There he saw a silver kettle over the fire. This seemed strange. He took the kettle and ran along the path to the ships. And when he had run for a while, he looked behind him and saw a terrifying giant running after him. Ketil hurried faster, yet the giant was catching up to him. He set the kettle down and took off the hanging chain and ran off as fast as he could, although from time to time he looked behind him. He saw that the giant came to a stop when he reached the kettle. At times the giant came towards him, and at times he walked away from him, but finally he picked up the kettle and walked to the house. Garda-Ketil got to the ship and broke the chain and laid it in his footlocker.

In the morning, when the men awoke and went ashore, they saw a track leading from the ship, because dew had fallen. They told Yngvar. He ordered Ketil to say whether he had gone there, because he said that no one else could have gone, and he said that he wouldn't kill him if he told the truth. Ketil told the truth, and he asked for mercy for his disobedience. He showed Yngvar the chain. Yngvar ordered him not to do it again, and they left it at that.

Then they sailed for many days and through many countries, until they saw that the animals looked and behaved differently. That's how they realized that they had left their own lands and countries far behind.

One evening they saw something like a half moon resting on the ground, far away. That night, Valdimar stood watch. He went ashore to search for the place that they had seen. He came to where a hill stood before him, colored like gold, and he saw the reason for that: it was completely covered with serpents. Since they were asleep, he reached out with his spearshaft towards a gold ring, and he pulled it towards him. A tiny serpent awoke, and at once it awakened another one next to it, until the jaculus was awakened.[20]

Valdimar hurried back to the ship and told Yngvar the whole truth. Yngvar ordered his men to brace themselves for the serpents and to steer the ships to another anchorage across the river, and so they did. Then they saw a terrifying dragon flying towards them over the river. Many men fainted from terror. And when the jaculus flew over the ship that two priests were steering, he spewed such venom that both the ship and its crew were lost. Then he flew back across the river to his own lair.

Yngvar traveled down the river for many days. Then fortresses and large houses appeared, and they saw a splendid city built out of white marble. As they neared the town, they saw a great multitude of women and men. They found the handsomeness of the inhabitants, and the courtliness of the women, to be outstanding, for many of them were noble to see. Yet one woman excelled them all, both in her dress and in her beauty. This stately woman beckoned to Yngvar that they should come to meet her.

Yngvar disembarked from his ship and went to meet this noble woman. She asked who they might be and what they might be doing, but Yngvar didn't answer, because he wanted to find out if she could speak more languages. As it turned out, she knew how to speak Latin, German, Norse, and Greek, and many others that are spoken in the Eastern realms.[21] When Yngvar found out that she could speak these languages, he told her his name, and asked what her name was and what rank she might hold.

"My name is Silkisif," she said, "and I am the queen of this land and realm."

She invited Yngvar to go to the city with her, along with all his men. He accepted. The townsmen picked up their ships with all their rigging and carried them up to the city. Yngvar settled all his men in one hall and locked it carefully, because there was heathen sorcery all around. Yngvar ordered them to beware of all dealings with the heathens, and he forbade all women to enter his hall, except for the queen. Some men paid little heed to his speech. He had them killed. Then no one dared to disobey his orders.

That winter Yngvar stayed there, highly honored, because the queen and her wise men sat and talked with him every day, and each of them told the other many new things. Yngvar always spoke to her about Almighty God, and she was pleased with this faith. She loved Yngvar so much that she invited him to possess the entire kingdom and take the title of king—and in the end, she gave herself to him, should he want to settle down there. But he said that first he wanted to search out the length of the river, and then he would accept that offer.

When spring came, Yngvar prepared to depart, and he wished the queen and her people well. Yngvar traveled down the river until he came to a great waterfall and deep chasms. There were high cliffs, so they hauled their ships up with ropes.[22] Then they hauled them back down to the river, and they traveled for a long time in which they didn't notice anything.

But as summer was passing, they saw a host of ships rowing towards them. They were all circular, with oars out on all sides.[23] They sailed out towards them so that Yngvar had no choice but to hold still, because their ships traveled like a bird flying. Before they met, one man stood up from among the fleet. He was clothed in a king's finery and spoke in many languages. Yngvar was silent. Then he said some words in Greek. Yngvar understood that his name was Jolf and that he was from the city of Heliopolis.[24] And when the king learned Yngvar's name and where he had come from and where he was going, he invited him to stay with him in his city all winter long. Yngvar said that it didn't suit him to delay, and he refused. The king made it clear to him that they would stay there that winter. Yngvar said that it would have to be that way. Then he and his men sailed into the harbor and went ashore and came to the city. And when they looked back, they saw that the townsmen were carrying their ships on their shoulders up to the city, where they could be locked in. They saw many heathen practices on all the streets there. Yngvar ordered his men to be diligent in prayer and hold fast to their faith. Jolf gave them a hall, and that winter Yngvar watched over his men so that none should be harmed by dealings with women or other heathen doings. When they went out to use the toilets, they went fully armed, and locked the hall in the meantime. No man was to come in except for the king. He sat and talked with Yngvar every day, and each of them told the other much news, new and old, from their countries.

Yngvar asked whether the king knew from where the river flowed. Jolf said that he knew truly that it flowed out of the source "which we call Lindibelti.[25] From there, another river descends to the Red Sea, and there is a great whirlpool there, called Gapi. Between the seas and the rivers is the peninsula called Siggeum.[26] The river flows a short distance before it falls from a cliff into the Red Sea, and we call that place the end of the world. But out on this river that you have followed, there lurk evildoers in huge ships. They have their ships completely concealed with reeds, so that men think that they are islands. They have all manner of weapons and blasting fire, and they destroy more men with the fire than with weapons."

The townsmen felt that their king was paying no attention to their needs on account of Yngvar. They swore to drive him from the kingdom and take another king for themselves. And when Yngvar heard that, he asked the king to do as his people willed. He did so. The king asked Yngvar to give him assistance in fighting against his brother. He was the more powerful of the two and treated his brother most unfairly. Yngvar promised to lend him aid when he returned.

CHAPTER VI

When winter had passed, Yngvar steered his entire fleet away from Jolf's realm. When they had traveled for a while, they came to a huge waterfall. There was such turbulence from it that they had to head for land. But when they approached the shore, they saw the footprint of a terrifying giant—the print was eight feet long. The cliffs were so high that they could not haul up their ships with ropes. They sailed their ships along the banks until they could drift out of the river currents. There was a little break in the cliffs on the bank, and there they landed, where the land was flat and marshy. Yngvar ordered them to fell trees and make digging tools, and they did so. They began to dig, and they measured the depth and width of the canal from the point where the river should rush in. They were at this for months before they could sail their ships there.

When they had traveled for a long time, they saw a house with a terrifying giant nearby, so wicked-looking that they thought it must be the Devil. They were badly frightened and begged God for mercy. Yngvar ordered Hjalmvigi to sing psalms to the glory of God, because he was a good cleric, and they vowed six days of fasting and prayers. Then the giant walked away from the house in another direction down the river. Once he had left, they went up to the house and saw a strong rampart around it. When they entered the house, they saw that one column held it up; it was made of clay. They began to chop at the column all around, at ground level, until the house trembled when they shook it. Yngvar ordered them to take large stones and carry them to the house, and they did so. When evening came on, Yngvar ordered them to get behind the rampart and hide in the reeds. And as night was falling, they saw the giant coming; he had many men fastened under his belt. He carefully closed up the ramparts and also the house. Then he had his meal. When a little time had passed, they grew curious about what he was doing, and they heard his loud snoring. Yngvar ordered them to pick up the stones they had brought, and they bombarded the column until the house collapsed. The giant struggled so hard that one of his feet came free. Yngvar and his companions came up and struck off the giant's foot with timber axes, because it was as hard as a tree. When that was done, they realized that the giant was dead. They dragged the foot to the ships and pickled it in white salt.[27]

Now they traveled until the river divided in two. They saw five islands stir and move towards them. Yngvar ordered his men to prepare themselves. He had fire lit from the consecrated flint and steel. One of the islands came at them fast and flung a heavy volley of stones at them, but they defended themselves and flung stones back at them. But when the raiders encountered resistance, they began to pump the bellows of a fiery furnace, and this caused a tremendous racket. There was a copper tube sticking out, and a huge flame flowed out of it onto one ship, and in a short time it burned the entire ship to pale ashes.[28] When Yngvar saw that, he grieved for his losses and ordered his men to bring him tinder with the consecrated fire. Then he bent his bow and nocked an arrow on the string and placed the tinder with the consecrated fire on the arrowhead. The arrow flew from the bow, carrying the fire into the tube sticking out of the furnace. The flame was turned back onto the heathens themselves, and in just a moment the island burned up, men and ships all together. The other islands had come up. But as soon as Yngvar heard the blowing of the bellows, he shot with the consecrated fire, and he destroyed the Devil's people with God's help, so that nothing was left but ashes.

A little later, Yngvar reached the spring from which the river flowed. There they saw a dragon. They had never before seen a dragon so large, and a great pile of gold lay underneath him. They anchored close by, and everyone came ashore, and they came to the track where the dragon was accustomed to slither down to the water. This path was extremely broad. Yngvar ordered them to scatter salt along the path and drag the giant's foot there, and he said that he thought that the dragon would stay there for a while. They kept silent and sought shelter for themselves. And when the usual time had come for the dragon to slither down to the water, when he crawled onto the path he saw that there was salt on the path before him, and he began to lick it up. When he came to where the giant's foot was lying, he swallowed it at once. He was on the path for longer than usual, because he turned back three times when he was halfway up, in order to drink.

Yngvar and his men went to the dragon's den and saw a huge amount of gold, as hot as if it had been newly cast in the furnace. At once they cut off a lump with timber axes. It was a huge amount of wealth that they got. Then they saw that the dragon was coming closer. They turned and ran away with the great heap of gold and hid it where the reeds were thick. Yngvar ordered them not to look too closely at the dragon. They did as he ordered, except for a few men who stood up and saw that the dragon took his loss badly. He reared up on his tail and made a noise like a man whistling, and coiled up in a circle on the gold. These men told what they had seen, and at once they fell down dead.[29]

CHAPTER VII

After this happened, Yngvar and his men sailed away. They explored the cape that they reached. There they found a castle, and they saw a great keep standing within. When they entered the keep, they saw that it was richly ornamented inside, and they found a great store of wealth and many treasures. Yngvar asked if anyone was willing to stay behind that night and find out whatever news he could learn. Soti said that he wouldn't refuse.

When evening came, Yngvar went to the ships with his men, and Soti hid in a certain place. Once it had grown late, the Devil appeared to him in the form of a man. He said: "There was a man named Siggeus, strong and mighty. He had three daughters. To them he gave much gold. But when he died, he was buried where you saw the dragon. After his death, the eldest sister begrudged her sisters the gold and treasures. She killed herself. The second sister followed her example. The third sister lived the longest, and claimed her father's inheritance and rulership of this place, and not only while she was alive. She gave the cape its name and called it Siggeum. She fills the hall with a host of devils every night, and I am one of them, sent to tell you of these events. Dragons ate the corpses of the king and his daughters, but some men think that they were turned into dragons. You must know, Soti, and you must tell your king Yngvar, that Harald the king of Sweden came this way a long time ago. He and all his men were lost in the Red Sea whirlpool, and now he has come here to rule.[30] As proof of my story, his banner is kept here, in this hall. Yngvar is to take that with him and send it to the Swedes, so that they are not kept ignorant of their king's fate. You must also tell Yngvar that he will die on this journey, along with a great number of his men. You, Soti, are unrighteous and faithless, and therefore you shall stay behind with us, but Yngvar will be helped by the faith that he has in God."

Once he had said this, the devil fell silent. All that night there was a terrible uproar and shrieking. When morning came, Yngvar arrived, and Soti told him what he had seen and heard. And when Soti had finished his story, he fell down dead in front of all the onlookers.

Yngvar took the banner that stood in the hall, and he and his men brought it to his ship. Now he turned his prows around. He gave a name to the huge waterfall, and called it Belgsoti.[31] Nothing of note happened until he came to the realm of King Hromund, who was Jolf by another name. When they sailed once again to the city of Heliopolis, King Jolf sailed out with many ships to meet them. He ordered Yngvar to lower his sails—"because now you must help me against my brother Bjolf, who is also called Solmund, because he himself and his eight sons want to plunder my kingdom."

Yngvar and his men went to the city and prepared for battle. Yngvar had large wheels built, fitted all over with sharp points and spikes on the outside. Besides that, he had caltrops forged.

Now both kings summoned their forces and came to the place that they had agreed upon. When Yngvar had readied his forces, Bjolf had far more men. King Jolf formed up his ranks to face his brother.

When both sides were ready, they screamed their battle cries. Yngvar and his men pushed out the wheels with all their battle-trappings, and this caused a dreadful slaughter, and the ranks were broken up. Then Yngvar attacked them on the flanks and killed all of King Bjolf's sons, but Bjolf himself escaped. King Jolf attacked fiercely and pursued the fleeing men, but Yngvar ordered his men to stay behind and not go so far from their own ships—"because our enemies could capture them. Instead, take plenty of plunder from our enemies whom we have killed here!"

They took many kinds of treasures and a great store of wealth, and carried them to the ships. Then Jolf came with his forces and formed up his ranks and shouted out battle cries. This caught Yngvar by surprise and forced him to retreat. He had the caltrops thrown before their feet. They didn't know how to protect themselves and ran right onto them. When they felt the sharpness of the points, they thought that they had been struck by sorcery.

Yngvar stayed by his tents, and his men chose plenty of treasures. Then they saw a great group of women coming to the tents, and they began to perform beautifully. Yngvar ordered his men to be as wary of the women as of the deadliest venomous serpents. And when evening came on and the host prepared to go to sleep, the women came to them in their tents. The most regal one got into bed next to Yngvar. He became angry and drew his knife and stabbed her in the genitals. When his men saw what he had done, they began to drive away these disreputable women. Yet there were some who could not resist their caresses because of devilish sorcery, and they lay with them.[32] When Yngvar heard about that, his joy in his wealth and his happiness in his friends turned to terrible grief, for in the morning, when they mustered their forces, eighteen men were lying dead. At once Yngvar ordered that the dead men be buried.

CHAPTER VIII

After that, Yngvar and all his men hurriedly prepared to leave. They set out on their way and traveled day and night as fast as they could. But a sickness began to spread in their ranks, so that all their best men died, and more died than survived. Yngvar also fell sick. By that time, they had reached Silkisif's kingdom. He summoned his men and ordered them to bury the dead. Then he called Garda-Ketil and other friends to him and said, "I have fallen ill, and I guess that it will be the death of me. May I then reach the place that I have striven for! I believe that God's Son will grant me His promise, by God's mercy, because with all my heart I entrust myself into God's hands every day, soul and body. I have watched over this folk as best I could. I want you to know that it is by God's just judgment that we are stricken with this deadly sickness, and this sickness and sorcery is meant for me most of all, because as soon as I am dead, the sickness will abate. This will I ask of you, and you most of all, Ketil: that you bring my body to Sweden and have it buried inside a church. My share of the wealth that I have here in gold and silver and costly clothes, I want to to have divided into three parts. One third I give to churches and priests, another third I give to poor men, and my father and my son are to have the third. Give my greetings to Queen Silkisif! For the sake of everything I want to beg you to stay united. If you disagree on what course to take, let Garda-Ketil decide, because he has the best memory of all of you."

Then he bade them farewell and wished for them to meet on the day of resurrection. He made a good impression in many ways. He didn't live for many days after that. They prepared his body carefully and laid it in a coffin, and then they turned from their course and landed at the city of Citopolis.[33]

When the queen recognized their ships, she went to meet them with great honors. When she saw them coming ashore, she was saddened, and she felt that something terrible had happened: she could not see the man who meant more to her than all the others. She asked them what had happened, and she demanded exact details about Yngvar's death and where they had left his body. They said that they had buried him in the earth. She said that was a lie, and she swore that she would have them killed if they didn't tell the truth. They told her the arrangements that Yngvar had ordered them to make for his body and his wealth, and then they brought her Yngvar's body. She had it brought to the city with great honor, and had it prepared for burial with costly unguents. Then the queen told them to go in God's peace and Yngvar's. "He who is your God is mine. Greet Yngvar's kinsmen when you reach Sweden, and invite some of them to come here with priests and bring Christianity to this people. Then I shall build a church here, where Yngvar shall rest."

When Yngvar died, 1041 years had passed since the birth of Jesus Christ. He was twenty-five years old when he died. This was nine years after the fall of Saint and King Olaf Haraldson.[34]

Ketil and his men prepared to leave, and they bid the queen farewell. They set out on their way, and they had twelve ships. And when they had traveled for a while, they disagreed over which way to go, and they separated, because no one wanted to follow the others. Ketil sailed the correct route and came to Russia, but Valdimar reached Constantinople in a single ship. We do not know anything for certain about where the other ships landed, because men think that most of them were lost, and we cannot say anything more about Yngvar. Yet we know that he accomplished many mighty deeds on this voyage, about which wise men must have said much.

Ketil, whom we mentioned before, spent the winter in Russia. He returned to Sweden in the summer and told of what had happened on this journey. He brought Yngvar's share of wealth to his son, who was named Svein, and he brought him the queen's greetings and her message. Svein was young and had grown tall. He was a strong man and most like his father. He set out on raids and wanted to prove himself above all. And when several years had passed, he went east into Russia with many men, and stayed there over the winter.

CHAPTER IX

It is also said that that winter, Svein entered the school where he learned to speak many languages that men knew were common in the Eastern realms. Then he prepared thirty ships and said that he wanted to sail this fleet to meet the queen. He brought many priests with him. Their highest-ranking bishop was named Rodgeir. The bishop consecrated the lots three times and drew lots three times, and each time the lots indicated that God wished for him to go. The bishop said then that he was ready and willing to travel.

Now Svein set out on his journey from Russia. And when they had traveled along the river for two days, heathens came upon them unawares with ninety ships; Norsemen call them galleys. The heathens prepared themselves for battle, as did the other side. Neither side could make out what the others were saying. As they were arming themselves, Svein appealed his case to God and had lots cast to show what God's will might be, to fight or to flee against such an overwhelming force. The lots told them to fight, and Svein promised to give up raiding if God would give him victory. After that they began to fight, and Svein and his men killed the heathens at will. In the end, the heathens fled away in twenty ships, and all the rest were killed. Svein suffered few casualties, and they took all the wealth they wanted, in gold and all sorts of treasures.

Then they went on their way until they reached the land where Ketil had taken the hanging chain from the kettle. Svein ordered the greater part of his men to arm themselves, and they did so. And they traveled only a short while before they saw a large house and a huge man nearby. He was shouting in a terrifying voice. At once people drew near from every direction. Humans call this kind of people Cyclopes. They had clubs in their hands, as huge as roof beams. They were making an uproar, and they had neither armor nor weapons. Svein ordered his archers to shoot them quickly and told them it was no use waiting there, "because they are as strong as lions and tall as houses or trees." At once they shot at them and killed many and wounded some. Then a wondrous event came to pass: the strongest ones fled. Svein forbade his men from pursuing them and said that there would be no shelter. They ran into the house and plundered great riches in pelts and clothes and silver and all precious metals. Then they returned to the ships and set out on their way.

When they had traveled for a long time, Svein saw a fjord cutting into the land. He ordered them to steer the ships there. They were eager to do this, because many young men were there. And when they approached the land, they saw castles and many houses. Eight people saw them sailing in and were amazed at their journey. One of the natives had a feather in his hand, and he straightened the feather quill and then the feather itself. This looked to them like a sign of peace. Svein also made a sign of peace on his side. Then they reached land, and the natives assembled under a certain cliff, with various sorts of trade goods. Svein told his men to go ashore, and they traded with the inhabitants, but neither could understand what the others were saying.

The next day, Svein's men went to trade with the inhabitants again, and they traded with them for a while. Then a Russian man[35] tried to break a deal that they had just made. The heathen got angry and punched him in the nose so that blood gushed onto the ground. The Russian drew a sword and chopped the heathen in two. Then the natives ran away with loud cries and shouts, and suddenly an overwhelming force assembled. Svein ordered his men to arm themselves and attack. A fierce and savage battle broke out between them, and a multitude of the heathens fell, because they were all unarmored. When they saw that they were overcome by superior forces, they fled. Svein and his men took a great share of wealth that the other side had abandoned, and they carried it to their ships.

After this happened, Svein and his men sailed away from there and praised God for their victory. They traveled for a while until they saw a large herd of pigs on a headland under a certain mountain peak by the river. Some of the men rushed onto land and wanted to kill them, and they did so. The pigs that escaped began to squeal loudly, and they stampeded up onto the land.

Just then they saw a huge army coming from the land down towards the ships. One man was walking a bit ahead of the army. This man was carrying three apples. He threw one up into the air, and it landed in front of Svein's feet. Then the next one followed it and landed in the same place. Svein said that he wasn't going to wait for the third apple.[36] "There's some devilish power and strong sorcery that accompanies this man."

Svein nocked an arrow on his bowstring and shot at him. The arrow struck him on the nose. There was a sound like a horn breaking in pieces, and the man twisted his head around and they saw that he had a bird's beak.[37] He screamed out loud and ran towards his men, and when they saw what had happened, they all ran back up onto land as fast as they could go.

CHAPTER X

After that, Svein returned to his ships and went on his way. When they had traveled for a short while, it is said that one day they saw ten men leading some beast behind them. They found that rather astonishing, because they saw a huge wooden tower standing on the beast's back.[38] Fifty men went ashore—the ones who were the most curious about the nature of the beast. When the men leading the beast saw the sailors, they hid themselves and abandoned the beast. Svein's men went up to the beast and wanted to lead it behind them, but the beast pushed its head down so that it wouldn't move, even though they all began to pull the reins attached to the beast's head. They thought that those ten men must be able to lead the beast with some sort of trick that they couldn't figure out. They devised a plan, and they left the beast and hid in the reeds so that they could see everything that happened to the beast. A little while later, the natives stood up and went to the beast. They took the reins and laid them back against the beast's neck on both sides and pushed them through a crossbeam in the tower. They brought up the beast's head that way, because there was a pulley in the hole bored in the crossbeam. When Svein's men saw the beast standing straight, they rushed to it as fast as they could. They seized the reins and led the beast wherever they wanted. But since they didn't know what sort of beast it was, or what it needed for food, they stabbed the beast with spears until it dropped dead. Then they went down to their ships and began rowing.

Next, they saw a multitude of heathens up on land. They walked out onto the shore and made signs of peace to Svein and his men, who steered their ships to land there. There was a fine harbor. They arranged a meeting between them, and Svein bought many treasures there. Then the heathens invited their trading partners into a house for a feast, and they accepted. When they came into the house, they saw all manner of delicacies set out, and plenty of the best drink. When Svein's men sat at the table, they crossed themselves. But when the heathens saw them make the sign of the cross, they were furious and charged at them. Some punched them with their fists, and some scratched them, and both sides called for help.

When Svein heard his men's shouts and saw their situation, he said, "Who knows if this feast will turn into great sorrow for us?" He joined his men and ordered them all to arm themselves. When Svein had drawn up his forces in ranks, they saw that the heathens had drawn up their ranks, and that they were carrying a bloody man in front of their ranks and were using him for a battle standard.

Svein consulted with Bishop Rodgeir about what course of action to take. The bishop said, "If the pagans hope for victory from the likeness of some wicked man, let us think of how we are bound to hope for assistance from heaven, where Christ the Lord himself lives and shows mercy. He is the ruler of all Christians, taking care of all the living and the dead. Bear the victory standard of our Christ Crucified before our ranks, with invocation of His name, and from it, we may expect victory for ourselves, but loss of life for the heathens!"

After the bishop gave this encouragement, they took the Holy Cross with the likeness of our Lord and used that as a standard and carried it before the ranks. Then they charged at the heathens without fear, while the priests went to their prayers. And when the ranks clashed, the heathens were blinded, and many were filled with fear and fled quickly. Every heathen ran in a different direction, some into the river, and some into swamps or forests. Many thousands of heathens were destroyed there.

Once the fleeing host was driven away, Svein had the bodies buried of those who had fallen there. And when that was done, Svein ordered his men to beware of curiosity about the customs of the heathens; "because there has been more slaughter than fruitfulness on this journey," he said.

CHAPTER XI

Svein departed, and they sailed until they seemed to see a half moon standing on the Earth. There they headed for land and disembarked. Ketil told Svein what had happened when he and Yngvar were there. Svein ordered his men to leave the ships and find the dragon. They walked until they entered a huge forest that stood by the dragon's lair, and there they hid themselves.

Svein sent some young men to the dragon to find out what was going on there. They saw that the serpents were asleep and were very numerous, but the jaculus lay curled in a ring that surrounded all the others. One of them began to reach out with his spear shaft towards a certain gold ring, and the shaft touched a tiny serpent. But when the serpent awoke, it wakened another one next to it, and then each serpent awakened another, until the jaculus reared up. Svein stood against a huge oak tree and nocked an arrow to his bowstring, and a piece of tinder as big as a man's head was set on the arrow point, bearing consecrated fire. When Svein saw that the jaculus was hauling himself aloft and heading for their ships, flying with gaping mouth, Svein shot the arrow with the consecrated fire into the serpent's mouth. The arrow pierced it to the heart, so that in an instant it fell down dead. When Svein and his men saw that, they praised God joyfully.

CHAPTER XII

After that happened, Svein ordered them to hurry away on account of the resulting stench and foulness. At once they turned and quickly headed for the ships, and almost all of them made it, except for six men who went up to the dragon for curiosity's sake—they dropped dead. The stench still gave many men a great deal of trouble, although no one else lost his life because of it.

Svein prepared to leave quickly, and he traveled until he entered the realm of Queen Silkisif. She came to meet him with great honor. As soon as Svein and his men landed, Ketil came first to meet the queen, but she paid him no heed, and she turned towards Svein and wanted to kiss him. But he pushed her away and said that he didn't want to kiss her, a heathen woman. "Why do you want to kiss me?"

She replied, "Because it seems to me that you have Yngvar's eyes."

Then they were received with honor and respect. When she found out that a bishop had come, she was glad. The bishop preached the faith before her, and they had an interpreter between them, because the bishop couldn't speak the language that she spoke.[39] She quickly gained understanding of spiritual wisdom and let herself be baptized. In that same month, all the people of the city were baptized.

Not long afterwards, the queen summoned a great assembly to consult with the men of the land. And when a huge multitude had assembled, Yngvar's son Svein was clothed in purple and a crown was set upon his head, and everyone called him their king. In addition to that, the queen was betrothed to him.

CHAPTER XIII

After this feast, King Svein traveled with a great host throughout his kingdom, and the queen went with him. The bishop and priests were also on this journey, because King Svein had the country made Christian, along with all the realms that the queen had formerly ruled.

At the beginning of summer, when the power of God's mercy had grown so strong in that land that it had become completely Christian, King Svein and his companions wanted to prepare to travel home to Sweden and let their kinsmen know the truth about his journey. When the queen found out about these intentions, she begged him to send his men home, but to stay behind peacefully himself. Svein answered, "I am not willing to send my men ahead of me, because there are many sorts of great risks for those who have to set out on this journey, as was proved earlier when there was no leader and all the men perished and wandered in all directions."

When the queen heard these words from the king and saw what his will was, she said, "You must not go so quickly, if I have any say in the matter, because maybe you won't want to return to this kingdom, or else you'll be lost on such a dreadfully dangerous journey, as you yourself have said. What's more proper for you is to strengthen Christianity and have churches built, because first you must have a huge and splendid church built in the city. If it turns out the way that I want, then you shall bury your father's body there. But when three winters have passed, you shall go in peace."

It was done as the queen asked. In the end, King Svein stayed there for three winters. During the third winter, a great church was competed in the city. Then the queen ordered the bishop to come. And when the bishop was in his vestments, he asked, "In whose name, o queen, do you wish me to consecrate the church?"

She answered, "To the glory of the holy King Yngvar, who lies here, shall you consecrate the church."

The bishop replied, "Why do you want such a thing, o queen? Has Yngvar manifested miracles after his death? Because them alone do we call saints who manifest miracles once their bodies are buried in earth."

She answered, "From your own mouth, I heard that the steadfastness of true faith and the habit of holy love is of greater worth in the eyes of God than the glory of miracles;[40] and I judge, as I have found, that Yngvar was steadfast in the holy love of God."

When the queen had pronounced that it should be so, the bishop consecrated the temple to the glory of God and all the saints, in the name of Yngvar. Then a new stone coffin was carved, and the body of Yngvar laid inside, and a precious cross with splendid fittings was set over it. The bishop had Mass sung frequently for Yngvar's soul, although he allowed the people to call it St. Yngvar's Church.[41]

CHAPTER XIV

When these matters were over and done, Svein prepared to sail away. He traveled from the south until he came to Sweden. The Swedes received him with joy and great honor. He was offered the kingdom, but when he heard that, he quickly refused it and said that he had won a better and more fertile land for himself and wanted to visit it again.

When two winters had passed, Svein sailed from Sweden, but Ketil stayed behind. He said that he had heard reports that Svein was in Russia over the winter and preparing to leave it in the spring. Svein sailed from Russia at the height of summer, and the last that people knew of him, he was sailing on the river. Ketil went to Iceland to meet his kinsmen, and he settled down there. He was the first to tell this story.

We know that some saga authors say that Yngvar was the son of Eymund Olafsson, because they feel it does him greater honor to call him a king's son. Onund would gladly have given all his kingdom if he could trade it for Yngvar's life, because all the chieftains in Sweden were eager to have him as king over them. Some men still ask why Yngvar was not the son of Eymund Olafson, and we will answer in this way: Eymund Olafsson had a son named Onund. He was the most similar to Yngvar in many respects, and most of all on his own far travels, as is shown in the book called *Gesta Saxonum*, where it is written: "*It is reported that Emundus the King of the Swedes sent his son Onundus by the Baltic Sea, who, after coming to the Amazons, was killed by them.*"[42]

Some men say that Yngvar and his men traveled for two weeks without seeing anything unless they lit a candle, because the cliffs closed up together above the river, and it was as if they were rowing in a cave for that half month.[43] But wise men feel that that cannot be likely unless the river channel were so narrow that the cliff peaks were touching, or there were forests so thick that the trees were touching between the cliff peaks. Although that may be possible, it isn't likely.

We have heard and written this saga according to the stories in the books that Brother Odd the Wise had made according to the stories of wise men, whom he mentions himself in the letter that he sent to Jon Loptsson and Gizur Hallsson.[44] Let those who think they know more details augment it where it seems to be lacking now. Brother Odd said that he had heard the saga told by the priest named Isleif, and also by Glum Thorgeirson, and a third man named Thorir. From their accounts he took what seemed most noteworthy to him. Isleif said that he had heard Yngvar's saga from a merchant, and that man said that he had learned it in the household of the King of Sweden. Glum had learned it from his father, and Thorir had learned it from Klakka Samsson, and Klakka had first heard it told by his kinsmen.

And here we end this saga.

The Saga of Eirek the Far-Traveler

Eireks saga víðförla

Eireks saga víðförla, *or* The Saga of Eirek the Far-Traveler, *comes from* Flateyjarbók, *the famous manuscript copied out and illuminated by two Icelandic priests, Jón Þórðarson and Magnús Þórhallsson, between 1387 and 1394. As discussed in the preface to* Sörla þáttr, *the writers of* Flateyjarbók *included a great deal of legendary material into their versions of the sagas of the missionary kings Olaf Tryggvason and Olaf Haraldson. Some had already been added by previous redactors, and some was added by Jón and Magnús themselves.*

Eireks saga víðförla *was probably written between 1300 and 1350, and is known from over fifty manuscripts, falling into three main recensions. Although traditionally classed as a* fornaldarsaga *and included as such in compilations of* fornaldarsögur, *it has almost nothing to do with traditional Norse heroic themes. On the other hand, it draws heavily on the theological writings of Honorius Augustodunensis, notably his* Elucidarius *and* Imago Mundi, *written around the year 1100. Fragments of a Norse translation of the Elucidarius survive, the oldest dated to the 12th century.*[1] *No translation survives of the* Imago Mundi, *but quotations and paraphrases in other texts suggest that it was well known in Iceland.*[2]

Jón Þórðarson selected and somewhat reworked Eireks saga víðförla *for inclusion in* Flateyjarbók *to serve as a prologue for his expanded saga of Olaf Tryggvason. His purpose was to show that Christianity had been known in Scandinavia in ancient times, but had been lost through centuries of error—from which the missionary-kings had saved their people. Parallels between Eirek and Olaf drive home the point; in the* Flateyjarbók *version of his saga, Olaf has a vision of a floating pillar or tower in a beautiful and sweet-smelling land, and in that vision he is commanded to go to Byzantium to receive baptism and learn the Christian faith. Like Eirek, Olaf returned to Scandinavia with a divine mission to preach and uphold Christianity.*[3]

The Flateyjarbók *text*[4] *is the oldest surviving manuscript of this saga and the primary exemplar of the A redaction. I have checked it against variants given in Jensen's edition.*

CHAPTER I

Thrand was the name of the first king to rule over Trondheim.[5] He had a son named Eirek. He was well-loved from a young age. He was physically strong, bold, and daring in every endeavor, and he grew up to be a valiant man.

It is said that one Yule evening, Eirek swore an oath to travel through all lands to see whether he might find the place that heathens call Odainsakr, the Field of the Undying, but that Christians call the Land of Living Men, or Paradise.[6] The swearing of this oath became famous throughout Norway.

The next summer, Eirek readied a splendid ship and sailed from Norway to Denmark. There were twelve men on the ship. The King of Denmark had a son, and he was also called Eirek. Father and son invited Thrand's son Eirek to stay with them that winter, and he accepted. The two Eireks made a pact of fellowship, and they got along well. They were alike in many ways.

The next spring, Eirek of Denmark set out on the journey with his namesake, and he also had twelve men all together. They set sail and headed for Constantinople, and they arrived there just as the King of the Greeks had mustered his army against the raiders that were invading his realm. When the King of the Greeks heard of the arrival of the Norsemen, he invited them to stay with him, and he received them in grand style. Then he inquired as to who they might be and from where they had come, and where they intended to go. Eirek said that they were Norsemen and sons of kings, and they intended to explore lands far and wide. The King of the Greeks honored them most excellently in all respects. When they had stayed there for some time, they accomplished many mighty deeds, with wise counsels and great bravery, and they gave powerful support to the authority of the King of the Greeks. When the king saw that they were stronger than almost all the other men in his land, he valued them more highly than anyone, and he bestowed great honors on them and made them his retainers and gave them the greatest share of all his men. It is said that that's when Norsemen first came to be honored in Constantinople.[7]

CHAPTER II
Eirek's Questions to the King

It was said that one day Eirek of Norway asked the king who had made heaven or earth. The king said, "One person made both of them."

Eirek asked, "Who is he?"

The king answered, "God Almighty, who is One in Godhead, but Three in His persons."

Eirek said, "Who are these three persons?"

The king said, "Look at the sun. In it are three distinctions: fire, light, and heat, and yet it is one sun.[8] So in God there are Father and Son and Holy Spirit, and yet He is one in His own omnipotence."

Eirek said, "This God is great, who made heaven and earth. Tell me something of his greatness now."

The king said, "God is One, indescribable and insurmountable. He is over all things and suffers all things, and He holds all the ends of the earth in His hand."

Eirek said, "Does God know all things?"

The king said, "He alone knows everything in His sight."

When the king had said that, Eirek was astonished at the greatness of God. Eirek said, "Does God live in heaven or on earth?"

The king said, "He rules in heaven, and His realm is there. There is no sickness nor wailing, no death, no grief and no misery. There is always rejoicing and eternal bliss and gladness and heavenly feasting without end."

Eirek said, "Who is there with God?"

The king said, "Holy angels are there. God Himself created them for His service in the beginning. God Almighty built a bright hall for himself; that hall He called the Kingdom of Heaven. Then he made a dark dungeon; that is this world that we inhabit. Within it, God set a deep pit; that is Hell.[9] In that place is every kind of misery, along with flames, and there the spirits of unrighteous men are tormented. Over that pit rules Satan, the enemy of all mankind. But after suffering death on the Cross, God Almighty bound him firmly. Then God arose on the third day after the death of His body, and on the fortieth day He ascended to the heavenly kingdom which was prepared with all God's might for His knights and retainers. Everyone is obliged to strive towards that place and fill the gap that came into being when the angels fell, and then God will complete their number with men who have lived in purity."[10]

Eirek said, "Where is that pit which you said was in the earth?"

The king said, "That is the land of death that has been prepared for sinful men, and it is called Hell. In that place there is all manner of misery, along with eternal fire. There wicked men are tormented."

Eirek said, "Who are they?"

The king said, "All heathens and apostates."

Eirek said, "Why are all heathens evil?"

The king said, "Because they are not willing to worship God, their Creator."

Eirek said, "Is it not God that we worship?"

The king said, "That is not God, because wretched things are said of how shamefully they died, or how wickedly they led their lives while they lived. Their spirits are now in eternal fire and unquenchable suffering."

Then Eirek said, "I have never heard such things said about them before."

The king said, "You are astray in your faith if you have never heard such things said. If you are willing to believe in the eternal God who is Three in One, then after death you will be with Him in eternal bliss."

Eirek said, "This is my wish: that I might inherit eternal life, after my death."

The king said, "This wish will be granted to you, if you believe in the eternal God who is Three in One, and receive holy baptism. Then you will receive new life by His flesh and blood, and you will become God's friend. Accept Christianity and honor God rightly in all things."

Eirek said, "It is fitting to do as you encourage. Tell me what I ask of you: Where is Hell?"

The king said, "Under the earth."

Eirek said, "What is above the earth?"

The king said, "The air."

Eirek said, "What is above the air?"

The king said, "The Firmament of Heaven. In this heaven are all the heavenly bodies, just like burning fire."

Eirek said, "What is above the Firmament of Heaven?"

The king said, "There the waters are fixed, like clouds."

Eirek said, "What is above the waters?"

The king said, "The Spiritual Heaven. Men believe that angels live there."

Eirek said, "What is above that heaven?"

The king answered, "The Intellectual Heaven. In this heaven, those who are worthy of it may see God Himself and His power."[11]

Then Eirek was amazed at how wise the king was, and he said, "Your wisdom is great and sublime and insurmountable. Say, if you know, how great is the breadth of the earth."

The king said, "You are inquisitive, Eirek, and you will want to know many things that are unnecessary and unheard-of and little known. So that I may satisfy your curiosity, hear what I tell you, and then leave off. Wise men reckon the circumference of the earth to be a hundred thousand leagues and eighty thousand more.[12] No pillars hold it up, but rather, God's power."

Eirek said, "How long is the distance between heaven and earth?

The king answered, "You are inquisitive. It is said that from the earth all the way to the highest heaven it is a hundred thousand miles, plus three hundred and eighty-five miles."[13]

Eirek said, "What is beyond the land?"

The king said, "A great sea called Oceanus."

Eirek said, "Where is the outermost land in the southern half of the world?"

The king answered, "We say that India is the end of lands in that half of the world."

Eirek said, "Where is the place that is called the Field of the Undying?

The king said, "We call that Paradise, or the Land of the Living."

Eirek said, "Where is that place?"

The king said, "That land is in the east, beyond the outermost India."

Eirek said, "Can one get there?"

"It is not certain," said the king, "because a wall of flames stands before it, which reaches up all the way to heaven."

When the king had told Eirek this and many other things, he fell at the king's feet and said, "I beg of you, best of kings, that I may be sped upon my journey by your aid, for I am compelled to fulfil the oath I swore, because I swore this oath: to travel to the south of the world to seek the Fields of the Undying. I know that I have no chance of reaching that place unless I may have the benefit of your assistance."

The king said, "Stay here with us for the next three winters and then go, because you must have help from my counsels. Heed my persuasions in every way. Accept baptism, and then I will assist you."

Eirek carefully asked the king about the rewards of righteousness and the torments of Hell. He also asked about the appearances of peoples and the particulars of countries, about harbors and foreign lands and about the entire eastern half and southern half of the world, about mighty kings and about various islands, about deserted lands and about the places that they would have to travel through, about strange people and their manner of dress and the customs of many nations, about venomous serpents and flying dragons and all manner of beasts and birds, and about the abundance of gold and gemstones. The king answered these and many other questions, wisely and well. Afterwards, Eirek and his men were baptized.

CHAPTER III
The Parting of the Namesakes at the Stone Bridge

When three winters had passed, and Eirek had learned such lore and much else, he traveled to Syria with his men. They carried the seal of the King of the Greeks. After that, they traveled sometimes by ship and sometimes on horseback, but most often they walked. Several years passed in this way, until they came to farthest India. No matter what strange land they reached, they were received well, and all the people sped them on their journey, because they had with them a letter and seal from the King of the Greeks and the Patriarch of Constantinople, written in all the languages of the nations that that they might expect to reach. The letter also stated who they were and where they intended to go. In this it was evident what great divine grace was with them, and how great a friend of God was the King of the Greeks: wherever his letter was seen, they had to be offered honor and never harmed, because God's mercy protected Eirek and his traveling companions, and the good luck of the King of the Greeks protected them, by his wise counsels, against the dangers of the journey.

But when they had traveled through the district of India for forty-four miles, they finally came to a land of darkness, where they saw the stars just as clearly by day as by night. All over the land they found huge nuggets of gold. They beheld many more wonders in that land. When they had been walking for a long time through a thick and wondrously tall forest, they finally came out of the woods. It began to grow light, and they saw a great river before them. There was a stone bridge over it. On the other side of the river, they saw a beautiful land with huge flowers and abundance of honey, and they smelled the sweet scent coming from there. It was bright to look at. They saw neither hills nor heights nor mountains in that land. Eirek realized that that river must divide these lands, as the King of the Greeks had told him. It occurred to him that that river must flow out of Paradise, and it must be the Phison. But as they approached the stone bridge, they saw that a terrifying dragon was lying on it and gaping his mouth, and he seemed to be growling savagely. Eirik turned towards it and intended to get over the river in some way. But when Eirek of Denmark saw that, be forbade his namesake to go, saying that the dragon would swallow him up at once.

Eirek of Norway said that he would not fear the dragon—"and he shall not hinder my going."

Eirek of Denmark said, "I beg you, best of friends, not to give yourself up to death. Go back home with us instead, because you will die as soon as you step forward."

Eirek said that he would not turn back, and each of them wished the other well. Now Eirek of Norway drew his sword and held it in his right hand, but with his left hand he took one of his travelling companions by the hand. They rushed into the dragon's mouth, and it looked to Eirek of Denmark as if the dragon had swallowed them both. He turned back by the way he had come, with his own followers, and after many winters had passed, he reached his native land. Then he told what he had last seen of Eirek of Norway. The man became renowned for his journey, and he was thought to be the most magnificent man. There is no more to tell of him.

CHAPTER IV
Eirek's Visions and Revelations in Paradise

But when Eirek of Norway and his companion rushed into the mouth of the dragon, they felt as if they were wading through smoke. When they passed out of the smoke, they saw a beautiful land, with plants as bright as the finest cloth, with a sweet smell and large flowers. Streams of honey were flowing all through the land. The land was wide and flat. There was such sunshine there that there was never darkness, and nothing cast shadows.[14] The air was calm above, but there was a light breeze towards the ground, so that they smelled the sweet smell more than before. They walked for a very long time and wondered if they would see any settlements or populated districts, or whether they could find out how wide this land might be. They saw something that most closely resembled a pillar; it was hanging in the air with no supports underneath. They approached it, and there they saw that it was a tower, hanging in the air without supports. A ladder stood against the tower on the south side. They were much astonished at this work of craft and found it extraordinary. They climbed the ladder and entered the tower. They saw that it was hung with the finest velvet. There stood a table, beautifully set, and a silver dish was on the table. On it there were all sorts of delicacies, and it was laden with white bread with a sweet aroma. There was a jug, set with gold and gemstones. There was a chalice full of wine. There were beds there, well prepared and spread with cloths woven with gold and the finest velvet.

Eirek said, "Here I see the Field of the Undying, which we have searched for on many roads, with great hardships."

They praised God and said, "God is great, that He allows us to see such a sight."

After that, they enjoyed their food and drink, and then they went to sleep.

But as Eirek was sleeping, a young man, beautiful and bright, appeared to him. The man said to him, "Great is the steadfastness of your faith, Eirek. Tell me how this land seems to you."

Eirek said, "Everything is just as I could wish for, and no land pleases me more than this one. But who are you, speaking with me? There is a great difference in our knowledge, for you knew me and called me by name, but I do not know who you are."

The young man looked upon him gently and said, "I am an angel of God, one of those that guard the gates of Paradise. I was standing nearby when you swore the oath to travel to the south of the world to search for the Field of the Undying. I encouraged you to sail to Constantinople, and by Divine Providence and my will, you accepted baptism. I count you blessed, because you heeded the profitable admonitions and counsels of the King of the Greeks and accepted his seal and washed yourself in the holy River Jordan. The Lord has sent me to you. I am your guardian angel, and I have protected you on sea and on land through all your perilous journeys, and defended you against all evils. But we are not humans, but rather spirits, living in Heaven as our native land. The place that you see here is like a desert compared with Paradise, but that place is a short distance from here, and that river that you saw flows from there. No living being can come there, and the spirits of righteous men must live there.[15] But the place that you have found is called the Land of Living Men. Before you came here, God commanded us to watch over this place and show you the Land of Living Men in some fashion, and prepare the feast for you and reward you for your troubles."

Then Eirek asked the angel, "Where do you live?"

The angel said, "We live in heaven, where we see the spiritual God. But for the sake of necessity we are sent into the world to offer our service to men, as you shall not doubt."

Eirek said, "What holds up this steeple, which seems to me to hang in the air?"

The angel said, "God's power alone holds it up. On account of such signs, you shall not doubt that God created all things from nothing."

Eirek said, "I shall not doubt that."

The angel asked Eirek, "Do you wish to stay here, or do you wish to return to your native land?"

Eirek said, "I wish to return."

The angel said, "Why do you wish that?"

Eirek said, "Because I want to tell my acquaintances about such glorious works of God's might. If I do not come back, then they will believe that I have died an evil death."

The angel said, "Though there be sacrifices to heathen gods in the Northlands now, that time will yet come when that people will be released from error, and God will call them to faith in Him. Now I give you leave to return to your native land and to tell your friends about God's mercy, which you have seen and heard, because they will believe in God's message and all His commandments all the sooner, if they hear such tales. Be often at prayer. I will come for you, some years from now, and bear your soul into bliss and guard your bones in the place where they must await judgment. Stay here for six days and rest, and then take provisions and return to the north."

Now the angel seemed to disappear from sight. Eirek did everything concerning their stay and departure just as the angel had commanded him.

CHAPTER V
The Death of King Eirek

At the appointed time, they descended from the tower and traveled until they came to the river. Then great darkness fell upon them. They came forth from the mouth of the dragon and began their journey. They saw many wonders, yet no harm came to them, and they discovered much knowledge.

They came to Constantinople after four winters had passed. Eirek told of his journey to the King, and it seemed a most excellent thing that he had returned. The king allowed Eirek to stay there for three winters. After that, Eirek set out on his journey from Constantinople and traveled north to Norway, and all the people welcomed him. He stayed there for ten winters. During the eleventh winter, early on a certain day, he went to pray. Then God's spirit seized him, and he was searched for but not found.

Eirek had told his traveling companion the dream that he had dreamed in the tower. That man told it, and he believed that God's angel must have taken Eirek and kept him safe. This Eirek was called Eirek the Far-Traveler. Many have affirmed this story, according to Eirek's own words. Now we will end this story here.

But the one who wrote this book set this tale first16 because he wished every man to know that no protection is sure unless it comes from God. For although heathen men may gain great fame from their deeds of bravery, when they end this earthly life it makes a great difference—they have taken their reward for their excellence from the praises of men, but then they have woeful chastisement for their transgression and faithlessness, since they did not know their Creator. But those who have loved God, and placed all their faith in Him, and fought for the liberty of holy Christendom, have received yet greater praise from the wisest of men, and the very greatest thing besides: that when they have gone forward through the doors of death common to all men, which no flesh may avoid, they have taken their own reward: that is to say, eternal reign with Almighty God without end, like this Eirek, as now has been told.

The Tale of Helgi Thorisson

Helga þáttr Þórissonar

A common theme in the legendary sagas is the hero who visits the far north and ends up as the lover of a female giant.[1] Helga þáttr Þórissonar, *a tale preserved as part of the expanded saga of King Olaf Tryggvason, neatly fuses the legendary motif of a giantess lover with the chivalric motif of a fairy lover. The immediate source was almost certainly Marie de France's* Lanval *or its translation* Janual; *both texts share details like the retinue of ladies, the richly ornamented tent, the lady's gift of wealth and her order not to reveal its source; and the mysterious land to which the hero is whisked.*[2] *The ruler of this "Avalon" is Godmund of Glæsisvellir, seen also in* Samsons saga *in this volume and in several other sagas, as well as Saxo's* History of the Danes. *Godmund's portrayal in the sagas varies considerably; in some he is helpful to the protagonist, but in* Helga þáttr *he is a diabolical figure who contends with the Christian king Olaf for Helgi's soul.*[3]

Helga þáttr Þórissonar *has been grouped with the "pagan contact tales" in* Flateyjarbók, *a set of tales in which a Christian king makes contact with a representative of the pagan past, with the rhetorical purpose of showing the superiority of Christianity.* Helga þáttr Þórissonar *immediately follows another "pagan contact tale",* Norna-Gests þáttr, *which presents an exemplary pagan who had known the greatest heroes of the past.* Helga þáttr Þórissonar *may have been deliberately paired with* Norna-Gests þáttr *as a reminder that the old ways had a dark side, that paganism was fundamentally incompatible with Christianity, and that only the wisest of men could discern the difference between the noble aspects of paganism and its dangers.*[4] *Thus we have a Christian theological message conveyed through a fusion of pagan lore and chivalric romance, all within the confines of this short story.*

Helga þáttr Þórissonar *is preserved in* Flateyjarbók *and two other manuscripts. I have translated from the* Flateyjarbók *text.*

CHAPTER I

There was a man named Thorir who lived in Norway on the farm named Raudaberg. This farm is a short distance from Viken.[5] Thorir had two sons. One was named Helgi, and the other was Thorstein. Both of them were well-mannered men, but Helgi was more accomplished. Their father was a hersir[6] in rank. He was a friend of King Olaf.[7]

One summer, the brothers made a trading journey north to Finnmark; they had butter and bacon to trade with the Finns.[8] They had a successful journey and set out for home towards the end of summer. One day they came to the cape called Vimund. There was a splendid forest there. They went on land and cut some maples. Helgi went farther into the forest than the other men. Suddenly a great darkness came up, so that he couldn't find their ship before evening, and night began falling quickly.

Then Helgi saw twelve women riding out of the forest. They were all on red horses and wearing red riding clothes. They dismounted. All of the horses' harnesses were gleaming with gold. One of these women excelled all the others in beauty, and all the others served her, this imposing woman. Their horses went to graze. After that, they set up a beautiful tent. It was striped with various colors and shot through all over with gold, and all the heads of the poles which held up the tent were made of gold, and so was the center pole, with a great golden knob on top. When they had pitched the tent, they set up a table and brought many kinds of delicacies. Then they began to wash their hands, with a pitcher and wash-basins made of silver, and everything inlaid with gold.

Helgi stood close to their tent and turned to look at it. The woman who led them said, "Helgi, come here and have food and drink with us." He did so. Helgi saw that there were excellent drinks and other foods, and beautiful vessels. Then the table was taken away and beds were prepared, and they were far more splendid than the bed of anyone else.

The woman who excelled all the rest asked Helgi whether he would prefer to sleep alone, or next to her. Helgi asked her name. She answered, "My name is Ingibjorg, the daughter of Gudmund of Glaesisvellir."

Helgi said, "I'd like to sleep with you."

And so they did, for three nights without interruption. Then the weather was clear. They stood up and dressed. Then Ingibjorg said, "Now we two must part here. Here are two small chests, which I will give you. One is full of silver, and the other is full of gold. Tell no one where they come from."

After that the women rode away by the same way they had come, and he went to his ship. His men welcomed him warmly and asked where he had been staying, but he wasn't willing to say anything about it. They set sail southwards, along the coast, and came home to his father. They had earned a great deal of money. The father of Helgi and his brother asked how such riches as he had in the chests had come to him, but he didn't want to tell.

CHAPTER II

Now time passed until Yule. One night, an ominous wind sprang up. Thorstein said to his brother, "We two should get up and find out what's passing by our ship." They did so, and the ship was quite secure. Helgi had had a dragon's head carved up on the prow of their ship, and he had it fixed well above the waterline. The money that King Gudmund's daughter Ingibjorg had given him had gone for this, and some of it he enclosed in the dragon's neck.

Then they heard a great crash. Two men rode at them and dragged Helgi away with them. Thorstein didn't know what had become of him. The wind quickly died down. Thorstein came home and told his father what had happened, and it seemed to be terrible news. He went at once to meet King Olaf, and he told him what had happened, and begged him to find out where his son had disappeared to. The king said that he would do as he asked, yet he said that he couldn't say with certainty whether Helgi would be of any use to his kinfolk.

Thorir went home, and so the year passed until the next Yule. The king stayed at Alrekstad[9] that winter. Then came the eighth day of Yule, and in the evening, three men came into the hall before King Olaf, where he was sitting at the table. They greeted him well. The king greeted them well in return. Helgi had come, but men didn't recognize the other two. The king asked them their names, and each of them said that he was named Grim.[10] "We have been sent here to you by Gudmund of Glæsisvellir. He sends you his greetings, and two horns along with them."

The king accepted them. They were worked with gold and were splendid treasures. King Olaf had two horns that were called the Hyrnings, but although they were quite good, these that Gudmund had sent him were even better.[11] "King Gudmund asks this of you, lord: that you and your men should be his friends. Having your goodwill is of great worth to him, more so than that of all other kings."

The king didn't answer that, but had them shown to their seats. The king had the horns of the Grims filled with good drink, and had the bishop bless them, and had them brought to the Grims so that they should be the first to drink from them. Then the king spoke this verse:

The guests in turn
must take the horns,
as Gudmund's thanes
are given their rest,
and drink their draughts
from their dear namesakes;
the ale shall prove good
for the Grims today.

The Grims accepted the horns, and realized what the bishop had spoken over the drink. They said, "Our King Gudmund's guesses weren't far off. This king is deceitful and knows how to reward good with evil,[12] for our king showed him honor. Let's all rise up now and get away from here."

So they did. There was a great commotion in the room. They flung the drink out of the horns and put out the fire. Then everyone heard a loud crash. The king asked God for protection, and ordered his men to stand up and stay calm before this uproar. At once the Grims went outside, and Helgi went with them. A light was kindled in the king's hall. They saw three men killed, but there lay the Grims' horns on the floor, next to the dead men.

"This is a great wonder," said the king, "and it would be better for such things to happen rarely. I have heard it said about Gudmund of Glæsisvellir that he is a great sorceror and it can be especially hard to deal with him, and the men who are under his power are in a bad fix, even if we could do something."

The king had the Grims' horns kept and drunk from, and they served well. The route that the Grims took from the east to Alreksstad is now called Grims' Pass, and no one has gone that way since then.

CHAPTER III

Now a year passed, and the eighth day of Yule came again, and the king and his retainers were in church to hear Mass. Three men came to the church doors, and one stayed behind. The other two went away, but first they said, "Here we've brought you Sulky, king, but it's not certain when you'll get rid of him." The people recognized that it was Helgi there. The king went to his feasting, and when men spoke with Helgi, they realized that he was blind.

The king asked what his condition meant, and where he had been all this time. He first told the king about how he encountered the women in the forest, and then about how the Grims sent the storm at the brothers when they wanted to save the ship. Then the Grims had taken him with them to Gudmund of Glæsisvellir and brought him to Ingibjorg, Gudmund's daughter.

Then the king said, "How did being there seem to you?"

"Perfectly good," he said, "I've never known better."

Then the king asked about King Gudmund's customs, and about his subjects and deeds. He spoke well of everything, and said that they were far greater than he could tell.

The king said, "Why did you go away so quickly the previous winter?"

"King Gudmund sent the Grims to deceive you," he said, "and because of your prayers, he let me go free, so that you might know what had become of me. But the reason we went away so quickly the last time was that the Grims didn't have the sort of nature that they could drink that drink which you had blessed. They became angry when they realized that they were beaten, and they killed your men because King Gudmund had told them to, if they couldn't do any harm to you. But he showed his own high rank by sending you the horns, so that you would remember less to seek for me."

The king asked, "Why have you come away for a second time?"

He answered, "Ingibjorg caused that. She felt that she couldn't lie with me except with discomfort, if she lay against me naked, and mostly for that reason I went away. And King Gudmund didn't want to oppose you as soon as he found out that you wanted to take me away. But about the high estate and munificence of King Gudmund and about the great multitude of men with him, I cannot tell in few words."

The king asked, "Why are you blind?"

He answered, "Gudmund's daughter Ingibjorg ripped both my eyes out when we parted. She said that the women in Norway wouldn't enjoy me for long."

The king said, "Gudmund would deserve harm from me for the killings that he did, if God wills it so."

Helgi's father Thorir was sent for at once, and he thanked him very much that his son had come back out of the hands of the trolls. He then went home, but Helgi stayed behind with the king, and lived until the same time next year. The king had the horns of the Grims with him when he sailed out from land for the last time. Men say that when King Olaf disappeared from the *Long Serpent*, the horns also disappeared, and no one has seen them since.[13]

And here ends the tale of the Grims.

BIBLIOGRAPHY

CSI in footnotes refers to Viðar Hreinsson, ed. *The Complete Sagas of Icelanders.* 5 vols. Reykjavík: Leifur Eiríksson Publishing, 1997.

Primary Source Texts

Aðalheiður Guðmundsdóttir (ed.) *Strengleikar*. Reykjavík: Bókmenntafræðistofnun Háskóla Íslands, 2006.

Andrews, A. Le Roy (ed.) *Hálfs saga ok Hálfsrekka.* Halle: Max Niemeyer, 1909.

Bjarni Vilhjálmson (ed.) *Riddarasuogur.* 6 vols. Reykjavík: Íslendingasagnaútgafan, 1961-1982.

Cook, Robert, and Matthias Tveitane (eds.) *Strengleikar: An Old Norse Translation of Twenty-One Old French Lais.* Oslo: Norsk Historisk Kjeldeskrift-Institut, 1979.

Cucina, Carla. "The Rainbow Allegory in the Old Icelandic Physiologus Manuscript." *Gripla*, vol. 22 (2011), pp. 63-118.

Detter, Ferdinand (ed.) *Zwei Fornadarsögur*. Halle: Max Niemeyer, 1891.

Finnur Jónsson (ed.) *Norsk-Islandske Skjaldedigtning*. 4 vols. Copenhagen: Villadsen and Christensen, 1912-15.

Gammelnorsk Ordboksverk / EDD (eds.) *Strengleikar. MENOTA: Medieval Nordic Text Archive.* http://www.menota.org/ Accessed December 17, 2017.

Guðbrandr Vigfússon and Carl Rikard Unger (eds.) *Flateyjarbók: En Samling af Norske Konge-sagaer med Indskudte Mindre Fortællinger om Begivenheder i og Udenfor Norge Samt Annaler.* 3 vols. Christiana: P. T. Malling, 1860-1862.

Guðni Jónsson (ed.) *Þiðreks saga af Bern.* Reykjavík: Íslendingasagnaútgáfan, 1954.

— and Bjarni Vilhjálmson (eds.) *Fornaldarsögur Norðurlanda.* 3 vols. Reykjavík: Bókaútgáfan Forni, 1943.

Halldór Hermannsson. *The Icelandic Physiologus: Facsimile Edition. Islandica,* vol. 27. Ithaca, N.Y.: Cornell University Press, 1938.

Heusler, Andreas, and Wilhelm Ranisch (ed.) *Eddica Minora.* Dortmund: Fr. Wilh. Ruhfus, 1903.

Kalinke, Marianne E. (ed.) *Möttuls Saga.* Editiones Arnamagnæanæ Ser. B, vol. 30. Copenhagen: C. A. Reitzels Forlag, 1987.

Kålund, Kristian (ed.) *Alfræði Íslenzk: Islandsk Encyklopædisk Litteratur. Vol. 1: Cod. Mbr. Am. 194, 8vo.* København (Copenhagen): S. L. Møller, 1908.

Loth, Agnete (ed.) *Late Medieval Icelandic Romances. Vol. IV.* Editiones Arnamagnæanæ, Series B, vol. 23. Copenhagen: Munksgaard, 1964.

Ólafur Halldórsson (ed.) *Sögur úr Skarðsbók.* Reykjavík: Almenna Bókfélagið, 1967.

Olson, Emil (ed.) *Yngvars Saga Víðförla: Jämte Ett Bihang om Ingvarsinskrifterna.* København (Copenhagen): S. L. Møllers Bogtrykkeri, 1912.

Seelow, Hubert (ed.) *Hálfs saga ok Hálfsrekka.* Reyjkavík: Stofnun Árna Magnússonar, 1981.

Unger, C. R. (ed.) *Heilagra Manna Søgur: Fortællinger og Legender om Hellige Mænd og Kvinder.* 2 vols. Christiania: B. M. Bentzen, 1877.

Wolf, Kirsten (ed.); Helen Maclean (transl.) *Parcevals saga: Valvens þáttr.* Marianne E. Kalinke, ed. *Norse Romance. Vol. II: The Knights of the Round Table.* Cambridge: D. S. Brewer, 1999. Pp. 105-216.

Alternate Translations and Source Texts

Auden, W. H. and Paul B. Taylor. *Norse Poems.* London: Athlone Press, 1981.

Bachmann, W. Bryant, and Guðmundur Erlingsson. "The Saga of Asmund the Champion-Killer." pp. 85-102. *Six Old Icelandic Sagas.* Lanham, Md.: University Press of America, 1993.

Burgess, Glyn S. and Keith Busby. *The Lais of Marie de France.* 2nd ed. London: Penguin, 1999.

Chrétien de Troyes (Daniel Poirion, ed.) *Œuvres Complètes.* Paris: Gallimard, 1994.

— (Robert White Linker, transl.) *The Story of the Grail.* 2nd ed. Chapel Hill, N.C.: University of North Carolina Press, 1952.

— (David Staines, transl.) *The Complete Romances of Chrétien de Troyes.* Bloomington: Indiana University Press, 1990.

Hardman, George L. (transl.) "The Saga of Asmund the Champion Slayer." *The Complete Fornaldarsögur Norðurlanda*, 2011. http://tinyurl.com/asmundr Accessed December 16, 2017.

Haymes, Edward R. *The Saga of Thidrek of Bern.* New York: Garland, 1988.

Hollander, Lee M. (transl.) *Old Norse Poems: The Most Important Non-Skaldic Verse Not Included in the Poetic Edda.* New York: Columbia University Press, 1936.

Jensen, Helle (ed.) *Eiríks saga víðförla.* Editiones Arnamagnæanæ, ser. B, vol. 29. Copenhagen: Reitzel, 1983.

Marie de France (Alfred Ewert, ed.; Glyn Burgess, intro.) *Lais.* London: Bristol Classical Press, 1995.

Pálsson, Herman, and Paul Edwards (transl.) *Seven Viking Romances.* London: Penguin, 1985.

Wilson, John (ed.) *Samsons Saga Fagra.* Samfund til Udgivelse af Gammel Nordisk Literatur. Copenhagen: J. Jørgensen & Co., 1953.

Secondary Literature

Aarne, Antti (Stith Thompson, ed. transl.). *The Types of the Folktale: A Classification and Bibliography.* 2nd Revision. Helsinki: Suomalainen Tiedeakatemia, 1981.

Adam of Bremen (Francis J. Tschan, transl.) *History of the Archbishops of Hamburg-Bremen.* New York: Columbia University Press, 2002.

Aðalheiður Guðmundsdóttir. "The Werewolf in Medieval Icelandic Literature." *Journal of English and Germanic Philology*, vol. 106, no. 3 (2007): pp. 277-305.

—. "*Strengleikar* in Iceland." *Rittersagas: Übersetzing, Überlieferung, Tradition.* Jürg Glauser and Susanne Kramarz-Bein, eds. Tübingen: A. Franke Verlag, 2014, pp. 119-132.

Aesop (Olivia Temple and Robert Temple, transl.) *The Complete Fables.* London: Penguin, 1998.

Aho, Gary L. "*Niðrstigningarsaga:* An Old Norse Version of Christ's Harrowing of Hell." *Scandinavian Studies*, vol. 41, no. 2 (1969), pp. 150-159.

Alfrún Gunnlaugsdóttir. "Um Parcevals Sögu." *Gripla*, vol. 6 (1984), pp. 218-240.

Andersson, Theodore M. "An Interpretation of *Þiðreks saga.*" *Structure and Meaning in Old Norse Literature: New Approaches to Textual Analysis and Literary Criticism.* John Lindow, Lars Lönnroth, and Gerd Wolfgang Weber, eds. Odense: Odense University Press, 1986, pp. 347-377.

—. "Composition and Literary Culture in *Þiðreks saga.*" *Studien zum Altgermanischen: Festschrift für Heinrich Beck.* Heiko Uecker, ed. Berlin and New York: Walter de Gruyter, 1994, pp. 1-23.

—. "Exoticism in Early Iceland." *International Scandinavian and Medieval Studies in Memory of Gerd Wolfgang Weber.* M. Dallapiazza, Olaf Hansen, Preben Meulengracht Sørensen, and Yvonne Bonnetain, eds. Trieste: Parnaso, 2000, pp. 19-28.

Augustine (Bernard M. Peebles, transl.) *[Enchiridion de Fide, Spe et Caritate] Faith, Hope and Charity. Writings of Saint Augustine*, vol. 4; *The Fathers of the Church*, vol. 2. Washington, DC: Catholic University of America Press, 1947.

— (Eva Matthews Sanford and William McAllen Green, transl. *[De Civitate Dei] The City of God Against the Pagans.* Cambridge, Mass.: Harvard University Press, 1965.

Bachman, W. Bryant Jr. and Guðmundur Erlingsson (transl.) *Six Old Icelandic Sagas.* Lanham, Md.: University Press of America, 1995.

Barnes, Geraldine. "Arthurian Chivalry in Old Norse." *Arthurian Literature*, vol. 7 (1987), pp. 50-103.

—. "Romance in Iceland." *Old Icelandic Literature and Society*. Margaret Clunies Ross, ed. Cambridge: Cambridge University Press, 2000, pp. 266-286.

Barraclough, Eleanor Rosamund. *Beyond the Northlands: Viking Voyages and the Old Norse Sagas*. Oxford: Oxford University Press, 2016.

Battista, Simone. "Translation or Redaction in Old Norse Hagiography." *Pratiques de Traduction au Moyen Age: Actes du Colloque de l'Université de Copenhague, 25 et 26 Octobre 2002 / Medieval Translation Practices: Papers from the Symposium at the University of Copenhagen, 25th and 26th October 2002*. Peter Andersen, ed. Copenhagen: Museum Tusculanum Press, 2004, pp. 100-110.

Battles, Paul. "Dwarfs in Germanic Literature: *Deutsche Mythologie* or Grimm's Myths?" *The Shadow-Walkers: Jacob Grimm's Mythology of the Monstrous*. Tom Shippey, ed. Tempe, Ariz.: Arizona Center for Medieval and Renaissance Studies, 2005, pp. 29-82.

Bell, L. Michael. "'Hel Our Queen': An Old Norse Analogue to an Old English Female Hell." *Harvard Theological Review*, vol. 76, no. 2 (1983), pp. 263-268.

Benati, Chiara. "Ásmund *á austrvega*: The Faroese Oral Tradition on Ásmund and its Relation to the Icelandic Saga." *Á austrvega: Saga and East Scandinavia. Preprint Papers of the 14th International Saga Conference*. Volume 1. Agneta Ney, Henrik Williams, and Fredrik Charpentier Ljungqvist, eds. Gävle: Gävle University Press, 2009, pp. 110-118.

Bjarni Aðalbjarnason, ed. *Heimskringla I. Íslenzk Fornrit*, vol. XXVI. Reykjavík: Íslenzka Fornritafélag, 2002.

Blaising, Craig A. "Bartholomew (First Century)." *Encyclopedia of Early Christianity*. Everett Ferguson, ed. New York: Garland, 1997, p. 169.

Blake, N. F. *The Phoenix*. Manchester: Manchester University Press, 1964.

Blamires, David. *Herzog Ernst and the Otherworld Voyage: A Comparative Study*. Manchester: Manchester University Press, 1979.

Bloch, R. Howard. *The Anonymous Marie de France*. Chicago: University of Chicago, 2003.

Blom, Grethe Authen. "The Participation of the Kings in the Early Norwegian Sailing to Bjarmeland (Kola Peninsula and Russian Waters), and the Development of a Royal Policy Concerning the Northern Waters in the Middle Ages." *Arctic*, vol. 37, no. 4 (1984), pp. 385-388.

Bostock, J. Knight. *A Handbook on Old High German Literature*. 2nd ed. Oxford: Clarendon Press, 1976.

Boyer, Régis. "The Influence of Pope Gregory's *Dialogues* on Old Icelandic Literature." *Proceedings of the First International Saga Conference*. Peter Foote, Hermann Pálsson, and Desmond Slay, eds. London: Viking Society for Northern Resesarch, 1973, pp. 1-27.

Browne, Clare. "Salamander's Wool: The Historical Evidence for Textiles Woven with Asbestos Fibre." *Textile History*, vol. 34, no. 1 (2003), pp. 64-73.

Budal, Ingvil Brügger. "The Genesis of *Strengleikar*: Scribes, Translators, and Place of Origin." *Eddic, Skaldic, and Beyond: Poetic Variety in Medieval Iceland and Norway*. Martin Chase, ed. New York: Fordham University Press, 2014, pp. 31-43.

—. "A Wave of Reading Women: The Purpose and Function of the Translated French Courtly Literature in Thirteenth-Century Norway." *Riddarasogur: The Translation of European Court Culture in Medieval Scandinavia*. Karl G. Johansson and Else Mundal, eds. Oslo: Novus Forlag, 2015, pp. 129-154.

Bullock-Davies, Constance. "Lanval and Avalon." *Bulletin of the Board of Celtic Studies*, vol. 23 (1969), pp. 128-142.

Byock, Jesse. "History and the Sagas: The Effect of Nationalism." *From Sagas to Society: Comparative Approaches to Early Iceland.* Gísli Pálsson, ed. London: Hisarlik Press, 1992, pp. 44-59.

— (transl.) *The Saga of King Hrolf Kraki.* London: Penguin, 1998.

— (transl.) *The Saga of the Volsungs: The Norse Epic of Sigurd the Dragon-Slayer.* London: Penguin, 1999.

—. 2001. *Viking Age Iceland.* London: Penguin, 2001.

Cartlidge, David R., and J. Keith Elliott. *Art and the Christian Apocrypha.* London: Routledge, 2001.

Cederschiöld, Gustaf. *Fornsögur Suðrlanda.* Lund: Berling, 1884.

Chambers, Raymond W. *Widsith: A Study in Old English Heroic Legend.* Cambridge: Cambridge University Press, 1912.

Chesnutt, Michael. "The Three Laughs: A Celtic-Norse Tale in Oral Tradition and Medieval Literature." *Islanders and Water-Dwellers: Proceedings of the Celtic-Nordic-Baltic Folklore Symposium Held at University College Dublin, 16-19 June, 1996.* Patricia Lysaght, Séamas Ó Catháin, and Dáithí Ó hÓgáin, eds. Dublin: DBA Publications Ltd., 1999. pp 37-50.

Christiansen, Eric. *The Norsemen in the Viking Age.* Malden, Mass.: Blackwell, 2002.

Ciklamini, Marlene. "The Combat Between Two Half-Brothers: A Literary Study of the Motif in *Ásmundar saga kappabana* and *Saxonis gesta Danorum.*" *Neophilologus*, vol. 50 (1966), pp. 269-279, 370-379.

Clopper, Lawrence M. "Midsummer." *Medieval Folklore: An Encyclopedia of Myths, Legends, Tales, Beliefs, and Customs.* Carl Lindahl, John McNamara, and John Lindow, eds. Santa Barbara, Calif.: ABC-Clio, 2000, pp. 662-663.

Clover, Carol. "*Völsunga saga* and the Missing Lai of Marie de France." *Sagnaskemmtun: Studies in Honor of Hermann Pálsson on his 65th Birthday, 26 May 1986.* Rudolf Simek, Jónas Kristjánsson, and Hans Bekker-Nielsen, eds. Vienna: Hermann Böhlaus Nachf, 1986, pp. 79-84.

Cole, Richard. "Echoes of the Book of Joseph and Aseneth, Particularly in *Yngvars saga Víðförla.*" *Saga-Book,* vol. 41 (2017), pp. 5-34.

Cross, Tom Peete. "The Celtic Elements in the Lays of *Lanval* and *Graelent.*" *Modern Philology*, vol. 12, no. 10 (1915), pp. 586-644.

Cucina, Carla. "The Rainbow Allegory in the Old Icelandic Physiologus Manuscript." *Gripla*, vol. 22 (2011), pp. 63-118.

Curley, Michael J. *Physiologus.* Austin, Tx.: University of Texas Press, 1979.

Curschmann, Michael. "The Prologue of *Þiðreks Saga*: Thirteenth-Century Reflections on Oral Traditional Literature." *Scandinavian Studies*, vol. 56 (1984), pp. 140-151.

Dahlerup, Verner. "Physiologus i to Islandske bearbejdelser." *Aarbøger for Nordisk Oldkyndighed og Historie*, ser. II, vol. 4 (1889), pp. 199-290, pl. 1-16.

Damico, Helen. "*Sörla þáttr.*" *Medieval Scandinavia.* Phillip Pulsiano and Kirsten Wolf, eds. London: Routledge, 1993, p. 638.

Davidson, H. R. Ellis. *The Sword in Anglo-Saxon England.* Corrected ed. Woodbridge: Boydell, 1994.

Davið Erlingsson. "Ormur, Marmennill, Nykur: Three Creatures of the Watery World." *Islanders and Water-Dwellers: Proceedings of the Celtic-*

Nordic-Baltic Folklore Symposium Held at University College Dublin, 16-19 June, 1996. Patricia Lysaght, Séamas Ó Catháin, and Dáithí Ó hÓgáin, eds. Dublin: DBA Publications Ltd., 1999, pp 61-80.

Delumeau, Jean (Matther O'Connell, transl.) *History of Paradise: The Garden of Eden in Myth and Tradition*. Urbana and Chicago: University of Illinois Press, 2000.

Diodorus of Sicily (Charles Henry Oldfather, transl.) *Diodorus of Sicily*. Loeb Classical Library. Cambridge, Mass.: Harvard University Press, 1933.

Dolcetti Corazza, Vittoria. "Crossing Paths in the Middle Ages: The *Physiologus* in Iceland." *The Garden of Crossing Paths*. Marina Buzzoni and Massimiliano Bampi, eds. Venice: Cafoscarina, 2007, pp. 225-248.

Driscoll, Matthew. "Fornaldarsögur Norðurlanda: The Stories That Wouldn't Die." *Fornaldarsagornas Struktur och Ideologi*. Ármann Jakobsson, Annette Lassen, and Agneta Ney, eds. Uppsala: Swedish Science Press, 2003, pp. 257-267.

—. *The Unwashed Children of Eve: The Production, Dissemination, and Reception of Popular Literature in Post-Reformation Iceland*. Enfield Lock: Hisarlik, 1998.

—. "Late Prose Fiction (*lygisögur*)." *A Companion to Old Norse-Icelandic Literature and Culture*. Rory McTurk, ed. Malden, Mass.: Blackwell, 2005, pp. 190-204.

Driscoll, Matthew, and Silvia Hufnagel. "Stories for All Time: The Icelandic *Fornaldarsögur*." Arnamagnæan Institute, Copenhagen. http://fasnl.ku.dk/ Accessed October 1, 2017.

Duff, J. Wright, and Arnold M. Duff. *Minor Latin Poets*. Loeb Classical Library. Cambridge, Mass.: Harvard University Press, 1956.

Einar Ól. Sveinsson, ed. *Brennu-Njáls Saga. Íslenzk Fornrit*, vol. XII. Reykjavík: Íslenzka Fornritafélag, 1954.

Eusebius of Caesarea (Kirsopp Lake, transl.) *The Ecclesiastical History.* Loeb Classical Library. Cambridge, Mass.: Harvard University Press, 1959.

Finlay, Alison. "The Saga of Ásmundr, Killer of Champions." *Making History: Essays on the Fornaldarsögur.* Martin Arnold and Alison Finlay, eds. London: Viking Society for Northern Research, 2010, pp. 119-139.

—. "Kappar in *Ásmundar saga kappabana* and *Bjarnar saga Hítdœlakappa.*" Tatjana N. Jackson and Elena A. Melnikova, eds. *Skemmtiligastar Lygisögur: Studies in Honour of Galina Glazyrina.* Moscow: Dmitriy Pozharskiy University, 2012, pp. 34-42.

Finnur Jónsson, ed. *Hauksbók.* København (Copenhagen): Thieles Bogtrykkeri, 1892–1896.

—. *Tilnavne i den Islandske Oldlitteratur.* Copenhagen: H. H. Thiel, 1908.

—. *Ordbog over det Norsk-Islandske Skjaldesprog.* 2nd ed. Copenhagen: S. L. Møller, 1931.

Firchow, Evelyn Scherabon. *The Old Norse* Elucidarius*: Original Text and English Translation.* Columbia, S.C.: Camden House, 1992.

Foote, Peter G. "Sagnaskemtan: Reykjahólar 1119." *Saga-Book of the Viking Society* , vol. 14 (1953-57), pp. 226-239.

Friedman, John Block. *The Monstrous Races in Medieval Art and Thought.* Syracuse, N.Y.: Syracuse University Press, 2000.

Friesen, William. "Family Resemblances: Textual Sources of Animal Fylgjur in Icelandic Saga." *Scandinavian Studies*, vol. 87, no. 2 (2015), pp. 255-280.

Gade, Kari Ellen. "Poetry and its Changing Importance in Medieval Icelandic Culture." *Old Icelandic Literature and Society.* Margaret Clunies Ross, ed. Cambridge: Cambridge University Press, 2000, pp. 61-95.

Gantz, Jeffrey. *Early Irish Myths and Sagas.* London: Penguin, 1981.

Gentry, Francis G. and James K. Walter. *German Epic Poetry.* New York: Continuum, 1995.

—, Winder McConnell, Ulrich Müller, and Werner Wunderlich, eds. *The Nibelungen Tradition: An Encyclopedia.* New York: Routledge, 2002.

Gerstein, Mary R. "Germanic *Warg*: The Outlaw as Werewolf." *Myth in Indo-European Antiquity.* Gerald James Larson, C. Scott Littleton, and Jaan Puhvel, eds. Berkeley: University of California Press, 1974, pp. 131-156..

Glauser, Jürg. "Bærings saga." *Medieval Scandinavia.* Phillip Pulsiano and Kirsten Wolf, eds. London: Routledge, 1993, p. 60.

—. "Vilmundar saga viðutan." *Medieval Scandinavia.* Phillip Pulsiano and Kirsten Wolf, eds. London: Routledge, 1993, pp. 702-703.

Glazyrina, Galina. "The Viking Age and the Crusades Era in *Yngvars sags víðförla.*" *Sagas and Societies: Conference at Borgarnes, Iceland, 2002.* Stefanie Wirth, Tõnno Jonuks, and Axel Kristinsson, eds. http://hdl.handle.net/10900/46206 Accessed December 16, 2017.

—. "On Heliopolis in *Yngvars sags víðförla.*" *Scandinavia and Christian Europe in the Middle Ages: Papers of the 12th International Saga Conference, Bonn/Germany, 28th July—2nd August 2003.* Rudolf Simek and Judith Meurer, eds. Bonn: Hausdr. der Univ. Bonn, 2005. http://www.sagaconference.org/SC12/SC12_Glazyrina.pdf Accessed December 16, 2017.

Goetinck, Glenys Witchard. "The Quest for Origins." *The Grail: A Casebook.* Dhira B. Mahoney, ed. New York: Garland, 2000, pp. 117-148.

Gregorius Magnus [Gregory the Great] (J. P. Migné, ed.). *Moralium Libri sive Expositio in Librum Beati Job, Pars II. Patriologiæ Cursus Completus, Series Latina.* Vol. 76, pp. 9-762. Paris: Garnier, 1895.

—. (J. Bliss, transl.) *Morals on the Book of Job.* Vol. III, part 2. Oxford: J. H. Parker, 1850.

—. (Odo John Zimmerman, transl.) *Dialogues.* Washington, D.C.: Catholic University of America, 1959.

Gregorius Turonensis [Gregory of Tours] (J. P Migné, ed.) *Libri Miraculorum. Liber Primus: De Gloria Beatorum Martyrum.* Vol. 71, pp. 705-828. Paris: Garnier, 1879.

Greenfield, Jeanette. *The Return of Cultural Treasures.* Cambridge: Cambridge University Press, 1989.

Grundy, Stephan. "Frigg and Freyja." *The Concept of the Goddess.* Sandra Billington and Miranda Green, ed. London: Routledge, 1996, pp. 56-67.

—. *The Cult of Óðinn: God of Death?* New Haven, Conn.: The Troth, 2014.

Gudbrand Vigfusson, ed. *Sturlunga Saga: Including the Islendinga Saga of Lawman Sturla Thordsson and Other Works.* Oxford: Clarendon Press, 1878.

Guðni Jónsson. *Byskupa sögur.* 3 vols. Reykjavík: Íslendingasagnaútgáfan, 1953-1962.

—. *Sturlunga saga.* 3 vols. Reykjavík: Íslendingasagnaútgáfan, 1963.

Guðvarður Már Gunlaugsson. "The Origin and Development of Icelandic Script." *Régionalisme et Internationalisme: Problèmes de Paléographie et de Codicologie du Moyen Age.* Otto Kresten and Franz Lackner, eds. Vienna: Verlag der Österreichischen Akademie der Wissenschaften, 2008, pp. 87-94.

Gunnell, Terry. "The Relationship Between Icelandic *Knattleikur* and Early Irish Hurling." *Béaloideas*, vol. 80 (2012), pp. 52-69.

Gunnlaugur Þórðarson. *Bragða-Mágus Saga með Tilheyrendi Þáttum*. Copenhagen: Páll Sveinsson, 1858.

Haki Antonsson. "The Lives of St Thomas Becket and Early Scandinavian Literature." *Le Saghe Islandesi e la Storiografia Medieval Europea*. Carla del Zotto Tozzoli, ed. Rome: Morcelliana, 2015, pp. 394-413.

Hallmundsson, May, and Hallberg Hallmundsson, transl. *Icelandic Folk and Fairy Tales*. Reykjavík: Iceland Review, 2005.

Halvorsen, Eyvind Fjeld. "On the Sources of the *Ásmundarsaga kappabana*." *Studia Norvegica Ethnologica & Folkloristica*, vol. 2, no. 5 (1951), pp. 1-57.

Harris, Joseph. "Folktale and Thattr: The Case of Rognvald and Raud." *Folklore Forum* vol. 13, no. 2/3 (1980), pp. 158-198.

—. "The Prosimetrum of Icelandic Saga and Some Relatives." *Prosimetrum: Cross-Cultural Perspectives on Narrative in Prose and Verse*. Ed. Joseph Harris and Karl Reichl. Cambridge: D. S. Brewer, 1997. Pp. 131-163.

Hatto, A. T. "On the Excellence of the 'Hildebrandslied': A Comparative Study in Dynamics." *Modern Language Review*, vol. 68 (1973), pp. 820-838.

Heide, Eldar. "*j Giardeyiar geíma*. Eit hamnenamn i *Halfs saga* – med nogo attåt." *Namn og Nemme*, vol. 30 (2013), pp. 105-110.

Heizmann, Wilhelm. *Wörterbuch der Pflanzennamen im Altwestnordischen*. Berlin: Walter de Gruyter, 2003.

Herodotus (A. D. Godley, transl.) *Herodotus*. 4 vols. Cambridge, Mass.: Harvard University Press, 1960.

Hieatt, Constance B. *Karlamagnús Saga: The Saga of Charlemagne and His Heroes.* 3 vols. Toronto: Pontifical Institute of Medieval Studies, 1975.

Higley, Sarah L. "Finding the Man Under the Skin: Identity, Monstrosity, Expulsion, and the Werewolf." *The Shadow-Walkers: Jacob Grimm's Mythology of the Monstrous.* Tom Shippey, ed. Tempe, Ariz.: Arizona Center for Medieval and Renaissance Studies, 2005, pp. 335-378.

Hill, John Spencer. "The Phoenix." *Religion & Literature*, vol. 16, no. 2 (1984), pp. 61-66.

Hofstra, Tette, and Kees Samplonius. "Viking Expansion Northwards: Mediæval Sources." *Arctic*, vol. 48, no. 3 (1995), pp. 235-247.

Hollander, Lee M. (transl.) *The Saga of the Jómsvíkings.* Austin: University of Texas Press, 1955.

— (transl.) *The Poetic Edda.* 2nd ed. Austin: University of Texas Press, 1962.

Holthausen, Ferdinand. *Studien zur Thidrekssaga.* Halle: E. Karras, 1884.

Homer (A. T. Murray, transl.; George E. Dimmock, rev.) *The Odyssey.* Cambridge, Mass.: Harvard University Press, 1995.

Honorius Augustoduniensis [Honorius of Autun] (J. P. Migné, ed.) *Elucidarium. Patriologiæ Cursus Completus, Series Latina.* Vol. 172, pp. 1109-1177. Paris: Garnier, 1895.

Isidore of Seville (Stephen A. Barney, W. J. Lewis, J. A. Beach, and Oliver Berghof, transl.) *The* Etymologies *of Isidore of Seville.* Cambridge: Cambridge University Press, 2006.

Jackson, Tatjana N. "*Bjarmaland* Revisited." *Acta Borealia*, vol. 2, pp. 165-179.

Jacobs, Kenna. "Crossing Cultures: The Old Norse Adaptations of Marie de France's Lais." *The Quiet Corner Interdisciplinary Journal*, vol. 1, no 1, 2015.

Jacobus de Voragine (William Granger Ryan, transl.) *The Golden Legend: Readings on the Saints*. Princeton, N.J.: Princeton University Press, 2012.

Jakob Benediktsson. *Íslendingabók, Landnámabók. Íslensk Fornrit I.* Reykjavík: Hið Íslenska Fornritafélag, 1986.

Jensson, Gottskálk. "Were the Earliest Fornaldarsögur Written in Latin?" *Fornaldarsagaerne: Myter og Virkilighed*. Agneta Ney, Ármann Jakobsson, and Annette Lassen, eds. Copenhagen: Museum Tusculanums Forlag, 2009, pp. 79-92.

Jerome (Thomas P. Halton, transl.) *On Illustrious Men*. Washington DC: Catholic University of America Press, 1999.

Jesch, Judith. "Hrómundr Gripsson Revisited." *Skandinavistik*, vol. 14 (1984), pp. 89–105.

—. "Race and Ethnicity in the Old Norse World." *Viator*, vol. 30 (1999), pp. 79-104.

—. *Ships and Men in the Late Viking Age: The Vocabulary of Runic Inscriptions and Skaldic Verse*. Woodbridge: Boydell, 2011.

— (ed.) "Sigvatr Þórðarson, Víkingarvísur 3". *Poetry from the Kings' Sagas 1: From Mythical Times to c. 1035. Skaldic Poetry of the Scandinavian Middle Ages* vol. 1. Diana Whaley, ed. Brepols: Turnhout, 2012, p. 537.

Jochens, Jenny. *Women in Old Norse Society*. Ithaca, N.Y.: Cornell University Press, 1995.

Johansson, Karl G., ed. "AM 242 fol—Codex Wormianus v. 0.9.9." *MENOTA: Medieval Nordic Text Archive*. http://www.menota.org/ Accessed November 29, 2017.

Jón Árnason. *Íslenzkar Þjóðsögur og Æfintýri.* 2 vols. Leipzig: J. C. Hinrich, 1862.

Jónas Kristjánsson (ed.) *Biskupasögur I. Íslensk Fornrit*, vol. XV. Reykjavík: Íslenzka Fornritafélag, 1998.

Josephus (H. St. J. Thackeray, transl.) *Josephus*. 9 vols. Loeb Classical Library. Cambridge, Mass.: Harvard University Press, 1959.

Kalinke, Marianne E. "The Foreign Language Requirement in Medieval Icelandic Romance." *Modern Language Review*, vol. 78, no. 4 (1983), pp. 850-861.

—. *Norse Romance I: The Tristan Legend.* London: D. S. Brewer, 1999.

Kalinke, Marianne E. "The Saga of Parceval the Knight." *Perceval/Parzifal: A Casebook*. Arthur Groos, and Norris J. Lacey, eds. New York: Routledge, 2002, pp 219-236.

Ker, William P. *Epic and Romance: Essays on Medieval Literature.* 2nd ed. London: Macmillan, 1922.

Kongelige Nordiske Oldskrift-Selskab. *Íslendinga Sögur: Udgivne efter Gamle Haandskrifter*. Kjöbenhavn (Copenhagen): S. J. Möller, 1848.

Knorr, Birgit. "Hildebrandlied." *Idunna*, no. 33, pp. 5-6.

Krapp, George Philip and Elliott van Kirk Dobbie, eds. *The Anglo-Saxon Poetic Records, Volume III: The Exeter Book.* New York: Columbia University Press, 1936.

Kratz, Henry. "The *Parcevals Saga* and *Li Contes Del Graal.*" *Scandinavian Studies*, vol. 49, no. 1 (1977), pp. 13-47.

Kristinsson, Axel. "Lords and Literature: The Icelandic Sagas as Political and Social Instruments." *Scandinavian Journal of History*, vol. 28 (2003), pp. 1-28.

Kunin, Devra. *A History of Norway and the Passion and Miracles of the Blessed Óláfr.* London: Viking Society for Northern Research, 2001.

Kålund, Kristian. *Alfræði Íslenzk: Islandsk Encyklopædisk Litteratur.* 3 vols. Copenhagen: S. L. Møller, 1908-1918.

La Rocca, Cristina. "*Mores tuos fabricae loquuntur*: Building Activity and the Rhetoric of Power in Ostrogothic Italy". *Haskins Society Journal* (2014), pp. 1-29.

Lagerholm, Åke. *Drei Lygisögur.* Halle: Niemeyer, 1927.

Larrington, Carolyne. "The Translated *Lais.*" *The Arthur of the North: The Arthurian Legend in the Norse and Rus' Realms*. Marianne E. Kalinke, ed. Cardiff: University of Wales Press, 2011, pp. 77-97.

Larsen, Hennig. "Notes on the Phoenix." *Journal of English and Germanic Philology*, vol. 41, no. 1 (1942), pp. 79-84.

Larson, Laurence M. (transl.). *The King's Mirror (Speculum regale—Konungs skuggsjá)*. Scandinavian Monographs 3. New York, 1917.

Larsson, Mats G. "Vart for Ingvar den vittfarne?" *Fornvännen*, vol. 78 (1983), pp. 95-104.

—. "Yngvarr's Expedition and the *Georgian Chronicle.*" *Saga-Book of the Viking Society*, vol. 22 (1986–1989), pp. 98-108.

Lincoln, Bruce. "On the Imagery of Paradise." *Death, War, and Sacrifice: Studies in Ideology and Practice*. Chicago: University of Chicago Press, 1991, pp. 23-31.

Lindow, John. "Supernatural Others and Ethnic Others: A Millennium of World View." Scandinavian Studies, vol. 67, no. 1 (1995), pp. 8-32.

—. "Norse Mythology and the Lives of the Saints." *Scandinavian Studies*, vol. 73, no. 3 (2001), pp. 437-456.

—. *Norse Mythology: A Guide to the Gods, Heroes, Rituals, and Beliefs.* Oxford: Oxford University Press, 2001.

Lionarons, Joyce Tally. "Dísir, Valkyries, Völur, and Norns: The *Weise Frauen* of the Deutsche Mythologie." *The Shadow-Walkers: Jacob Grimm's Mythology of the Monstrous.* Tom Shippey, ed. Tempe, Ariz.: Arizona Center for Medieval and Renaissance Studies, 2005, pp. 271-297.

Lipsius, Richard Adelbert, and Maximilian Bonnet. *Acta Apostolorum Apocrypha.* Leipzig: Hermann Mendelssohn, 1898.

Lönnroth, Lars. "From History to Myth: The Ingvar Stones and *Yngvars saga víðförla.*" *Nordic Mythologies: Interpretations, Intersections, and Institutions.* Timothy Tangherlini, ed. Berkeley, Calif.: North Pinehurst Press, 2014, pp. 100-114.

Lucan (M. Annaeus Lucanus) (J. D. Duff, ed. transl.) *Lucan.* Cambridge, Mass.: Harvard University Press, 1962.

Machinskij, D. A. and M. V. Pankratova. "Severnaja Rus' i Sagi o Drevnikh Vremenakh [Northern Russia in the Sagas of Olden Times]." *Evropa–Azija: Problemy Étnokul'turnykh Kontaktov. K 300-Letiju Sankt-Peterburga.* Gleb S. Lebedev, ed. St. Petersburg: LEMA, 2002, pp. 23-46.

Mahoney, Dhira B. "Introduction and Comparative Table of Medieval Texts." *The Grail: A Casebook.* Dhira B. Mahoney, ed. New York: Garland, 2000, pp. 1-116.

Marchand, James W. "Leviathan and the Mousetrap in the *Niðrstigningarsaga.*" *Scandinavian Studies*, vol. 47, no. 3 (1975), pp. 328-338.

—. "Two Notes on the Old Icelandic Physiologus Manuscript." *MLN*, vol. 91, no. 3 (1976), pp. 501-505.

Marti, Suzanne. "Translation or Adaptation? *Parcevals saga* as a Result of Cultural Transformation." *Arthuriana*, vol. 22, no. 1 (2012), pp. 39-52.

—. "*Tristrams saga* Revisited." *Maal og Minne*, vol. 1 (2013), pp. 39-68.

McConnell, Winder, transl. *Kudrun.* Columbia, S.C.: Camden House, 1992.

McCready, William D. *Signs of Sanctity: Miracles in the Thought of Gregory the Great.* Toronto: Pontifical Institute of Medieval Studies, 1992.

McDougall, Ian. "Foreigners and Foreign Languages in Medieval Iceland." *Saga-Book of the Viking Society*, vol. 22 (1986–1989), pp. 180-233.

McKinnell, John. *Meeting the Other in Norse Myth and Legend.* Cambridge: D. S. Brewer, 2005.

McTurk, Rory. *Studies in* Ragnars saga loðbrókar *and its Major Scandinavian Analogues.* Medium Ævum Monographs, New Series, vol. 15. Oxford: Society for the Study of Mediæval Languages and Literature, 1991.

Meulengracht Sørensen, Preben (Joan Turville-Petre, transl.) *The Unmanly Man: Concepts of Sexual Defamation in Early Northern Society.* Odense: Odense University Press, 1983.

Mickel, Emanuel J. "Marie de France and the Learned Tradition." *A Companion to Marie de France*. Logan Whalen, ed. Leiden: Brill, 2011, pp. 31-54.

Mitchell, P. M. "The Grail in the *Parcevals Saga.*" *Modern Language Notes*, vol. 73, no. 8 (1958), pp. 591-594.

Mitchell, Stephen A. "Scandinavian Balladry and the Old Norse Legacy: Álvur kongur (CCF 14), Stolt Herr Alf (ST 5) and *Hálfs saga*." *Arv*, vol. 41 (1985), pp.123-131.

—. "The Sagaman and Oral Literature: The Icelandic Traditions of Hjörleifr inn kvensami and Geirmundr heljarskinn." *Comparative Research on Oral Traditions: A Memorial for Milman Parry*. John Miles Foley, ed. Columbus: Slavica, 1987, pp. 395-423.

—. *Heroic Sagas and Ballads.* Ithaca, N.Y.: Cornell University Press, 1991.

—. "Heroic Legend and Onomastics: *Hálfs saga*, *Das Hildebrandslied*, and the Listerby Stones." *Donum natalicium digitaliter confectum Gregorio Nagy septuagenario a discipulis collegis familiaribus oblatum: A Virtual Birthday Gift Presented to Gregory Nagy on Turning Seventy by his Students, Colleagues, and Friends.* Leonard Mueller and David Elmer, ed. Washington DC: Center for Hellenic Studies, 2012. https://chs.harvard.edu/CHS/article/display/4360 Accessed December 17, 2017.

Motz, Lotte. "The Families of Giants." *Arkiv för Nordisk Filologi*, vol. 102 (1987), pp. 216-236.

Murdoch, Brian O. *Old High German Literature.* Boston: Twayne, 1983.

—. *The Medieval Popular Bible: Expansions of Genesis in the Middle Ages.* Cambridge: D. S. Brewer, 2003.

O'Connor, Ralph. *Icelandic Histories and Romances.* 2nd ed. Stroud: Tempus, 2006.

Odd Snorrason (Theodore M. Andersson, transl.) *The Saga of Olaf Tryggvason.* Ithaca, N.Y.: Cornell University Press, 2003.

Ogden, Daniel. *Drakon: Dragon Myth and Serpent Cult in the Greek and Roman Worlds.* Oxford: Oxford University Press, 2013.

Ólafur Halldórsson, ed. *Færeyinga saga; Ólafs saga Odds. Íslenzk fornrit*, vol. XXV. Reykjavík: Hið Íslenzka Fornritafélag, 2006.

Olrik, Axel. *A Book of Danish Ballads.* Transl. E. M. Smith-Dampier. Princeton: Princeton University Press, 1939.

Pliny the Elder (H. Rackham, transl.) *Natural History.* Cambridge, Mass.: Harvard University Press, 1942.

Plutarch (Bernadotte Perrin, transl.), *Lives.* Cambridge, Mass.: Harvard University Press, 1959.

Poole, Russell G. *Viking Poems on War and Peace: A Study in Skaldic Narrative.* Toronto: University of Toronto Press, 1991.

Power, Rosemary. "Saxo in Iceland." *Gripla*, vol. 6 (1984), pp. 241-258.

—. "Le Lai de Lanval and Helga þáttr Þórissonar." *Bibliotheca Arnamagnæana* vol. 38, *Opuscula VIII* (1985), pp. 158-161.

Procopius of Caesarea; H. B. Dewing, transl. *History of the Wars.* Loeb Classical Library. Cambridge, Mass.: Harvard University Press, 1962.

Psaki, F. Regina. "Women's Counsel in the Riddarasögur: The Case of *Parcevals saga.*" *Cold Counsel: Women in Old Norse Literature and Mythology.* Sarah M. Anderson and Karen Swenson, eds. New York: Routledge 2002, pp. 201-224.

Quinn, Judy. "From Orality to Literacy in Medieval Iceland." *Old Icelandic Literature and Society*. Margaret Clunies Ross, ed. Cambridge: Cambridge University Press, 2000, pp. 30-60

—. "The End of a Fantasy: *Sörla þáttr* and the Rewriting of the Revivification Myth." *13th International Saga Conference, Durham and York, 6th-12th August 2006.* John McKinnell, David Ashurst, and Donata Kick, eds. Durham: Centre for Medieval and Renaissance Studies, 2006. http://

www.sagaconference.org/SC13/SC13_Quinn.pdf Accessed December 16, 2017.

Raw, Barbara C. *Trinity and Incarnation in Anglo-Saxon Art and Thought.* Cambridge Studies in Anglo-Saxon England no. 21. Cambridge: Cambridge University Press, 1997.

Rose, Els. *Ritual Memory: The Apocryphal Acts and Liturgical Commemoration in the Early Medieval West (c. 500–1215).* Leiden: Brill, 2009.

Ross, Margaret Clunies. "The Development of Old Norse Textual Worlds: Genealogical Structure as a Principle of Literary Organisation in Early Iceland." *Journal of English and Germanic Philology*, vol. 92, no. 3 (1993), pp. 372-385.

—. *The Bookish* Riddarasögur: *Writing Romance in Late Medieval Iceland.* Odense: University Press of Southern Denmark, 2014.

Roughton, Philip. "Stylistics and Sources of the *Postola Sögur* in AM 645 4to And AM 652/630 4to." *Gripla*, vol. 16 (2005): pp. 7-50.

Rowe, Elizabeth Ashliman. "*Sörla þáttr*: The Literary Adaptation of Myth and Legend." *Saga-Book of the Viking Society*, vol. 26 (2002), pp. 38-66.

Rowe, Elizabeth Ashman. "*Þorsteins þáttr uxafóts, Helga þáttr Þórissonar,* and the Conversion *Þættir*". *Scandinavian Studies*, vol. 76 (2004), pp. 459-474.

—. *The Development of Flateyjarbók: Iceland and the Norwegian Dynastic Crisis of 1389.* Odense: University Press of Southern Denmark, 2005.

—. "*Fornaldarsögur* and Heroic Legends of the Edda." *Revisiting the Poetic Edda: Essays on Old Norse Heroic Legend.* Paul Acker and Carolyne Larrington, eds. New York and London: Routledge, 2013, pp. 202-218.

Russom, Geoffrey R. "A Germanic Concept of Nobility in *The Gifts of Men* and *Beowulf.*" *Speculum*, vol. 53 (1978), pp. 1-15.

Rögnvaldr Jarl and Hallr Þórarinsson. *Háttalykill. Poetry from Treatises on Poetics. Skaldic Poetry of the Scandinavian Middle Ages* vol. 3. Kari Ellen Gade and Edith Marold, eds. Turnhout: Brepols, 2017, p. 1001. http://skaldic.abdn.ac.uk/db.php?id=1347&if=default&table=text Accessed December 16, 2017.

Sallust (J. C. Rolfe, transl.) *Sallust.* Cambridge, Mass.: Harvard University Press, 1921.

Saxo Grammaticus (Hilda R. Ellis-Davidson, ed; Peter Fisher, transl.) *The History of the Danes: Books I-IX.* Ed. Rochester, N.Y.: D.S. Brewer, 1996.

Sayers, William. "Karlsefni's 'Húsasnotra': The Divestment of Vinland." *Scandinavian Studies,* vol. 75, no. 3 (2003), pp. 341-350.

Scheidweiler, F. "The Gospel of Nicodemus: Acts of Pilate and Christ's Descent into Hell." *New Testament Apocrypha. Volume 1: Gospels and Related Writings.* Edgar Hennecke and Wilhelm Schneemelcher, eds. Philadelphia: Westminster, 1963, pp. 470-481.

Schlauch, Margaret. *Romance in Iceland.* Princeton, N.J.: Princeton University Press, 1934.

Shepard, Jonathan. "Yngvarr's Expedition to the East and a Russian Inscribed Stone Cross". *Saga-Book of the Viking Society,* vol. 21 (1982-1985), pp. 222-292.

Seelow, Hubert. "Hálfs saga ok Hálfsrekka." *Medieval Scandinavia.* Phillip Pulsiano and Kirsten Wolf, eds. London: Routledge, 1993, p. 262.

Sigurdson, Erika. *The Church in Fourteenth-Century Iceland: The Formation of an Elite Clerical Identity.* Leiden: Brill, 2016.

Simek, Rudolf. *Altnordische Kosmographie: Studien und Quellen zu Weltbild und Weltbescreibung in Norwegen und Island vom 12. bis zum 14. Jahrhundert.* Berlin and New York: Walter de Gruyter, 1990.

Simpson, Jacqueline. *Icelandic Folktales and Legends.* Berkeley: University of California Press, 1972.

Smyser, Hamilton Martin. "The Middle English and Old Norse Story of Olive." *Proceedings of the Modern Language Association*, vol. 56, no. 1 (1941), pp. 69-84.

Snorri Sturluson. *Edda.* Vol. 1: *Prologue and Gylfaginning.* Vol. 2a: *Skaldskaparmál: Introduction, Text, and Notes.* Vol. 2b: *Skáldskaparmál: Glossary and Index of Names.* Ed. Anthony Faulkes. London: Viking Society for Northern Research, 2005-2008.

—. *Heimskringla: History of the Kings of Norway.* Transl. Lee M. Hollander. Austin: University of Texas Press, 1964.

Stitt, J. Michael. *Beowulf and the Bear's Son: Epic, Saga, and Fairytale in Northern Germanic Tradition.* New York and London: Garland, 1992.

Ström, Folke. *Níð, Ergi, and Old Norse Moral Attitudes.* London: Viking Society for Northern Research, 1974.

Svanhildur Óskarsdóttir. "Prose of Christian Instruction." *A Companion to Old Norse–Icelandic Literature and Culture.* Rory McTurk, ed. Malden, Mass.: Blackwell Publishing, 2005, pp. 338-353.

Sørensen, Preben M. "Þorr's Fishing Expedition (Hymiskviða)." *The Poetic Edda: Essays on Old Norse Mythology.* Paul Acker and Carolyne Larrington, eds. New York: Routledge, 2002, pp. 119-137.

Theodore the Studite (Giorgia Di Maria, transl.) "Encomio di San Bartolomeo Apostolo." *Tre* Laudationes *Bizantine in Onore di San Bartolomeo Apostolo.* Vittorio Giustolisi, ed. Palermo: Centro di Documentazone e Ricerca per la Sicilia Antica "Paolo Orsi"—ONLUS, 2004, pp. 57-64.

Theodoricus Monachus (David and Ian McDougall, transl.) *Historia de Antiquitate Regum Norwagiensium: An Account of the Ancient History of the Norwegian Kings.* London: Viking Society for Northern Research, 1998.

Thompson, Stith. *Motif-Index of Folk Literature.* 5 vols. Revised ed. Bloomington: Indiana University Press, 1973.

Thurber, B. A. "The Viking Ball Game." *Scandinavian Studies,* vol. 87 (2015), pp. 167-188.

Tolkien, Christopher (transl.) *The Saga of King Heiðrek the Wise.* London: Thomas Nelson and Sons, 1960.

Tulinius, Torfi. *The Matter of the North: The Rise of Literary Fiction in Thirteenth-Century Iceland.* Odense: Odense University Press, 2002.

Turville-Petre, Gabriel. *Origins of Icelandic Literature.* Rev. ed. Oxford: Clarendon Press, 1967.

—. "Dreams in Icelandic Tradition." *Nine Norse Studies.* London: Viking Society for Northern Research, 1972, pp. 30-51.

Unger, C. R. *Stjorn: Gammelnorske Bibelhistorie Fra Verdens Skabelse Til Det Babyloniske Fangenskab.* Christiana: Feilberg & Landmarks Forlag, 1862.

Viðar Hreinsson (ed.) *The Complete Sagas of Icelanders.* Reykjavík: Leifur Ericsson, 1997.

Waggoner, Ben (transl.) *The Sagas of Ragnar Lodbrok.* New Haven, Conn.: The Troth, 2009.

—. *The Sagas of Fridthjof the Bold.* New Haven, Conn.: The Troth, 2009.

—. *Sagas of Giants and Heroes.* New Haven, Conn.: The Troth, 2010.

—. *Norse Magical and Herbal Healing.* New Haven, Conn.: The Troth, 2011.

—. *Six Sagas of Adventure.* New Haven, Conn.: The Troth, 2014.

White, T. H. *The Book of Beasts.* New York: G. P. Putnam's Sons, 1954.

Wolf, Kirsten. "*Gyðinga saga, Alexanders saga,* and Bishop Brandr Jónsson." *Scandinavian Studies,* vol. 60, no. 3 (1988), pp. 371-400.

—. "Postola Sögur". *Medieval Scandinavia.* Phillip Pulsiano and Kirsten Wolf, eds. London: Routledge, 1993, pp. 511-512.

—. "Skarðsbók." *Medieval Scandinavia.* Phillip Pulsiano and Kirsten Wolf, eds. London: Routledge, 1993, p. 596.

—. "The Influence of the *Evangelium Nicodemi* on Norse Literature: A Survey." *The Medieval* Gospel of Nicodemus: *Texts, Intertexts, and Contexts in Western Europe.* Zbigniew Izydorczyk, ed. Tempe, Ariz.: Medieval and Renaissance Texts and Studies, 1997, pp. 261-286.

Þórir Óskarsson. "Rhetoric and Style." *A Companion to Old Norse-Icelandic Literature and Culture.* Rory McTurk, ed. Malden, Mass.: Blackwell, 2005, pp. 354-371.

ENDNOTES

Introduction

1. My translation from Einar Ól. Sveinsson, ed. *Íslenzk Fornrit* XII, pp. 182-183.
2. My translation; Waggoner, *Six Sagas*, pp. 244-245.
3. Quoted in Byock, "History and the Sagas", p. 54.
4. Ker, William P. *Epic and Romance*, p. 282.
5. Quoted in Driscoll, "Late Prose Fiction," p. 196.
6. My translation from *Jóns saga baptista* II; Unger, *Postola sögur*, p. 849.
7. Driscoll, "Fornaldarsögur Norðurlanda", pp. 258-259. He points out that only three "sagas of Icelanders" have come down to us in fifty or more surviving manuscripts, while at least half of the "legendary sagas"—about fifteen out of twenty-five or so—have survived in fifty or more manuscripts.
8. Driscoll, *The Unwashed Children of Eve*.
9. Driscoll, "Late Prose Fiction," pp. 191-193.
10. *Íslendingabók* 1, in Jakob Benediktson, ed., *Íslenzk Fornrit* I, p. 4.
11. Tulinius, *The Matter of the North*, pp. 59-60; Mitchell, *Heroic Sagas and Ballads*, pp. 122-126.
12. Kristinsson, "Lords and Literature," pp. 7-8; this paper discusses the use of written sagas to create solidarity in the 13th century, but at some level the process probably operated in the realm of oral tradition before the introduction of writing.
13. Quinn, "From Orality to Literacy," p. 46.
14. Byock, *Viking Age Iceland*, p. 143, 156-158.
15. Jakob Benediktsson, ed., *Íslenzk Fornrit* I, p. cii.
16. For example, in *Bjarnar saga Hítdælakappa* 1 (*CSI* I:255), Thord Kolbeinson is a great skald who often travels abroad and is esteemed by high-ranking men for his skill. Gunnlaug Serpent-Tongue receives rich gifts from the kings of England and Ireland, the earl of Orkney, two Norwegian earls, and the king of Sweden, in exchange for praise-poems (*Gunnlaugs saga örmstungu* 7-10; *CSI* I:315-321)
17. Guðni Jónsson, *Byskupa sögur*, vol. 2, p. 39.

18. Johansson, ed. *Codex Wormianus* (AM 242 fol.), fol. 84.
19. Ch. 1; my translation from Kahle, p. 87.
20. My translation from Bjarni Aðalbjarnason, ed. *Íslenzk Fornrit* XXVI, pp. 3-5.
21. transl. Gade, "Poetry and its Changing Importance," p. 67.
22. Theodoricus, *Historia*, ch. 1.4-10; transl. McDougall and McDougall, p. 5.
23. *History of The Danes*, Preface; transl. Fisher, p. 5.
24. My translation from the text in Guðni Jónsson, ed. *Sturlunga Saga*, vol. 1.
25. Jesch, "Hrómundr Gripsson Revisited," pp. 95-96. For a discussion of the *Þorgils saga* passage and its authenticity and textual history, see Foote, "Sagnaskemtan." For the saga, see Waggoner, *Six Sagas*, pp. xxv-xxix, 241-251.
26. *Landnámabók* SH6-9; Jakob Benediktsson, ed. *Íslenzk Fornrit* vol. 1, pp. 38-46. See also *Flóamanna saga* 2 (*CSI* III:272).
27. E.g. Kjalnesinga saga 1-2 (CSI III:305-306), Eiriks saga rauða 1 (CSI I:2).
28. Guðvarður Már Gunlaugsson, "The Origin and Development of Icelandic Script," p. 88, table 1.
29. Svanildur Óskarsdóttir, "Prose of Christian Instruction," pp. 343-347.
30. Quoted in Haki Antonsson, "The Lives of St Thomas Becket," p. 407.
31. *Jóns saga ins helga* ch. 8; Jónas Kristjánsson, ed. *Íslenzk Fornrit* XV, pp. 211-212.
32. Andersson, "Exoticism in Early Iceland," p. 22.
33. Kalinke, "The Introduction of the Arthurian Legend," pp. 9-10.
34. Glauser, "Romance," pp. 375-376.
35. Barnes, "Arthurian Chivalry," pp. 84-85.
36. Budal, "A Wave of Reading Women," pp. 151-152.
37. Kalinke, "The Introduction of the Arthurian Legend," p. 10; Barnes, "Arthurian Chivalry," pp. 68-69.
38. Smyser, "The Middle English and Old Norse Story of Olive," p. 69.
39. Glauser, "Romance," p. 375.
40. Kalinke, "The Introduction of the Arthurian Legend," p. 18 n9.
41. Driscoll, "Late Prose Fiction," p. 192.
42. Bishop Brandr's identity as the translator has been questioned, but at the very least, the two texts do seem to be by the same person; see Wolf, "*Gyðinga saga, Alexanders saga*, and Bishop Brandr Jónsson".
43. For example, a motif from *Eliduc*, a *lai* by Marie de France that does not appear in the Norse compilation *Strengleikar*, appears in *Völsunga saga.* (Clover, "*Völsunga saga* and the Missing Lai of Marie de France," pp. 79-84.) The "punch line" of a French *fabliau*, "La damoisele qui ne pooit oïr parler de foutre", has evidently been borrowed into *Bósa saga* 11 (transl. Waggoner, *Six Sagas*, pp. 125-126).
44. Gunnlaugur Þórðarson, *Bragða-Mágus saga*, p. 177.
45. Kalinke, "Norse Romance," pp. 334-340.
46. See Marti, "Translation or Adaptation?" for a detailed discussion of the issue; also Glauser, "Romance," p. 380.
47. Clover, "*Völsunga saga* and the Missing Lai of Marie de France," pp. 79-84.
48. *Örvar-Odds saga* 21, 30; transl. Waggoner, *The Hrafnista Sagas*, pp. 102-103, 134.
49. Reviewed in Ross, *The Bookish* Riddarasögur, pp. 9-29.
50. Lindow, "Norse Mythology and the Lives of the Saints," pp. 438-446.

51. Driscoll, "Late Prose Fiction", pp. 201-202.
52. McKinnell, *Meeting the Other*, e.g. ch. 12.
53. Driscoll, "Late Prose Fiction", p. 198.
54. Byock, *Viking Age Iceland*, pp. 254-255; see e.g. *Eyrbyggja saga* 4 (*CSI* V:133-134); *Egils saga* 84 (*CSI* I:174). In *Vápnfirðinga saga* 5 (*CSI* IV:318) a priestess (*gyðja*) maintains the temple and collects the tolls.
55. Byock, *Viking Age Iceland*, pp. 326-328.
56. My translation, *Kristni saga* 17, in Finnur Jónsson (ed.), *Hauksbók*, p. 146.
57. Jón Viðar Sigurðsson, "The Education of Sturla Þórðarson", pp. 21-22.
58. Sigurdson, *The Church in Fourteenth-Century Iceland*, pp. 21-26.
59. Sigurdson, *The Church in Fourteenth-Century Iceland*, pp. 24-25.
60. Tulinius, *The Matter of the North*, pp. 64-65.
61. Jón Viðar Sigurðsson, "The Education of Sturla Þórðarson", pp. 25-30.
62. Gade, "Poetry and Its Changing Importance", p. 85.
63. Turville-Petre, *Origins of Icelandic Literature*, p. 142.
64. My translation from Lagerholm, *Drei Lygisögur*, p. 121.
65. Þórir Óskarsson, "Rhetoric and Style", pp. 356-360.
66. Isidore of Seville, *Etymologies*, I.xliv.5; transl. Barney et al. p. 67.
67. Isidore of Seville, *Etymologies*, I.xli.1; transl. Barney et al. p. 67.
68. Isidore of Seville, *Etymologies*, I.xl.1,2; transl. Barney et al. p. 66.
69. My translation from Jakob Benediktsson, ed. *Íslenzk Fornrit* I, p. 4.
70. O'Connor, "History or Fiction?", pp. 129-130.
71. O'Connor, "History or Fiction?", pp. 115-117.
72, My translation from Lagerholm, *Drei Lygisögur*, p. 121.
73. My translation; Waggoner, *Six Sagas*, p. 170.
74. Tulinius, *The Matter of the North*, pp. 45-46.

The Saga of Half and his Warband

1. See, for example, Mitchell, "Heroic Legend and Onomastics."
2. Tulinius, *The Matter of the North*, pp. 120-123.
3. Now Årstad, a district of the city of Bergen.
4. The Norse word *mungát*, used here, is nearly synonymous with *öl*, "ale", but seems to mean a stronger drink than ordinary *öl*. (Fell, "Old English *beor*," p. 86) Further references to ale-brewing in this chapter use only the word *öl*.
5. *Höttr* literally means "hood"; compare Odin's name *Síðhöttr*, "long hood", in *Grímnismál*.
6. Hardsae (*Harðsær*) is the present-day Bjørnafjorden and Korsfjorden, north of the Hardangerfjord. Kollsey ("Koll's island") cannot be identified now, although it may have been the present-day island of Tysnesø. (Andrews, *Hálfs saga*, p. 70)
7. The manuscript has *Geirhildr getta*. *Getta* may be a word, not otherwise recorded in the sagas, for a young girl (Cleasby and Vigfusson, *An Icelandic-English Dictionary*, pp. 197, 774). This is the interpretation followed by Tunstall. On the other hand, it may be a nickname or "pet name" for Geirhildr herself (Finnnur Jónsson, *Lexicon Poeticum*, p. 181), as it follows a similar phonetic pattern to attested nicknames such as *Todda* for *Þórdís* and *Ubbi* for *Úlfr* (Finnur Jónsson, *Tilnavne i den islandske oldlitteratur*, p. 301).

Andrews emends it to *Geirhildr, gættu*: "Geirhild, watch yourself"; "Geirhild, be careful."

8. *Gautreks saga* 3-6 and Saxo's *Danish History* both preserve the story of how Vikar came to be sacrificed to Odin, although *Gautreks saga* gives Vikar a different parentage and childhood from *Hálfs saga* (Waggoner, *Six Sagas*, p. 8; Saxo, *History of the Danes* VI.184-185, transl. Fisher, pp. 171-172). The Danish ballad "German Gladensvend" also preserves the motif of a queen trading away "what lies beneath her belt", unwittingly condemning her unborn child (Olrik, *A Book of Danish Ballads*, pp. 99-103). So do Scandinavian folktales such as "The Three Princesses in Hvidtenland" (Mitchell, "The Sagaman and Oral Literature", pp. 399-400). This is a variant (S242.1) of the well-known international folktale motif S240, "Children unwittingly promised" (Thompson, *Motif-Index of Folk Litterature*, vol. 5, pp. 316-317)
9. In the genealogy *Hversu Nóregr byggðist* in *Flateyjarbók*, Josur is the son of Hord, the ruler who gives his name to Hordaland, and Ogvald is the grandson of Hord's brother Rugalf. The Josurheid is the present-day Jusureid farm, while Vidi is identified with present-day Veum, both place names in south Telemark (Andrews, p. 73). Stord is a large island that in part separates the Hardangerfjord and Bjørnafjord.
10. Ogvald's life and death are briefly recounted in *Óláfs saga Tryggvasonar* 64 (*Heimskringla,* transl. Hollander, pp. 203-204); here, his killer is named Varin. Ogvaldsnes is present-day Avaldsnes, Norway—the site of several burial mounds, ranging from the Bronze Age to the Viking era.
11. Finn the Wealthy is mentioned in *Landnámabók* (S26/H23; ed. Jakob Benediktsson, pp. 64-66) and in *Harðar saga ok Hólmverja* 2 (*CSI* II: 194).
12. An almost identical stanza appears at the end of the best-known redaction of *Ragnars saga loðbrókar*, where it is spoken by a dead king in a mound. Several scholars have argued that the verse was borrowed from *Hálfs saga* into the Y-redaction of *Ragnars saga* (e.g. McTurk, *Studies in* Ragnars saga loðbrókar, p. 18). Poole (*Viking Poems*, pp. 20-22) has argued that the borrowing went the other way: the stanza was borrowed into *Hálfs saga* from *Ragnars saga*, and also points out influence from stanzas 49 and 50 of the *Hávamál.*
13. A small inlet on the south side of Byfjorden, just west of present-day Bergen.
14. Norse *Kvennaherað*; modern Kvinnherad, in Hordaland, Norway.
15. The appendices (*Viðrauki*) to the *Skarðsárbók* manuscript of *Landnámabók* include an anecdote that a certain Norwegian trader, who had told an otherwise unknown saga about King Vatnar, was visited by Vatnar in a dream and granted permission to take treasure from his mound, which is said to be south of Hákonarhella (now Håkonshella, near Bergen). Later, King Harald Hardradi anchored by *Bræðrahaugr* ("brothers' mound"), near Glaumstein in Halland, Sweden (now Glumsten, near the present-day town of Falkenberg,) and two of his men also had dream-encounters with the inhabitants. Both Snjall and Hjall were said to be ancestors of early settlers of Iceland; Snjall's grandson was Olvir Child-Sparer, while Hjall's grandson was Bjorn Buna, father of Ketil Flat-Nose. (*Íslendinga Sögur*, pp. 326-328).
16. Bjarmaland is the White Sea coast of what is now Russia, inhabited by a settled Finnic-speaking people known as the *Bjarmar*, probably Karelians. Several historical Norwegians traveled around the northern cape of Scandinavia to reach Bjarmaland. In legendary sagas, it is usually depicted as a place to win great wealth by trading and by looting, but also as a place of monsters and sorcery. (Hofstra and Samplonius, "Viking Expansion

Northward", pp. 235-247; Jackson, "Bjarmaland Revisited", pp. 165-173)

17. *Njarðey*, "island of the god Njörðr", is now known as Nærøya. Namdalen, the valley of the Nauma River, is in central Norway, in the present-day Nord-Trøndelag county.
18. This episode must take place on King Hjorleif's return voyage. This place, called *Gjarðeyjargeimi* in the text, is identified as the island of Gjerøy or Gjerdøya, located in what is now central Nordland in Norway. The *geymi* element is related to Norse *geyma*, "to conceal", so the place name is literally "the concealed place on Gjerdøya." This island does in fact contain a natural harbor, now called Gjømma, close to the sea lanes but screened from them by cliffs. (Heide, "*j Gjardeyiar geíma*", pp. 105-108)
19. Norse *brunnmigi*, "one who pisses in wells". The saga text also calls it both a *tröll* (troll) and a *þurs* (a giant, usually wicked or hostile).
20. The original text is missing the fifth half-line. My translation follows Finnur Jónsson's emendation of lines 5-7, with the restored half-line in brackets: [*mun ást sýna*] *óverðum þér Hildr Hjörleifi* (*Skjaldedigtning* vol. B2, p. 277). *Eddica Minora* has *óverðum þér* [*eld mun sløkkva*] *Hildr, Hiörleifi*, "Hild will extinguish the fire for you, unworthy Hjorleif," making the verse a clearer prophecy of what will happen soon. Andrews does not fill in the missing line, but reads the sixth half-line as *vér undum þér* instead of *óverðum þér*, which could mean "we wind for you" or "we were happy for you". (*Hálfs saga*, p. 79) Finally, Mitchell reads the last two lines as a complete sentence: *Hildr Hjörleifi haltu nær loga*, "Hild, you will hold Hjorleif near the fire." ("The Sagaman and Oral Literature", p. 396)
21. It has been argued that this episode is an appearance of the "Polyphemus story", best known from the *Odyssey*, in which a hero stabs a hostile giant in the eye with a burning spear (Andrews, *Hálfs Saga*, pp. 11-12). Other legendary saga episodes are closer in detail to the *Odyssey*; for example, in *Egils saga einhendi* 10 (transl. Pálsson and Edwards, *Seven Viking Romances*, pp. 242-246) and *Hrólfs saga Gautrekssonar* 19 (transl. Waggoner, *Six Sagas*, p. 73), the hero is imprisoned in the giant's house, blinds the giant with a heated skewer, and then must escape from the house.
22. *Konungahella* is now Kungahälla, in Kungälv municipality north of Gothenburg (Göteborg) on the Göta älv river in Sweden. Andrews (p. 80) points out that it appears several times in the "kings' sagas" as a royal meeting place, not surprising given its central location in Scandinavia.
23. Booths (*búðir*) were permanent enclosures of stone or turf, with no roof. They were built at the sites of regular gatherings, and tented over with cloth awnings when occupied.
24. The word *marmennill* or *marbendill* is sometimes translated "merman", but is not a human-fish hybrid like the stereotypical "mermaid". The *marmennill* is fully human-shaped (to the extent that its shape is described at all), and a tale recorded by Jón Árnason calls it a *sjódverg*, "sea-dwarf". An episode in *Landnámabók* mentions a captured *marmennill* who speaks prophecies, including the death of his captor (S68/H56; ed. Jakob Benediktsson, pp. 95-97). See Davíð Erlingsson, "*Ormur, Marmennill, Nykur*," pp. 65-73.
25. *Hálfs saga* is the oldest appearance of a well-known folktale from Scandinavia, Scotland, an Ireland, in which a captured sea-being laughs ironically at his captor's foolishness. In one variant, when the fisherman and *marmennill* come home, the fisherman beats his dog, trips over a tussock and curses it, and embraces his wife. The *marmennill* laughs,

but not until he is released does he inform the fisherman that his dog loves him, the tussock hides buried treasure, and his wife has cuckolded him. In some variants, the *marmennill* also prophesies the imminent death of the fisherman. (See Jón Árnason, *Íslenzkar Þjóðsögur og Æfintýri*, vol. 1, p. 132-134; Simpson, *Icelandic Folktales and Legends*, pp. 92-94; Hallmundson and Hallmundson, *Icelandic Folk and Fairy Tales*, pp. 29-31; Thompson, Motif-Index, N456, "Enigmatical smile reveals secret knowledge," vol. 5, p. 108; Chesnutt, "The Three Laughs".) The tale has Celtic counterparts in medieval stories of Merlin's knowing laughter, and in fact a Talmudic story (*Gittin* 68), in which Solomon captures the demon Asmodai, is surprisingly similar. The story of Merlin has been claimed as the source for the folktale, but Mitchell ("The Sagaman and Oral Literature," pp. 397-399) has argued that the reverse is more likely, with the Norse tale inspiring the accounts of Merlin's life.

26. Finnur Jónsson (*Skjaldedigtning*, vol. B2, p. 277) has *Högna dottir* here, which I have followed. Guðni Jónsson, Andrews, and Heusler and Ranisch's *Eddica Minora* follow the original manuscript here: *Svarðar dottir*, "daughter of Svörðr". Svörðr does not seem to be known from any other source. The reference to Hogni's daughter seems odd, because Hogni's daughter Hild is Hjorleif's wife, and she is already with him. But the goblin is probably referring to the legend of the *Hjaðningavíg*, the eternal battle, in which the ancient kings Heðinn and Högni eternally fight, die, and are resurrected (see *Sörla þáttr*, this volume). Hild is the daughter of Högni in the *Hjaðningavíg*, and she seems to be a spirit or personification of war—her name means "battle", and some sources list her as a valkyrie. In several versions of the legend, it is her magic that resurrects the fighters and keeps the battle from ending. (Rowe, "*Sörla þáttr*", pp. 44-55) The poet would thus be equating Hjorleif with Heðinn, who kidnapped Högni's daughter Hildr to try to improve his own standing, setting up the monstrous conflict with her father.

27. The manuscript ends the fourth half-line with *af letta*, which Andrews reads as meaning "willingly". But Andrews emends the text to *a fléttum*, "on [her] braided hair", which I've followed. Finnur Jónsson emends it to *of leika*, "game," setting up the kenning "game of Heðinn" as a kenning for war. In any case, the verse again refers to the legend of the eternal battle, the *Hjaðningavíg*, and the Hildr referred to is not Hjorleif's wife, but rather a valkyrie-like personification of battle.

28. Guðni Jónsson and Andrews have *brá mær augum. . . hegna til þegna*, "the maid opens [her] eyes to the leaders of thanes". Heusler and Ranich have *brá mær augum. . . Högna til þegna*, "Hogni's maid opens her eyes to the thanes" (*Eddica Minora*, p. 91). I have followed Finnur Jónsson's edition here, which has *brá mér fyr augu. . . höggna mjök þegna*, "there appears before my eyes a great hewing of thanes." (*Skjaldedigtning*, vol. B2, p. 278) This particular stanza approaches the style of formal skaldic poetry, with several instances of internal rhyme and half-rhyme, and longer lines than typical Eddic meters. As such, it seems stylistically out of place in the saga and may have been borrowed from another source. I've tried to retain some of the rhymes and metrical pattern.

29. The manuscript reads *hafa skal huer dreingr híor níot ok morg spíot*. Guðni Jónsson and Andrews both delete a word: *Hafa skal hverr drengr hjör ok mörg spjót*, "every warrior must have a sword and many spears." I have followed Finnur Jónsson, who emended it to *hafa skal hverr drengr hjörnjóts mörg spjót* (*Skjaldedigtning*, vol. B2, p. 278; also Heusler, *Eddica Minora*, p. 91.)

30. The manuscript has *kuett*, emended *kveitt* by Finnur Jónsson. There's been some debate as to what this rare word means; it may be a variant of *kjöt*, "meat," as Bachman and Erlingsson assume (*The Sagas of King Half and King Hrolf*, p. 11). Cleasby and Vigfússon cite *kveita* as meaning "flounder; halibut" (*Icelandic-English Dictionary*, p. 362), while Andrews cites sources suggesting that it means "whale meat" (*Hálfs saga*, p. 86).
31. Norse *herör*: an arrow that was passed from house to house as a summons to assemble for war. Snorri Sturluson refers to it repeatedly in *Heimskringla* (e.g. *Hákonar saga góða* 23, *Óláfs sags Tryggvasonar* 17, 37, 48, 59; transl. Hollander, pp. 115, 156, 177, 190, 199; etc.).
32. Presumably King Hreidar has taken Hjorleif's wives as plunder.
33. This method of torture appears in the Eddic poem *Grímnismál*; it may have originally been a rite of purification or protection (Grundy, *The Cult of Óðinn*, pp. 199-200).
34. Guðni Jónsson and Finnur Jónsson both have *Minntist Hreiðarr, hvar Hera fellduð*, "Hreidar remembered where you felled Heri." This seems awkward, unless we can assume that the first part of the verse was originally spoken to Hjorleif. Andrews has emended the verse as *Minnztu, Hreiðarr! hver Hera feldi*, "Remember, Hreidar, who felled Heri", which seems to make better sense.
35. This genealogy appears in *Fóstbræðra saga* 2 (*CSI* II:331), and also in *Landnamabók*, although with Otrygg given as the father of Oblaud (S112/H86; ed. Jakob Benediktsson, p. 150).
36. The Norse name *Hálfr* is spelled identically with *hálfr* meaning "half", and this is punned on later in the saga, when Half has to come with half his warband. But the name derives from Proto-Norse **Haþuwulafr*, "war-wolf", documented as far back as 7th century rune inscriptions from Sweden (Mitchell, "Heroic Legend and Onomastics").
37. *Hversu Nóregr byggðist* calls Half a berserk, although this is not mentioned in any other source.
38. A hersir was a local leader of lesser rank than a jarl.
39. The name *Hrókr* means "rook" (*Corvus frugilegus*), a close relative of crows and ravens. Rooks are normally black, but all-white rooks are occasionally seen.
40. *Haukr* and *Valr* mean "hawk" and "falcon". There seems to have been a legendary tradition of paired heroes named for identical or similar birds or animals; the brothers *Hrókr* of this saga are another example. Brothers named Örn and Valr ("Eagle and Hawk") appear in *Eyrbyggja saga* 18 (*CSI* V:148). *Göngu-Hrólfs saga* 9 (transl. Waggoner, *Six Sagas*, p. 183) includes two brothers who take the pseudonyms Hrafn and Krákr ("Raven and Crow"). *Hálfdanar saga Eysteinssonar* may be satirizing this custom with its paired warriors named Haukr and Gaukr ("Hawk and Cuckoo") and Köttr and Kisi ("Cat and Kitty") (see this volume, p. 250 note 36). Whether this is purely a literary convention or draws on actual naming practices is not clear. It is tempting to speculate that these were originally totemic names, taken to signify a strong bond between two members of a warband, whether they were actual brothers or not.
41. Norse *Útsteinn*, "Outside Stein", as opposed to *Innsteinn*, "Inside Stein".
42. An ell was about eighteen inches (46 cm), although the precise definition varied. Saxo Grammaticus claims that the legendary King Frothi introduced a similar provision in his law code; disputes were to be settled by duels, but if a commoner had to fight a champion warrior, the champion was to be handicapped by fighting with a club one ell

in length, while the commoner could be fully armed. (*History of the Danes* V.153; transl. Fisher, p. 143)

43. The "Viking laws" kept by Hjalmar in *Örvar-Odds saga* 9 also forbade robbing or abducting women (Waggoner, *The Hrafnista Sagas*, p. 65). The code of the Jómsvíkings forbade bringing a woman to the Jómsvíkings' base, and also forbade cowardice and fearful speech, as well as setting a younger age limit of eighteen (transl. Hollander, *The Saga of the Jómsvíkings*, pp. 63-64). Finally, some of the laws of the legendary King Frothi mirror the laws of Half's warband: women must be married legally and of their own free will, and warriors may not retreat from an even fight (*History of the Danes* V.153, 157; transl. Fisher, pp. 143, 148)
44. In other words, to anchor in the most exposed and dangerous places, not in sheltered harbors.
45. To be "straw-dead" (*strádauða*) meant to die on a straw mattress in bed—a much less glorious ending for a noble Viking than laying down his life for his fellow warriors. The point of this episode, aside from underscoring the suicidal bravery of Half's warband, may be to emphasize the danger that Half is in from Asmund's treachery; when he meets Asmund, he has already lost some of his bravest men, and then can only take half of the survivors with him to Asmund's hall.
46. The motif of a man who hears of ominous dreams but insists on interpreting them in a foolishly optimistic light, appears in the Völsung legend (*Atlamál* 14-26; *Völsunga saga* 35-36, transl. Byock, *The Saga of the Volsungs*, pp. 96-98) and in *Hrómundar saga Grípssonar* 9 (transl. Waggoner, *Six Sagas*, pp. 250-251).
47. We're not told why King Asmund wants to kill his stepson, but a parallel situation appears in *Hrólfs saga kraka*, in which Hrolf visits his stepfather King Adils with a fraction of his forces, and Adils tries to burn Hrolf alive. The reason in this case is that Adils has not only killed Hrolf's father, but is withholding Hrolf's rightful inheritance. Something similar may be going on here, which the saga writer did not bother to mention, probably because his audience was already familiar with Half's legend and Hrolf's legend. (Tulinius, *The Matter of the North*, p. 126)
48. Wax may have been used to protect blades from rust.
49. *Skogkarl* means "forester; old man of the forest".
50. *Dísir* are supernatural female beings, often depicted as protectors of a person or family line and sometimes as embodying destiny or fortune. See Lionarons, "Dísir, Valkyries, Völur, and Norns," pp. 275-282.
51. The text has *dritmenn*; *drit* is cognate with English "dirt" but usually has the specific meaning of "excrement."
52. The text has *ragmenn*, "unmanly men; men who are *argr*." *Argr* is a hard word to translate; its basic meaning is "unmanly", but it can be applied to men who are cowardly, who follow feminine social roles, or who are sexually penetrated. See Ström, *Níð, Ergi, and Old Norse Moral Attitudes*, pp. 5-8.
53. *Annisnes* is probably a variant spelling of *Andsnes*, a cape at the mouth of Kvænang Fjord, northeast of Tromsø. (Andrews, *Hálfs Saga*, p. 117)
54. The word translated "black sheep" is *aukvisi*, meaning a weakling. The verse alludes to the proverb *einn er aukvisi ættar hverrar*, "there's one weakling in every family".
55. The manuscript's *Bersi* may be an error for *Bárðr*; Björn is paired with Bárðr in chapters

10 and 14 of this saga and in *Tóka þáttr Tókasonar* in *Flateyjarbók.* Both *Björn* and *Bersi* mean "bear"; see note 40.

56. Hrok calls himself a *hornungr,* literally "man in the corner": an outcast, one who must sit in the corner away from the company of others. The word is also a legal term for an illegitimate child, specifically the child of a free-born woman and a slave man, adding extra force to Hrok's complaint that no one knows his ancestry. (Andrews, *Hálfs Saga,* pp. 130-131)
57. Hromund Gripsson has a saga of his own; see Waggoner, *Six Sagas,* pp. 241-251.
58. In the version of this story in *Landnámabók,* the mother of Hamund and Geirmund is named Ljúfvina, the daughter of the king of Bjarmaland, whom Hjor abducts on a raid. The name *Ljúfvina* is intelligible in Norse, meaning "beloved friend", but possibly borrowed from the Old English name *Leofwine* with the same meaning. (*Landnámabók* S112/H86; ed. Jakob Benediktsson, pp. 150-151, n3) The third major source, *Geirmundar þáttr* in *Sturlunga saga,* does not give Hjor's queen's name or origins.
59. Guðni Jónsson's edition has *fæddir eigi þú þann mög, kona,* which my translation follows; but Finnur Jónsson gives *fæðat þú þann; fár mun enn verri*—"you didn't bear him; there must be few that are worse," following the S recension of *Landnámabók* (*Skjaldedigtning,* vol. B1, p. 5) The H recension of *Landnámabók* has *fæð hann, kona, í fjörð mun han verri*—"feed him, woman, next year he'll be worse" (Jakob Beneditksson, p. 151, n6).
60. Espihóll is a large farm near the head of Eyjafjord in the north of Iceland. The Esphæling family are Víga-Glum's adversaries in *Víga-Glúms saga.*
61. Medalfellsstrond, now Fellsstrond, is in western Iceland. According to *Landnámabók* (ed. Jakob Benediktsson, M30, p. 151; S115/H87, pp. 156-157; S125/H97, pp. 166-169), Geirmund's daughter Ýri (or Ýrr) married Ketill gufa ("Mist") Örlygsson, and their descendants included relatives of the Sturlung clan by marriage.

The Saga of Asmund Champions' Bane

1. transl. Gantz, *Early Irish Myths and Sagas,* pp. 147-152.
2. For a comparison of the Persian, Irish, Russian, and German legends, see Hatto, "On the Excellence of the 'Hildebrandslied'".
3. See translation and discussion in Bostock, *Handbook,* pp. 43-82; translation by Walter, "The Older Lay of Hildebrand," in Gentry and Walter, *German Epic Poetry,* pp. 1-8; and discussion in Murdoch, *Old High German Literature,* pp. 55-64.
4. For the Middle High German *Jüngeres Hildebrandslied* see Walter, "The Younger Lay of Hildebrand," in Gentry and Walter, *German Epic Poetry,* pp. 295-302; Knorr, "Hildebrandlied," pp. 5-6.
5. For example, at the end of *Kjalnesinga saga*—where, however, the son is fully aware of his parentage and tells his father, but the father refuses to believe it (*CSI* III:326-328). Unlike the tale of Cú Chulainn, which may have influenced it, the son kills the father. A similar combat with a happy ending appears in *Áns saga bogsveigis* 7 (transl. Waggoner, *The Hrafnista Sagas,* pp. 182-184), and additional variants turn up in other sagas, mostly post-Reformation romances. (Schlauch, *Romance in Iceland,* pp. 113-118)
6. Harris, "Prosimetrum", pp. 145-146.
7. Einar Halvorsen called it "a rather complicated and confused narrative," and added

that the sagaman was "a mediocre author" who "has made very little out of a promising subject" ("On The Sources of the *Ásmundarsaga kappabana*," pp. 10, 27, 53). Marlene Ciklamini called it "unsophisticated" and an "adaptation to the taste of an undemanding peasant audience" ("The Combat Between Two Half-Brothers," p. 270).

8. Auden and Taylor, *Norse Poems*, pp. 58-59.
9. Hollander, *Old Norse Poems*, pp. 52-55.
10. It was a royal accomplishment to be a good judge of craftwork; *Óláfs saga helga* 3 records that King Olaf Haraldsson was *hagr ok sjónhannarr um smíðir allar, hvárt er hann gerði eða aðrir menn*, "skillful and keen-eyed for all works of craftsmanship, whether he or others had made them" (transl. Hollander, *Heimskringla*, pp. 245-246). See also Russom, "A Germanic Concept of Nobility," pp. 7-9.
11. A poem at the end of this saga may suggest that these "men" are dwarves, although the verses are unclear and have been emended in different ways (see note 34). In any case, their names (pseudonyms?) are Latin: if *Olíus* is derived from *ollus*, which is a form of *ille*, they mean "That One" and "The Other One".
12. This episode may be inspired by one in *Þiðreks saga af Bern* 63-64 (Guðni Jónsson, *Þiðreks saga af Bern*, pp. 90-91; transl. Haymes, *The Saga of Thidrek of Bern*, p. 43), in which Velent the Smith forges a knife for King Nidung, so unexpectedly sharp that when the king slices a bread roll, the knife also slices the table that the bread sits on.
13. A similar test of sword quality appears in *Svarfdæla saga* 2 (*CSI* IV:151); both may owe something to Charlemagne's testing of the swords Cortana, Almace, and Durendal, which was known in Norse literature (*Karlamagnús saga* I:xliv; transl. Hieatt, vol. 1, p. 133. Swords had to be made to flex under high stress (otherwise they would break), but a sword that could not spring back to its original shape was a liability, as its wielder would have to break off fighting to bend it straight, as in *Laxdæla saga* 49 (*CSI* V:79). (Ellis Davidson, *The Sword in Anglo-Saxon England*, pp. 164-165)
14. This is a hole in the plot: the sword only kills one of the sons.
15. Agnafit is at Lake Mälaren's outlet to the Baltic Sea. According to a 12th-century Latin history, it is the site where Stockholm was later founded. (transl. Kunin, *History of Norway*, pp. 11-12)
16. The text calls Eyvind *skinnhöll*, which would mean "skin-hall"; but Halvorsen suggests that this should be emended to *skinnhæll* ("On the Sources of the *Ásmundarsaga kappabana*," p. 37 n53). *Hæll* is literally "heel," but can figuratively mean a peg fastened in the earth, possibly used for stretching skins or hides. This is still a rather odd nickname.
17. The word *hönd* (pl. *hendr*) can mean "hand" as in English, but it can also mean the hand and arm together.
18. The original reads *at standa tveir fyrir einum*, "for two to stand before one." This could mean that the two berserks thought it unworthy to fight one man—but that contradicts the fact that they *do* fight Asmund. But *standa* can figuratively mean "to stop, to rest, to pause", and I've assumed that this is the intended sense.
19. The Norse term is *spádísir*, literally "prophetic female guardian spirits." *Völsunga saga* 11 (transl. Byock, *The Saga of the Volsungs*, p. 53) also mentions *spádísir* who defend King Sigmundr against being wounded in battle.
20. The older tradition that Hildibrand had killed his son seems tacked on awkwardly, probably because it was preserved in Hildibrand's death-poem and had to be explained

in the prose.

21. The original text is defective here; Guðni Jónsson's edition reads *of borinn öðrum*, "beaten by another". Heusler and Ranisch (*Eddica Minora*, p. 53) has *barmi öðrum*, "brother [slain] by the other", and other emendations have been proposed. I have followed Guðni Jónsson's text here.
22. The original calls the queen *drótt*, which Saxo evidently took to be her personal name. The saga author seems to have interpreted the word as a title or poetic word, possibly a variant of *drótning*, "queen" (*drótt* literally means "royal household; warband"), and given the queen the name Hild.
23. Guðni Jónsson's text follows the main manuscript and has *tyrvir gjarnir*, "eager fir-trees", which sounds more like a kenning for warriors (often called trees in skaldic poetry) than a kenning for swords. Heusler and Ranisch (*Eddica Minora*, p. 53) conjecturally amend this to *tiörvar görvir*, "weapons made"; but I have followed Finnur Jónsson's edition (*Skjaldedigtning* B2, p. 340) which has *til vígs gjarnir*, "eager for battle".
24. Guðni Jónsson's text says *Svá höfðu dvergar dauðir smíðat*, "Thus had dead dwarves smithed". Finnur Jónsson emends this to *Svá höfðu dvergar Dáinsleif smíðat*, "Thus had dwarves forged Dainsleif." Dainsleif, "Dainn's leavings", is described in Snorri's *Edda* as a dwarven-forged sword that never fails to strike or to slay its victim (*Skáldskaparmál* ch. 50, ed. Faulkes, p. 72). This Dainsleif is not Asmund's sword; Hildibrand is simply comparing it to Asmund's sword, or using the name metaphorically.
25. The Norse phrase *svási sonr*, literally "dear son" or "beloved son", echoes a phrase in the Old High German *Hildebrandslied*, when Hildebrand says that his *suâsat chind*, "dear child", must now strike him with a sword (line 53). A similar phrase turns up in *Þiðreks saga af Bern* (ch. 409; see p. 177 note 24 in this volume); after Hildibrand has been reconciled with his son Alibrand, his mother addresses Alibrand as *minn sæti son*, "my sweet son".
26. This detail seems wrong, since Hildibrand is said to have killed his son before going to meet Asmund. In Saxo's rendering, Hildiger (Hildibrand) says that he has painted his son on his shield; this may be Saxo's attempt to rationalize an awkward detail preserved from a time when the legend dealt with a father-son conflict.
27. This is tough. Guðni Jónsson's text has *at mik manns einskis ófyrr kvæði*, probably "that they would say I was not before any man", i.e. "that they would say that I was not superior to anyone else". Finnur Jónsson's edition (*Skjaldedigtning* B2, p. 341) changes *ófyrr*, literally "un-fore", to *øfra*, "higher". Jónsson's text seems to make more sense in this context, and it seems to fit Saxo's version, in which Haldan (Asmund) says that he wasn't expecting "woman's false fabrications" (VII.245; Ellis-Davidson and Fisher, p. 224).
28. *þá er mik til kappa / kuru Húnmegir* could also be rendered "when the Huns chose me as their champion"—since Asmund is not the Huns' champion, this verse would presumably have belonged to Hildibrand originally (Finlay, "*Kappar* in *Ásmundar saga kappabana*", p. 39), assuming the verse is not just corrupt (Halvorsen, "On the Sources of the *Ásmundarsaga kappabana*," pp. 18-19). But *kappa* could be either the genitive singular or plural of *kappi*, "champion", or the genitive plural of *kapp*, "contest, combat." If the latter, *kuru til kappa* means "they chose [me] for the purpose of combats", which might not imply that Asmund is the Huns' champion, but rather that they've chosen him as their adversary. This is the sense I was aiming for, and in fact "called me out" could also

be read in two different ways: "summoned me" or "challenged me."

29. The warriors are called *fletmegningr*, an obscure word that means something like "floor-mighty" or "bench-mighty." I've followed Finnur Jónsson's interpretation of this word as meaning "unwarlike", denoting one who has plenty of strength for sitting on benches and drinking ale, but no stomach for real fighting. (*Ordbog over det Norsk-Islandske Skjaldesprog* p. 141)
30. Another problematic verse; Guðni Jónsson's text has *meðan*, "meanwhile", while Finnur Jónsson (*Skjaldedigtning* B2, p. 342) has *mæki*, "[with] a sword".
31. According to Saxo Grammaticus's *History of the Danes*, the man was Sivar, "noblest of the Saxon race." Haldan (Saxo's equivalent of Asmund) not only killed him, but massacred the entire wedding party (VII.246; Ellis-Davidson and Fisher, p. 225).

The Tale of Sorli

1. Rowe, *Development of* Flateyjarbók, pp. 22-25.
2. See Greenfield, *The Return of Cultural Treasures*, pp. 12-41, and Rowe, *The Development of* Flateyjarbók, pp. 403-406, for fuller accounts.
3. Ross, "*Sörla þáttr*," pp. 44-52, gives more detail on the variants of the story.
4. Damico, "*Sörla þáttr*", p. 638.
5. For versions of the Everlasting Battle in Norse sources, see *Skáldskaparmál* 50, transl. Faulkes, pp. 122-123; *Háttalykill* 45-46, in *Skaldic Poetry* database; *History of the Danes* V.158, transl. Ellis-Davidson and Fisher, p. 147.
6. A German version of the story is preserved in the 13th-century epic *Kudrun* (chs. 4-8; transl. McConnell, pp. 23-58.) No Old English source tells the story, but names and references in the poems *Deor* and *Widsith* suggest that the Anglo-Saxons knew it; see Chambers, *Widsith*, p. 100-109, for detailed discussion.
7 .Quinn, pp. 6-8.
8. This paragraph draws on what is called the Learned Prehistory, which also appears in Snorri Sturluson's *Edda*, his *Heimskringla* (*Prologue* and *Ynglinga saga* 1-4), and several other texts. According to the Learned Prehistory, the Norse gods were really mighty humans; the Æsir came from Asia, and the Vanir came from the Vana or Tana River (the Don River in present-day Ukraine). The Learned Prehistory has no historical or mythological basis; medieval scholars often rationalized stories by appealing to similarities in names.
9. The word translated "spells" is *álög*, literally "things laid on". Appearing in many legendary sagas, the word implies magical compulsion; it resembles the *geasa* of Irish legend and may have been borrowed from Celtic sources. (Schlauch, *Romance in Iceland*, pp. 125-134)
10, *Frið-Fróði*, "Peace-Frodi," was a legendary king whose reign was marked by a long spell of peace. Medieval scholars imagined him as a contemporary of Jesus; see Saxo, *History of the Danes* V.169-170 (transl. Ellis-Davidson and Fisher, pp. 156-157), or the introductory prose to *Gróttasöngr* in the *Poetic Edda* (transl. Hollander, pp. 153-154).
11. Chapters 3 and 4 summarize events told at much greater length in *Sörla saga sterka* (transl. Waggoner, *Sagas of Giants and Heroes*, pp. 111-139).
12. *Elliði* was the legendary ship of Fridthjof the Bold (*Friðþjófs saga ins frækna* 1, transl.

Waggoner, *Sagas of Fridthjof the Bold*, p. 57). *Gnoð* was the legendary ship of Asmund Berserks'-Bane, briefly mentioned in several sagas (e.g. *Egils saga einhenda* 18, transl. Pálsson and Edwards, *Seven Viking Romances*, p. 257). *The Long Serpent* (*Ormr inn Langi*) was King Olaf Tryggvason's huge flagship (*Óláfs saga Tryggvasonar* 88; transl. Hollander, *Heimskringla*, pp. 220-221).

13. Old Norse *Austrveg*; a rather nebulous term for the eastern Baltic lands.
14. The Norse reads *Serkland*, which was rather nebulously defined but more or less means the Middle East. In *Göngu-Hrólfs saga* 17 (transl. Waggoner, *Six Sagas*, p. 196), Hjarrandi is said to rule India.
15. The wandering hero who finds a mysterious woman in a grove turns up in a few other sagas, and is probably borrowed from medieval French lays of chivalry. The direct source is probably the Breton lay *Lanval*, in which the mysterious lady is a *fée* or "fairy". (See this volume, pp. 214-223; also Kalinké, *Norse Romance*, pp. 10-11)
16. In other sources, Heidrek Wolfskin is said to have ruled Reidgotaland (probably Jutland in Denmark) and to have a daughter named Hild (*Hervarar saga* 11, transl. Tolkein, *Saga of King Heidrek*, p. 59).
17. Again, I've used "spells" to translate the word *álög* (see note 9)
18. Hoy is an island in the Orkneys (Norse *Háey*, "High Island").
19. Ivar's son Thorstein is the hero of *Þorsteins þáttr uxafóts* (*CSI* IV: 340-348), which appears just before *Sörla þáttr* in *Flateyjarbók*. This tale includes Thorstein's defeat of the giant *Járnskjöldr* ("Iron-Shield"), after which Thorstein takes his sword.
20. Helm of Awe = *ægishjálmr*. In later folklore this is a magical sign worn on the brow to make one invincible. See Waggoner, *Norse Magical and Herbal Healing*, pp. 5, 50.

The Saga of Bartholomew the Apostle

1. It is possible that Bartholomew was confused with the apostle Thomas, who has a stronger tradition of having evangelized in India, where the Saint Thomas Christians still trace the founding of their church to him. The confusion may have arisen from a misunderstanding of *Mar Thoma* (St. Thomas in Aramaic) as *Bar Tolmai*. See Blaising, "Bartholomew", *Encyclopedia of Early Christianity*, p. 169.
2. Eusebius, *Historia Ecclesiastica*, V.x.3, pp. 462-463; Jerome, *De Viris Illustribus* XXXVI.2, p. 59.
3. See Roughton, "Stylistics and Sources", pp. 8-9 and n3-4, for an overview of the textual history of "pseudo-Abdias."
4. Lipsius and Bonnet, *Acta Apostolorum*, vol. 1, part 2, pp. 128-150.
5. Wolf, "Postola sögur", pp. 511-512.
6. Bell, "Hel Our Queen", pp. 263-266; however, Bell does not affirm that the female Hel in *Bartholomeus saga* is inspired by the pre-Christian goddess Hel.
7. Lindow, "Supernatural Others and Ethnic Others", pp. 13-17.
8. Roughton, "Stylistics and Sources", pp. 10-13.
9 .For an overview of the manuscript history, see Bell, "Hell Our Queen", pp. 265-266 n11, and Roughton, "Stylistics and Sources", pp. 7-8 n2; and sources therein.
10. Ólafur Halldórsson, *Sögur úr Skarðsbók*, pp. 174-185. See Wolf, "Skarðsbók", p. 596, for a brief overview of the Skarðsbók manuscript.

11. This chapter does not appear in the oldest Icelandic collection of saints' lives (AM 645); nor does it appear in *Skarðsbók*, which is very close to AM 645. Not part of the saint's life proper, it is a homily that would have been read before reading the saint's life on his feast day, and it was added to the initial translation at a later date (Battista, "Translation or Redaction," pp. 102-104)
12. *Bar* does mean "son" in Aramaic, and Bartholomew's name would have been *Bar Tolmai*. Many medieval sources interpret his name as "son of one who bears [or suspends] the waters", or "son of one who suspends himself" (e.g. Jacobus de Viragine, *Golden Legend* no. 133, transl. Ryan, p. 495; Isidore of Seville, *Etymologiae* VII.ix.16, transl. Barney et al., p. 169). This etymology, which is not generally accepted today, first appears in the anonymous *Breviarium Apostolorum* written around 600 (Rose, *Ritual Memory*, p. 86). The suggestion that Bartholomew was descended from the Ptolemaic dynasty periodically crops up in later references, but I have not been able to trace the source of this idea in the saga.
13. Debates among the apostles over who is greatest are reported in Luke 9:46-48 and Luke 22:24-30 (parallel with Matthew 20:20-28; Mark 10:35-45). The saga does not closely follow any of these Bible passages.
14. Alliteration is present in the original.
15. *Skarðsbók* adds that "And when he arrived, he was unknown to everyone there, and a foreigner." (*Og er hann kom þangað, þá ver hann þar öllum ókunnigur og útlendur*; Ólafur Halldórsson, p. 175)
16. The writer of *Skarðsbók* appears to have independently checked the Norse translation against the Latin, but occasionally he slips up. AM 652/630 has *En er nott þa leið ok lysti fyrir degi*, "when night had passed and day was breaking", which is close to the Latin *cum transisset nox et aurora diei futurae inciperet*, "when the night ended and the dawn of the next day began". *Skarðsbók*, however, has *En hina nærstu nott eptir ok lysti fyrir degi*, "and the following night and day broke". (Battista, "Translation or Redaction," pp. 103-104)
17. As mentioned, the writer of *Skarðsbók* appears to have tried to edit the Norse translation to be closer to the Latin. Here AM 652/630 has *þviat ek ætla eigi manni at giptaz*, "because I do not intend to be betrothed to a man", while *Skarðsbók* has *þviat ek hefi æigi karllman kennt*, "because I have not known a man," which is closer to the Latin text *quia uirum non cognosco*, "since I don't know any man." (Battista, "Translation or Redaction," pp. 103-104)
18. Norse *blótbyskupar*, literally "sacrifice-bishops".
19. A different recension of this saga, from manuscript AM 655 4to XIII (ca. 1250–1275), calls the devil *ogorlegr blamaþr biki svartari*, "a terrifying black man, blacker than pitch." (Unger, p. 763) "Black man" (*blámaðr*) evidently translates the word "Egyptian" in the original text (Lipsius and Bonnet, *Acta Apostolorum*, vol. 1, part 2, p. 146). Although *blámaðr* is used in historical sagas for Africans, the description of this devil as a *blámaðr* probably influenced the later legendary sagas, in which *blámenn* appear as trollish monsters. (Lindow, "Supernatural Others and Ethnic Others", pp. 13-17)
20. The *Passio Bartholomaei* states only that Bartholomew was beaten and beheaded (Lipsius and Bonnet, *Acta Apostolorum*, vol. 1, part 2, p. 149). The tradition that he was flayed alive comes from Armenia, but it seems to have been introduced into Latin texts as early as the 9th century, in which *decollari* (beheaded) is corrected to *decoriari* (flayed). (Rose,

Ritual Memory, p. 84)

21. This chapter is not part of the saint's life itself, and does not appear in the earliest manuscript AM 645, nor in *Skarðsbók*. It is a *translatio*, an account of the removal of relics from one location to another.
22, The tradition that Bartholomew's casket had floated all the way to Lipari appears in the 6th century, in Gregory of Tours's *De Gloria Martyrum* XXXIII (Migné, *Patrologia Latina*, vol. 71, p. 734). The added details that it led the caskets of four other saints' relics, that it was too heavy for people to lift and had to be drawn by bulls, and that it stopped a volcanic eruption may be Byzantine in origin; the saga text here is fairly close to a Greek homily by Theodore the Studite, from the 9th century (transl. Di Maria, "Encomio di San Bartolomeo Apostolo," pp. 62-63).
23. From this point to the departure for Benevento, the text is very close to a section of Jacobus de Voragine's *Legenda aurea* or *Golden Legend* (transl. Ryan, p. 499), and presumably derives from one of Jacobus's sources, if not from the *Legenda* itself.
24. I.e., Norse speakers call the Saracens *Serki.*

The Saga of the Descent into Hell

1. Cartlidge and Elliott, *Art and the Christian Apocrypha*, pp. 126-131.
2. *Moralia in Job* XXXIII.vii.14, ix.17; ed. Migné, *Patrologia Latina* vol. 76, pp. 680, 682; transl. Bliss, pp. 569-570, 572-573.
3. *Heilagra Manna Sögur*, vol. II, pp. 1-20. See Wolf, "The Influence of the *Evangelium Nicodemi*", pp. 262-265, for an overview of the available manuscripts and filiation.
4. Scheidweiler, "The Gospel of Nicodemus," pp. 470-481.
5. In the original *Gospel of Nicodemus*, Charinus and Leucius are the sons of Simeon, the old priest in the Jerusalem Temple who had seen the infant Jesus. They are dead by the time of Jesus's crucifixion, but are suddenly resurrected at the moment of Jesus's death. Unable to speak what they have seen, they write down accounts of the Harrowing of Hell, since they were with their father at the moment of Jesus's entry. After writing their accounts, they ascend to Heaven. The episode is an expansion of Matthew 27:52-53, which alleges that at the moment of Jesus's death, "the graves were opened; and many bodies of the saints which slept arose, and came out of the graves after his resurrection, and went into the holy city, and appeared unto many." (KJV)
6. The Norse phrase *verk grøðerans* renders the Latin *Gesta Salvatoris*, which was the usual title for the *Gospel of Nicodemus* before the 11th century. (Roughton, "Stylistics and Sources", p. 45)
7. The original refers only to Hell being dark. The addition of "foggy" (*þocusamt*) in the translation may be an allusion to the world of Niflheim or Niflhel mentioned in Norse mythological texts.
8. The Norse *er oss hefer heitet at senda lios sit* could be "who has promised to us to send his own light" or "who has promised to send his own light to us". The Greek text just has "This shining comes from a great light". (Scheidweiler, "Gospel of Nicodemus", p. 471)
9. All Latin quotations from the Vulgate Bible have been translated as quotes from the King James Version of the Bible (KJV), and printed in italics. Chapter and verse citations follow the KJV. This is a quotation of Isaiah 9:1-2, with verse 9:1 abbreviated.

10. The text has Simeon saying only "*Nunc dimitis Vsque in finem*", or "*Nunc dimittis* to the end", presumably an abbreviation for the entirety of the prayer *Nunc dimittis.* I have included the prayer in full. The source is Luke 1:29–32.
11. Again, the text says only "*Ecce agnus dei usque in finem*", "*Ecce Agnus Dei* to the end", presumably meaning that the reader should insert the entire Latin prayer *Agnus dei.* The quotation is from John 1:29.
12. Matthew 3:17.
13. Note that John the Baptist is the forerunner of Jesus in Hell, as he was on Earth.
14. In the original, this section is a discussion between Satan and Hades (Latin *Inferus*), the personification of Hell itself. The translator has replaced Hades with a collective crowd of devils along with beings drawn from Norse mythology, giants (*jötnar*) and trolls (*tröll*). Satan himself is explicitly called a giant (*jötunn*) as well as a dragon (*dreki*), and the phrase that mentions his heads and his dragon shape does not appear in the Greek or Latin texts. The original text's triad of Christ, Inferus, and Satan has been reduced by the translator to the binary opposition of Christ and Satan (Wolf, "The Influence of the *Evangelium Nicodemi*", p. 266)
15. The Greek text has Satan mentioning here that he has heard Jesus express fear by saying "My soul is very sorrowful, even to death" (Matthew 26:38; Scheidweiler, "Gospel of Nicodemus", p. 472). The point is that Satan believes that Jesus is only a human, since if Jesus were God, he could not truly be afraid of death. The usual answer from theologians was that Jesus's fearful words were a *pia fraus*, "pious fraud," to trick Satan into trying to claim him (Marchand, "Leviathan and the Mousetrap", p. 333).
16. A few words are missing at this point in manuscript AM 645 and have been restored according to AM 623. AM 238 follows the Latin more closely, with Satan listing torments in more detail: "I sharpened the spear, and I urged that it be stabbed into his side; I mixed sour gall to give him as a drink for his thirst; I built a gallows to crucify him. . ." AM 238 also has Satan speaking to a singular Prince of Hell (*helvitis hofdingi*), equivalent to Inferus in the Latin text, instead of to a crowd of devils.
17. A few missing words in this passage have been restored from AM 623.
18. Chapter IV is the first interpolation that has no counterpart in the Latin text. The description of the rider is based on Revelations 19:11-16.
19. The fact that Satan is called the Midgard Serpent, and that Christ is depicted as catching him with a hook, has drawn attention for its similarity with a Norse myth in which the god Thor fishes for the world-encircling Midgard Serpent, hooks it, and nearly kills it (e.g. Aho, "*Niðrstigningarsaga*", pp. 154-155). Marchand ("Leviathan and the Mousetrap", pp. 330-333) has pointed out that the source is likelier to be Christian. Comparing Christ on the cross to a hook baited for Satan was a common medieval allegory; among many other texts, it appears in an Icelandic book of sermons from around 1200 (*Hómiliubók*), which in turn derives it from Gregory the Great (*Morals on the Book of Job* XXXIII.14, 17; transl. Bliss, pp. 569-570, 572-573). Nonetheless, even though the source for this interpolation is probably Christian, for the translator to choose to insert it in this text at this point would have reminded his audience very pointedly of the older myth. Marchand suggests that Christian theology could have influenced the Norse myth, but there are artistic depictions of Thor's fishing expedition which date back to the 8th century, and descriptions in poetry going back to the 9th

century. This would not absolutely rule out Christian influence, but it shows that the myth existed before there was extensive Christian influence in Scandinavia. (Sørensen, "Thorr's Fishing Expedition", pp. 121-127)

20. The quotation is from Psalms 24:7.
21. This paragraph is the second interpolation not found in the Latin text. Like the first, it is reminiscent of the myth of Thor fishing up the Midgard Serpent, although its proximate textual source is almost certainly Christian. The image of the Cross as a mousetrap is also derived from Christian sources, notably Augustine (Marchand, "Leviathan and the Mousetrap", p. 333-335).
22. The quote is a conflation of Psalms 105:1, 105:6, and 107:16-17.
23. Paraphrased from Isaiah 26:19.
24. Psalm 24:8. In the original Greek text, Hades only says "Who is this King of Glory?", and it is the angels who respond "The Lord strong and mighty, the Lord mighty in battle." (Scheidweiler, "Gospel of Nicodemus", p. 474)
25. A conflation of Psalm 24:8 and 102:19-20.
26. The sentence is slightly garbled in AM 645 and has been amended from AM 623.
27. Psalm 30. In the Latin gospel, Adam quotes the first five verses of this psalm. The Norse translator or scribe evidently had a Latin text with all five verses, but opted to trim them. (Wolf, "The Influence of the *Evangelium Nicodemi* on Norse Literature", p. 265)
28. Psalm 98:1. The original text has David quoting the first two verses in full; the translator has trimmed this to the first half of the first verse.
29. Habakkuk 3:13. Habakkuk and Micah do not appear in the earliest Greek text.
30. A paraphrase of Micah 7:18-19.
31. As noted in *Landafræði* (p. 97 note 10) and *Eireks saga víðförla* (pp. 353-354 note 15), it was widely held in the early Church that the souls of the blessed dead inhabited Paradise, where they awaited the resurrection of their bodies at the Last Judgment, when they would finally enjoy the full presence of God in the spiritual Kingdom of Heaven. Most authorities, if not all, equated Paradise with the Garden of Eden, inaccessible to living humans but still a physical place in the farthest East of the world. Most agreed that the good thief, Adam, Enoch, and Elijah inhabited Paradise; whether or not other righteous souls would reach Paradise was an unresolved question. (Delumeau, *History of Paradise*, pp. 27-33)
32. Jesus's words here are taken from Luke 23:43.
33. This chapter implies that the translator knew a more complete version of the *Descent* that included a fuller account of who Leucius and Carinus were and how they had written matching accounts of what they had seen in Hell. (Scheidweiler, "The Gospel of Nicodemus," pp. 470-471)

Geography

1. e.g. Homer, *Odyssey*, IV.561-569, transl. Murray, vol. 1, pp. 158-161; Plutarch, *Life of Sertorius* VIII.2-3, transl. Perrin, vol. 8, pp. 20-23.
2. Delumeau, *History of Paradise*, pp. 18-21.
3. transl. Duff and Duff, *Minor Latin Poems*, pp. 641-665.
4. The phoenix ultimately derives from Egyptian myths about the *bennu* bird as transmitted

by classical authors, e.g. *Herodotus* II.73; transl. Godley, pp. 358-361. For overviews of the origin and history of the phoenix legend, see Blake, *The Phoenix*, pp. 8-16, and Hill, "The Phoenix", pp. 62-63.

5. *Altnordische Kosmographie*, pp. 276-280.
6. The word used for "world" here is *heimstöð*, "homestead".
7. The description of Paradise and the phoenix that lives in it is very close to an anonymous Old English "Homily on the Phoenix," preserved in two manuscripts: the 12th-century Cotton Vespasian D.xiv, and the 11th-century Cambridge, Corpus Christi College 198. All are related to the Old English poem *The Phoenix*, which in turn draws on a Latin poem by Lactantius. Blake (*The Phoenix*, pp. 94-99) gives the Old English and Old Norse texts. He suggests that both are based on the same Latin original (p. 97), whereas Larsen ("Notes on the Phoenix", pp. 79-84) argued that the relationship is so close that the Norse text must have been translated directly from the Old English homily.
8. The Old English homily that the Norse is based on has *feowrtig fedmen*, "forty fathoms". (Blake, *The Phoenix*, p. 94)
9. *Saltus* is Latin for "woodland"; *Radion* is unclear, although the name could be an error for *radians saltus* or *radiosus saltus*, "shining woods". This name is found in the Old English homily on the phoenix, but not in Lactantius or anywhere else I could trace.
10. Jesus had promised one of the thieves who were crucified beside him, "Verily I say unto thee, today shalt thou be with me in paradise." (Luke 23:43, KJV; see also *Niðrstigningar saga*, this volume.) The belief that the souls of good men enjoyed life in the Earthly Paradise until the Last Judgment, when they would enter Heaven and experience the full presence of God, was condemned in the 14th century by the Catholic Church. Before that time, however, it was a widely held belief, originating in Jewish esoteric thought and entering Christianity through texts like the *Apocalypse of Paul*, that the souls of the blessed—possibly only martyrs, possibly all good people—would inhabit the Earthly Paradise until their final summons to Heaven. Isidore of Seville and the Venerable Bede were two well-known authorities that supported this view. (Delumeau, *History of Paradise*, pp. 23-38)
11. This sentence is in Latin in the manuscript: *Hoc dicit Iohannes apostolus de Paradiso.* It seems to be misplaced, as it has been put in the middle of the account of the phoenix. The Old English homily that this text is probably based on begins with a brief account of how the Apostle John was taken to Paradise by an angel, giving the account of Paradise a "framing story" derived from the Apocalypse of St. John. (Larsen, "Notes on the Phoenix", pp. 80-81)
12. This scene of birds building the pyre may be depicted in the *Physiologus* Fragment A, although the *Physiologus* text does not mention it. (See illustration on p. 106, lower row.)
13. It was thought that the four rivers of Paradise flowed into underground caverns, which allowed them to reappear in four different parts of the world, even crossing oceans. (Delumeau, *History of Paradise*, pp. 40-41)
14. In the more historical sagas, *Serkland* is more or less the name for the lands ruled by the Islamic Caliphate. Here it has no concise equivalent. "The Middle East" is not entirely satisfactory as a translation, since the text goes on to assign Jerusalem and Antioch to Asia, not to Africa.
15. The names of the sons of Shem, Ham, and Japheth are taken from Genesis 10, the

"Table of Nations." The Bible does not precisely specify which territories their sons are said to have settled and founded; the traditional assignments found here can be traced at least back to Josephus. (*Jewish Antiquities* I.122-147; transl. Thackeray, vol. IV, pp. 58-73)

16. The text has *Svíþiod en mikla*, literally "Sweden the Great", the usual name for Siberia or Scythia.
17. The Bible refers to the building of the Tower of Babel, which caused God to replace humanity's common language with many languages, so that the builders could no longer communicate. (Genesis 11:1-9) While the Bible states that the builders were human and does not name them, a widespread medieval tradition going back at least to Augustine (*De civitate dei* 16.4) assigns the building of the Tower to Nimrod the son of Cush, and makes him a giant. The Bible itself refers to Nimrod only as a mighty hunter and ruler who founded cities in the Near East (Genesis 10:8-12). See Murdoch, *The Medieval Popular Bible*, pp. 133-134.
18. According to Josephus (*Jewish Antiquities* I:124, transl. Thackeray, vol. IV, pp. 60-61), Madai founded the nation of Medes living in Iran and Mesopotamia. The *Kylfingar* appear in *Egils saga* 10 (*CSI* I:43) as a people living to the east of Finnmark in northern Norway; whether they were Finnic, Norse, or some other ethnicity is not known.
19. Josephus assigns Gomer to Galatia in Asia Minor, and Tubal to the Caucasus (*Jewish Antiquities* I.123-125; transl. Thackeray, vol. IV, pp. 58-61). Isidore of Seville mostly agrees (*Etymologies* IX.ii.26-29; transl. Barney et al., p. 193); elsewhere he links the Goths with Magog (IX.ii.89, transl. Barney et al., p. 197). I am not sure on what authority Scandinavia is linked with Gomer, unless it is to provide a link with Rome and nationalistic pride at being descended from the firstborn of Japheth's sons.
20. *Serkland* is the usual term in the sagas for the Islamic Caliphate, more or less, although this translation would be anachronistic here.
21. Gaetulia was the Roman name for the land south of the Atlas Mountains and extending into the Sahara Desert, mostly in present-day Morocco. (e.g. Pliny, *Natural History* V.i.9-13, 17; transl. Rackham, vol. II, pp. 224-231; Sallust, *Jugurtha* XVIII-XIX, transl. Rolfe, pp. 170-177.) The Gaetulians were plausibly ancestors or relatives of the Berbers.
22. Roman-era Numidia referred to the Mediterranean coastal regions of present-day Algeria and Tunisia.
23. Mauretania in Roman times referred to what is now northern Morocco along the Mediterranean and Atlantic Coasts. Little if any of ancient Mauretania overlapped with the modern country of Mauritania.
24. The term *Bláland*, "black [people's] land" is more or less synonymous with Africa, although here it seems to refer more specifically to sub-Saharan Africa.
25. In most medieval Christian commentaries on Genesis, seventy-two is the standard number of languages spoken in the world. Usually the descendants of Shem speak 27, the descendants of Ham speak 30, and the descendants of Japheth speak 15; the numbers are somewhat different here. (Murdoch, *The Medieval Popular Bible*, pp. 139-144)
26. *Miklagarðr* means "great city".
27. The Latin *Historia Norwegiae* agrees that *Vegistafr* (possibly "way-staff" or "signpost") is the northern limit of Norway (transl. Kunin, p. 3). It has been identified with the modern Cape Svyatoj Nos on the Kola Peninsula (Binns, "Participation of the Kings",

p. 386).

28. Anglesey Sound, *Aunguls-eyjar-sund*, is part of the Irish Sea, between Wales and Ireland. This seems nonsensical at first, but the writer was evidently including the Norwegian settlements in northern and western Scotland and the Isle of Man as part of the kingdom of Norway.
29. St. Sunniva is the patron saint of western Norway; her relics were placed in the cathedral at Bergen in 1170.
30. St. Hallvard Vebjörnsson is the patron saint of Oslo and a first cousin of St. Olaf. He is said to have died in the year 1043; by 1130 a cathedral was built in his honor in Oslo.
31. This is Knut IV of Denmark, who was killed in Odense in 1086; he was canonized in 1101.
32. "Knut the Younger" is St. Knut Lavard, a nephew of Knut IV, killed near Ringsted in 1131 and buried there, and canonized in 1170.
33. Margaret of Ølsemagle was murdered by her husband in 1176. Miracles allegedly occurred where her body had been thrown, and it was moved to Our Lady's Abbey in Roskilde. Margaret's shrine became a place of pilgrimage for centuries, although she was never formally canonized.
34. Helluland ("rock-slab land") is thought to be Baffin Island; Markland ("forest land") is probably Labrador; and Vinland ("wine land", from wild grapes or similar berries found there) is Newfoundland.
35. The word is *husa-snotro*, normalized as *húsasnotra*; *Grænlandinga saga* tells how Thorfinn Karlsefni cut down a maple tree to make a *húsasnotra*. The obscure word literally means something like "wise lady of the house"; I have followed Sayers in translating it as "weathervane." ("Karlsefni's *Húsasnotra*", pp. 341-350)
36. The Norse settlement of *Garðar* was located in south Greenland, in the former Eastern Settlement, near the present-day town of Igaliku. The bishopric was established in 1124; the last bishop died in 1378.

The Physiologus and Related Texts

1. Curley, *Physiologus*; see pp. ix-xxxiii for a discussion of the origins and transmission of the *Physiologus*. T. H. White's *A Book of Beasts* is a complete (and quite charming) translation of a mid-12th century Latin bestiary from England, not much older than the Icelandic fragments.
2. Dolcetta Corazza, "Crossing Paths," p. 226.
3. *Historia Naturalis* VII.ii.9-32; transl. Rackham, pp. 513-527.
4. *Etymologies* XL.iii.12-27, transl. Barney, pp. 244-245. For an overview see Friedman, *Monstrous Races*.
5. Friedman, *Monstrous Races*, pp. 123-124; Dolcetta Corazza, "Crossing Paths" p. 229.
6. Friesen, "Family Resemblances".
7. Hermannson, *The Icelandic* Physiologus.
8. Cucina, "The Rainbow Allegory", pp. 69-74.
9. Kålund, *Alfræði Íslenzk*, pp. 34-36 (Plinian races), 39-40 (serpents).
10. Dahlerup, "Physiologus i to Islandske Bearbejdelser," pls. 1-16.
11. Barraclough, *Beyond the Northlands*, pp. 139-140.

12. The *Physiologus* claimes that hoopoes care for their parents by preening their feathers and licking their eyes; see Curley, *Physiologus*, pp. 14-15; White, *The Book of Beasts*, pp. 131-132. The use of ashes as a remedy for dim sight may be a bit of folk medicine; ashes of various substances were used as salves for different ailments (Waggoner, *Norse Magical and Herbal Healing*, pp. 10, 12).
13. This is based on the *Physiologus* description of ants—although the translator seems to have altered the usual meaning; ants in the *Physiologus* carry off wheat seeds from fields but leave barley grains alone, symbolizing the need to separate sound doctrine from heresy. In any case, since Iceland has no native ant species, the translator seems to have substituted another insect, *kleggjur*, "horseflies".
14. The onocentaur (Greek *onokentauros*) has a human forepart and the body of a donkey. (The more familiar type of centaur, with a horse's body, is specifically called a hippocentaur or *hippokentauros*). The Norse *finngálkn* appears in a few legendary sagas as a similar human-equine monster (e.g. *Hjálmþés saga ok Ölvis* 7, transl. O'Connor, p. 133).
15. The crocodile-killing *hydrus* is usually depicted as a snake or lizard, not a bird. In some versions of the text the name is *niluus* (e.g. Curley, *Physiologus*, pp. 53-54).
16. Hermannsson notes that the manuscript uses the word *gát* instead of the standard spelling *geit. Gát* is Old English and early Middle English for "goat;" thus it's possible that the translator was working from an English manuscript of the *Physiologus.*
17. The quote is from 1 Peter 5:8.
18. Some Latin texts make a pun here that the Norse translator did not attempt to render: just as apes have no *cauda*, "tail", the Devil has no *caudex*, i.e. *codex*, "book; Scripture". (White, *The Book of Beasts*, pp. 34-35)
19. The quote is based on 2 Timothy 3:5.
20. Based on Psalm 49:20. The illustration shows the onocentaur speaking to two men, one of whom is naked, the other of whom is dressed in long robes and holds a sword. The naked man may represent those who are prey to temptation, while the clothed man may represent those who successfully defend against temptation. (Dolcetti Corazza, "Crossing Paths," p. 239)
21. The text has *marsus*. The Marsi were an Italic tribe who claimed to have the ability to destroy or charm snakes and cure snakebite. (See Ogden, *Drakon*, pp. 213-214.) However, the illustration depicts both the *marsus* and the asps as quadrupedal beasts
22. This entry goes back to Psalm 58:4-5: "They [the wicked] are like the deaf adder that stoppeth her ear; which will not hearken to the voice of charmers, charming never so wisely."
23. The quote is Psalm 42:1.
24. The reference is to Proverbs 30:28. *Stellio* means a type of lizard; in the Latin Vulgate, the word is *stilio.*
25. Ananias, Misael, and Azarias are better known by their Babylonian names: Shadrach, Meshach, and Abednego (Daniel 1:7). The story of their survival in the furnace is told in Daniel 3.
26. Based on 2 Corinthians 4:9.
27. The entries on the kite, boar, and owl are not part of the *Physiologus* proper; they are brief glosses to animals mentioned in the Psalms, and are rather cryptic out of context. The entry on the kite is a gloss to Psalm 104:17, which mentions the home of a bird in

the fir trees. Jerome had translated the bird's Hebrew name as *herodius*, "stork" in the Latin Vulgate, but suggested in a letter that the name should be rendered *milvus*, "kite". See Marchand, "Two Notes", pp. 502-503.

28. The quotation is Psalms 79:14; the boar is said to destroy "a vine out of Egypt", a metaphor for the Jewish people.
29. The quotation is Psalms 102:6.
30. Norse *fill* is borrowed from Arabic *fīl*, which comes from Persian *pīl*.
31. The section on the elephant is in different handwriting from the rest of Fragment B. As with the phoenix, the illustration conveys information that is not included in the Icelandic text but that is typical of the *Physiologus* in general: the elephant is said to have no knees, and is drawn without knees. (e.g. White, *The Book of Beasts*, pp. 24-26). The trapezoid covering the elephant's face in the illustration is evidently some sort of armor.
32. The reference is to 1 Maccabees 6:37, which describes war elephants in the forces of King Antiochus Eupator, each of which bore a wooden tower that held thirty-two men. The number thirty-two is not completely clear in the *Physiologus* text, and is restored from the text of the Bible. See *Yngvars saga víðförla* 10 (pp. 338-339, this volume).
33. The Norse text reads *hann er stor sem ormar*, "it is as large as serpents". I have emended this based on Isidore of Seville, *Etymologies* XII.iv.4; transl. Barney et al., p. 255.
34. This odd fact may be derived from Isidore of Seville's account of a precious stone called *dracontites*, which is extracted from a dragon's brain. Bold men cut off dragons' heads to extract the stone. (*Etymologies* XVI.xiv.7; transl. Barney et al., p. 326) Isidore also notes that the dragon is native to Ethiopia (XII.iv.5; transl. Barney et al., p. 255). The Land of Black Men (*Bláland*, "Black Land") is often used for Africa; see "Geography" in this book, note 22.
35. *Emorvis* is a variant spelling of *haemorrhois*; *ipialis* is a variant of *hypnalis*; *difsa* is a variant of *dipsa*. These serpents, along with the basilisk and the dragon, appear in Lucan's *Pharsalia* in a section describing the serpents of Libya and the horrible deaths that their victims suffer (IX.700-838; transl. Duff, pp. 558-567). This is the ultimate source for much of the serpent-lore in the *Physiologus*.
36. According to Isidore of Seville, the *prester* serpent has its mouth perpetually open and steaming, and its bite causes death from swelling up enormously and putrefying. (Isidore, *Etymologies* XII.iv.16; transl. Barney et al. p. 256)
37. The translation may be garbled here; the sources state only that the *amphisbaena* is the only snake that can withstand cold. (Isidore, *Etymologies* XII.iv.20 transl. Barney et al. p. 256)
38. The description of the *rimotrix* is based on accounts of the salamander, which was said not only to resist fire, but to be able to poison springs or trees by simple contact. (Isidore, *Etymologies* XII.iv.36; transl. Barney et al. p. 257; White, *A Book of Beasts*, pp. 182-184). The name *rimotrix* may derive from a scribal error for *natrix*, "water snake", which is called a "polluter of waters" by Lucan in *Pharsalia / De Bello Civili* (IX.720; transl. Duff, pp. 558-559) and allegedly poisons any spring in which it finds itself (Isidore, *Etymologies* XII.iv.26; transl. Barney et al. pp. 256-257).
39. Asbestos was claimed to be "salamander wool" in the later Middle Ages and Renaissance (Browne, "Salamander's Wool", pp. 66-67). This idea goes back to the famous *Prester John Letter*, a forgery written in Latin around 1165-1170, which purported to describe

marvels of the distant East. The oldest version of the *Letter* mentions salamanders in terms strikingly close to the Norse text: *faciunt pelliculam quandam circa se. . . . inde habemus vestes et pannos ad omnem usum excellentiae nostrae. Isti panni non nisi in igne fortiter accenso lavantur* (*Epistola Presbiteri Iohannis* 42-43, in Brewer, *Prester John,* p. 52). "They make certain little skins around themselves. . . . from them we have clothes and garments for our excellency's every use. These garments are not washed except by burning them strongly in fire." (transl. Brewer, *Prester John*, p. 76) Prester John's Letter is mentioned in *Konungs skuggsjá*, written around 1250, as having recently come to Norway (transl. Larson, *The King's Mirror*, pp. 101-102), so it seems reasonable that some "fact" from it could have been inserted here.

40. Typical medieval scholarly opinion, including the sources of the Biblical compilation known as *Stjórn*, associated only two colors of the rainbow with judgments: blue, the color of water, was associated with the Flood; and red, the color of fire, was associated with the Last Judgment. (I.20; ed. Unger, p. 62) Other writers assigned four colors to the rainbow, each associated with one of the four elements. A fragment of a Latin homily has survived that uses the same three-color interpretation as this passage, and it may represent the source of the Icelandic text. (See Marchand, "Two Notes", pp. 503-505.) This learned tradition may have influenced Snorri Sturluson, whose *Edda* also states that the rainbow has three colors, and that the red color is fire. (*Gylfaginning* 13, 15 ; Faulkes, ed., p. 15, 18)

41. The length of the Viking-era ell ranged from 47 cm to 63 cm, or between 18 and 25 inches. (Christiansen, *Norsemen in the Viking Age*, p. 333).

42. See *Samsons saga fagra* 13 and 14 (this volume, pp. 272-273) for its mention of *Smámeyjaland*, "the Land of Little Girls," which may be derived from accounts like this.

43. Most of this paragraph, from the Cicopli (Cyclopes) to the Indian women who only live to the age of eight, is a direct but somewhat abridged translation of a section of Isidore's *Etymologies* (XI.iii.16-27, transl. Barney et al., p. 245). Most of the names are easily recognizable in the writings of Pliny and others; those that may be troublesome include Lamnies (*Blemmyae*); Panadios (*Panotii*, "all-ears"); Ardabadites (*Artibatirae*); Acrobi (*Macrobioi*); and Skioppodas (*Sciopods*, "shadow-foot").

44. The African races are derived from Pliny, who writes of the Panphagi ("eaters of everything"; spelled here as Pagasi), Troglodytes ("cave dwellers"), Anthiophagi ("eaters of wild game"), and Anthropophagi ("eaters of humans").

45. The women who bear only one child in their lives, and whose white hair at birth turns black with age, are called the the Pandae in the writings of Ctesias (Friedman, *The Monstrous Races*, p. 18). Long-lived tribes also are mentioned in *Samsons saga fagra* 13 (this volume, p. 272).

46. The mouthless tribe that lives on the scent of apples is usually called the Astomi ("mouthless"), or the "Apple-Smellers" (Friedman, *The Monstrous Races*, p. 11). Accounts of "trees that bear wool" in India ultimately derive from Greek and Roman accounts of the use of cotton (e.g. Herodotus, *Histories*, III.106, transl. Godley, vol. 2, pp. 132-135; Pliny, *Natural History*, XII.xxxi-xii; transl. Rackham, vol. IV, pp. 26-29). In fact, one Asian species, *Gossypium arboreum*, does grow as a tree, or at least as a woody shrub, and has been cultivated in India since at least the second millennium BCE.

47. Hairy people are sometimes called Pilosi, but descriptions of them in medieval sources

are quite variable. The wild fish-eating people are usually called Ichthiophagi, "fish-eaters". (Friedman, *The Monstrous Races*, p. 15-17)

48. The text uses the word *Svíþiod enni miclo,* literally "Sweden the Great", but commonly used for the lands east of Russia.
49. Norse *Kvennaland.* Adam of Bremen also mentions a land of women warriors to the north of Sweden (*History of the Archbishops of Hamburg-Bremen* IV.xix; Tschan, transl., p. 200.) It is possible that some of these references result from misinterpreting the name *Kvenland*, the land of the Kvens, a Finnic-speaking ethnic group. The Latin *Historia Norvegiae* mentions "a country of maidens" somewhere in the far North (transl. Kunin, pp. 2-3).
50. The *Historia Norvegiae* mentions *cornuti Finni*, "horned Finns", living somewhere in northern Norway or east of it (transl. Kunin, p. 2). *Finni* usually refers to the nomadic Saami or "Lapps", not the Finnish people in the modern sense.

The Saga of Parceval

1. Marti, "Tristrams saga Revisited", pp. 46-66.
2. Kalinke, "The Saga of Parceval the Knight", pp. 222-226.
3. Linker, transl. *The Story of the Grail*; Staines, transl., *The Complete Romances*, pp. 339-449.
4. This opening paragraph does not correspond to the original and was probably added by the translator or a later copyist. Its statement that Parceval's father is "a farmer by rank" (*bóndi at nafnbót*) contradicts Parceval's mother's later claim that he and she were both "of the best families" (*af hinum beztum ættum*). It resembles Vilmund's origin story in *Vilmundar saga viðutan* 8 (this volume, p. 293), which shares several other motifs with *Parcevals saga.* Similar tales of abducted brides appear in *Orkneyinga saga* 93 and the romance-like saga of Icelanders, *Víglunds saga* 6 (*CSI* II: 416-417; see Kalinke, "The Saga of Parceval the Knight", pp. 221-22)
5. This diverges from the original, which simply says that Parceval took three javelins with him. (Kratz, "The *Parcevals Saga* and *Li Contes Del Graal*", p. 15)
6. These rhyming phrases, often proverbial or gnomic in character, appear throughout the saga. As noted in the introduction, they seem to be the translator's stylistic innovation.
7. The proverbial-sounding *Dirfist maðr af manni* seems to echo *Hávamál* 57: *maðr af manni verðr at máli kuðr*, "a man becomes known to [another] man by his speech."
8. The three loaves (Norse *hleifar*) are venison meat pies (*pastez de chevrel*) in the original.
9. In the original, the maiden weeps and says that she will not commend him to God (*a Deu ne le comandera*). Expressions like "may trolls take you" are more idiomatically Norse.
10. In the original, King Arthur is said to have fought against *roi Ryon. . . Li rois des Isles*—"King Ryon, the King of the Isles" (lines 851-852). *Rimeyja borg*, "the fortress or city of the Rim Islands", is presumably a copyist's error, possibly a misreading of *Rion eyia k*, "Rion k[ing] of the Isles]", as *Rimeyia b*, "f[ortress] of the Rim Islands" (Wolf and Maclean, *Parcevals saga*, p. 211 n5).
11. *Yvonés* in French.
12. *Quinqueroi* in French.

13. The Norse word *ræðismaðr* means "manager", translating the French title *seneschal*, Kay's usual position in the Arthurian romances.
14. Another change, possibly an error: the original has Yonez leaving *without* companions.
15. The text has "sword" (*sverð*), but this seems to be an error (Wolf and Maclean, *Parcevals saga*, p. 211 n7).
16. Another minor translation error. In the original, Parceval says that he will have to cut the dead man into *charbonees*, "collops; pieces of meat for grilling" (line 1136). The translator seems to have read the word as *charbon*, "coals; ashes." (Kratz, "The *Parcevals Saga* and *Li Contes Del Graal*", pp. 15-16)
17. *Seint er at kenna fóli vísdóm.* A proverb with the same meaning, *seint er afglapa at snotra*, appears in *Hálfdanar saga Brönufóstra* 13 (transl. Waggoner, *Sagas of Giants and Heroes*, p. 105).
18. Norse *nú nálgaz gjafar yðrar*, translating the French *Ore aprochent vos aventures*, "Now [the time of] your adventures is approaching" (1257; Wolf and Maclean, *Parcevals saga*, p. 211 n11). It is possible that *gjafar* is an error for *gipta*, "luck; fortune", used in the sense of "what's coming to you; what you're fated to receive."
19. The reference to St. Julian is not in the French text. There were several saints named Julian; the intended one is presumably St. Julian the Hospitaller, invoked by travellers seeking a night's lodging.
20. *Gornemanz de Goorz* in the original.
21. Psaki ("Women's Counsel in the Riddarasögur", pp. 205-208) points out that in the saga, but not in the original French text, Gormanz's advice subtly reverses Parceval's mother's priorities. His mother's first advice is to fear God, with advice on how to treat others placed later; Gormanz's first advice is to treat knights properly, with honoring God placed later. Gormanz's advice not to be too inquisitive contrasts with the mother's advice that "every wise man asks questions." Parceval's acceptance of Gormanz's advice over his mother's sets up his failure to ask about the Grail.
22. The French text (1910) has *miches*, "small loaves made with white flour"; the translator has rendered them *munkahleifir*, "monks' loaves". (Wolf and Maclean, *Parcevals saga*, p. 212 n18)
23. The three hundred and ten knights of the original (*trois cenz chevaliers et dis*; line 1999), of whom fifty remain, have somehow become thirteen thousand knights, of whom sixty remain.
24. In the French he is simply *Clamadeu des Illes*, "of the Isles" (line 2005); here he is *Klamadius ór Suðreyjum*, literally "Klamadius from the Southern Isles"—but *Suðreyjar* specifically means the Hebrides, the "southern isles" from the viewpoint of Norway. The French *Anguinguerrons* has turned into Norse *Gingvarus*.
25. Manuscript Holm Perg. 6 4to resumes at this point.
26. Norse *Fögruborg* translates *Biaurepaire* (Modern French *Beaurepaire*), "beautiful retreat".
27. In the French text, throughout this scene, Clamadeu is said to have fifteen hundred fighting men—five hundred knights and a thousand men-at-arms (lines 2433-2434, 2460-2461), twenty of whom are sent to the gates. The Norse text is inconsistent: Klamadius has fifteen thousand knights, sixty of whom are sent to the gates, while the main body soon turns into four hundred knights and two thousand foot soldiers.
28. The passage beginning "He was esteemed highly" has no counterpart in the French text.

Characterizations like this are common in the sagas, and the translator or a copyist may have added this to make the style more familiar to his audience. (Marti, "Translation or Adaptation?", pp. 41-43)

29. The Norse word *siklát* here is a borrowing of Middle High German *sigelât*, "silk cloth worked with gold"; it replaces the original *sebelin*, "sable fur" (line 3089).
30. The bleeding lance is never explained in *Perceval*. The later First and Third Continuations of *Perceval* identify it as the spear thrust into the side of the crucified Jesus, but it is not clear whether this is what Chrétien de Troyes originally had in mind.
31. The French text simply says that the maiden bore a *graal*—a word that originally meant simply a dish or platter (possibly from the Latin *gradale*, "in stages", designating a dish brought to the table at various stages during a meal; see Mahoney, "Introduction", p. 5, and Goetinck, "Quest for Origins", p. 133). In Chrétien de Troyes's *Perceval*, the *graal* is bright and beautiful, but not otherwise spiritually or magically charged. It was Robert de Boron's *Joseph d'Arimathie*, written about ten years after Chrétien de Troyes's *Perceval*, that identified the *graal* as Jesus's cup at the Last Supper, which also caught his blood during the Crucifixion. The Norse translator probably did not know what the word *graal* meant, and his attempts to explain it are rather confusing. The translator uses the Latin word *textus* to describe it. Richard Heinzel suggested that this was the scribe's attempt to explain one meaning of the word *graal*, "gradual; book of music for the Mass" (Latin *graduale;* French *grael*, *graal*, etc.), but P. M. Mitchell points out that the translator could have used Norse *gradal* or *graðall* if he meant to indicate a gradual book, and also that *textus* would mean a book of the Gospels, not a gradual ("The Grail in the *Parcevals Saga*," p. 592). Álfrún Gunnlaugsdóttir suggested that *textus* was a mistake for *pyxis*, a round box used to transport the consecrated Host, the bread used in the celebration of the Mass. ("Um Parcevals Sögu", p. 230)
32. The manuscript has *braull*, presumably a mistake for the French *graal*. This may have resulted from misreading a capital *G* as a *b* (Wolf and Maclean, *Parcevals saga*, p. 213 n29)
33. The Norse phrase *gangandi greiði* is especially obscure, and scholars do not agree on what the translator meant (Mitchell, "The Grail in the *Parcevals Saga*," pp. 593-594). *Greiði* in modern Icelandic can mean "food; provisions" or "favor; help; kindness"; according to Cleasby and Vígfússon's *Dictionary* (p. 213) its primary meaning is "disentanglement; arrangement; ordering", and it can refer to the settlement of legal cases, although it can also mean "entertainment; refreshment"; Wolf and Maclean render it as "processional provision" (p. 149
34. The Norse word *tön* is a hapax legomenon; the word *tailleoir* at the corresponding point in the French text (line 3231) means a tray.
35. The Norse word *sirop* is a direct borrowing from the French; the word could mean more or less what English *syrup* does, but it also could mean a sweetened wine or other thick, sweet drink.
36. In the original, Perceval simply gives his name as *Percevax li Galois*, "Perceval the Welsh" (3575), and the maiden says that he must have changed it, because his name should be *Percevax li cheitis*, "Perceval the Wretch" (3582). Somewhere in the textual transmission of this saga, *Percevax li Galois* evidently became compressed into *Pacuvaleis*.
37. The original (line 3675) has Parceval ordered to go "to the lake below Cotouatre", *au*

lac qui est sor Cotouatre (Wolf and Maclean, *Parcevals saga*, p. 213 n34). The "mighty man named Loth" seems to be a misreading of *Loth* for *lac*, "lake", by the translator, influenced by the name of King Lot or Loth, the father of Gawain.

38. French *Trabuchet*. The sword never reappears in *Perceval*, but its eventual breaking and later reforging is told in the Second and Third Continuations, where it is identified eventually as the sword that wounded the Fisher Kimng and killed his brother. (Mahoney, "Introduction", p. 7)
39. French *Carlion*, or Caerleon in Wales, long associated with Arthur's court.
40. In Chrétien's text, the hermit reveals that the Grail carries a single Host (consecrated bread wafer, literally transsubstantiated into the Body of Christ in Catholic doctrine). This is enough to sustain the life of the Fisher King's father, who is fed inside the side room that the Grail procession enters.
41. The rather abrupt happy ending is the translator's creation; Chrétien de Troyes did not finish *Perceval*.

The Saga of Theodoric of Verona: Theodoric Claims His Kingdom

1. Andersson, "An Interpretation," pp. 356-366; he suggests that the source reached Norway even before the reign of Hákon IV, the king who sponsored so many translations of chivalric literature.
2. Andersson (e.g. "An Interpretation," pp. 347-351) argues that the saga was translated from a single German prose compilation. Haymes (in Gentry et al., *The Nibelungen Tradition*, p. 41) argues that the translator himself compiled the saga from multiple German songs and stories.
3. Andersson, "Composition and Literary Culture," pp. 3-5.
4. Andersson, "Composition and Literary Culture," pp. 17-23.
5. Guðni Jónsson, *Þiðreks saga af Bern*, vol. 2, pp. 531-560.
6. Bertelsen, *Þiðreks saga af Bern*, vol. 2, pp. 328-359.
7. The Amelungs are Theodoric's family and lineage.
8. Hildibrand is frequently given the honorific title of *meistari*, "master", a loanword from Middle High German *meister*. *Meister* has multiple senses; it can mean "teacher", "learned man", "expert craftsman", "overseer", "owner", or "champion". A literal transition at this point would be *King Theodoric and his master Hildibrand*, but in English that could imply that Hildibrand has control over Theodoric, which is not the case. Hildibrand is Theodoric's foster-father; he taught him in his youth and fights for him, but he is not in authority over Theodoric. I have therefore translated *meistari* as "champion" or "foster-father" whenever translating it as "master" seemed to give the wrong impression; however, I have left it in when it is used as an honorific title.
9. Amelungland (Norse *Ömlungaland*) is located in northern Italy.
10. Sifka is Ermanaric's counselor and treasurer. Earlier in *Þiðreks saga*, in the section called *Hefndir Sifka* ("Sifka's Vengeance"), Ermanaric sends Sifka on an errand and then rapes Sifka's wife. In revenge, Sifka plots the death of Ermanaric and all his kinsmen, who are killed one by one. Theodoric is Ermanaric's nephew, and Sifka's accusations force Theodoric to flee his kingdom and take refuge with Attila. (Hugus, "Sifka", in Gentry et al., *The Nibelungen Tradition*, p. 117)

11. Herrat (Norse *Herað*) is Theodoric's wife, but also Attila's kin by marriage: she is the niece of Attila's first wife, Helche (Norse *Erke*).
12. Soest (Norse *Susat*) is a town in Westphalia, presented as Attila's royal seat in *Þiðreks saga*. The *Nibelungenlied* places Attila's capital at Etzelnburg, usually identified with Esztergom in Hungary. However, the German source of *Þiðreks saga* set much of the action around the lower Rhine. In some cases, this creates geographical implausibilities that cannot easily be resolved.
13. Pöchlarn (Norse *Bakalar*, Middle German *Bechelaren*) is a city in present-day Lower Austria. Its ruler Rudiger (Norse *Roðingeirr*) is depicted in the sources as exceptionally hospitable, loyal to Attila but helpful and generous both to Theodoric and to the Nibelungs. His death is deeply mourned by both sides. (McConnell, "Rüdiger", in Gentry, *The Nibelungen Tradition*, pp. 112-113)
14. The sentence rhymes in the Norse text.
15. Rudiger's rescue of Hildibrand is told in ch. 308 of *Þiðreks saga*, in the section *Ófriðr Húna ok Rúzimanna* ("Hostility of the Huns and Russians").
16. Samson's story begins the entire *Þiðreks saga*; his son Dietmar (Norse *Þéttmarr*) is Theodoric's father.
17. *Hildigrímr* means "masked for battle." According to the section of *Þiðreks saga* known as *Æska Þiðreks konungs* ("The Youth of King Theodoric"; ch. 17), Theodoric won the helmet from two giants named Hildr and Grímr, who had named it after themselves.
18. *Ekkisax* is one of Theodoric's two famous swords. The Norse translator of *Þiðreks saga* explained the name with a pun that could not have been made in German; *ekki sax* means "no knife" in Norse, and the saga states that "no knife, nor sword, that is better has ever been taken from the forge" (*Þáttr af Ekka, Fasold ok Sistram*, ch. 99). In the German material, the sword's name *Eckesahs* comes from the giant Ecke (Norse *Ekka*), from whom Theodoric wins the sword. The original meaning of the name is probably just "sword with a sharp edge" (compare modern German *Eck*, "corner")
19. Possibly an error for Bavaria (Middle High German *Beier lant*)?
20. Norse *Hlöðver*; etymologically close to Old High German *Lothar*, Old Frankish *Chlothar*.
21. The Wolfings ("descendants of the wolf"; Norse *Ylfingar*) are Hildibrand's family line. A family by that name appears in various Norse legends, and in *Beowulf* as the ruling clan of the Geats (the Wulfingas); it's not clear whether these were considered identical to Hildibrand's family.
22. Hildebrand makes the same offer in the *Jüngere Hildebrandslied* after he has knocked Alebrand down: *bistu ein jünger Wölfinger, von mir magst du wol genesen* (Gentry and Walter, eds. *German Epic Poetry*, p. 297)
23. The insult is preserved in the *Jüngere Hildebrandslied* 10: *den streich lert dich ein wîb!* (Gentry and Walter, eds. *German Epic Poetry*, p. 297)
24. The phrase "my sweet son", *minn sæti son*, echoes both *Ásmundar saga kappabana* and the older *Hildebrandslied*, where it appears as *suâsat chind*. (See note 25 to *Ásmundar saga kappabana*).
25. Gregenborg's identity is not certain; it's been suggested that it is the present-day Greve in Chianti, near Florence, Italy. (Holthausen, "Studien zur Thidrekssaga," p. 19)
26. *Leiðarvísir*, written around 1150 as a guide for Scandinavian pilgrims to Rome,

mentions the Baths of Theodoric at Viterbo (*Boternisborg*), just north of Rome (ed. Kålund, *Alfræði Íslenzk*, vol. 1, p. 17). There are many thermal springs in the Viterbo region which have been used since Roman times; the specific Baths of Theodoric may refer to Bagnoregio, originally *Balneum regis* or "Baths of the king".

27. Statues of Theodoric were erected in Rome, Ravenna, and Constantinople during his lifetime (La Rocca, "Building and Power in Ostrogothic Italy", pp. 25-26), but it is not clear whether the statues existed at the time that the saga was written. Theodoric's statues in Rome were allegedly destroyed (Procopius, *History of the Wars* VII.xx.29, transl. Dewing, vol. IV, pp. 332-333).
28. The Arian heresy is the belief that Jesus is not coequal in nature with God the Father. The historical Theodoric was a lifelong Arian. During his reign, several Arian rulers in Europe converted to Catholic Christianity, and hostility between Arian and Catholic factions rose, but Arianism was not effectively ended until the Byzantines ended Ostrogothic rule in Italy in the mid-6th century.

The Saga of the Mantle

1. Motifs D1053, "Magic mantle (cloak); H411.7, "Mantle as chastity test"; Thompson, *Motif-Index of Folk Literature*, vol. 2 pp. 131-132; vol. 3 p. 411.
2. Kalinke, *Möttuls Saga*, pp. xix-xx.
3. Kalinke, *Möttuls Saga*, pp. lix-lxi.
4. The text from the beginning to this point does not correspond to anything in the French text, and was presumably composed by the translator.
5. The text has *valskann*, literally "Welsh", but used in other texts, including *Parcevals saga*, to mean northern French.
6. The text has *pickisdaga* (normalized, *pikkisdagar*).
7. *Alf kona*, "elf woman", translates *fee*, "fairy", in the original (195; ed. Kalinke, p. 24)
8. Meon corresponds to Yvain in the French; this suggests that the translator did not know Chretien de Troyes's poem *Yvain*, and that *Ívens saga* had not yet been translated. (Kalinke, *Möttuls Saga*, p. lx)
9. In the French text he is Tor, son of Arés.
10. In French he is Ydier son of Nu (Welsh *Edern ap Nudd*).
11. Bodendur corresponds to *Bedoër* in the French text, or Bedivere in English. His Norse name looks like a pun on *boða*, "to proclaim; to preach"; the word *boðendur* in modern Icelandic means "proclaimers; preachers".
12. The French text simply states that Kay seats Gawain's lover beside his own (lines 484-486). The Norse translator has added a ribald pun, stating that "no clouds are more alike than you are" (*ongur eru lijkari mökur enn þid erud*), punning on the similarity between *mökur*, "clouds", and *mök*, "sexual intercourse". The translator has tried to convey the general spirit of the pun.
13. Geres is *Guivres* in the French text.
14. In the French text Paternas is Perceval; like the substitution of Meon for Yvain, this substitution suggests that this translation by someone who was not familiar with the Arthurian corpus, probably before *Parcevals saga* was translated.
15. These two sayings are common Norse proverbs and are not found in the French text.

The first, *ad kuelldi er dagur lofanndi,* is close to *Hávamál* 81, *At kveldi skal dag leyfa*, "At evening one must praise the day" (in other words, don't declare that something is good until you have seen it completely). The second, *margt kann audrvvijs til ad bera enn menn hÿggia*, belongs to a family of proverbs that mean, in effect, "nothing ever goes as expected." Compare *margt gengr verr en varir*, "much goes worse than is expected" (*Hávamál* 4); *marger hluter verda nu audruuis enn menn ættludu,* "many things now turn out otherwise than men expected" (*Samsons saga fagra* 11, ed. Wilson, p. 29; this volume, p. 270); *mart verðr annann veg enn maðrinn ætlar fyrir sér*, "much turns out differently than the man thinks will happen to him" (*Jómsvíkinga saga* in *Flateyjarbók* 160; ed. Vigfússon and Unger, p. 160); and so on.

16. In the saga it is not clear who speaks this line. In some versions of the French text it is spoken by several knights at once. (Kalinke, *Möttuls saga*, p. 77)
17. The statement that it is more honorable not to speak up about others' transgressions is not in the French text, and seems to be based on a verse in *Hugsvinnsmál*, itself a translation of the didactic Latin poem *Disticha Catonis.* (Kalinke, *Möttuls saga*, p. 78)

1. She gives her name as Marie at the beginning of the *lai Guigemar*: *Oëz, seignurs, ke dit Marie*, "Hear, lords, what Marie says." (line 3; ed. Ewers, *Lais*, p. 3) The *de France* was added in the 16th century. There are several known aristocratic women named Marie from England and France in the late 12th century, but which one (if any) wrote the *lais* is unknown. For an overview of speculations on Marie's identity and location, see Bloch, *The Anonymous Marie de France*, pp. 1-13.
2. Four of the *lais* in *Strengleikar* do not correspond to any surviving original texts in French.
3. Budal, "The Genesis of *Strengleikar*", pp. 31-43. Budal identifies no fewer than sixteen Norwegian men with court connections who were in England during this time frame. The main manuscript of *Strengleikar*, DG 4-7, also includes *Elis saga ok Rosamundu*, a translation of the *chanson de geste*, *Élie de Sainte-Gilles*. A note in *Elis saga* attributes the translation to "Abbot Robert," but there is no reason to assume that the same Abbot Robert translated the *Strengleikar*, or even that all the *Strengleikar* were translated by one person.
4. For a handy summary of the translator's deletions and additions, see Jacobs, "Crossing Cultures".
5. Two of the missing leaves were discovered in 1703, having been cut up and used to stiffen an Icelandic bishop's miter. They are now conserved as AM 666b 4°. See Cook and Tveitane, *Strengleikar*, pp. ix-x, for an overview of the manuscript.
6. Larrington, "Translated *Lais*", p. 79. The manuscript is Lbs. 840 4to.
7. For a thorough overview, see Aðalheiður Guðmundsdóttir, "*Strengleikar* in Iceland". Marie's *Eliduc* is not in the surviving manuscript of *Strengleikar* but may have been known in Iceland, because an episode in *Völsunga saga* seems to have been borrowed from it. (Clover, "*Völsunga saga* and the Missing Lai of Marie de France"; although see Aðalheiður Guðmundsdóttir, "*Strengleikar* in Iceland", pp. 125-126). *Lanval* (*Januals ljóð*) is apparently a source for *Helgis þáttr Þórissonar* (this volume). A version of *Bisclaret* that was independent of the existing text was rewritten as *Tiódels saga.*

8. Other examples include Pwyll and Rhiannon in the *Mabinogion*, the Irish *Aidead Muirchertag maic Erca* ("Death of Muirchertach mac Erca") and *Noinden Ulad* ("Nine Days' Sickness of the Ulstermen"), as well as the Breton *lais* of *Desiré*, *Grælent*, and *Guingamor.* (Cross, "Celtic Elements") One might also add the myth of Aphrodite and Anchises. Compare motif C31.5, "Tabu: boasting of supernatural wife", in Stith Thompson, *Motif-Index*, vol. 1, p. 490.
9. The text has *i syðra brætlande*, "in the farther-south Britain".
10. The original has Marie proposing to translate from Latin into French; this is probably a translator's error, although it has been suggested that the word *bókmál* or "book-language", usually translated as "Latin", might mean some other language in this passage. (Cook and Tveitane, *Strengleikar*, p. xix)
11. The king is presumably Henry II of England (ruled 1154–1189), although it could have been his son, Henry "the Young King", who was titular king from 1170 to 1183, although he never ruled in his own right.
12. The alliterative "courteous clerks and mannerly men" (*kurtæisom klærkom ok hæverskom hirðmonnom*) does not correspond to anything in the original French, and is an example of the typically Norse device of alliteration, probably used here by the translator to convey a "higher", more poetic style.
13. The name appears as *Bisclavret* in the French text, and is probably Breton. The first syllable is derived from *bleiz* or *bleid*, "wolf". The rest of the name may come from *laveret*, "rational; capable of speech"; *claff*, "sick"; or *claffret*, "false". (Mickel, "Marie de France and the Learned Tradition", p. 34)
14. The original text gives the Norman French name *garwaf*; the Norse translator has replaced this with a Norse equivalent, *vargúlfr*. *Vargr* and *úlfr* both could be used for the wolf as a natural animal, but *vargr* also meant a human outcast, outlawed for especially heinous crimes (Gerstein, "Germanic *Warg*", pp. 137-139; Higley, "Finding the Man Under the Skin," pp. 352-358).
15. This was actually a contentious point in the Middle Ages: could a man literally transform into an animal? The general opinion of theologians, beginning with Augustine (*De Civitate Dei* 18.17; transl. Sanford and Green, vol. 5, pp. 422-425), was that a human could not change himself into a wolf, or be changed into a wolf; at best, demons might create the illusion of a man becoming a wolf. Burchard of Worms considered it heretical to believe that "the Divine Image [the human body] can be turned by somebody into another form or species—except by God omnipotent". (Higley, "Finding the Man Under the Skin", pp. 342-345). It's interesting that both Marie de France and her translator never dispute that Bisclaret really becomes a wolf; this would have been a heretical position outside of the fictional world. Nor do they blame demonic forces for the transformation; Bisclaret's lycathropy is uncanny, but he himself is not evil or demonic. This sympathetic view of werewolves is common to several courtly stories from 12th century Britain and Brittany (Aðalheiður Guðmundsdóttir, "The Werewolf in Medieval Icelandic Literature," pp. 292-294).
16. In the original, Bisclavret tears off his wife's nose. The translator may have felt that public nakedness was a more shameful punishment than mutilation.
17. The translator has for some reason substituted *ástsemð*, "love, affection", for *destrece*, "compulsion; distress": compare Norse *sakar astsemdar oc ognar konongs*, "for love and

fear of the king" with French *tant par destrece e par poür*, "as much from compulsion as from fear" (line 265; ed. Ewert, *Lais*, p. 55). I've followed Aðalheiður Guðmundsdóttir's suggestion that her love is for her new husband who is being held hostage. (*Strengleikar*, p. 95 n176)

18. The translator has retained the original text's claim that the faithless wife's female descendants were born with no nose, even though the point of this claim is now missing.
19. This brief personal note from the translator, the only such note in *Strengleikar*, is evidence for the folk belief in werewolves. Men transforming into wolves are widespread in Icelandic literature; the motif appears in *Völsunga saga* and Eddic poetry, where it appears to be very old (Aðalheiður Guðmundsdóttir, "The Werewolf in Medieval Icelandic Literature," pp. 284-288).
20. The name of the nightingale in old Breton is *austic* (modern Breton *eostig*; cf. Welsh *eos*). The initial *l* resulted from combining the Breton word with the French definite article: *l'austic*. (Burgess, "Introduction", *Lais*, p.xi)
21. The last two sentences have been added by the Norse translator, presumably because nightingales are not native to Norway or Iceland. A French or English audience would not need to be told what a nightingale is.
22. Saint Malo (also Maloù or Maclou) was one of seven missionaries who came from Wales in the 7th century and founded dioceses in Brittany. The French text refers only to the district of Saint-Malo (*En Seint Mallo en la cuntree / ot une vile renumee*; lines 7-8, ed. Ewert, *Lais*, p. 97); the Norse translator evidently took "Saint Malo" to refer to the saint, not the city.
23. A brief section describing the knight's prowess, and another brief section describing the lovers' homes, have been omitted by the translator. In general, this lay seems to contain more brief deletions compared to the French text than the other lays in *Strengleikar.*
24. The Norse translator has left out a few lines that describe the nightingale's fate explicitly. When the lady begs for the nightingale's life, the lord breaks the nightingale's neck before throwing it at her: *E il l'ocist par engresté / Le col li rumpt a ses deus meins / De ceo fist il que trop vileins*; "And he killed it by violence; he broke the neck with both hands; what he did was too base." (lines 114-116; ed. Ewert, *Lais*, p. 100)
25. *Chefrefuill* (modern French *Chèvrefeuille*) is the word for the honeysuckle—the Norse translator has made a rare mistake and attached the Norse definite article *–inn* to the French name. Marie calqued the English translation as *Gotelef*, "goat-leaf", and the Norse translator followed her lead and calqued the Norse name as *Geitarlauf.* The text of the lay uses the usual Norse word for the honeysuckle, *viðvindill*, cognate with Middle English *wodewinde.*
26. Depending on how it is punctuated, the French text could read either "This was the gist of the message he had sent her: he had been there a long time. . ." or "That was all he wrote, because he had sent her word that he had been there a long time. . ." In other words, the French is unclear as to whether or not Tristram carves that he has been waiting for a long time. (Burgess and Busby, *The Lais of Marie de France*, p. 127 n1; Kalinke, "Norse Romance," p. 346) The Norse text is unambiguous: Tristram does carve this longer message.
27. The first quarter of *Janual* is missing from the manuscript. It has been restored here from lines 1-156 of the Old French text (Ewert, *Lais*, pp. 58-62). I have substituted the

Norse name *Janual* for the French name *Lanval* to maintain consistency throughout. Bullock-Davies points out that the name *Lanval* resembles the name of a Celtic god, *Lanovalus*, known from inscriptions from southeastern France; the name would mean something like "powerful in full flow" and apply to a river god. Given that Lanval's encounter with his lover takes place beside a river, it is perhaps just possible that this *lai* might preserve a fragment of a Celtic myth. ("Lanval and Avalon", pp. 131-133)

28. Semiramis was a legendary queen of Assyria, famous both for her military leadership and for her alleged luxury and sensuality. (Diodoris Siculus, *Library of History* II:4-20; transl. Oldfather, pp. 357-419)
29. Octavian is better known as Augustus, the first Roman emperor.
30. The surviving Norse text begins at this point.
31. The French text has *n'i ot estrange ne privé*, "there was no stranger nor close friend" (line 213; ed. Ewert, *Lais*, p. 63). While *estrange* in French can mean "outsider; stranger" or "foreigner", the Norse translator has specifically chosen "foreigner" (*útlenzcr*). The translator may also have read *privé* as "deprived" and interpreted it as one deprived of speech (*mallaus*, "speech-less").
32. St. John's Eve is the evening before June 24, on or very close to the summer solstice. St. John's Day is traditionally a day for games, dances, plays, and other outdoor celebrations. (Clopper, "Midsummer", pp. 662-663)
33. I have substituted the more familiar names Gawain and Ywain for Norse *Valvein* and *Ivein*.
34. The translator has deleted a sizable section of the original here (lines 433-468, ed. Ewert, *Lais*, pp. 69-70), in which the Count of Cornwall rules that Janual must be pardoned—if he can bring his lady into court and prove that she is fairer than the queen. Janual is told this ruling, but is unable to produce his lover. Compare motif M55, "Judgment: pardon given if hero produces the lady about whom he has boasted", in Stith Thompson, *Motif-Index*, vol. 5, p. 29.
35. The French text has the ladies riding *deus muls espanneis*, "two Spanish mules" (line 512; ed. Ewert, *Lais*, p. 71).
36. At this point in the French text, Ywain's knights point out the ladies to Lanval, who replies that he has no idea who they are (lines 519-526). This is a repetition of what Gawain and his knights have already done, and thus the translator may have seen fit to omit it.
37. The original text of *Lanval* includes a sizable passage (lines 555-572, ed. Ewert, *Lais*, p. 72) describing the lady's beauty here; the Norse translator has left it out, stating later that "there is no need to describe her beauty and refinement beyond what has already been said."
38. The standard French text (580) has *Ele veneit meins que le pas*, "She came at a slower pace", but alternate manuscripts have *plus que le pas*, "at a faster pace." The translator's text evidently had this alternate reading. (Cook and Tveitane, *Strengleikar*, pp. 224-225 n8)
39. The French (618-619) has *ne vueil mie qu'a mal li turt, / de ceo qu'il dist*; "I do not want him to suffer for what he said."
40. These last two sentences were inserted by the translator. Expressions like "Thanks to those who listened" are very common in the Icelandic sagas.

The Saga of Halfdan, Son of Eystein

1. Driscoll and Hufnagel, "Stories for All Time: The Icelandic *Fornaldarsögur.*"
2. Saeming is mentioned in Snorri Sturluson's *Prose Edda* as a son of Odin, appointed by Odin as the first ruler of Norway (*Prologue* 10; ed. Faulkes, p. 6). *Ynglingasaga* 8 in *Heimskringla* adds that he was the son of Odin and the giantess Skadi (transl. Hollander, p. 12).
3. *Hrómundar saga Grípssonar* 5 (transl. Waggoner, *Six Sagas*, p. 246) gives the sisters' names as Svanhvit and Dagny.
4. Eirek the Far-Traveler is the subject of *Eireks saga víðförla*, included in this book.
5. Sigurd Hart is mentioned in *Ragnarssona þáttr* 5 (transl. Waggoner, *The Sagas of Ragnar Lodbrok*, p. 75) and in *Saga Hálfdanar svarta* 5 in *Heimskringla* (transl. Hollander, p. 54), which confirm his ancestry as given here. Sigurd Snake-in-the-Eye is one of the sons of the legendary Ragnar Lodbrok.
6. Bjarmaland is the coast of the White Sea in present-day Russia. Several Norse voyages to Bjarmaland are attested in historical documents. In the legendary sagas, Bjarmaland is generally a rich place to plunder, but also the home of monsters and dangerous magic. See Hofstra and Samplonius, "Viking Expansion Northward," pp. 244-245.
7. Gold-Thorir has a saga of his own, alternately titled *Gull-Þóris saga* and *Þorskfirðinga saga*; he allegedly made a voyage to the far North and won a great treasure (*CSI* III:335-359). *Landnámabók* (the *Book of the Settlement of Iceland*) mentions him and his father (S114/H86, ed. Jakob Benediktsson, p. 154).
8. Tatjana Jackson identified *Álaborg* with the archaeological site of Gorodishche on the Syas River, settled around 700 and abandoned around 930. *Áluborg*, presumably a variant spelling of the same site, is mentioned in *Hrólfs saga Gautrekssonar* 3, 30 (transl. Waggoner, *Six Sagas*, pp. 176, 217). In both sagas, Alaborg is a rival of *Aldeigjuborg*, which is Ladoga. (Reviewed in Machinskijn and Pankratova, "Severnaja Rus' i Sagi o Drevnikh Vremenakh," pp. 23-26.)
9. A proverb (*bætr liggja til alls*) also found in *Örvar-Odds saga* 2 (transl. Waggoner, *The Hrafnista Sagas*, p. 47) and *Hrólfs saga Gautrekssonar* 19 (transl. Waggoner, *Six Sagas*, p. 72)
10. The Norse place name is *Bálagarðssíða*, "the coast of 'Bala-enclosure'", which is also mentioned in *Víkingarvísur* ("Viking Verses") by the skald Sigvatr Þórðarson, quoted in *Óláfs saga helga* 9 in *Heimskringla* (transl. Hollander, p. 250). The saga and the poem both imply that *Bálagarðssíða* is in Finland, and it's usually thought to lie on the southwest coast of Finland, which would place it close to the action in this saga; however, the *Legendary Saga of St. Olaf* places *Bálagarðssíða* in Zealand, the largest island in Denmark. (Jesch, "Sigvatr Þórðarson, *Víkingarvísur* 3", p. 537)
11. People in the sagas who are traveling incognito often give their names as *Grímr*, "hooded man; masked man". The name is related to the word *gríma*, "cowl; deep hood".
12. The ball game is called *knattleikr*; its exact rules are not known, but from descriptions in other sagas it seems to have been a ball-and-stick game similar to, and possibly derived from, Irish hurling. See Gunnell, "The Relationship Between Icelandic *Knattleikur* and Early Irish Hurling"; also Thurber, "The Viking Ball Game", pp. 170-184.

13. This seems to be a type of magical compulsion known in other sagas as an *álög*, although the word is not used here. See *Sörla þáttr*, this volume, note 9.
14. These are appropriate false names. *Vígfúss* means "eager to kill"; *Ófeigr* means "unafraid."
15. *Krakunes* means "Cape Crow" or "Crow Point"; its location in this saga has not been determined.
16. The significance of the name "Little Bag" (*böggull*) is unclear, but in several sagas, bags hold magic charms (e.g. *Kormáks saga* 9, 12). The implication may be that Ivar is a sorceror.
17. *Hlynskógr* means "Maple Forest"; *Klyfandanes* means "Division Cape". Although the action is supposedly taking place in northernmost Scandinavia and Russia, Boris Kleiber pointed out that maples do not grow north of 61°N. He suggested that the saga describes travel over a portage route from Lake Ladoga via the Svir' River to Lake Onega, and from there over to the White Sea, more or less following the route of the White Sea Canal. He identified *Hlynskógr* with a Russian village called *Klenovaja* ("Maple"), 10 km northeast of Vytegra and within the limits of maple growth. *Klyfandanes* may be the Andoma Ridge, a local high point 25 km northeast of Klenovaja that divides the Baltic and White Sea watersheds. ("Zu einigen Ortsnamen aus Gardarike", pp. 219-220)
18. The motif of the poor man or couple who nurse the hero back to health appears in several legendary sagas (e.g. *Hálfs saga* 14, this volume, p. 20; *Hrómundar saga Grípssonar* 7, transl. Waggoner, *Six Sagas*, p. 249; *Áns saga bogsveigis* 7, transl. Waggoner, *The Hrafnista Sagas*, pp. 181-182). *Hriflingr* means a rawhide shoe, commonly worn by poor laborers (cognate with the archaic English word *rivelin* for such a shoe). *Arghyrna* means something like "cowardly-horned"; it appears as a poetic name for an axe (Snorri Sturluson, *Skáldskaparmál* 74, verse 463; ed. Faulkes, *Edda*, p. 121). Many axe-names are also names for female giants, and the implication may be that Arghyrna is a troll herself, or else looks like one—not unlike calling s "that old battle-axe".
19. An untranslatable pun: the word translated "wretched existence" is *hriflingabjörg*, literaslly meaning "subsistence by means of rawhide shoes" and also punning on Hrifling's name.
20. An expression also used in *Óláfs saga helga* 125 in *Heimskringla* (transl. Hollander, p. 395); the sense is "many would find it difficult to escape from the disaster that would result."
21. In the sagas, the *Finnar* are not Finns in the modern sense, but Saami, or "Lapps", reindeer-herding nomads. "Finns" in the sagas have a reputation for wielding powerful and dangerous magic.
22. The word translated "league" is *röst*, etymologically related to "rest" and meaning the distance a man would typically walk before taking a rest. It was approximately three miles, but the length varied with terrain, being shorter in difficult country. (Cleasby and Vigfusson, *Dictionary*, p. 508)
23. Kol's name, *Kolr*, is derived from the word for "coal", presumably alluding to a swarthy complexion. The name often appears in the sagas for swarthy, often violent or sinister characters (e.g. *Vilmundar saga* 2, this volume, p. 288 note 9; see Jesch, "Race and Ethnicity," p. 87). *Kolsskog* means "Kol's Forest". His daughter's name, Gullkula, means "gold ball".
24. Kol and his daughter have become *draugar*, undead revenants. Unlike the stereotype

of zombies, *draugar* in the sagas do not lose their strength, intelligence, or coordination, and fight as effectively as they did in life, if not more so.

25. There's a similar dog-taming scene, with a double-pointed stick used as a gag, in the tale *Ásmundar saga flagðagæfu*, based on a lost saga (transl. Waggoner, *Sagas of Giants*, p. 156). A sword is used as a similar gag on the wolf Fenrir in the myth of Fenrir's binding (Snorri Sturluson, *Gylfaginning* 34, *Edda*; ed. Faulkes, p. 29)
26. Sorcerous villains shapeshift into walruses in the "saga of Icelanders" *Kórmaks saga* 18 (*CSI* I:208) and in the legendary *Hjálmþes saga ok Ölvis* 11 (transl. O'Connor, *Icelandic Histories and Romances*, pp. 164-166).
27. It's tempting to identify this scene as a borrowing from the description of the *hidrus* in the *Physiologus* (this volume, p. 108).
28. The ability to blow weapons out of an opponent's hands is a fairly common skill for sorcerous villains in legendary sagas; see, e.g. *Göngu-Hrólfs saga* 3, *Hrómundar saga Grípssonar* 7 (transl. Waggoner, *Six Sagas*, pp. 174, 249).
29. A character with an identical name (*Sviði sókndjarfi*) appears in *Vilmundar saga* (this volume) and its prequel, *Bósa saga ok Herrauðs* (transl. Waggoner, *Six Sagas*, p. 134). A third *Sviði sókndjarfi* appears in *Illuga saga Gríðarfóstra* (Waggoner, *Sagas of Giants and Heroes*, p. 142). In the saga texts as we have them, these three Sviðis have contradictory biographies and do not appear to be the same person.
30. Hrolf the Walker, *Göngu-Hrólfr*, is the hero of a long legendary saga of his own (transl. Waggoner, *Six Sagas*, pp. 169-240). He is not the same as the historically attested *Göngu-Hrólfr* or Rollo who became the first Viking ruler of Normandy.
31. According to *Heimskringla* (*Óláfs saga helga* 96, transl. Hollander, pp. 350-351), *Eysteinn glumra*, Eystein Rattler or Eystein the Noisy, was a petty king in western Norway, whose son Sigurd became the first jarl of the Orkney Islands; however, in *Flateyjarbók* 178 (ed. Vigfússon and Unger, p. 221) he is said to be the son of Ivar the jarl of Uppland, and Halfdan is not mentioned. A man named Thorir Hart (*Þórir hjörtr*) is described in *Heimskringla* as resisting Olaf Tryggvason's missionary activities in northern Norway (*Óláfs saga Tryggvassonar* 78, transl. Hollander, pp. 212-213), but as he would have lived over 100 years after Eystein Rattler, either he is not the same as Halfdan's son, or the saga writer has committed an anachronism (and not the first).
32. As noted earlier, Odd the Showy and his settling in Iceland is briefly described in *Landnamabók* (S114/H86, ed. Jakob Benediktsson, p. 154).
33. The *Long Serpent* (*Ormr inn langi*) was King Olaf Tryggvason's flagship, allegedly built with 34 pairs of oars.
34. Norse *Helluland*, "rock slab land". In the Vinland sagas this land is said to lie along the sailing route from Greenland to Vinland; it has been identified as the east coast of Baffin Island.
35. Val hid a great hoard of treasure in the Arctic and turned into a flying dragon to guard it; his story is told in *Gull-Þóris saga.*
36. *Köttr* and *Kisi* mean "cat" and "kitty", more or less. As noted in *Hálfs saga ok Hálfsrekka* (this volume), there are several instances of paired warriors, usually brothers, given names of related animals or birds. This saga may be poking fun at this tradition with Kott and Kisi, and with Hauk and Gauk (see below).
37. It was believed that there was a "land bridge" across the northernmost parts of the known

world connecting Russia with Greenland—this is how a mountain could be "north of the Arctic Ocean." (See *Geography*, this book, p. 101; also Hofstra and Samplonius, "Viking Expansion Northwards," p. 245.) On the other hand, *Gull-Þóris saga* places the mountain Blesavergr in Finnmark (northernmost Scandinavia). Svadi the son of Thor is also mentioned in *Bárðar saga snæfellsáss* 2 (*CSI* II:239).

38. *Hornhjalti* means "horn hilt".
39. *Haukr* and *Gaukr* mean "hawk" and "cuckoo."
40. This may be inspired by an event in *Jómsvíkinga saga* 21, in which the wounded Viking Bui leaps overboard in the middle of a battle, holding two chests of gold (transl. Hollander, *Saga of the Jómsvíkings*, pp. 102-103). Like Val, Bui allegedly turned into a dragon on his gold (*Jómsvíkinga saga* 24, transl. Hollander, p. 115).
41. Both Agnar in the mound and Val and his sons turned into dragons appear in *Gull-Þóris saga*, although Agnar's parentage is different in that saga. Agnar's father Raknar appears as an undead mound-dweller in *Bárðar saga Snæfellsáss* 18-20 (*CSI* II:261-265).

The Saga of Samson the Fair

1. In AM 343a and most older manuscripts, her name is Filipia or Phillippia.
2. Vilhjálmsson's text and AM 181b describe the dance as being held *vel ok kurteisliga*, "well and courteously"; this may be an accidental scribal repetition of the same phrase used a few lines above (Wilson, *Samsons Saga Fagra*, p. 3 line 7). I have emended the text to follow AM 343a.
3. AM 343a gives her name as *Ingiam.*
4. *Galinn* literally means "bewitched, enchanted", but often has the sense of "crazy."
5. The word translated "ogress" is *gyðja*, literally "[pagan] priestess". This could be a mistake for *gygr*, "ogre", but it could also be an example of an originally pagan concept becoming monstrous. The motif of a miller making a pact with a water-spirit in the millstream that allows the spirit to capture innocent people is common in European folklore (e.g. "The Nix of the Mill-Pond", type 316 in Aarne, *Types of the Folktale*, p. 111; see also Ivanits, *Russian Folk Belief*, p. 73).
6. AM 181b just has *stolpann*, "the pillar". AM 343a has *sængurstolpann*, "the bed-pillar." I'm not quite sure what this is and have assumed it's a bedpost.
7. This episode, and the preceding episode with the greyhound, are both borrowings of Æsop's fable "The House-Ferret and Aphrodite", more commonly known as "Venus and the Cat" (transl. Temple and Temple, *The Complete Fables*, #76, p. 62). The origin of the cat's tail stripes seems out of place and is probably a borrowed motif; there are many tales that explain how an animal got the type of tail that it has (e.g. A2378.8, "Origin of color of animal's tail", Thompson, *Motif-Index*, p. 297)
8. In AM 343a, Samson pays sixty marks.
9. The underwater fight against the female ogre parallels Beowulf's fight with Grendel's mother, including details such as the water turning bloody and the discovery of a cave filled with treasures. Variants of this episode are widespread in the legendary sagas. (Stitt, *Beowulf and the Bear's Son*, pp. 98-100)
10. A commonplace of Norse legend is that dwarves live inside stones and can pass into them and out of them (e.g. *Sörla þáttr* 1, this volume, p. 57; *Ynglinga saga* 12, transl.

Hollander, *Heimskringla*, pp. 15-16). *Áns saga bogsveigis* 1 includes the motif of a human blocking a dwarf from entering his stone until the dwarf promises a favor (transl. Waggoner, *The Hrafnista Sagas*, p. 161). The name Grelant, on the other hand, may have been borrowed from the anonymous Breton *lai* translated as *Grelent* in the *Strengleikar* collection. (Aðalheiður Guðmundsdóttir, "*Strengleikar* in Iceland", p. 124)

11. Vilhjálmsson's text has *með undarlegum hagleik og hjálmi*, "with wondrous skill and a helmet", although the helmet is never mentioned again. AM 343a has *med undarligum hagleik. Rann hun a hiolum*, "with wondrous skill; it ran on wheels". I assume that *hjálmi* is an error for *hjólum*.
12. The section of Chapter 9 from the beginning to this point is placed after the section from this point to the end of Chapter 9 in the older manuscripts.
13. The motif of the hero pursuing an uncatchable stag appears in several legendary sagas (*Göngu-Hrólfs saga* 15; *Gautreks saga* 1; *Hjálmþes saga ok Ölvis* 9; see Waggoner, *Six Sagas*, pp. 284-285, n20-21). The motif is probably borrowed from Arthurian or other Celtic sources; several of the *lais* known in Norse translation as *Strengleikar* include it, notably *Grelent* and *Guiamar*. (Aðalheiður Guðmundsdóttir, "*Strengleikar* in Iceland", p. 129) Usually, the stag leads the hunter to the Otherworld; however, the motif is being burlesqued here, since Samson does not reach the magical Otherworld but instead falls into a trap. (See also Thompson, *Motif-Index*, F159.1, "Otherworld reached by hunting animal", vol. 3, p. 27; N774, "Adventures from pursuing enchanted animal", vol. 5, pp. 130-131).
14. The cart may have been borrowed from Chrétien de Troye's *Lancelot*, in which Lancelot is forced to ride in a cart driven by an ugly dwarf, on his way to rescue the abducted Guinevere. (Kalinké, *The Arthur of the North*, p. 161)
15. Aside from its comic value, this strike to the buttocks has further significance. In Norse legal codes, the word for a strike on the buttocks was *klámhögg*, "foul blow" or "shaming-stroke". It was disgraceful for a man to receive one, because it symbolically "womanized" him. Law codes ranked the *klámhögg* as equal to castration in severity. (Meulengracht Sørensen, *The Unmanly Man*, pp. 68-70)
16. In the legendary sagas, dwarves allied with the villains can often be quickly persuaded by threats of violence to switch sides (e.g. *Göngu-Hrólfs saga* 25, transl. Waggoner, *Six Sagas*, p. 209).
17. AM 343a has *ok syndizt þa vera ein mær su hin vonda gygr*, "and then that wicked ogress appeared to be a maiden."
18. *Glæsisvellir* means "amber plains" and appears in several legendary sagas as a land in or on the border of Jötunheimr, the land of giants.
19. *Risaland* and *Jötunheimr* both mean "land of giants"; *risar* and *jötnar* both mean giants. The words are often used more or less interchangeably, but Lotte Motz points out that the word *jötnar* tends to refer to giants in the sense of huge beings associated with wild nature, while *risar* is a relatively rare word ("Families of Giants", pp. 218-222, 235). Several legendary sagas mention specifically that *risar* are more attractive and more civilized than other giants (Waggoner, *Sagas of Giants and Heroes*, pp. xv-xvi).
20. The discovery of *Svalbarði* is mentioned in Icelandic annals for the year 1194; however, the land discovered is more likely to have been Jan Mayen, not the island called Svalbard today, formerly Spitsbergen (Hofstra and Samplonius, "Viking Expansion Northwards",

pp. 236-238). Several sources suggest that the Norse believed in a land bridge across the northern Arctic, connecting Bjarmaland (the White Sea region of present-day Russia) with Greenland. (See *Geography*, this book, p. 101; *Hálfdanar saga Eysteinssonar*, this book, p. 250 note 37; also Hofstra and Samplonius, "Viking Expansion Northward, p. 245.)

21. Short-lived people are one of the "Plinian races"; they may have been borrowed from Isidore of Seville, who places them in India and has them living to the age of eight and bearing children at the age of five (*Etymologies* XI.iii.27; transl. Barney et al., p. 245). Tribes of exceptionally long-lived people who rarely have children are also commonly found among the "Plinian races"; see "The Nations of Giants", this volume, p. 116.
22. "Trolls take it!" is a common idiom expressing frustration or exasperation, similar to "Damn it!" or "Devil take it!"
23. The motif of cooks finding a beautiful woman while they are on land cooking food, and bringing her back to their king on his ship, may have been borrowed from *Ragnars saga Loðbrókar* 5 (transl. Waggoner, *Sagas of Ragnar Lodbrok*, pp. 8-9).
24. Under pre-Christian law codes, deformed, illegitimate, or otherwise unwanted infants could be abandoned in the wilderness to die of exposure (*útburðr*, "carrying out"). The trope of an abandoned infant growing up to be a mighty warrior, often after rescue by a poor peasant couple, is fairly common in the sagas of Icelanders and legendary sagas (e.g. *Vatnsdæla saga* 37, *CSI* III:49; *Þórsteins saga uxafóts* 4-5, *CSI* IV:343-344; *Finnboga saga ramma* 2-3, *CSI* III:222-223; *Ála flekks saga* 2, transl. Bachman and Erlingsson, *Six Old Icelandic Sagas*, p. 44), as it is in world history and legend (e.g. Moses, Sargon of Akkad, Oedipus).
25. Both names mean "crooked", more or less—implying that their owners are hunchbacked or otherwise deformed.
26. All texts have *Þau voru rík*, "they were powerful", but Wilson suggests this might be a scribal error for **Þau voru órík*, "they were weak" (*Samsons saga fagra* p. 33 n10).
27. The pun relies on the similarity between *Sigurðr* and *suga*, a cake made for babies to suck on. The *suga* and the pun are not found in AM 343a or AM 181b.
28. In legendary sagas, powerful or ruling giants are often named Skrimnir, or seemingly related names (Skram, Skrýmir); e.g. *Sörla saga sterka* 2-4; *Jökuls þáttr Búasonar* 3 (transl. Waggoner, *Sagas of Giants and Heroes* pp. 59-60, 117); Snorri Sturluson, *Gylfaginning* 45-47, *Edda* (ed. Faulkes, pp. 37-43). The name is probably related to words for "monster", e.g. Icelandic *skrimsl* (McKinnell, *Meeting the Other*, p. 245 n22).
29. The text has *álfkonur*, "elf-women". Terms for supernatural beings are often used interchangeably in Norse.
30. Literally, "You aren't from our country" (*ekki ertu af voru landi*).
31. In AM 343a and AM 181b, Sigurd is invited to come when he leaves Skrymir.
32. Vilhjálmsson's text has *Bjarmaland, Kirjaland* (Karelia, east of Finland proper) *og Smálönd* (the "Small Lands", present-day Småland in Sweden). AM 343a has *Biarmaland ok Kwrland* (Courland, in present-day Latvia) *ok Samland* (Sambia, on the Baltic coast of the present-day Kaliningrad region).
33. No saga of Sigurd Hring has survived, but he is mentioned in Saxo's *Danish History* and in *Sögubrot*, a saga fragment that may have been part of the lost *Skjöldunga saga* (transl. Waggoner, *Sagas of Ragnar Lodbrok*, pp. 52-58). Ulfhedin is not mentioned in

the surviving *Sögubrot.* His name, meaning "Wolf-Skin", is used elsewhere for a type of berserk warrior (Lindow, *Norse Mythology*, p. 76). In *Þorsteins þáttr bæjarmagns* 5, it is said that every ruler of Glæsisvellir takes the named Godmund, and that a previous ruler was named Ulfhedin before taking the throne and the name Godmund (transl. Pálsson and Edwards, *Seven Viking Romances*, p. 264).

34. Jarl Agdi of Gnipaland or Gnipalund appears in *Þorsteins þáttr bæjarmagns* 5-13 (transl. Pálsson and Edwards, *Seven Viking Romances*, p. 265-275).

35. *Geirröðargarðar*, "Geirrod's Towns", appears in *Þorsteins þáttr bæjarmagns* and in Snorri Sturluson's *Edda* (*Skáldskaparmál* 18, ed. Faulkes, pp. 24-25), although in these instances Geirrod is alive and Geirrodargardar is his home.

36. The giant is called *Aper* in MS 343a; a giant by that name also appears in *Valdimars saga* (McKinnell, *Meeting the Other*, p. 188). However, a giant named Asprian appears in *Þiðreks saga* and its German sources, and it's possible that *Þiðreks saga* suggested this name, among others, to the writer of *Samsons saga.* In either case, the names show evidence of Latin learning: *Aper* means "wild boar", whereas *Asper* means "rough; severe; savage". Either name would be fitting for a giant.

37. This sentence follows AM 343a (Wilson, p. 43); Vilhjálmsson's edition has *Fóru menn á skóg að fá perur og plummur*, "Men went to the forest to get pears and plums"; this may be haplography, with the writer accidentally skipping words between two identical phrases.

38. AM 343a is much more direct: *þa hun var sordin,* "when she was fucked."

39. Note that this thief-detecting property of the mantle does not appear in *Möttuls saga*, where the mantle only reveals infidelity.

40. The mantle has been said to fall off a thief. It may not fall off here because Kvintelin is disguised as a woman (Kalinke, *King Arthur North-by-Northwest*, p. 225).

41. *Rúðuborg* is the name of Rouen, France in both the sagas and in modern Icelandic. I have not been able to find a Norse placename in Ireland that could have been turned into *Rúðuborg* by a plausible scribal error. It is possible that the *Rúðu-* is related to Irish *ráth*, "fort; rampart"; *Rúðuborg* would then mean "Fort Fort", more or less.

42. *Myrkjol* is also not identifiable as a place in Ireland. The name looks like the Norse root *myrk-*, "dark; darkness", or possibly *mýrr*, "swamp; marsh".

43. Walter the Duke of Holstein and his wife Gertrude are the parents of Baering, the eponymous hero of *Bærings saga* (Cederschiöld, *Fornsögur Suðrlanda*, pp. 85-123). *Bærings saga* dates to the early 14th century, and is thus one of the earliest original Icelandic chivalric romances. (Glauser, "Bærings saga", p. 60)

44. *Sigurðar saga þögla* 15 mentions that the elder Sigurd, Samson's son-in-law, was known as *Mánaleggr*, "Moon-Leg". His grandson Sigurd, son of Ulf and called *hinn frækna,* "the Bold", fought Blót-Haraldr (Harald the Sacrificer) of Greece, "as is told in the Saga of Cecilia the Fair (*Saga Seciliu hinnar vænu*), daughter of King Svein of Sicily." (ed. Bjarni Vilhjálmsson, *Riddarasögur*, vol. 3, p. 144) This saga of Cecilia does not seem to exist today, at least under that title.

45. His name is *Gujmar* in AM 343a, which could have been borrowed from *Guimar* or *Guiamar*, a lay in *Strengleikar* (*Guigemar* in French). *Grímar*, however, is related to *Gríma*, "cowl; mask"; names like Grímr are common for characters who conceal their identities (see *Hálfdanar saga Eysteinssonar* 7, note 11).

The Saga of Vilmund the Outsider

1. McKinnell, *Meeting the Other*, pp. 188-189.
2. McKinnell, *Meeting the Other*, pp. 126-127, 188-190.
3. Loth, ed. *Late Medieval Icelandic Romances*, vol. IV, pp. 139-201.
4. *Vissevaldr* is the Norse version of the Slavic name *Vsevolod*, "all-ruler." There were several medieval Russian princes of that name, but none can be identified with the saga king.
5. The manuscript has *skarefifel* (normalized *skarififill*), the autumn hawkbit, *Scorzoneroides autumnalis*. This plant is noted for its bright yellow, dandelion-like flowers. (Heizmann, *Wörterbuch der Pflanzennamen*, p. 58)
6. *Sóley*, originally *sól-eyg* or "sun-eye", is the name for buttercups (*Ranunculus* spp.; in Iceland, this would be either *R. acris* or *R. repens*). (Heizmann, *Wörterbuch der Pflanzennamen*, p. 59)
7. *Gullbrá*, literally "gold-brow" or "gold-eyelid". This name is used in modern Icelandic to translate "Goldilocks". It is also a name for *Saxifraga hirculus*, marsh saxifrage (Heizmann, *Wörterbuch der Pflanzennamen*, p. 76). Like buttercups and hawkbit, marsh saxifrage is noted for its bright yellow flowers.
8. *Gunnvaldsborg* is named in *Heimskringla* (*Óláfs saga helga* 17; transl. Hollander, p. 257) as a castle that King Óláfr Haraldson (St. Olaf) raided, probably located in present-day Spain or Portugal. Evidently the geography is a little confused.
9. Norse *Kolr krýppa*; another instance of a swarthy, sinister character named "coal". Several *fornaldarsögur* feature hunchbacked villains with essentially synonymous names; *Kolr kroppi* in *Sturlaugs saga starfsama* 6 (transl Waggoner, *Six Sagas*, p. 139), and *Kolr kroppinbaki* in *Þorsteins saga Víkingssonar* 2-3 (transl. Waggoner, *Sagas of Fridthjof the Bold*, pp. 4-7).
10. Manuscript AM 586 has *af Einglandj* here; presumably this is a simple error.
11. The first element of the name *Öskubuska* is "ashes" (*aska*), and Oskubuska is still the Icelandic name used to translate Cinderella. This saga shares several other motifs with Cinderella fairy tales, such as the lost shoe. (Glauser, "Vilmundar saga", p. 703)
12. Norse *Viðbjóðr*, literally "disgust".
13. Norse *Ulfr illt eitt*, literally "Ulf evil only". He somewhat resembles *Úlfr inn illr*, "Ulf the Wicked", in *Hálfdanar saga Eysteinssonar* (this volume).
14. A double-pointed iron rod appears as the weapon of the trollish Harek Ironskull in *Þórsteins saga Víkingssonar* 2 (transl. Waggoner, *Sagas of Fridthjof the Bold*, p. 4).
15. Note the appearance of the same motif in *Hálfdanar saga Eysteinssonar* 5 (this volume, pp.229-230)
16. The idea that an animal may be worshipped by humans and thus turn into a monster is fairly common in the legendary sagas, although usually the animal is a cow. Examples include Sibilja the cow in *Ragnars saga loðbrókar* 9 (transl. Waggoner, *Sagas of Ragnar Lodbrok*, p. 14); *Sturlaugs saga starfsama* 22 (transl. Waggoner, *Six Sagas,* pp. 162-163); and *Bósa saga* 8 (transl. Waggoner, *Six Sagas*, p. 121).
17. Bosi is the hero of *Bósa saga ok Herrauðs*, and his saga mentions his son and grandson at the very end (transl. Waggoner, *Six Sagas*, p. 134). The father of Illugi, hero of *Illuga saga Gríðarfóstra*, is also named Svidi Bold-Attacker (*Sviði sókndjarfi*), and although his life differs in detail from the Svidi in *Vilmundar saga*, his son Illugi is raised in poverty

but exceeds the king's son Sigurd in competitive skills, and the two swear brotherhood—parallelling Vilmund and Hjarrandi in *Vilmundar saga* (Waggoner, *Sagas of Giants and Heroes*, p. 142). A character named *Sviði sókndjarfi* also appears in *Hálfdanar saga Eysteinssonar* (this volume); whether he is identical with either of the other Svidis is not clear.

18. McKinnell (*Meeting the Other*, p. 188 n16) notes that this reference to a hot spring strongly suggests that the saga was composed in Iceland.
19. At this point the main manuscript (AM 586 4°) is missing a leaf. The text is restored from two other manuscripts, AM 577 4° and GKS 1006 fol. (Loth, *Late Medieval Icelandic Romances,* vol. 4, p. 154)
20. This simile appears in, and may have been borrowed from, *Þiðreks saga* 15 (ed. Guðni Jónsson, p. 20), where it is applied to Hildibrand.
21. At this point the main manuscript (AM 586 4°) resumes. (Loth, *Late Medieval Icelandic Romances,* vol. 4, p. 159)
22. Several folk motifs are recorded in which an animal has an unusual name that is taken literally; e.g. J2462.1, "The dog Parsley in the soup"; J2493, "Names of dogs literally interpreted" (Thompson, *Motif-Index*, vol. 4, pp. 216, 220-221).
23. In legendary sagas and in later folklore, every person has a *fylgja* (literally "follower"), a sort of guardian spirit that usually takes the form of an animal whose nature is like that of the person. Kings may have "noble" *fylgjur* such as stags; warriors may have aggressive beasts such as bears or boars; villains may have foxes or dragons; and so on. It's common for dreams to foretell events by showing the *fylgjur* of the people involved. (Turville-Petre, "Dreams in Icelandic Tradition", pp. 37-39) Similar dreams to this one include *Hrólfs saga Gautrekssonar* 7, 12 (transl. Waggoner, *Six Sagas*, pp. 47, 56-57) and *Hálfdanar saga Brönufóstra* 1 (transl. Waggoner, *Sagas of Giants and Heroes*, pp. 88-89)
24. In the sagas and later folklore, a shapeshifted person can be recognized by his or her eyes. (*Ketils saga hængs* 3, transl. Waggoner, *The Hrafnista Sagas* p. 9; *Kormaks saga* 18, *CSI* I:208; *Ála flekks saga* 10, transl. Bachmann and Erlingson, *Six Old Icelandic Sagas*, p. 51).
25. Usually in the legendary sagas, fighters who stamp or push so hard that they sink into the earth are giants or supernatural beings (e.g. *Sörla saga sterka* 3, transl. Waggoner, *Sagas of Giants*, p. 116; *Göngu-Hrólfs saga* 31, 33, transl. Waggoner, *Six Sagas*, p. 221, 226).
26. It's common in the legendary sagas for a hero to defeat a villain at wrestling by breaking him over a stone or sharp edge. Examples include *Sturlaugs saga starfsama* 12 (transl. Waggoner, *Six Sagas*, p. 146); *Áns saga bogsveigis* 5 (transl. Waggoner, *The Hrafnista Sagas*, p. 174); *Kjalnesinga saga* 15, 18 (transl. Waggoner, *Sagas of Giants and Heroes* p. 46-47, 51).
27. Hjarrandi's stone weighs one *skippund* or "ship pound", a measure of weight commonly used for cargo. The *skippund* was approximately 160 kg, over 350 pounds. Twelve *skippundar* made one *lest*, which was about the maximum load that a ship could carry.
28. The unit translated "yard" here is *stikr*, equal to two ells. The precise length of the ell varied from place to place and also changed over time, but was approximately between eighteen inches and two feet.
29. A very common form of swimming contest was "competitive dunking", in which

competitors tried to hold each other under the water.

30. Several saga heroes fight bears (e.g. *Grettis saga* 21, *CSI* II:83-85), but this episode resembles one in *Finnboga saga ramma* 17 (*CSI* III:239), in which the hero Finnbogi wrestles Jarl Hakon's pet bear in a swimming contest and wins by stabbing it with a small knife.
31. "One of those fools who sits around in the cookhouse" (*eldhúsfífl*, "fire-house fool") refers to a common trope in legendary sagas and later folk tales: the "ash-lad" (Norwegian *askeladden*), "coal-biter" (Icelandic *kolbitr*), or "male Cinderella": a seemingly idle young man who lies by the fire all the time, but who rises to the occasion when a challenge comes.
32. "Black men" (*blámenn*) can refer to Africans in more historical sagas. In the legendary sagas, *blámenn* are legendary monstrous beings from unspecified distant lands; most of the reference to historical Africans is gone. Several other sagas link them with berserks (Lindow, "Supernatural and Ethnic Others", pp. 11-18).
33. *Blaukumannalandj*, normalized *Blökumannaland*, is a common name for Africa along with *Bláland*, "Black Land". See *Geography*, this volume, p. 100 note 24.
34. *Örvar-Odds saga* 23 (transl. Waggoner, *The Hrafnista Sagas*, p. 107), *Göngu-Hrólfs saga* 33 (transl. Waggoner, *Six Sagas*, p. 228), and *Órms þáttr Stórólfssonar* 9 (*CSI* III:465) include other instances of a hero who tears the face from a sorcerous opponent who is immune to bladed weapons. (transl. Waggoner, *The Hrafnista Sagas*, p. 107)
35. Literally, *þeir drecka satter saman*, "they drink the agreement together", implying the ritual shared drinking of ale to mark formal occasions (Jochens, *Women in Old Norse Society*, p. 106).
36. Since Galicia is later said to be "far away in the west of the world" (ch. 21), it is presumably Galicia in what is now northwestern Spain, not the eastern European land now divided between Poland and the Ukraine.
37. "Concluding remarks" at the end of sagas are usually simple phrases such as "Here ends this saga", sometimes with kindly wishes such as "Go in peace" or "Thanks to the one who wrote this and the one who read it," or occasionally short prayers or poems. Some romances end with jokes or satirical remarks (e.g. *Bósa saga* and *Vilhjálms saga sjóðs*; Waggoner, *Six Sagas*, pp. 134, 302 n38), and some end with reproach for anyone who didn't enjoy the tale (e.g. *Göngu-Hrólfs saga* 38, transl. Waggoner, *Six Sagas*, p. 239), but this is probably the rudest ending, all the more comical when juxtaposed with the lofty conclusion of the saga. Geraldine Barnes suggests that the insult to those who don't pay taxes suggests that the intended audience consisted of upwardly mobile, well-to-do Icelanders, who might have seen their own social aspirations reflected in the courtly settings of the romances in general. ("Romance in Iceland", p. 282)'

The Saga of Yngvar the Far-Traveler

1. For a useful overview, see Jesch, *Ships and Men*, pp. 103-107.
2. Lönnroth, "From History to Myth", pp. 100-106.
3. Larsson ("Vart for Ingvar den vittfarne?") proposed that Yngvar's expedition ended up in Georgia, fighting at the Battle of Sasireti. They would have traveled down to the Black Sea along the usual trade route to Constantinople, but then gone up the Rioni River and

portaged across to the Kura (Mtkvari) River, ending their voyage on the Caspian Sea. Shepard, "Yngvarr's Expedition to the East", gives a detailed overview of the evidence bearing on Yngvar's expedition; while he feels that Yngvar did make a real expedition, he is skeptical of Larsson's hypothesis. Larsson ("Yngvarr's Expedition") responds with additional supporting information.

4. Cole, "Echoes of the *Book of Joseph and Aseneth*", pp. 5-16.
5. Glazyrina, "The Viking Age and the Crusades Era," p. 4.
6. Glazyrina, "The Viking Age and the Crusades Era," pp. 4-13, suggests that the rhetoric of the saga, with the sharp distinction it draws between Christians and heathens, could have been influenced by accounts of the Crusades.
7. ". . . the renowned King Olaf Tryggvason was not known to men for the making of miracles after his death. Still, we believe him to be a glorious man and outstandingly devoted to God." (Andersson, transl. *The Saga of Olaf Tryggvason*, p. 35) Odd's goal in writing both sagas may have been political; the Church was contending with secular leaders at the time over which should control Church property, a contest known as *staðamál fyrri* or "first case of the proprietary churches". The chieftains Gizurr Hallson and Jón Loptsson—to whom Odd sent *Yngvars saga*, as we find out at the very end—supported secular control, and they won the debate in 1179 (although the Church would later win control over property in 1297). Odd's purpose may have been to show that secular leaders, outside of the clergy, could be just as effective as saints and priests as promoters and protectors of the Church's best interests. (Lönnroth, "From History to Myth", pp. 107-108)
8. Driscoll and Hufnagel, "Stories for All Time".
9. Sigríð *stórráða*, also known as Sigrid the Haughty, is famous for having refused to marry Olaf Tryggvason after he refused to allow her to keep her pagan religion. She went on to assemble the alliance that brought him down at the Battle of Svold. (*Óláfs saga Tryggvassonar* chs. 60-61; transl. Hollander, *Heimskringla*, pp. 200-201)
10. *Óláfr sænski* (Olaf the Swedish) is better known as *Óláfr Skotkonungr*, possibly meaning Olaf the Tribute-King. He died in 1022.
11. *Sjálfdæmi*, "self-judgment", was a feature of Norse law codes; both parties in a dispute could agree to allow one party to set terms for the settlement between them.
12. This is Yaroslav I of Kiev, also known as Yaroslav the Wise. He married Ingigerd in 1019, after which she took the name Irene.
13. Yaroslav fought for four years against the forces of his half-brother Svyatopolk, who was supported by Boleslaw I the Brave of Poland. It seems likely that Boleslaw's name (Norse *Burizleifr*) has been transferred to the historical Svyatopolk. Eymund may be the same as the Eymund who aids Yaroslav in *Eymundar þáttr hrings* in *Flateyjarbók* (Vigfusson and Ungerm vol. 2, pp. 118-134), although in *Flateyjarbók* Eymund is a Norwegian, rather than a Swede.
14. Onund, also known as Anund Jakob, was king of Sweden after his father (1022-1050).
15. According to *Flateyjarbók* Styrbjorn, the nephew of Eirik the Victorious, also yearned to be king and pressed his claim to the throne; his revolt against his uncle ended badly. (Vigfússon and Unger, *Flateyjarbók*, vol. 2, pp. 70-73)
16. The Semigallians lived on the west bank of the Daugava River, south of the Gulf of Riga; their territory is now part of both Latvia and Lithuania. A now-lost runestone

from Steninge, Sweden (U 439), known from a woodcut made in the 1600s, may have commemorated a warrior who "steered his ship east with Yngvar to Estland", presumably Estonia. This might confirm this detail in the saga, but there is some controversy over how to read the last word of the inscription, and Estonia and Semigallia usually appear as clearly separate and distinct places. (Shepard, "Yngvarr's Expedition to the East", pp. 243-244; Jesch, *Ships and Men*, pp. 90-93)

17. Heroes in the legendary sagas and Icelandic romances are often said to learn many languages; Yngvar's son Svein will also learn many languages in chapter 9 of this saga. (Kalinke, "The Foreign Language Requirement", pp. 852-856; McDougall, "Foreigners and Foreign Languages", pp. 210-211)
18. This is usually taken to be either the Dniepr—the usual route to the Black Sea and then to Constantinople—or the Volga. The problem is that neither one flows out of the east, and neither is the largest of a trio of rivers. The preposition is ambiguous; *um Garðaríki* would normally mean "around Russia" but could also be "beyond Russia" or even "across Russia." Larsson's solution is that Yngvar took the Dniepr to the Black Sea, but from there he ascended the Rioni River in the Caucasus, which does flow from the east and is paralleled by two smaller rivers. ("Yngvarr's Expedition," p. 104)
19. *Hjálmvígi* is probably meant to be a German (the Norse version of the name Helmwig), *Valdimarr* is probably meant to be a Russian (the Norse version of the name Vladimir), and *Sóti* may have been a Swede (Glazyrina, "The Viking Age and the Crusades Era", p. 2).
20. According to medieval bestiaries (e.g. White, *The Book of Beasts*, p. 180; see also "On Serpents" in this volume) and going back to Pliny (*Natural History* VIII.xxxv.85; transl. Rackham, vol. 3, pp. 62-63) and Lucan (IX.720-721, 822-827; transl. Duff, pp. 558-559, 566-567), the *jaculus* is a serpent that leaps or springs from tree branches. According to Lucan, it springs fast enough to pierce its victim completely through, and does not need venom. In the saga, however, the jaculus has become a flying dragon.
21. Heroines of Icelandic romances, like their heroes, are often said to speak many languages. (Kalinke, "The Foreign Language Requirement", pp. 855-856)
22. Larsson points out that this description does not fit the Dneipr River, which is rather wide; there are rapids on the Dneipr which required portaging, but no steep cliffs. It does, however, fit the gorges on the Tscherimela River, a tributary of the Rioni River, from which the Surami Pass leads over the Likhi Mountains to the watershed of the Kura ("Vart for Ingvar den Vittfarne?", pp. 98-99, 101).
23. These circular boats just might be based on the *quffa* or "kuphars", coracles used on the Tigris and Euphrates Rivers from the time of Herodotus into the 20th century. (Larssen, "Vart For Ingvar den Vittfarne?", p. 99; "Yngvar's Expedition," p. 106)
24. There were two cities in the ancient world known as Heliopolis (Greek, "City of the Sun"), one in Egypt (now part of Cairo) and one in Syria (now Baalbek in Lebanon). Heliopolis in Egypt was listed in Isidore of Seville's *Etymologies* (XV.i.31, transl. Barney et al., p. 303), while Heliopolis in Syria was known as the site of the martyrdom and burial of St. Barbara, who was popular in Iceland. If Yngvar's historical expedition went to Georgia, then he could not have visited either city; presumably this detail was added by the saga writer. (Glazyrina, "On *Heliopolis* in *Yngvars saga víðförla*", pp. 175-177)
25. If Yngvar's saga reflects an actual expedition into present-day Georgia, Lindibelti might

be the Caspian Sea itself, as proposed by Larsson ("Vart for Ingvar den vittfarne?", p. 97; "Yngvarr's Expedition", pp. 106-107). The word used to describe it, *uppspretta*, usually means "spring" and does not normally apply to a sea. On the other hand, *Belti* is the word for the Baltic Sea, and the name *Lindibelti* might reflect a perceived similarity between the Baltic and the Caspian, both being surrounded by land and having lower salinity than the open sea. The *lindi-* element might derive from *lind*, "spring; brook", or possibly *lind*, "linden tree", which does grow in the Caucasus near the Caspian coast.

26. Presumably derived from *Sigeion* or *Sigeum*, a peninsula and city in Anatolia near the site of Troy. Again, if Yngvar's expedition really went to Georgia, they could not have seen Sigeum, which is on the Mediterranean Sea at the mouth of the Hellespont. The saga writer may have taken the name from Isidore of Seville (*Etymologies* XIV.vii.2; transl. Barney *et al.*, p. 297). If Yngvar's saga reflects an actual expedition into present-day Georgia, the peninsula might be Kara-Bugaz ("Black Strait" in Turkic) on the eastern side of the Caspian, where water does at times cascade through narrow straits from the Caspian Sea into the Garabogazköl lagoon, creating waterfalls and whirlpools that could correspond to Gapi and Belgsoti (Larsson, "Vart for Ingvar den vittfarne?", p. 97; "Yngvarr's Expedition", pp. 106-107). Because the Kara-Bugaz is a peninsula at the entrance to a narrow strait, the saga writer may have identified it with Sigeum because Sigeum is the only promontory in Asia mentioned in Isidore's *Etymologies*.

27. This is a version of a common scene in *fornaldarsögur*: the hero sneaks into a giant's dwelling during the day, sees the giant coming home bringing game and/or human flesh as a meal, and then kills the giant in the night. (e.g. *Ketils saga hængs* 2, transl. Waggoner, *The Hrafnista Sagas*, pp. 7-8; *Þórsteins saga Víkingssonar* 15, transl. Waggoner, *The Sagas of Fridthjof*, pp. 28-29)

28. This is clearly based on "Greek fire", the sticky inflammable substance that could be pumped from nozzles on Byzantine warships.

29. This detail may be borrowed from bestiary accounts of the serpent known as *prester*, which constantly breathes out poisonous vapors (White, *A Book of Beasts*, p. 175 ; see also "On Serpents" in this volume). Isidore of Seville also mentions the *sibilus* as a snake that kills by hissing (*Etymologies* XII.iv.9; transl. Barney, p. 255)

30. The only known King Harald of Sweden is the legendary Harald Wartooth, who is not otherwise reported to have traveled in the east. However, this entire episode may have been added for hagiographic reasons; King Harald is reminiscent of Pharaoh, who was drowned with his army in the Red Sea as they pursued the fleeing Israelites. Yngvar is thus identified with the Israelites, who will escape the Red Sea, but who must continue wandering in the wilderness. (H. Antonsson; quoted in Lönnroth, "The Ingvar Stones", pp. 111-112)

31. *Belgsóti* looks like it should mean "Soti's bag" or "Soti's bellows".

32. Lönnroth ("The Yngvar Stones", p. 107) points out that this may be yet another borrowed Classical theme: these women are reminiscent of the Amazons, and they live in the same region of the world that the Amazons were said to inhabit, Scythia.

33. Queen Ellisif's city is finally named. Larsson ("Yngvarr's Expedition", pp. 104-105) argued that Citopolis can be identified with Kutaisi (Latin *Cytaea*), which was ruled by a woman at the time of Yngvar's expedition (Mariam, the mother of Bagrat IV of Georgia). Kutaisi's monumental Bagrati Cathedral would certainly fit the saga description of

splendid buildings of white marble.

34. Manuscript GKS 2845 places Yngvar's death in 1040 and gives his age as thirty, eleven years after the fall of Olaf. (Olson, *Yngvars Saga Víðförla*, p. 30)
35. The word for "Russian" (*gerðskr, gerzkr*; derived from *Garðar*, "Towns", the usual name for Russia) is often confused with the word for "Greek" (*grískr*, often metathesized to *girskr*). Manusript AM 343 has *girdzkur*, which looks like it should be "Russian"; GKS 2845 has *griske*, which looks more like "Greek".
36. This is echoed by an event in Odd Snorrason's *Saga of Olaf Tryggvason*: Olaf's bowman Einar fires two arrows at Jarl Eirik, who says *Ekki em ek fúss at bíða ennar þriðju*, "I am not eager to wait for the third," and then orders his archer to shoot. (Ólafur Halldórsson, ed., *ÍF* XXV, p. 342)
37. The usual lists of "Plinian races" do not include bird-headed or bird-beaked men (Friedman, *The Monstrous Races*, pp. 8-24. One possible source might be the German poem *Herzog Ernst*, whose hero encounters an army of crane-headed men on his journey in the mysterious East. *Herzog Ernst* may have borrowed this motif from a Turkish tale. (Blamires, *Herzog Ernst and the Otherworld Voyage*, pp. 32-40, 87-89) *Herzog Ernst* has already been suggested as a possible inspiration for one *fornaldarsaga*, *Bósa saga ok Herrauðs* (Waggoner, *Six Sagas*, p. xviii). On the other hand, bird-headed men do occasionally appear in medieval geography, notably the Hereford *mappa mundi*; perhaps something like that was the source (Barraclough, *Beyond the Northlands*, p.216).
38. This unnamed beast is based on descriptions of the elephant, which is usually drawn with a tower on its back for carrying soldiers (White, *The Book of Beasts*, pp. 24-25; see *Physiologus* B in this volume, p. 113.)
39. It has already been established that Silkisif can speak Latin and Norse. Unless this is an authorial mistake, it is possible that Silkisif is only pretending not to understand the bishop, perhaps because she wants to make his job harder, or because she is reminding the bishop that he is inferior to Yngvar in skill. (Kalinke, "The Foreign Language Requirement", p. 859)
40. A theological point articulated by many medieval theologians, including Gregory the Great: "The true estimate of life, after all, lies in acts of virtue, not in the display of miracles. There are many, Peter, who without performing miracles, are not at all inferior to those who perform them." (*Dialogues* 1.12.4; transl. Zimmerman, p. 51; see McCready, *Signs of Sanctity*, pp. 66-68, for additional examples) Gregory's works were well known in medieval Iceland, and the *Dialogues* were especially well known, since episodes borrowed from or inspired by the *Dialogues* turn up all over the saga literature. See Boyer, "The Influence of Pope Gregory's *Dialogues* on Old Icelandic Literature"; also see *Niðrstigninga saga*, this volume.
41. This indirectly shows the bishop's skepticism over Yngvar's sanctity. Masses would only be said for Yngvar's soul if Yngvar were thought to be in Purgatory—in which case he could not be a saint.
42. This quotation is in Latin in the original. *Gesta Saxonum*, "History of the Saxons", is probably Adam of Bremen's history now usually known as *Gesta Hammaburgensis ecclesiae pontificum*, "History of the Bishops of the Church of Hamburg." Onund's fate at the hands of the Amazons is told in Adam's *Gesta* twice (3.15 and Scholion 123; transl. Tschan, pp. 126-127, 200), although not in exactly these words; Odd Snorrason was

probably quoting from memory. This quote may in fact be the only surviving fragment of Odd's original Latin account of Yngvar's voyage, preserved because the translator thought it was a direct quote from Adam of Bremen (Jensson, "Were the Earliest Fornaldarsögur Written in Latin?", pp. 82-84).

43. As noted above, Larsson points out that this description does not fit the wide Dneipr River. Allowing for some exaggeration, however, it does fit the gorges of the Tscherimela River in the Caucasus. ("Yngvarr's Expedition and the *Georgian Chronicle*", p. 105.)
44. Gizurr Hallsson, who served as Lawspeaker of Iceland, died in 1206. Jón Loptsson, chieftain of the Oddaverjar clan, died in 1197. Thus 1197 is the latest possible date for the composition of Odd's Latin saga of Yngvar.

The Saga of Eirek the Far-Traveller

1. Firchow, *The Old Norse* Elucidarius.
2. Svanhildur Óskarsdóttir, "Prose of Christian Instruction", pp. 342-343.
3. *Óláfs saga Tryggvasonar* ch. 89, in *Flateyjarbók*, ed. Vigfússon and Unger, vol. 1, pp. 116-117. See Rowe, *The Development of* Flateyjarbók, pp. 181-192.
4. Vigfússon and Unger, eds. *Flateyjarbók*, vol. 1, pp. 27-36.
5. According to the legendary genealogy *Hversu Nóregr byggðist,* which is also preserved in *Flateyjarbók* (ed. Vigfússon and Unger, vol. 1, pp. 21-24), Thrand is the son of Nórr, the hero who gave his name to all of Norway, and whose sons and grandsons settle and establish the historic districts of Norway. Thrand (*Þrándr*) is allotted Trondheim (*Þrándheim*), which takes its name from him. It is significant that the story starts here: Trondheim, later called Nidaros, would include the royal seat of the Norwegian kings and the site of its first diocese.
6. An unresolved question is whether the pre-Christian Norse really had a concept of *Ódáinsakr*—literally "un-dead's-field"—or whether this is a literary convention. Saxo Grammaticus mentions a place called *Undensakre* to which an exiled man retreats and seemingly vanishes (*History of the Danes* IV.105, transl. Fisher, p. 100). The longer redaction of *Hervarar saga* identifies Ódáinsakr with Glaesisvellir, the land ruled by Godmund, within or next to Jotunheim in the far north (Tolkien, *The Saga of King Heidrek the* Wise, p. 66); and there are a few other occurrences of the place name (p. 86). Lincoln ("On the Imagery of Paradise", pp. 26-27) has argued that Ódáinsakr is a reflex of a Proto-Indo-European concept, comparable with the Greek Elysian Fields and the Irish Emain Ablach. That said, the sources are few and problematic, and Lincoln does not discuss the possibility that the extensive early Christian writings on the Earthly Paradise have at least strongly influenced the concept of Ódáinsakr.
7. The reference is to the Varangian Guard, the elite Byzantine military unit and personal guard of the Emperor in the 10th through 14th centuries, in which many Scandinavian fighters took service.
8. The analogy of the Christian Trinity of Father, Son, and Holy Spirit with the substance, light, and heat of the sun is fairly widespread in the writings of several early medieval theologians (Raw, *Trinity and Incarnation*, pp. 34-35). The immediate source may be the *Elucidarius* of Honorius Augustodunensis (Migné, *Patrologia Latina* vol. 172, pp. 1110-1111), although the wording of *Eireks saga* does not correspond closely to the known

Norse *Elucidarius* (Firchow, *The Old Norse* Elucidarius, 1.3, pp. 2-5)

9. The explanation of Heaven as a bright hall, Earth as a dark dungeon, and Hell as a pit is a nearly direct quote from the Norse *Elucidarius* (Firchow, *The Old Norse* Elucidarius, 1.23, p. 9; cf. Migné, *Patrologia Latina* vol. 172, pp. 1116).
10. The idea that righteous humans will replace the fallen angels and complete God's original plan goes back at least to Augustine (*Enchiridion* IX.29; transl. Peebles, pp. 393-394) and is repeated in the *Elucidarius* (Firchow, *The Old Norse* Elucidarius, 1.77-78, p. 21; cf. Migné, *Patrologia Latina* vol. 172, pp. 1116, 1118).
11. The concept of a threefold Heaven—a visible Heaven or firmament, a Spiritual Heaven for angels, and an Intellectual Heaven where God himself resides—was widespread in medieval theology. The proximate source for *Eireks saga* is probably the *Elucidarius* again (I.3; Migné, *Patrologia Latina* vol. 172, p. 1111), although again the wording differs from the Norse *Elucidarius* text (Firchow, *The Old Norse* Elucidarius 1.11, p. 5).
12. Ptolemy of Alexandria had given the circumference of the Earth as 180,000 stadia, and this figure was widely copied by later authors. The direct source here may be Honorius Augustodunensis, *De imagine mundi* I.v (ed. Migné, *Patrologia Latina* vol. 172, p. 122)
13. Manuscript B gives the number as 100,000 plus 85 miles; manuscript C gives it as 100,000 plus 9382 miles; manuscript D gives it as 10,000 plus 3005 miles. (Jensen, *Eiríks saga,* pp. 42-45)
14. Ódáinsakr might have been influenced directly by Irish visionary writings, some of which are known to have been translated. For example, the *Navigatio Sancti Brendani* describes the Earthly Paradise as so bright that there are no shadows (Lincoln, "On the Imagery of Paradise", p. 25); the *Visio Tnugdali*, known in Norse as *Duggals leizla*, describes Paradise as a field of sweet-smelling flowers in eternal sunlight (ch. 16; Unger, *Heilagra Manna Sögur*, vol. 1 p. 352).
15. As noted in *Landafræði* (this volume, p.97 note 10), it was a common belief in the early medieval church that righteous souls would occupy the Earthly Paradise between their deaths and the Last Judgment, when they would enter Heaven and be united with God himself. (Delumeau, *History of Paradise*, pp. 23-38) Note that the angel reveals that, contrary to what is implicit up to this point, the Land of Living Men is not the same as the true Paradise.
16. The monk Jón Þórðarson wrote most of the core of the original *Flateyjarbók*, beginning with *Eireks saga* and continuing with the sagas of Olaf Tryggvason and Olaf Haraldsson. His colleague Magnús Þórhallsson drew the illustrations; after Jón stopped working on *Flateyjarbók*, Magnús completed the saga of Olaf Haraldsson, and then added material to the beginning and the end, so that *Eireks saga* is no longer first in *Flateyjarbók.*

The Tale of Helgi Thorisson

1. Waggoner, *Sagas of Giants and Heroes.*
2. Power, "*Le Lai de Lanval*", pp. 158-161; McKinnell, *Meeting the Other*, p. 177.
3. Barraclough, *Beyond the Northlands*, p. 86.
4. Rowe, "Conversion *Þættir*", pp. 468-472.
5. Viken (*Vík* in Norse) is the Oslofjord, near the modern city of Oslo.
6. A *hersir* was a local chieftain and military commander, of lesser rank than a jarl.

7. This is King Olaf Tryggvason (d. 1000).
8. Butter and bacon are commonly depicted as trade goods especially prized by the "Finns", the Saami people. (Barraclough, *Beyond the Northlands*, pp. 89-90)
9. A large royal estate on the Norwegian west coast; now Årstad, a district of the city of Bergen.
10. *Grimr* means "Mask". In the sagas, it's a fairly common name given by one who is disguised or otherwise not inclined to reveal his actual name (see *Hálfdanar saga Eysteinssonar*, this volume, p. 232-233, note 11).
11. *Þórsteins saga bæjarmagns* 8-13 (transl. Pálsson and Edwards, *Seven Viking Romances*, pp. 269-275) contains a story of how King Olaf gained two precious drinking horns from Godmund of Glæsisvellir; this saga shares a number of motifs with *Helga þáttr Þórissonar*.
12. An ironic allusion to Psalm 109:5: "And they have rewarded me evil for good, and hatred for my love."
13. The *Long Serpent* was Olaf Tryggvason's flagship. Defeated at the naval Battle of Svold in the western Baltic, the king is said to have leaped into the sea (*Óláfs saga Tryggvasonar* 111, *Heimskringla*, transl. Hollander, pp. 240-241).

www.ingramcontent.com/pod-product-compliance
Lightning Source LLC
Chambersburg PA
CBHW030822310726
48980CB00006B/602/J

* 9 7 8 1 9 4 1 1 3 6 1 7 1 *